Escher

F. H. Bool · Bruno Ernst · J. R. Kist

J. L. Locher · F. Wierda

Escher

With a complete catalogue
of the graphic works

Including essays by M. C. Escher

General Editor J. L. Locher

with 606 illustrations, including 36 in colour

 Thames and Hudson

The first five biographical chapters (pages 9–57) are by J. R. Kist, younger brother of Bas Kist who was Escher's intimate friend throughout his life.

For the following five biographical chapters (pages 59–133), the material – mostly consisting of writings by Escher himself – is selected by J. L. Locher, Professor of Art at the University of Groningen, formerly Curator of Modern Art at the Gemeentemuseum in The Hague.

The text of 'Voyage to Canada' (pages 103–14) is by Escher himself.

'The Vision of a Mathematician' (pages 135–54) is by Bruno Ernst, teacher of mathematics in Utrecht.

'The Regular Division of the Plane' (pages 155–72) is the first English translation of Escher's book *Regelmatige vlakverdeling*, published in 1958 by the De Roos Foundation in Utrecht.

The Catalogue (pages 175–343) is compiled by F. H. Bool, Curator of Prints at the Gemeentemuseum in The Hague, J. L. Locher and F. Wierda, Editor at Meulenhoff Publishers in Amsterdam.

Translated from the Dutch
Leven en werk van M.C. Escher
by Tony Langham and Plym Peters

This translation © 1982 Thames and Hudson, Ltd, London, and Harry N. Abrams, Inc, New York

Text © 1981 Meulenhoff & Co bv, Amsterdam

Illustrations © 1981 M.C. Escher Estate c/o Beeldrecht, Amsterdam

Printed and bound in the Netherlands

The illustrations in this book were produced from photographs supplied by the Gemeentemuseum in The Hague, with the exception of the following:

    page 75 (right): Gemeentemuseum, Arnhem;

    page 78: N V Philips Gloeilampenfabrieken, Eindhoven;

    pages 115, 151: Igno Cuypers, Amsterdam;

    page 138 (right): Bruno Ernst, Utrecht;

    pages 138 (below), 142 (after a design by Bruno Ernst), 147 (below): Lodewijk Sijses, Haastrecht, Netherlands;

    pages 147 (left), 154: Feddo van Gogh, Amsterdam;

    cat. nos. 18, 27, 31, 86, 394, 407, 440: Cornelius Van S. Roosevelt, Washington, D.C.;

    cat. no. 91: Museum Meermanno-Westreenianum, The Hague;

    cat. nos. 187, 301, 404: J.W. Vermeulen, Plascassier, France;

    cat. no. 447: National Gallery of Art, Washington, D.C. Gift of Mr and Mrs Seymour Schwartz.

Contents

Biographical Chronology

1898
Maurits Cornelis Escher is born on 17 June in Leeuwarden, in the Dutch province of Friesland

1903
The family moves to Arnhem

1912–18
Escher attends secondary school in Arnhem

1916
First graphic work

1917
The family moves to Oosterbeek

1919–22
Escher attends the School for Architecture and Decorative Arts in Haarlem; lessons from S. Jessurun de Mesquita

1921
March–May: holiday trip along the French Riviera and through Italy. In November the booklet *Flor de Pascua*, with woodcuts by Escher, is published

1922
April–June: journey through northern Italy. In September Escher travels by freighter to Tarragona; trip through Spain and first visit to the Alhambra; on to Italy, where he stays in Siena from mid-November onwards

1923
From March to June Escher stays in Ravello, where he meets Jetta Umiker. Back in Siena end of June. 13–26 August: first one-man exhibition in Siena. Moves to Rome in November

1924
In February first exhibition in Holland. Escher and Jetta are married on 12 June

1925
They live in their own house in Rome from October onwards

1926
2–16 May: exhibition in Rome. Son George is born on 23 July

1927–35
Yearly spring trips through inhospitable areas of Italy

1928
Son Arthur is born on 8 December

1932
In the summer the book *XXIV Emblemata*, with woodcuts by Escher, is published

1933
In the autumn *De vreeselijke avonturen van Scholastica* is published, also with woodcuts by Escher

1934
Escher's lithograph *Nonza* is awarded a third prize at an exhibition in Chicago, Ill. 12–22 December: exhibition at the Dutch Historical Institute in Rome

1935
In July the Escher family moves to Switzerland

1936
April–June: sea trip along the coasts of Italy and France to Spain, where Escher visits the Alhambra for the second time, as well as the mosque in Córdoba. Turning-point in Escher's work—from landscapes to 'mental imagery'

1937
In August the Eschers move to Brussels

1938
Son Jan is born on 6 March

1939
Escher's father dies on 14 June

1940
10 May: German invasion of the Low Countries. Escher's mother dies on 27 May

1941
In February the Eschers move to Baarn in Holland

1951
Articles on Escher are published in *The Studio* and *Time* and *Life* magazines

1954–61
Each year Escher makes a sea voyage to and/or from Italy

1954
In September, large one-man exhibition at the Stedelijk Museum in Amsterdam on the occasion of the International Mathemetical Conference. In October and November, exhibition in the Whyte Gallery, Washington, D.C.

1955
In February the Eschers move to a new house in Baarn. On 30 April Escher is knighted

1958
Early in the year Escher's book *Regelmatige vlakverdeling* (The Regular Division of the Plane) is published

1959
In November *Grafiek en tekeningen M. C. Escher* (*The Graphic Work of M. C. Escher*, 1961) is published

1960
In August, exhibition and lecture in Cambridge during an international conference of crystallographers. August–October: sea voyage to Canada. Lecture at MIT in Cambridge, Mass., end of October

1961
Article on Escher by E. H. Gombrich in *The Saturday Evening Post* of 29 July

1962
In April Escher is admitted to hospital for an emergency operation; he takes a long time to recover

1964
On 1 October Escher and Jetta fly to Canada, where he falls ill again and has to undergo another operation in Toronto

1965
In March Escher is awarded the cultural prize of the city of Hilversum. In August *Symmetry Aspects of M. C. Escher's Periodic Drawings* by Caroline H. MacGillavry is published. An article on Escher appears in the October issue of *Jardin des Arts*

1966
Scientific American publishes a long article on Escher in its April issue

1967
Second decoration

1968
Exhibitions in Washington, D.C. (Mickelson Gallery) and The Hague (Gemeentemuseum). In July Escher makes his last graphic work, a woodcut. At the end of the year Jetta leaves for Switzerland. Escher lives on his own with a housekeeper

1970
In the spring Escher is re-admitted to hospital for another major operation. In August he moves to the Rosa Spier House in Laren

1971
In December *De werelden van M. C. Escher* (*The World of M. C. Escher*, 1972) is published

1972
Escher dies on 27 March in the hospital in Hilversum

Preface

In honour of his seventieth birthday in 1968, a large retrospective exhibition of the work of the Dutch graphic artist M.C. Escher was held in the Gemeentemuseum in The Hague. It was by no means his first exhibition, but it was the first time that an important museum of art, on its own initiative, had put on an exhibition of his complete work, seen both from the point of view of art history and from Escher's own working methods. In addition, attention was paid to the numerous scientific and semi-scientific aspects. The exhibition was very successful and Escher, who had already acquired great fame in the Netherlands and abroad, became even more widely known as a result.

Also in 1968, the Escher Foundation was set up. One of its aims was to ensure that as complete a collection as possible of Escher's work would be held by a Dutch museum. This aim was achieved; the Gemeentemuseum of The Hague now contains a virtually complete collection of Escher's graphic work and an important series of drawings, as well as extensive archives containing photograph albums, writings and letters.

The catalogue for the 1968 exhibition prompted the book *The World of M.C. Escher*, published in 1971. The present publication is a sequel to it and also a complement. The material in The Hague made it possible to compile a survey of Escher's entire graphic oeuvre; this can be found in the catalogue section (pages 175 ff.). It is preceded by the story of Escher's life and a mathematician's view of his work, both containing numerous quotations from Escher's writings and correspondence. A concordance of print numbers and an index of works illustrated have been added to make the book easier to consult.

Anyone who has ever heard Escher speak about his work, or who has corresponded with him, knows that he had an unusual talent for communicating his interests. Although he often complained about all the writing he had to do, he could never stop himself from giving lecture after lecture—all of which he wrote out in full—or from remaining in contact with his family, friends and relations by means of an extensive correspondence. During the second half of his life particularly, he wrote letters almost daily. In fact, it is easy to follow his life virtually step by step in the abundant material of lectures, diaries and letters. Here the last twenty years of his life are largely recounted in quotations from Escher himself. It is possible for the reader by this means to gain an idea of Escher's life from the inside.

An important source for the first half of Escher's life is his father's diary. His father, who is separately introduced in the first chapter, had a clear influence on the formation of Escher's character: many of the traits of his father's personality can be seen again in the graphic artist. Escher's eldest son George has recounted for this book some of his memories of his life in Italy, and provides a typically Escherian account of the end of his father's life, which concludes the biography with a great deal of feeling but by no means sentimentally.

A subject on which Escher gave many lectures and which was closest to his heart was the regular division of the plane. He summarized his ideas on this in a lecture published in a small edition in 1958 by the De Roos Foundation in Utrecht. This important text is included here, and is thus made available to a wider public for the first time. The editors and the publisher are grateful to the De Roos Foundation for making this possible.

This book could never have appeared in its present form but for the material gathered in The Hague. The cooperation of two authors who knew Escher very well was also essential. J. R. Kist is the younger brother of Bas Kist who was one of Escher's closest friends from his youth. His acquaintance with Escher's family and friends has made it possible for him to locate many biographical sources and to introduce something of Escher's own individual outlook on life into the story. Bruno Ernst maintained close contact with Escher from the mid-1950s, and feels particularly at home with the mathematical side of Escher's graphic work. He has published various articles on this subject, as well as the book *De Toverspiegel van M.C. Escher* (The Magic Mirror of M.C. Escher). Escher himself believed consideration of his work from the mathematical point of view to be quite essential.

This book supplements the existing literature on Escher, on the one hand by providing an illustrated catalogue of his entire graphic work, and on the other hand by being the first definitive biography. Many people have collaborated in the preparation of the book. I should like to mention a few of these by name. First there are those at the Gemeentemuseum of The Hague, where the material of the Escher Foundation had to be put into order, catalogued and photographed before we could begin to use it: Flip Bool in particular worked extremely hard at this task. Then there is Cornelius Van S. Roosevelt, one of Escher's oldest American friends and his greatest collector, whose detailed knowledge and exceptionally helpful attitude were invaluable. Acknowledgment should also be made to J. W. Vermeulen who succeeded in convincing Escher that an Escher Foundation should be set up, for without this Foundation there would have been no collection or archives in The Hague and consequently no basis for the present book. By his involvement with the Escher Foundation and his contacts with Escher's sons, and as an ever-willing source of information, Mr Vermeulen has made an important contribution. Escher's sons have also contributed in making their father's letters readily available. Finally, I should like to express my admiration for the efforts of the Meulenhoff publishing house, whose enthusiasm and confidence remained unshaken through numerous setbacks and problems, and for the publisher's own contribution to the book.

J. L. LOCHER

Escher Senior   1843–1939

'S[arah] did not want to go along to Ameland. She was expecting another baby in June. As we had only boys, she dearly wanted a little girl, and this was why we had tried again just once more, although we were both—me especially—rather old to have more children. However, on 17 June it turned out to be another boy. We named him Maurits Cornelis after S[arah]'s beloved uncle Van Hall, and called him "Mauk" for short or, while he was still small, "Maukie".'

This is how George Arnold Escher (1843–1939) described the birth, in 1898, of his youngest son, who was later to become the graphic artist M. C. Escher. The description can be found in an account he wrote of his life, which precedes the diary he began writing in 1910.

He had five sons: Eddy and Beer from his first marriage to Charlotte de Hartitzsch; George, Nol and Mauk from his second marriage to Sarah Gleichman. This book is about the life and work of the youngest of these sons. But first we should take a look at the remarkable personality of the father, as it is revealed in his autobiography and his diary.

During the last years of his life the writing of his diary became an increasingly important activity for Escher senior. In 1919 he remarked that writing a diary was a suitable occupation for him because it made a change from reading, which was far more tiring for his eyes. Every day he noted exactly the names of all the people he had met, and made summaries of conversations, letters, articles and books, and anything else that interested him. When in 1934 he stayed at the hotel De Tafelberg in Oosterbeek, he was delighted to find the seat in the lounge at the writing-table with a lamp unoccupied, enabling him to continue writing his diary there, 'however unimportant it may be'. And when in the end his eyes, ears, legs and his digestive system (the weak point of the family) gave up on him almost entirely, and the last pages of volume 61 became all but illegible, he was still trying to note at least the date, wind direction and temperature every day.

PROFESSIONAL LIFE

One of Escher senior's most striking features was his matter-of-factness. The way in which as a young boy, even before going to secondary school, he systematically worked out what career was most suitable for him is typical. 'In this,' he writes in his autobiography, 'I was chiefly guided by my main shortcoming—a poor, slow memory and a generally slow intellect. As a result I found it very difficult to learn things by heart. I could not remember facts, expressions or phrases that I had heard or read, and could therefore make little use of them in telling a story or writing a composition. In other words, I was, and still am, a poor speaker and I also find it difficult to get things down on paper. Consequently, I sought a profession in which factual knowledge was not important and in which I would not have to make any speeches. Thus the professions of lawyer, magistrate, mayor, priest, teacher or actor were immediately ruled out.'

After turning down a whole series of other possibilities, he finally arrived at work that he considered himself capable of. 'However, I did feel that I had some talent for the study of the connections between natural phenomena and human constructions based on them. As it is difficult to find an occupation in the physical sciences without having to teach, there was not much left apart from construction work, that is, engineering. I have never regretted this choice.'

In 1859 he completed the science course at the *gymnasium* (secondary school) and began to study civil engineering in Delft. After qualifying on 22 June 1863 he worked for some years on the State Railway from Amsterdam to Den Helder, until on 1 January 1867 he sat an examination to work for the Ministry of Transport.

JAPAN

When he had been employed by the Ministry of Transport for a few years, a plan to work abroad for a while began to form in his mind. There were opportunities for entering the employment of the Japanese Government; two of his colleagues had preceded him there in 1872. A year later he was recommended as one of the engineers for the river and port improvement scheme in Osaka, and on 3 August 1873 he sailed from Marseilles on the *Iroaouaddy*. Escher travelled first class, his assistant De Rijke and his family travelled second class, and a bricklayer, Arnst, who had been appointed foreman, and his wife travelled third class.

The five years Escher spent in Japan were a culminating point in his engineering career. His memories of this period, and the objects that he brought back, coloured the rest of his life, as his diary repeatedly shows.

villa Rosande, Oosterbeek

In 1878 Escher left Japan. He did not find it difficult to get work back in Holland. After some fruitful visits to colleagues at the Ministry of Transport, he applied for the post of District Engineer in Maastricht. After his stay in Japan, and as the result of an inheritance, his financial position had improved. So he started to look for a wife.

'However, Catholic Maastricht was not very suitable in this respect,' he writes in his autobiography. 'I did know some gifted and attractive women and girls in the Protestant circle but these by no means fitted the equation $w = 1/2\,m + 10$, in which "w" is the right age for the girl and "m" represents the man's age. Some of them were too old and some too young, or they were not healthy enough. I felt it was particularly important for me to have this health requirement, as my own health—or at least the strength of my constitution—was not very good, and I still wanted a good chance of healthy children.'

After working in Maastricht for two years he was transferred to Breda, where the possibilities of marriage were more favourable. A colleague mentioned the chic, well-born young ladies of the De Hartitzsch family in Ginneken: Sidonie, Amélie, Edmée, Charlotte and Angeline.

He met them and was particularly taken with Charlotte. Because of an imminent transfer to Gorinchem on 1 January 1882, he had to declare his matrimonial intentions very quickly. He was accepted and the wedding took place on 1 June. They were married by his cousin, David Escher, in the church at Ginneken.

In 1883 Eddy was born, followed two years later by Beer. The births went well, but soon after the second one, Charlotte had to be operated on for a tumour and died aged 33. Charlotte's sisters took it in turns to come and stay for a couple of months to do the housekeeping, and, wrote Escher, 'in this way I managed. I regularly weighed the children and kept a record of their weights on a graph'.

THE SECOND MARRIAGE

After several more transfers, Escher settled in Leeuwarden in 1890, where he became Chief Engineer, second class. His brother-in-law drew his attention to Sarah Gleichman, daughter of the well-known liberal Minister of Finance, J.G. Gleichman; on her mother's side she was related to a patrician family, the Van Halls. He found her rosy-cheeked, fresh face, her simplicity and her open-mindedness very attractive. The great difference in their ages—seventeen years—did not satisfy the formula $w = 1/2\,m + 10$, but as she was extremely reliable and moderate, he was not particularly concerned. They were married on 27 October 1892 in The Hague by the Reverend P. Heering, with whom they afterwards maintained contact. In Leeuwarden, Escher rented a large and grand house, Het Oude Princessehof; there was plenty of room there for his office and study. His sons George (20 June 1894), Nol (20 February 1896) and Mauk (17 June 1898) were

Escher's father and mother, c. 1916

born there. Later, when the Princessehof became a municipal museum, his youngest son would hold an exhibition there.

KNIGHTHOOD

Escher senior was recommended for a knighthood in the order of the Nederlandse Leeuw: 'However, I certainly did not want this: in the first place, I considered myself to be inferior in knowledge, in diligence and therefore in useful achievement, compared with many others who had not been knighted. It seemed unfair that I should be raised above these people by knighthood. Secondly, I disapprove generally of the custom of giving decorations. However, the consideration that the chief engineers of the Ministry of Transport are all decorated, so that non-decoration becomes a mark of inadequacy, persuaded me to let the matter drop.' He was pleased to notice that there was no compulsion to wear the decoration. He would have considered this a show, which went against the grain with him.

ARNHEM

In 1903 Escher was transferred to Arnhem and bought a house there, Utrechtsestraat 19. The children liked it very much. Arnhem is in a beautiful part of Holland, with landscapes full of contrast; the family had many outings. There was a bridge over a railway embankment where the children liked to go to watch the trains.

Escher had an extension built into the garden so that Nol and Mauk had a room for their carpentry. There were two work benches, which Eddy and Beer had previously used in Leeuwarden. A contractor's apprentice, Van Eldik, regularly gave the boys lessons and inspired Mauk with a love for wood.

The 'Van Eldik technique', which consisted of endlessly wetting and scraping to remove the grain from the surface of a plank of pearwood, later on proved to be very useful to Escher when he made woodcuts.

RETIREMENT

On 1 July 1908 'old Es', as he was known to his friends, retired. He made good use of the free time he now had, going to meetings and lectures, serving on various boards and committees, where his technical expertise—and, when necessary, his ample means— proved a valuable asset. In addition, he was a respected member of the Royal Institute of Engineers. He attended meetings regularly, sitting on the front row wearing his visor, as his youngest son depicted him (cat. no. 274). There was always some problem or other with one of his five sons, and he regularly had to intervene and help. His wife did a lot of social work during this period.

The whole family became engrossed in one of his hobbies. In Paris he had bought a large telescope, which he installed on the flat roof of his house. There he studied the heavenly bodies with his children; Mauk in particular was fascinated, and this interest was to remain with him throughout his life (see page 154). Their communal interest in astronomy is repeatedly mentioned in 'old

Es's' diary. Thus he notes in July 1933 that Mauk was working on a lithograph of the phosphorescent sea (cat. no. 231) and wanted to show the Plough in the night sky. He noticed that his son had forgotten to do this constellation in mirror image (for what is drawn on the stone appears reversed in the print). Of course, this would not do, and 'old Es' notes that Mauk immediately corrected his mistake.

HOLIDAYS

Every year the family travelled abroad during the summer holidays. 'Apart from our own holiday we also provided the finance for the holidays of two other families, who needed a break for health reasons,' Escher says in his diary. For the same reasons Mauk usually stayed at Dutch seaside resorts, which he hated. In 1913 he convinced his father that the coasts abroad were more beautiful and just as healthy. They chose Brittany, and his mother, 'though reluctantly', gave her permission.

Their last holiday abroad before the First World War was to be cut short. They had gone to the Tyrol on 11 July 1914, two weeks after the murder at Sarajevo which precipitated the outbreak of war. When railway connections were threatened, the Eschers were forced to leave some of their luggage behind and return to Arnhem in a goods train.

OOSTERBEEK

When the first Belgian refugees crossed the border, Mauk was allowed to go to the railway station to give them milk and bread for their journey to Camp Oldenbroek. Later, when Antwerp fell, Sarah was appointed to a local committee for housing refugees in various buildings and looking after them. All this misery made a great impression on Mauk; for St Nicholas' Day he made a wooden figure of the Kaiser on his lathe, and wrote a satirical poem to go with it.

During the war the house in Arnhem was uncomfortable. The Stokvis factory behind the Eschers' house was extended for the manufacture of war materials, producing noise and soot. There was very little they could do about it, and as the house had become too large anyway, now that only Mauk was still living at home, on 31 March 1917 the family moved to the Villa Rosande in nearby Oosterbeek.

SILVER WEDDING

The Eschers celebrated their silver wedding on 27 October 1917. 'As an enemy of celebration, especially when I was forced to play a part myself, I would have preferred to let the day pass unnoticed, but Sarah thought differently and therefore we invited members of the family and a few friends, as well as our sons, to the Maison de Bruyn, on the Eusebiusbuitensingel.' The menus were decorated with portraits of the married couple, dating from 1892 and (probably) 1916. After the meal Mauk entertained as the 'instant artist' Velocitas. 'Our servants took part in the dinner in an

12

Top: A portrait of his father, drawn by Escher c. 1916

Above: A fragment from the diary of Escher's father

adjoining room.' One of the presents was a bowl designed by Mauk, made from embossed silver by an Arnhem silversmith called Holthuis. Mauk took a photograph of his parents in which the silver bowl can be seen.

NO TYRANT

Escher always put forward his point of view quietly and clearly to his children and was never overbearing. For example, when Mauk suggested in 1919 that he should give up architecture and take up the graphic arts, his father pointed out the difficulties of earning enough as an artist to be able to support a family, but said that, all the same, if Mauk really wanted to do this, he would not stand in his way. His sons had to decide for themselves. However, he could not help worrying about the increasing number of grandchildren, 'seeing that their parents are not earning anything'. A last straw was when a grandson, Ruud, Beer's son, decided to become an 'artist'. (Ruud was to become the composer Rudolf Escher.)

THE HAGUE

In 1927 the Eschers decided to move to The Hague. This was an old plan to be closer to 'our boys'. Nol had died on a mountaineering expedition. Mauk had become a graphic artist and was living in Italy, and in The Hague Sarah would be better able to help him to organize exhibitions in Holland. The couple felt at home immediately in the new house and 'old Es' became a member of the De Witte club, introduced by Lindo, a friend from his days in Japan.

Every time Escher saw one of his youngest son's works, he was interested in the technique Mauk had used, though his first question concerned its sale value. This attitude influenced his judgment. He certainly appreciated traditional subjects, but the unorthodox worried him. On the enigmatic woodcut *Metamorphosis* of 1937 (cat. no. 298), he remarks: 'Altogether it reminds me of the word-pictures he did some time ago for Bijenkorf wrapping-paper [cat. no. 232]. I consider this a continuation of his earlier productions, and very suitable to keep as an example of this sort of work.' After an enthusiastic letter from the art critic G. H. 's-Gravesande about the woodcut *Day and Night* of 1938 (cat. no. 303), he writes: 'Naturally we are pleased about this encouraging response. It seems to me that the price of 50 guilders he asked for this woodcut is too high. I do not think he will easily find a buyer at this price, although the effort that went into the work has certainly earned it.'

The official commission to illustrate a booklet on Delft, the purchase of his prints by the Ministry of Education, Arts and Sciences, the increasing interest in Mauk's work shown by the printrooms of the major museums, and the excellent reviews the prints received, all combined to set his father's mind somewhat at ease again.

Top: A portrait of his mother, drawn by Escher c. 1921

Above: Escher on holiday in Brittany, 1913

13

THE END

When he was over ninety, 'old Es' began to feel his age. In 1935 he had to cancel a two-day trip to South Limburg, organized by the Royal Institute of Engineers. 'Unfortunately I cannot go on this trip very easily, now that my sight and hearing are failing and I cannot walk very well.' He could still listen to music on the radio using headphones, and he could read reasonably well with a magnifying glass and a sodium lamp. His friend Lindo regularly fetched him to walk to De Witte. He liked to go on walks when somebody accompanied him. He felt happy quietly browsing through *De Ingenieur* (the journal of the Royal Institute of Engineers) in the evening or writing his diary. Towards the end of his life someone would read the newspaper to him and then he would continue himself. On 4 June 1939 the diary notes a visit from Lindo, who had just read in the newspaper that the engineer Frans Bourdrez had died in China: 'a descendant of my supervisor'. This is the last entry. George Arnold Escher died on 14 June.

Escher's father and mother at the party for their silver wedding on 27 October 1917.
The silver bowl designed by Escher is on the table next to his mother

14

Early Life 1898–1922

While the three youngest sons, George, Nol and Mauk, were small, their mother used to take them to the seaside resort of Zandvoort nearly every year, accompanied by a nanny. Mauk, the youngest of the three, was a sickly child. In 1905 his doctor prescribed a longer period by the sea, with the result that Mauk was put into a home for children, and had to attend the local village school after the summer holidays had ended. The worst memories of his childhood date back to this time. Walking through the village on his way to school in a bright red suit chosen for him by his mother, he was taunted by the other children.

In 1906 he returned home to Arnhem. In 1907 he started carpentry lessons with Van Eldik, and took piano lessons from Mrs Stenfert Kroese-Dupuy, the sister of a well-known music critic.

In 1912 he went to the *hogere burgerschool* (secondary school) in the Schoolstraat, where he remained until 1918. At school his marks were not especially good—except for drawing—and he had to repeat the second class. The art teacher, F. W. van der Haagen, took an interest in him and taught him how to make linocuts. Later they became close friends.

He failed his final examinations; and although he did not fail in mathematics, he was not outstandingly good in the subject either. Later, when his prints were particularly admired by mathematicians, he would exaggerate by claiming that he never got the hang of it. When he accepted the Hilversum cultural prize in 1965, he said that 'at school in Arnhem I was an extremely poor pupil in arithmetic and algebra, and I still have great difficulty with the abstractions of figures and letters. I was slightly better at solid geometry, because it appealed to my imagination, but even in that subject I never excelled at school.'

MUSIC

During his school years Mauk made some lifelong friends; among the closest were Roosje Ingen Housz, Jan van der Does de Willebois and his older sister Fiet, and Bas Kist. He formed a string quartet with Roosje, Bas and Conny Umgrove, in which he played the cello. He had by this time given up the piano. He had lessons from the principal cellist and Deputy Director of the Arnhem Orkestvereniging, Leo Ruijgrok. However, after a few years he began to neglect the cello too. With a characteristic mixture of sentiment and self-mockery he wrote to Roosje in 1919:

'Yesterday, in a sentimental mood, I picked up my cello again. It was covered with a thick layer of dust! Then I kept the family awake until half past two with my caterwauling; and all this on two strings only, since the G and the C broke a long time ago! I played by the eerie light from a skull into which I have fitted an electric light bulb. What is man, when all's said?'

Mauk would be the last to pretend to any real achievement in music. He could not manage the more difficult fingering on the cello because his hands were too small. His son George later remembered that he sometimes improvised on the piano, playing sombre chords that never turned into real melodies. When he settled in Baarn in the second half of his life, he took flute lessons for a short time from Adriaan Bonsel, principal flautist of the Radio Orchestra. He worked hard and enjoyed it, but his lower lip turned out to be too thin to play high notes, and after a while he gave it up. He continued to go to concerts all his life, and music was a great source of inspiration for his work, as we see repeatedly in his letters and essays.

THE FIRST GRAPHIC WORK

Mauk was not very religious, but his parents sent him to catechism classes, as was usual in those days. In October 1913 he joined the Reverend P. Heering's classes, and it was here that he met Bas Kist, who was also interested in printing techniques. Mauk experimented early on with linoleum cuts. For the first ones he made, he printed with purple ink from an ink pad. One of his first prints was a portrait of his father, dating from 1916 (cat. no. 1); probably the photograph of his parents on page 11 was used as a model for this.

For his visit to Brittany in 1913 Mauk was given a camera by his father. On this holiday he and his parents first visited Antwerp, Ghent and Bruges, where they bought reproductions of works by Memling and Jan van Eyck for Mauk's 'work and art corner'. These remained on his wall until his death. The greatest attraction in Paris was the Eiffel Tower, which lived up to all expectations.

On 7 January 1917 Mauk and Bas went together to visit the painter and etcher Gert Stegeman (1858–1940) in his new studio, which had a printing press, in the Sabelpoort in Arnhem. The small number of etchings that Mauk made during this period were printed here, including *Railway Bridge across the Rhine at Oosterbeek* (cat. no. 6).

Top: Self-portrait, c. 1917
(the estimated date which Escher
himself later put on the drawing is most
probably inaccurate)

Above: Escher's white cat; drawing,
c. 1919

LITERATURE

The three friends Mauk Escher, Jan van der Does de Willebois
and Bas Kist met regularly in Mauk's seven-sided living-room in
the Villa Rosande in Oosterbeek, where the Escher family lived
from 1917. According to Bas, they talked endlessly. All three were
attracted to literature with a psychological interest: Russian
novels such as Andreyev's *The Seven Who Were Hanged*,
Dostoevski's *Crime and Punishment* and Gogol's *Dead Souls*. They
read aloud many poems and prose pieces. Mauk would often go
for walks with Jan, frequently at night; sometimes they would go
on long hikes lasting a few days with members of the De Willebois
family. He also enjoyed playing billiards—at home, in a café or at
the Kists'.

During this period he also began to write his own poetry and
prose, some of which showed a developing ability to put his
observations and feelings clearly into words. Later he was to write
numerous letters and speeches, and essays on his own work.

A few compositions remain from his last school years. In one of
them he describes a Sunday morning in winter when he went for a
walk in the snowy landscape, carrying a sketchbook:

'You walk out into a light-white world as a small dark speck.
Everywhere is quiet, peaceful and tingling light. It gives you an
indescribable feeling, a lump in your throat, and you are ashamed
of being dark in all that light. I walked along the narrow path by
the railway track to the big bridge over the Rhine. I pulled myself
up onto the tip of the wide pillar jutting out and supporting the
first arch on the river bank. I sat in the hot sun and made a sketch
of the low summer dyke, which cast a beautiful blue shadow on
the white meadow below it. The town was hazy on the horizon; the
outlines of church towers could be clearly recognized. While I was
sitting there so quietly alone, a very small bird hopped over the
snow—perhaps it was a wren. It was enjoying the fine weather, it
chirped merrily and blinked at the sun. It skipped towards the
water and fluttered about a bit. Then it flew away, so I left too.'

DELFT

With Mauk in his fifth and last year at school it was time to be
thinking of a career. His parents thought that he should have a
'normal' job. A career in architecture seemed the most suitable to
them and also to Mauk himself. His mother went to Amsterdam
to talk to Professor Derkinderen, who recommended the Higher
Technical School in Delft, rather than the Royal Academy of Art
in Amsterdam, which Mauk preferred. But Mauk upset this
programme when in his final examination on 3 August 1918 he
failed in history, constitutional organization, political economy
and book-keeping. He consoled himself, as his father notes in his
diary, 'by drawing and making a linocut of a sunflower' (cat. no.
20).

However, there was still a chance for him to leave Oosterbeek.
At that time there was a rule that boys of conscription age who
had failed their final examination need only retake the subjects in

Escher and his schoolmates in Zandvoort, 1905 (Escher on front row, second from the left, wearing a sailor suit)

which they had failed. Mauk, who had been granted a deferment of military service, could enlist in 1919, and meanwhile in 1918 take private lessons and start his studies in Delft.

The Rector of the Higher Technical School in Delft agreed to this plan. Mauk attended lectures and became a member of the student body. He found a room with a servant of the club, designed sets for a play and did a drawing for the student almanac.

He repeatedly had to interrupt his studies. As a result of an intractable skin infection, he fell so far behind with his lectures that, as he wrote to Roosje Ingen Housz in January 1919, he was not even trying to catch up again. 'I think I will just do lots of drawings now, technical drawings too.' He asked whether he could make a portrait of her. In February he wrote to her about a visit to Professor R. N. Roland Holst: 'He strongly advised me to do some woodcuts and I immediately followed his advice, with the enclosed result. Large blocks of wood are too expensive and small ones are really only suitable for bookplates. I was therefore forced to make a bookplate.' It turned out to be one for his dearest friend Roosje. 'I send it to you, even though it isn't particularly good— but it is my first woodcut. It is wonderful work but far more difficult than working with linoleum, because this end-grain palmwood is terribly hard.' Five days later he sent her thirty prints: 'Here are 30 roses' (cat. no. 27).

In the accompanying letter he proudly quotes from a review, in the weekly paper *De Hofstad*, of his entry for the annual exhibition of the Artibus Sacrum society, of which he and Bas Kist were members: 'The works that first attract our attention include the beautiful woodcuts (?) by M. C. Escher, who entered a few portraits and a sunflower, soberly executed and with a beautiful contrast between black and white.' Mauk had inserted the question mark after 'woodcuts' because they were actually linocuts.

HAARLEM

In May 1919 the Ministry of Defence refused his request to enter military service. As a result he was not allowed to take the examinations in Delft without a complete final examination from secondary school. It was decided that he should break off his studies, which he did not regret in the slightest. He now tried to become apprenticed to an architect, but was advised first to acquire some practical experience and theoretical understanding of building at the School for Architecture and Decorative Arts in Haarlem. In September he moved to Haarlem, where he found a sitting-room with an adjoining bedroom. The landlady gave him a pure white cat as a present. A week after the start of classes he wrote to Jan van der Does de Willebois that he had met Samuel

17

Jessurun de Mesquita, who taught nature drawing and graphic arts. Mauk showed him his work, and De Mesquita saw enough in it to advise him to continue. The Director, H. C. Verkruysen, agreed with this opinion; and so, with his parents' permission, Mauk devoted himself entirely to what he called his favourite occupation: 'the graphic and decorative arts, in particular woodcuts'. He had finally arrived, and he much preferred Haarlem to Arnhem and Oosterbeek.

His new pet was pleasant company and an ideal model. It inspired him to make a woodcut (cat. no. 28), which he completed at the beginning of November. Two months later this woodcut appeared in the weekly paper *Eigen Haard*, with an article, 'De schoone eenvoud' (Beautiful Simplicity), written by his friend Henk Calkoen. (According to Escher's father, this piece was far too flattering.) Calkoen was engaged to Heleen van Thienen, for whom Mauk had once made a bookplate depicting two pelicans (cat. no. 16).

Pelicans as a symbol of parental care are shown in the design for a 1920 calendar for the Arnhem Life Insurance Company in a far more realistic way, because the Director of this company, Bas's father, had lent him a large book of photographs of the Hamburg Zoo. He also used this book for the wild animals that accompanied the naked figures in his prints of the Garden of Eden. He drew Eve from a live model in his room. He wrote to Jan: 'The model has now been to my room four times. It is wonderful work and I will finish the first study next week. A young girl's body is moving and beautiful.'

In another letter to Jan he described (in the third person) the tremendous experience he had had in a church, listening to the organ: 'Suddenly a storm wind chased through the pipes of the organ and a thundering voice announced the glory of God! Thereupon the young man lay down on his back on the cold flagstones, in the middle of the church at that. He felt his heart swelling amidst the hurricane, amidst the resounding thundering voice. The pillars of the church could no more bear this sound than he. They stretched out, like a man stretches when he wakes up in the morning, so forcefully that it seemed there might be an accident.

'The young man lay on his back on the cold flagstones of the church and stretched out his arms, as if he were going to be crucified. He grabbed hold of the huge stones with his fingers and was aware of lying on his great mother, Earth. He felt that Mother Earth was a sphere and his outstretched arms almost touched at the other side of the earth. Above him he could see the undulating, swaying pillars. Wind blew through the organ pipes even more forcefully and thunderously. The organ grew much larger; the pipes reached from Heaven down to the earth and the young man felt such a strong wind that he rose from the stones and flew into the air, right through the swaying pillars.'

In the summer of 1920 Mauk and Jan stayed for three weeks on the island of Texel, with a farmer called Zutphen. Mauk did many

Top: Portrait of farmer Zutphen, with whom Escher stayed during the summer of 1920; drawing, August 1920

Above: Self-portrait in a chair; drawing, 1920

drawings there, including some of his host and his fourteen-year-old daughter.

In December he went home to his parents. He showed them his latest drawings, including a study of the interior of the St Bavo church in Haarlem, where he often used to sit and draw in the cold. He also tried out on them a lecture on the Dance of Death in art. In February 1921 he gave this lecture, accompanied with lantern slides, to the pupils and teachers at the school in Haarlem. The performance lasted three hours. De Mesquita came over especially from Amsterdam, and Verkruysen was highly pleased. In October of the same year he also gave a talk on fairy-tales.

Notes have been kept of both lectures, showing how thoroughly and systematically Escher approached these subjects. He was not only concerned with depictions of the Dance of Death, but also with death itself, the fact that everything is doomed, as a general phenomenon. He began his lecture by outlining a scheme with categories such as 'The Living', 'The Lifeless', 'Moving' and 'Motionless', applied to the human condition, to nature and objects, and particularly to the various art forms.

In his lecture on fairy-tales, too, he tried to put forward a few basic principles. He pointed out that the nature of the fairy-tale is 'non-historical: timeless'. He added that this can be seen in three ways: '1. The fact that no one actually created it . . . 2. that the action itself is not dependent on the passage of time . . . 3. that the action takes place in the present.'

FRANCE AND ITALY

Mauk and his parents travelled along the Riviera and through Italy from 22 March to 16 May 1921. It is typical of Mauk's visual interests that he was not very impressed by the wealth of subtropical flowers. As he wrote to Jan from Menton: 'Of course, when you see all this for the first time, it is overwhelming and therefore interesting. But if you are in the middle of it for a week or so, it starts to become quite ordinary.' Rather than flowers, he drew large cacti and olive trees. He also went in search of high places to draw views—of harbours, for example. When his parents took the Pont Transbordeur to cross the mouth of the harbour in Marseilles, he took the elevator so that he could cross the aerial bridge. Much later, in 1936, he made a print of this bridge (cat. no. 290).

He had a stroke of luck when he won 1,150 francs at the roulette table in Monte Carlo. These winnings came in useful when the party went to Florence and he bought a coloured head of St Bernardino and a ceramic plaque of St Francis.

EASTER FLOWER AND ST FRANCIS

In October 1921 Mauk finished a series of woodcuts (cat. nos. 68–83) for the booklet *Flor de Pascua* (Easter Flower), semi-jocular, semi-serious philosophical texts written by his friend Aad van Stolk. In a very rudimentary form, the woodcuts in the booklet showed motifs that later were to become of central

Escher's 'working and drawing corner'
in Arnhem, c. 1915

significance: the mirror image (*The Scapegoat*), crystal shapes (*Beautiful*) and the spherical mirror (*The Sphere*). (In August he had already made his first spherical-mirror drawing; he had brought back the sphere from a visit to Innsbruck.) The cover for the booklet was designed by Van Stolk's wife, Fiet, the sister of Mauk's friend Jan. The booklet appeared in November.

In the same month Mauk wrote to Jan about a print he was thinking of making: 'A tree with countless birds in its branches, in a field full of flowers, animals and people, a distant horizon and a sky full of clouds.' And in January 1922: 'For seven whole days I have been working like a madman: thank God a gentle St Francis, surrounded by many marvellous birds, is coming into being.'

This large print (cat. no. 89) was the first to sell in great numbers. Nevertheless, his father wrote in his diary in March, Mauk was 'dissatisfied with the lack of success of his work and also with the signboard commissioned by the welfare organization of Van Wijk–Rom van Stolk in Rotterdam'. This was a sign for the De Arend (The Eagle) clubhouse: Mauk had received the commission through Rom, Aad's brother. He also did a woodcut vignette for De Arend (cat. no. 92).

As far as one can gather, he was never paid for these jobs. He did not mind, as we see from a letter written eighteen months later to Jan: 'Do tell Rom van Stolk that my mother sent me a piece to read by Van Wijk in the journal *Volksontwikkeling* (Social Development) about the activities in De Arend. After reading it I had the unpleasant feeling of being a good-for-nothing compared with the extremely hard, worthwhile and humane work that he carries out. I am sure that at the moment, because of lack of funds, they do not intend to pay for the eagle I did for them. They will therefore probably not be interested to learn that after reading this article I felt ashamed about ever having wanted any return.'

Mauk needed fresh inspiration and hoped to find it in Italy. He made plans with Bas and Jan to go to Florence in April. He gave up his room in Haarlem; a decisive step in his life had been taken.

Left: Bas Kist made a linocut portrait of his friend Mauk (left); the latter made some improvements by cutting away the surround and adding a whiff of tobacco smoke (right). Both states are printed on the same sheet of paper

Right: M.C. Escher, c. 1920

Italy and Spain 1922–1924

On 5 April 1922 Escher left Arnhem for Florence with Jan van der Does de Willebois and Bas Kist. In his travel diary he noted the last pieces of parental advice given at the station: 'Mrs Escher: "Son, don't smoke too much!" Mrs Kist: "Son, make sure you get enough to eat!" Mr Willebois: "Son, don't drink too much!"'

At the end of his life Bas Kist would still clearly remember this trip: 'As soon as the train started moving we felt enormously relieved, and we never stopped laughing until it arrived. We stayed in a pension on the Arno. To our eyes, only the Primitives and the early Renaissance artists were worth seeing. Michelangelo's *David*, which Mauk reckoned you encountered everywhere in Florence, was extremely boring. We particularly admired the design of the marble of the Medici Chapel. Our favourite artists included Cimabue and lesser gods like Margeritone d'Arezzo. We went several times to a small chapel outside the city, San Leonardo in Arceti (which Mauk had discovered the previous year), particularly for the marble pulpit with the Descent from the Cross.'

The three friends and Jan's sister, Lex, who had joined the group, were present on 15 April for the solemn occasion when a (mechanical) dove, flying to and fro between the Duomo and the Baptistery along a wire, set off an ear-shattering firework, while an enormous crowd cheered below. After a last visit to Santa Croce and the Baptistery, where they saw 'many new-born infants baptized', Bas had to return home on 17 April. He borrowed the money from Escher and had just enough over to buy a box of dates to eat on the journey. A few days later, Jan also returned to Holland, and Escher and Lex travelled on through Empoli to Poggibonsi and San Gimignano. They covered the last stretch in a carriage, 'while the 17 towers of San Gimignano drew nearer and nearer. It was like a dream, which could not possibly be real.' Escher began to do some serious drawing here. On 28 April 'I began in the morning by making a sketch of an olive tree, and in the background the silhouette of the towers of the town.'

On 2 May Lex returned to Florence and Escher to San Gimignano. On 5 May he visited Volterra and went on to Siena, where he found a room in the Pensione Giuseppa Alessandri at Via Salustro Bandini 19. He was to return there many times. He admired the Lorenzetti brothers and the early Sienese painters, of which there were many examples. He sketched the city, the view from his room, and in the following days found beautiful places to draw Siena from a distance.

On a 'very long' walk in the neighbourhood of Siena, he noted that in the hills of the Monte Maggio 'the earth was mostly dark red. I saw a large beetle which was pushing a big ball (of plant fibre and earth) up the mountainside, walking backwards. The ball had a diameter of about 3 cm. The female was following her mate. Both beetles were completely black.' A pair of these dung beetles appears in a wood engraving of 1935 (cat. no. 273).

On 15 May he travelled on to Orvieto. In the Duomo he saw 'beautiful frescoes by Signorelli, though as late as 15th century'. He made sketches of the town and of the sheer rock faces. The region, he wrote, was 'the most beautiful I have seen so far'.

On 22 May Escher left again. He travelled through Terontola and Perugia to Assisi. Here, in the Hotel Minerva, he met the Dutch painter and graphic artist Huub Gerretsen, with whom he had many acquaintances in common, some from the school in Haarlem. Shortly before his death Gerretsen described this encounter: 'One day a boy came in who turned out to be Dutch, of all amazing things. He had a striking nose, clear blue eyes, a rather unsure mouth and an expression of genial frankness. He told me how much he was enjoying Italy, a country that should never be left. After he had gone he sent me a card from Ravenna, and afterwards we met frequently. It's amazing how his face changed over the years; his cameo-like profile, the hawk-like nose, the wispy eyebrows like an insect's antennae—they fitted perfectly; but his eyes were still the same clear blue, his laugh still as sudden and generous as it had been under the Italian sun.'

On 29 May Escher travelled on to Urbino, writing that 'I shall probably have to stay here for months to learn to understand these wildly undulating hills and luxuriant plant life'. Again he explored the surrounding country, taking bus and train to Calmazzo and walking back to Urbino in six hours.

On 2 June he went to Ravenna. Waiting for a connection, he had plenty of time to visit the Duomo in Rimini and lie on the beach sunbathing. He did not stay long in Ravenna either: on 5 June he went to Venice and visited the Biennale. Then on 9 June he went to Padua; he would have liked to stay longer there but he felt restless. He left for Milan the next day and took the train back to Holland on 12 June; as he wrote to his parents, 'in order not to have too much to assimilate'. When he arrived home he showed his parents a folder of drawings from his travels, and 'old Es', with his usual love of detail, noted they were 'all in pen, mostly with black lines, and some with halftones obtained by scratching out'.

Italian landscape (surroundings of
Siena); drawing, January 1923

Escher had his furniture moved from Haarlem and went back to live at the Villa Rosande with his parents. He began to appear regularly in 'old Es's' diary again: on 6 August 'I looked with Mauk at the blackbird through the large telescope on the roof. As usual it sits singing high up in the dead beech tree in the Beukenlaan.... S. enjoys the singing while he is picking raspberries, peas and beans, and I enjoy it when I go to the wc, where I can see the bird clearly.'

But Escher could not find peace at home. He used one of his many Italian sketches for a woodcut (cat. no. 93), and that was the extent of it. He wanted to go back to the south, and an opportunity soon presented itself. His friends Aad and Fiet van Stolk were travelling to Alicante in Spain on a Dutch freighter, and Escher could go along with half his expenses paid if he was prepared to help look after their two small children.

Escher seized the opportunity eagerly. After a week's holiday on the island of Terschelling with Jan van der Does de Willebois, he filled a large trunk full of his belongings (including a pair of binoculars given by his parents). He did not plan to return soon, much to his mother's regret. On 13 September he embarked on the *Juno* in Amsterdam.

This was the first time he had travelled by freighter and he took to it immediately. He got on very well with the crew, and the food was excellent. In his diary he noted that, from the Bay of Biscay, the ship was regularly accompanied by schools of dolphins. One evening the first mate called him to the bows. 'I saw an unforgettably beautiful spectacle: some porpoises, illuminated by the phosphorescent sea, were playing just in front of the ship. They shot forwards leaving a tail of light behind them.' He made a drawing of it the next day, and in February 1923, a woodcut of this subject (cat. no. 97).

In Alicante the Van Stolks disembarked, but Escher had decided to sail on to Tarragona. When they passed the mouth of the Ebro the colour of the sea 'suddenly changed from dark blue to green, and then to an even lighter greenish yellow. The transition was extremely sudden. It was caused by the silt of the river. I did a sketch of this in colour' (see page 41).

BULLFIGHTS

On 30 September he disembarked in Tarragona. The same day he left by train for Barcelona, where he went sightseeing. He also went to a bullfight, which he found 'off-putting and barbaric. The large number of horses that is sacrificed is particularly sad and horrible to see. Many of them were led away walking, while large lumps and pieces of their insides hung out of their disembowelled bodies. In total, 17 horses and 6 bulls were slaughtered between half past three and 6 o'clock.' On 5 October he went on an excursion to Vich. The following day he left for Madrid, a train journey of fifteen hours. 'The journey was extremely interesting and the landscape very varied.'

In Madrid he naturally visited the Prado, 'which contains an enormous number of paintings by great artists who mean nothing to me, as well as some beautiful ones: Bosch, Memling, Breughel and primitive Spanish artists'. He went to another bullfight, 'which appealed to me more than the one in Barcelona, despite the gruesome murder of the horses'. After two days in Avila, where he saw the sights and admired the view, he travelled to Toledo on 12 October. He wrote to Jan van der Does de Willebois about this 'old, proud city': 'a tangled web of steep and narrow, winding alleyways, a mighty cathedral and many old churches—all set on a rock and encircled by the sluggish Tagus. Two high and wide-arched bridges give access to the city.' He wanted to draw one of these bridges, the Puente de San Martín, but it proved very difficult to find a good place—almost everywhere it was indescribably dirty or there were large rats. 'Finally I found a clean, smooth rock where I sat down exhausted and began to draw. This went wonderfully well and the result filled me with joy.'

A MARATHON TRAIN JOURNEY

After a few days he wanted to go on to Granada. There was a good train connection once every two days. He was to leave at 8.35 on the morning of 17 October. He was at the station at 8.15 but it took a long time to buy a ticket and marshal his luggage. He later wrote to Jan: 'At 8.35 I stormed onto the platform, and for the first time I saw a Spanish train leave on time before my very eyes. (I later heard that King Alphonse came in person to give the station-master a medal.) Furious and powerless, I stood and watched as the train drew out of the station.' Because he did not want to wait two days for the next connection, he decided to leave for Granada anyway later that day, 'on a wretched local train with extremely bad connections'.

The journey took more than twenty-four hours; he sent Jan descriptions of his fellow-travellers. Of a two-year-old girl he wrote: 'She sat down next to her mother, picked a bunch of grapes out of a basket and began to eat them one by one with a very serious expression on her face. She had a system for this: first she examined the grape attentively from every angle, then she put it in her mouth, took it out again, then looked again at the beautifully shining and now transparent grape and finally ate it up with relish, spitting the pips and the skin neatly on the floor.' In his diary he described an 'amorous couple': 'The male was disgustingly ugly with a two-week-old stubbly beard, rotten teeth and a few brown hairs glued onto his skull. It was strange to see the woman—hardly a beauty herself—look on this disgusting creature with rapture.'

GRANADA AND SEVILLE

In Granada Escher visited the Alhambra. He did not have great expectations of it, but was pleasantly surprised. 'It was amazingly Eastern. The strange thing for me was the great wealth of decoration (bas-relief in stucco), and the great dignity and simple

23

beauty of the whole. Those Arabs were aristocrats, such as are no longer found today,' he wrote in his diary. 'The strange thing about this Moorish decoration is the total absence of any human or animal form—even, almost, of any plant form. Perhaps this is a strength and a weakness at the same time.' On 20 October he made a drawing of a section of tile-work that interested him 'for its great complexity and geometric artistry' (see page 41).

On 24 October he left for Seville. Here he asked the Dutch consul about the possibility of travelling to Italy on a Dutch ship. This was indeed possible, and on 6 November he embarked at Cádiz on the freighter *Bacchus* for Genoa.

BACK IN ITALY

Again he enjoyed the sea voyage immensely. When the weather was fine, he sketched the ship. In the evenings he played cards with the captain, the first mate and the chief engineer, 'while I laughed myself sick about the ungodly language which the captain would spew up in his songs'.

On 11 November they arrived in Genoa. Escher stayed there and then in Pisa for a few days, before going on to Siena, where he returned to the familiar Pensione Alessandri. He settled for a long time and worked very hard. On Christmas Day he wrote to Jan: 'My heart would not be able to absorb with sufficient gratitude, nor my brain with sufficient susceptibility, the absolutely new atmosphere in which I am living, the surprising, unexpected happenings and unfamiliar moods that are offered to me every day anew in this blessed place, if I did not try to share them with others to some extent in letters, and if I did not try to get down the abundance to which I am exposed here (like a child's sandcastle on a beach to the laughing waves) with a drawing-pen or a woodcut goudge, and save it from cursed oblivion for a while.' He was ecstatic about the light-blue sky over the hills of Tuscany: 'Bluer than the Mediterranean Sea, bluer than the blue of the Dutch flag—bluer than snow is white and bluer than pitch is black.' The town itself also charmed him greatly: 'Oh, the nocturnal streets of Siena! I made a woodcut of them, which I finished yesterday' (probably cat. no 95).

On New Year's Eve he wrote Jan a lyrical letter about a walk in the rain. 'On my way back, a great joy awaits my childlike mind: my eye is caught by the sparkle of quartz crystals. . . . They are lying by the road—tens, hundreds, thousands of them. I bend down, choose the most beautiful and take them home, as happy as if they had been diamonds.'

He was certainly happy. In January he wrote: 'Rarely, if ever, have I felt calmer, more pleased, more content than in recent times. Many wonderful prints are springing from my mostly industrious hands, and the question whether they contain any beauty I leave to be answered by the miserable generations to come.' He did have sexual problems, however, 'mainly because of the abundant presence of the fair female sex in this town'. As a 'cure' he went to San Gimignano for a few days, 'also to do a few

sketches there. It was not much better: I was the only stranger, surrounded by a large crowd of inquisitive young ladies.' The Fascist regime in Italy also worried him: he saw Mussolini as being fatal for the country, 'and as for the actions of his supporters, the Fascists—any unprejudiced person can see how impossibly, how childishly and criminally they behave'.

In the middle of February he wrote to his parents that lately he had not been able to do much work; he was thinking of going soon to Naples and then to Rome, to return to Siena in the summer, and possibly go to Sicily the following winter. Ten days later he sent them four prints from woodcuts (cat. nos. 94–97); the view of San Gimignano pleased his father most.

On 1 March he left for Naples, where he arrived the next day. He found it very busy and expensive, but he did admire the view of the bay. After a week he had had enough of the city. On 12 March he visited Pompeii and on 14 March he left for Ravello (about twenty miles south-east of Naples, just north of Amalfi), enjoying a three-hour drive in a carriage along the beautiful Amalfi coast. He moved into the Albergo del Toro, where he planned to stay for a long time, as he wrote to his parents and Jan.

At the end of March he noted the arrival at the pension of a 'Mr Umiker with his wife and daughter. A Swiss industrialist who has lived in Russia for twenty years.'

FLORA AND FAUNA

On 2 April he wrote to Jan: 'I am working hard! This is the main reason for my happiness, for the very lovely countryside, the warm spring and my excellent lodgings would not alone make me happy. . . . I am working in pen and ink only—I left woodcuts behind in Siena.' The drawings 'serve only as a diary [his written diary had now come to an end], so that I shall know later what I saw here, and see better what I see now'. He hoped to improve his drawing technique through practice. 'I want to find happiness in the tiniest things—a minute moss plant, 2 cm across, on a rock— and I want to try to do what I've been wanting to do for so long, that is, to copy these infinitesimally small things as precisely as possible and to be aware of their size.' But even the simplest plants he found very difficult to do. 'I won't start on all the beautiful little flowers yet—for colour, even if it is not essential for them, is desirable, and I don't want to use colour.'

Later in April he described a walk through the woods. 'I was peculiarly moved by the angelic life growing on the ground. I have no idea what sorts of flowers grow there in profusion—I don't know their names. But I was so moved that I sat down, trying to flatten as few grasses and plants as possible with my clumsy backside. . . . This brought my head quite close to the silent, joyful, exuberant, celestial children of heaven. They are so humble, so quiet, and they do not mind if you observe them, if you think they are beautiful. . . . Nor do they mind if you don't look at all—they just stand there together all by themselves in the huge stretch of woods and grow and bloom just the same, peacefully, joyfully and

Midsland, on the isle of Terschelling;
drawing, 2 September 1922. The figure
in the chair is probably Jan van der
Does de Willebois

25

silently. I am absolutely sure that they know nothing of the swinish and filthy behaviour of people in their dirty stinking houses—they know only about heaven.'

He also paid a great deal of attention to the local wildlife. He gave a humorous eye-witness account of two lizards mating. 'An enormously fat and beautiful gentleman-lizard, speckled green, black and white, lay basking in the sun when a small, slim, grey lady-lizard came slipping coquettishly from under the dry leaves, wiggling suggestively. They saw each other clearly enough, of course, but they both pretended to be oblivious of the other's presence. The fat male lay snoring, his eyes half shut, and the female looked at the sun. Suddenly, quick as a flash, the male took the uttermost tip of the female's tail in his teeth. She still pretended no to know what was going on, and continued to look at the sun. The male, eyes sparkling, lay quite still for a minute, a silly look on his face and the tip of the female's tail between his teeth. Then with small tugs he hauled his way up and up the tail until at last he was holding the female's body at its middle. You can imagine how he must have felt with a naked female in his teeth! However, the female gradually began to get livelier; she squirmed anxiously in her lover's teeth, as if wondering, "What have I done? What have I started?" Then, with an amazing twist, the male turned his body in such a way that his underside touched the female's and it was then that they must have coupled. The male was still holding the female in his teeth. I'm sure people would never be successful that way.'

IN LOVE DESPITE HIMSELF

On 5 June Escher wrote to Jan: 'Next to me at the small table where I'm writing is a girl of twenty-five. She is eating a biscuit, and seeing her, I am suddenly terribly moved, because it is warm and she is wearing a sleeveless blouse. Girls' arms always have a great effect on me. Not if they are fat red arms, but if they are rather thin and young and slightly sunburnt. . . . It seems, dearest friend, that I haven't written to you for a very long time; and if this is true, this girl is the delightful cause of it. She has taken up a great deal of my thoughts for the past month.'

The girl was Jetta Umiker. Her father was a German-Swiss who had owned a silk-spinning factory near Moscow and fled to Finland and then Switzerland after the Revolution. For the last five years the Umikers had been moving from place to place—in Italy in the winter, in Switzerland in the summer. Jetta's health was poor, 'since she had suffered from starvation for six months in Finland and had seen too many people being murdered', wrote Escher. He had become very involved with her, partly because her father was preventing her from becoming a Catholic. Umiker was strongly anti-religious, seeing religion as the source of all evil. He was an embittered man; however, Escher got on very well with him.

Escher realized that he was falling more and more in love with Jetta. He described the symptoms to Jan with characteristic objectivity: 'When a young man lives in the immediate proximity

A page from Escher's travel diary, April 1922

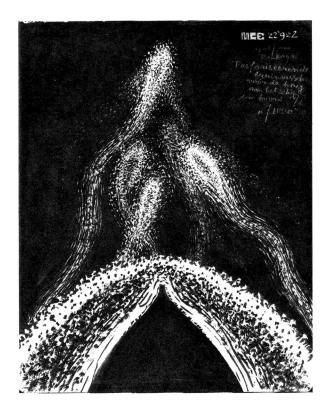

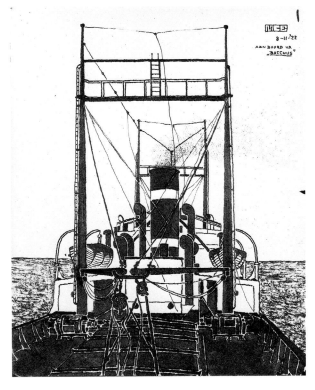

Top: Phosphorescent 'porpoises' (actually dolphins) in front of the bows of the *Juno*; drawing, 29 September 1922

Above: The deck of the *Bacchus*; drawing, 8 November 1922

of a young girl and suddenly notices one day, to his surprise, that he is doing all he can to dazzle that girl, as far as his shyness will let him, and in the most ridiculous ways . . . it is crystal clear that the charm of the girl has taken root in the young man's thoughts. But the ridiculous young man himself—he wonders, his heart beating faster than ever, "Do I love the girl?"'

Escher doubted his capacity for love and compared himself to a little stray dog that scratched about in the neighbourhood of the pension begging for love—that is, attention. 'A week ago I was on the point of telling the girl that I loved her; a mistake which I have already made twice with other girls, and which is to say: "Love me!"; which actually means, I am a poor little dog with sad eyes and trembling legs; I have no master to feed me or house where I can sleep at night on my own cushion; I run around at night through the back streets of the town, my tail between my thin hind legs, and I bark now and then, annoying people who are not asleep; . . . and at half past twelve I creep towards people eating lunch in the garden under the vines and roses, and look up anxiously into their munching faces, and my sad eyes ask: "Feed me, love me!"'

Jetta would now and again throw scraps to the real dog during the course of a meal. Escher describes how this dog stopped him sleeping one night, and how he got up, walked into the garden and threw 'a heavy stone' in its direction. 'A high-pitched yelp showed that I had accidentally hit the animal. A long silence followed, and after half an hour of feeling uneasy, I slept undisturbed until the sun woke me. In the morning I remembered the little wounded dog and I hastened to the scene of the crime like a murderer who can't help returning to the body of his victim. However, the murdered dog was alive and kicking, and looked at me with its anxious, beady little eyes as if to say, "Love me." However, I felt only pity.'

Escher finished the letter with the assurance that 'I shall never again be as stupid as I was before'. However, Jetta's attraction proved too strong. On 21 June he wrote to Jan: 'The girl I wrote to you about a few days ago has left for Switzerland with her parents. Her influence on me was like an electromagnet on a piece of iron; a steadily strengthening current flowed through this electromagnet, so that the miserable bit of iron felt as though it was being drawn towards the magnet more and more forcibly. And although I had firmly resolved to keep my feelings about her loveliness secret, her influence finally became so powerful that on the last day before her departure the bit of iron lost its last vestige of resistance, and clanged into the magnet with a dull thud; which is to say that I unburdened my heart to her—insofar as a weakling could do so— on a walk we took together. In the event, the consequences were less disastrous than I had foreseen. We sat for a few hours on a table-shaped boulder and stared down at the wide expanse of blue sea, while I tried to express in bad French what I could no longer keep to myself. She was not too surprised and, what is more important, did not completely dash my hopes of a future paradise. She even said some things that flattered my self-esteem in the

A few days later Escher left Ravello for Siena. On 9 July his father noted: 'Letter from Mauk with photographs of two of the drawings he did in Ravello. He laments the absence of the Umiker family, especially of their daughter with whom he talked a great deal about art.' Escher also sent these photographs to Jan: '. . . the dark one, with the sea and the small town [Atrani] seen from high above, is about as large as a medium-sized napkin (used at lunch); the other is about half this size. Both of course only black and white and India ink.'

About Jetta he said: 'We write to each other. Yesterday I received a letter for which I had been waiting 9 days; that was almost too long, but now I am content.' He composed a poem about Jetta's hands: '*Tes doigts, longs comme ceux d'un voleur / M'ont doucement volé mon coeur*' ('Your fingers, long as a thief's, have softly stolen my heart'). He fantasized about the future, but he still had his doubts: 'Thinking of all this, we are drumming a triumphal march, a sort of music of the future, on the tanned skin of the bear that still has to be caught—which is pleasant but pointless.' Meanwhile he had grown a beard—an outward sign of the changes that had taken place inside him.

Escher's first one-man show was held from 13 to 26 August at the Circolo Artistico in Siena. This was a milestone, but he paid very little attention to it—Jetta was far more important. Henk and Heleen Calkoen, who visited him in the Pensione Alessandri, noted that he was struggling with dictionaries so that he could write letters in Italian. On 24 August his father noted: 'Letter from Mauk with a self-portrait with beard, informing us that he has asked the Umiker girl he met in Ravello to be his wife, and that he is soon leaving for Zurich to join the Umiker family and become better acquainted with the girl. He is optimistic about being accepted and asks if we will first come to Zurich rather than Siena [on a proposed trip to Italy], so that we can meet the Umiker family.'

Everything went according to plan. On 28 August Escher arrived in Zurich. For the first few days Jetta and he found it 'difficult to get closer to each other', but the ice was soon broken. They went for a lot of walks but were hardly interested in the scenery. Time flew. On 1 September his parents and brother George arrived. His father noted in his diary: 'Picked up by Mauk and his beard. Walk with Mr and Mrs Umiker, Mauk constantly with Jetta, who is slightly older than he and, like her sister, has black hair, large mouth and rather melancholy appearance. We speak German and French with Mr Umiker; Mrs Umiker is Italian and prefers to speak French—apart from Italian and Russian. Mauk likes to speak Italian with the family, while they prefer to speak Russian among themselves. Both daughters Russian type.'

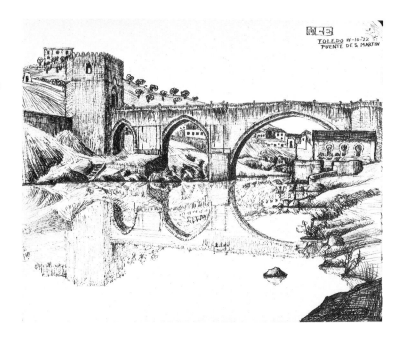

Top: Toledo, Puente de San Martín; drawing, 14 October 1922

Above: Plants and flowers, Ravello; drawing, April 1923

At a later meeting the two pairs of parents talked about Escher's financial prospects. They agreed that he should try to find work to earn a living. For the time being, however, Jetta and he would have to manage on the allowances they received from their parents; they should be able to live on 300 guilders a month in Italy. (Meanwhile Escher had told his parents that he wished to remain in Italy; he thought the people in Holland unpleasant. This saddened his mother.) On 19 September he wrote to Jan: 'I do not want to have a job and will never have one.' He and Jetta thought about opening a shop in Rome, but they did not want to marry yet. 'As you can understand, it was necessary, especially for my mother, to give an official label to the relationship between her son-with-the-beard and the daughter of the other party, and so, after careful deliberation and who knows how many sleepless nights, we were declared to be "in a state of engagement".'

FIRST EXHIBITION IN HOLLAND

On 6 September the engaged couple had to part. Escher left with his family on their tour through northern Italy. His father wrote in his diary: 'Mauk has become introverted about leaving his loved one.' They visited Genoa, Florence and Siena, where the whole Escher family naturally had to stay in the Pensione Alessandri.

Escher's father rather liked the pension, although the rooms were not clean and the furniture was scruffy. The pension took up the second floor of a palace. The town was dirty and an unpleasant smell pervaded the market square. 'Mauk doesn't mind; he thinks Siena is a wonderful town.' Of course they also visited San Gimignano. After Siena they went to Orvieto, Assisi and Ravenna. When they had reached Palanza, Jetta came over. Escher made a few more sketches before returning to Zurich with her.

In November the Umiker family moved to Rome and Escher accompanied them. His parents heard from him at the end of January. He was suffering from his eternal complaint—constipation and weakness caused by being too thin—and the doctor also thought Jetta was too thin. Until she was stronger, she was not to have any children. Nevertheless, they planned to marry in the spring, 'which will be good for Jetta, to escape from her father's uncomfortable company'.

In February Escher had his first exhibition in Holland. It was held in The Hague in the art gallery De Zonnebloem. It was not really a one-man show, for he shared the room with the glass-work of De Bazel. The press paid some attention and on the whole the reviews were favourable. For example, J. Dona wrote in *Elseviers Maandblad* of June 1924: 'This is the work of a young fresh mind which is not intimidated and quietly goes its own way. It is cultured like De Bazel's work, quiet, pure and powerful, and has a strong tendency towards decoration.' The woodcut *St Francis* (cat. no. 89) was bought as a present for the writer Jan Walch because of his play *The Life of a Saint*. Later Escher became a friend of his, and in 1932 illustrated one of his short stories.

Top: On the beach at Viareggio, 10 June 1924; Jetta and Escher, with their respective parents—the Umikers on the left, the Eschers on the right
Centre: After the marriage ceremony,

16 June 1924; the bride and groom with their parents, Jetta's sister Nina, and Escher's brother George
Above: Honeymoon in Annecy; Jetta on the terrace of their hotel

THE WEDDING

The couple decided to get married in Viareggio. The wedding caused many problems— Jetta's father made difficulties over the marriage contract. However, everything was arranged and on 12 June 1924 the wedding took place in the town hall. This was followed on 16 June by a religious ceremony in a room in a Catholic school, because Jetta had entered the Roman Catholic Church despite her father's opposition. The same afternoon the young couple left on their honeymoon to Genoa and then Annecy. Ten days later Escher's father noted: 'Letter from M. and J. from Annecy in a very cheerful and light-hearted mood.' They were to go to Holland for three months to visit family and friends.

The newly married couple in Leiden, 28 August 1924

Rome 1924–1935

On 19 July 1924 the Escher-Umiker couple arrived at the Villa Rosande after visiting Escher's brother and sister-in-law in Brussels. During the following months they travelled through Holland, staying with friends and family. Naturally Jetta was taken to see the old places; Escher took a photograph of her by the Borger Oak, of which he had once made a linocut (cat. no. 29). They also made a boat trip to the Kaag lake.

They returned on 15 October. They first travelled to Chartres, where they went to look at the cathedral, and by the end of October they were back in Italy to meet Jetta's parents. They went to Siena and naturally stayed in the Pensione Alessandri, and visited San Gimignano. In November they moved into the Pensione San Carlo in Frascati. This town, with its beautiful parks, was within easy reach of Rome; they would have liked to settle there, but could not find a suitable house. They did find one in Rome: they bought the top floor of a house that was still being built in a new part of the city on the slopes of the Monte Verde—Via Alessandro Poerio 100.

While they were waiting for the house to be completed, they spent the winter in the pension in Frascati. Escher made a large woodcut portrait of his wife (cat. no. 101) and a view of Vitorchiano, near Viterbo (cat. no. 102). In March the house was finished, but they decided to let it dry out all summer and for the time being moved into the Albergo del Toro in Ravello, the place where they had first met. Their memories and the beautiful scenery there were such strong attractions that the Eschers often spent the summer months in Ravello in subsequent years.

ROME

At the start of October they were finally able to furnish the house in Rome. Later that month Nol Escher lost his life during a mountaineering expedition in the Tyrol; Escher had to leave immediately for Merano to identify his brother's body. Shortly afterwards his parents came to Rome to see the new house. Escher's father made notes in his diary about the building's lack of solidity.

From December 1925 to March 1926 Escher worked on a series of six woodcuts of the Days of the Creation (cat. nos. 104–9). With sixteen other woodcuts and a good forty drawings he showed them from 2 to 16 May in the galleries of the Association of Roman Engravers, at the Palazzetto Venezia in Rome. The exhibition attracted a lot of attention and the general reaction of the critics was favourable. Reviews also appeared in Holland in the national newspapers *Nieuwe Rotterdamsche Courant* and *De Tijd;* the review in the former was written by Dr H. M. R. Leopold, a Dutch archaeologist working for the Dutch Historical Institute in Rome. Escher formed an excellent relationship with him and with the Director of the Institute, Dr G. J. Hoogewerff. The woodcut most praised at the exhibition was *The Second Day of the Creation (The Division of the Waters)*. Escher would sell many prints of it.

The Eschers were not satisfied with their house; it was too small, especially in view of the fact that there was soon to be an addition to the family. They found a better house not far away (Via Alessandro Poerio 94, renumbered a few years later to 122). The purchase was completed in June but they could not yet move in, for the house was not finished.

On 23 July George was born. Escher thought he was 'adorable, sweet and beautiful', as he wrote to his parents. In a letter to Roosje, who had meanwhile married his friend Jan, he gave an ironic description of the christening ceremony: 'When we arrived we found King Emmanuel and Mussolini patiently sitting on the stairs and the Fascist brass band of the Monte Verde played the Dutch national anthem. There were also a couple of cardinals and choirboys swinging incense about.'

At the end of September Escher received a telegram from Fiet van Stolk from Vietri; Aad, her husband, had died. Escher immediately travelled there. He found Fiet and her two children staying in a shabby, dirty neighbourhood and took them to a hotel nearby. Aad's funeral moved Escher deeply. His friendship with Fiet would last through the years.

In October Escher's parents again travelled to Rome and stayed a month. They looked at the new house; it was still far from being completed. Finally, in February 1927, the Eschers were able to move in. Escher had his own studio on the fourth floor, which fulfilled a wish he had had for a long time.

GROWING FAME

Meanwhile Escher had more and more exhibitions in Holland, sometimes on his own but often together with other artists. In 1926 he had exhibitions in Arnhem and Amsterdam; in 1927 another in Amsterdam, and in 1928 one in Leiden. By 1929 he had become so well known that he was able to hold exhibitions in five places, often on his own: in Rotterdam, Utrecht, Leeuwarden (in the house where he was born), Arnhem and The Hague. From then on the number of exhibitions steadily increased. In 1931 he became a member of De Grafische, and in 1932 of Pulchri Studio. These artists' associations held exhibitions of members' work once a year in Amsterdam in the Stedelijk Museum and three times a year in The Hague respectively. Escher always contributed a few prints.

The reviews were often lengthy and usually favourable. Escher's individual talent was recognized. Reviewers typically expressed a number of reactions to his work that were to reappear again and again over the years. It was considered 'unspontaneous', 'non-pictorial' and 'reasoned'.

For example, R. W. P. de Vries wrote in the *Nieuwe Rotterdamsche Courant* of 2 October 1927: 'Escher's pen-and-ink and brush drawings and woodcuts have a dogmatic assurance, a conscious, cool sobriety which precludes any spontaneity.... He devotes himself to technique and tries to keep this as pure as possible.... He seems to be at his best when he works purely mechanically in his woodcuts. He avoids any pictorial effect and shows landscapes and city views in a cool white and black ... and is fascinated not by the accidental or the picturesque but by the typical, the "whole", which often has a constructional quality.'

And Just Havelaar wrote in *Het Vaderland* of 1 February 1929: 'Escher is a patient, precise, cool draughtsman.... But it is possible to pursue an aim too rigorously.... The work becomes too intellectual. It is more patient than intensive. It gives an impression of coming too much from the head, which is something else than coming from the intuitive imagination!'

A number of dealers now had his work in stock, not only in Holland, but also in Paris, Zurich, Batavia (present-day Jakarta) and even in the United States. One of his acquaintances in Rome introduced him to William Douglas of New Haven, Connecticut, who sold Escher's works to students for a total of 220 dollars ('Good prospects', Escher's father noted in his diary) and managed to place the entire collection of prints with 'the best print man of New York'.

The woodcut *The Division of the Waters* (cat. no. 105) became extremely popular, because the VAEVO (an association for the promotion of aesthetics in higher education) bought three hundred prints from Escher at a reduced price; they were hung in schools.

JOURNEYS AND WANDERINGS
In Anticuli, not far from Rome, lived the modest Dutch painter Rudolf Bonnet. He had met Escher in Rome and admired his work. Escher visited him on 14 and 15 April 1927; they did drawings together and arranged to meet again after the summer.

Escher made a tour of Etruscan antiquities with Jetta and her father from 21 April to 5 May, visiting Tarquinia, Viterbo, Barbarano (see cat. no. 129) and Norchia. During this period

Jetta's sister, Nina Schibler, looked after George. Throughout the warm summer months the Eschers stayed with Nina in Steckborn in Switzerland. Then they visited The Hague, where Escher was given the room next to the garden to use as a studio in the new house on the Laan Copes.

When Bonnet came to Rome at the beginning of December 1927, the friendship was renewed. Escher and Jetta asked him to supper, together with Nina, who was staying with her parents in Rome. Bonnet described to them his plan to visit Tunisia, and both Escher and Nina became so enthusiastic that on the spur of the moment they decided to accompany him. Jetta, who preferred to stay at home with George, and Nina's husband—to whom they sent a telegram immediately—agreed to the plan. The three of them left via Naples and Palermo for Sidi-bou-Said, near Tunis, and went on to Kairouan; they enjoyed it immensely. In the evenings Escher would read aloud from *The Thousand and One Nights*, which was appropriate literature. Escher and Nina returned to Rome just before Christmas; the trip had taken a fortnight and had produced a folder full of drawings. Bonnet stayed behind in Tunisia.

At the start of 1928 Escher made the prints *Castle in the Air* (cat. no. 117) and *Tower of Babel* (cat. no. 118). The former was based on a fairy-tale that Escher had been reading to his son George. Of *Tower of Babel* he later wrote the following explanation in *The Graphic Work of M. C. Escher:* 'On the assumption that the period of language confusion coincided with the emergence of different races, some of the building workers are white and others black. The work is at a standstill because they are no longer able to understand each other. Seeing that the climax of the drama takes place at the summit of the tower which is under construction, the building has been shown from above, as though from a bird's-eye view. This called for a very sharply receding perspective. It was not until twenty years later that this problem was thoroughly thought out.'

From 10 to 19 April Escher made his first visit to the Abruzzi mountains. He travelled alone and covered large distances by bus. He went to Ascoli Piceno and Loreto, along the Adriatic to Ortona and back to Rome via Sulmona. In his diary he noted that he had made five drawings on the way; he used one of these for a woodcut (cat. no. 119). Shortly afterwards, from 23 May to 25 June, he travelled through Corsica with his father-in-law. Jetta could not join them, since she was expecting another baby. They explored Bonifacio, Calvi and Corte extensively, and this time Escher returned home with seventeen drawings; these produced three woodcuts (cat. nos. 120, 121, 123).

On 8 December Arthur was born (see cat. no. 122). He was

Alfedena, Abruzzi; scratch drawing, August 1929

8-29 MCE

christened on 3 February 1929 in the house in Rome. On the photograph (opposite) Grandmother Umiker is holding Arthur in her arms with Padre Costanzi next to her. Copies of the print *La Cathédrale engloutie* (cat. no. 124) can be seen drying in the background. Grandfather Escher's diary reveals that this print was inspired by a performance of Debussy's prelude of the same name, played by the pianist Erwin Fischer. Fischer received a copy as a token of Escher's esteem.

With a plan at the back of his mind to produce an illustrated book on the Abruzzi, Escher went on a second trip through this inhospitable area in the spring. His letter to Bas Kist, written shortly before his departure on 4 May, was quite lyrical: 'It grieves me more than I can say that I am not able to make this spring trip in your company. I have become accustomed to making such a journey each spring, refreshing my body and spirit and collecting material for the work of the following months. I know of no greater pleasure than to wander over hills and through vales, from village to village, feeling the effects of unspoiled nature and enjoying the unexpected and unlooked-for, in the greatest possible contrast to life at home. The most unpleasant things—a bed crawling with vermin, the often inferior food—not only seem inevitable but even a part of our enjoyment. I often think of making these trips in future with my son or sons; it must be the most enjoyable thing possible for children.'

The book on the Abruzzi never materialized—though the trip, from 12 May to 10 June 1929, in company with the Swiss artist Giuseppe Haas-Triverio, did produce twenty-eight drawings and a folder of prints (cat. nos. 126, 127, 130–32, 134).

REDISCOVERING LITHOGRAPHY

In the summer Escher stayed, alone, in The Hague. His father's diary mentions that when Bas visited on 6 July, 'we looked at the sketches Mauk made on his travels in the Abruzzi, one of them elaborated in Steckborn by a new procedure he worked out— namely, obtaining different degrees of brightness by scratching with a pocket knife in a layer of printing-ink spread on a thick piece of paper impervious to oil (like parchment). The technique is especially suitable for dark drawings, such as those of the interiors of churches and other buildings, since less effort is required to show light than to show dark. He used mounting paper in dark shades for sketches. To obtain the light in windows he stuck on pieces of white paper. Bas Kist looked at everything critically and advised Mauk to make lithographic prints.'

Escher decided to revive his knowledge of lithographic technique with the help of his former teacher at art college, Mr Dieperink. He purchased the necessary materials and set to work. His father followed the creation of the first lithograph of an Italian landscape (cat. no. 126) step by step. On 14 July he noted in his diary: 'Mauk covered a lithographic stone with *tusche* [lithographic ink] and water, using brushes from my paint-box. This stone is too small to reproduce on the same scale the sketches

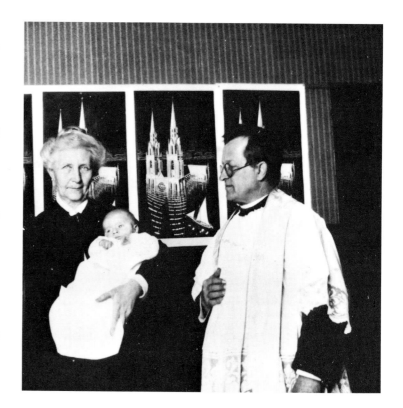

Top: Arthur's christening, 3 February 1929

Above: The Eschers' home, Via Alessandro Poerio, Rome, 1932. In the foreground, woodblock and proof of the (second) title page of *XXIV Emblemata*, with the printing materials

that he made in the Abruzzi. He therefore made a reduced drawing of one of these sketches [a study of Goriano Sicoli], using a set square.' 18 July: 'Using white transfer paper, M. traced his reduced sketch onto his stone covered in black ink. He then began to elaborate the drawing with a pocket knife by scratching in the shading.' 20 July: 'M. got up early, breakfasted alone and is now busy working on his lithographic stone in the bathroom.' 22 July: 'At about 11 o'clock Mauk showed me his completed drawing on the stone. It seemed very successful to both of us.' 25 July: 'M. returned from Amsterdam with an excellent print of the mountain village in the Abruzzi that he had drawn on the stone. It was made in the workshop of Mr Dieperink by a lithographic printer over 60 years old, who is very experienced in all sorts of lithography. The procedure used by Mauk is very rarely employed.' A second lithograph was started but not completed. Escher has become too 'restless'. The stone was wrapped up and sent to Rome; Escher returned to Italy.

CALABRIA

From 28 April to 25 May 1930 Escher visited Calabria. In addition to the faithful Haas, the painter Roberto Schiess accompanied him with his zither, as well as Jean Rousset, a young French historian who dragged along a large camera. The latter was a cultured man, with whom Escher got on famously; he excelled at epigrams. The party got off the train in Pizzo and followed the coast to the south. As soon as they left the main road and entered the impoverished inland districts, they had to use mule tracks or dried-up river-beds. From Pizzo they went via Tropea and Scilla to the southernmost tip of Calabria, Mélito. Here the trip began in earnest with a long walk along a river-bed to reach Pentedattilo, where they spent a few days. The first day Escher was drawing there, a praying mantis jumped onto his folder and stayed there immobile for such a long time that he was able to use it as a model. Five years later this praying mantis found an appropriate place in the wood engraving *Dream* (cat. no. 272). The journey continued to Palizzi and along the western coast to Stilo, Crotone, Santa Severina and Rossano. From here they reached Morona and Rocca Imperiale, travelling part of the way by train. Finally they returned to Naples. The trip eventually produced thirteen prints (cat. nos. 135–47).

Schiess had discovered an excellent way of overcoming the suspicious attitude of the local people. When he took out his zither and began to pluck it, they were instantly won over. In Spezzano he managed to get the station-master to dance to his music, so that he forgot to give the signal for the train's departure. Jean Rousset commemorated it: *'Barbu comme Apollon et joueur de cithare | il fit danser les muses et même un chef de gare.'* ('Bearded like Apollo and playing the zither, he made the muses dance, and even a station-master.')

THE EMBLEMATA

At the end of 1930 Escher wrote a depressed letter home. His health was failing and as a result of his own and his family's many illnesses, he could not make ends meet, especially since he was not selling any of his work. He doubted his own skills. These depressions recurred repeatedly throughout his life. However, as soon as he could gather fresh impressions or start on a new project, the mood would pass. This time that stimulus came from the art historian G. J. Hoogewerff, who was not only Director of the Dutch Historical Institute in Rome, but was also a regular contributor to *Elseviers Geïllustreerd Maandschrift*. Visiting Escher, he proposed that they should make *emblemata*— illustrated four-line epigrams introduced by a Latin motto, like those that were common in the seventeenth century. The editor of *Elsevier* did not consider them suitable for his paper, but he agreed to include an article by Hoogewerff about Escher's graphic work, which appeared in the October 1931 issue. It was the first time that a well-known art historian had taken an interest in Escher's work, and it was an excellent article.

For Hoogewerff, emotional and cerebral expression in art were not mutually exclusive. A work of art could contain a clearly thought-out message. He saw Escher's prints as syntheses or constructions requiring a thorough thinking through. He also pointed out the sobriety and humour in Escher's prints and dealt in detail with the most important works done up to that time. He concluded his article with a reference to the *Emblemata* (for which he had written the epigrams under the pseudonym A. E. Drijfhout). 'It may be that when one has seen the *Emblemata*, one will again judge Escher's art to be "cerebral". This term can be taken to mean anything one likes, but in my opinion his work is characterized in *all* its manifestations by deep thought and true spirituality.'

Hoogewerff and Escher found a publisher in Bussum, Van Dishoeck, who brought out the *Emblemata* as a book in 1932 (cat. nos. 159–86).

THE WITCH OF OUDEWATER

Escher spent the early part of the summer of 1931 in Ravello, a period which saw the creation of fifteen prints (cat. nos. 148–53 and 206–14). On 3 July the whole family travelled from Rome to The Hague. Escher visited the studio of the wood engraver Fokko Mees, where the advantages of working on end-grain wood with a burin were discussed. He was stimulated to attempt this technique. On 3 September he bought a burin and a magnifying glass for distinguishing the fine grooves, and on the same day he began a wood engraving—the invitation card incorporating the lion of St Mark from Ravello for the exhibition at Liernur in The Hague, from 1 to 31 October (cat. no. 149). *Het Vaderland* said: 'An attractive card, showing a cleverly engraved lion with an archaic appeal, invites us to visit the exhibition; anyone who takes up the invitation will not be disappointed.'

Meanwhile Escher had become acquainted with Jan Walch who wrote the daily column 'Goeden Morgen' (Good Morning) in *Het Vaderland*. Some time before, Walch had received one of Escher's prints as a present from friends. Many years earlier he had written a story about 'the Witch of Oudewater'. He was ecstatic about this little town with its old tower, its Witch's Scales and its tiny canal with the market bridge. Escher had never been there but had read the story. He visited Walch and soon both were enthusiastic about producing a fine edition of the story illustrated with woodcuts. They went to Oudewater in the early morning, walking the last stretch to see something of the surrounding countryside. Escher took photographs and bought a few postcards. Three weeks later he sent Walch the first woodcut (cat. no. 194).

MUMMIES OF PRIESTS

In February and March 1932 Escher's prints first appeared in the Gemeentemuseum in The Hague; he contributed to the exhibition 'Modern Dutch Woodcuts', showing the *Emblemata*. At the same time the Post Office announced a prize for a design for a 'peace stamp'. Escher's design (cat. no. 215) was considered one of the fifteen best of the 807 entries, but it was not finally used.

From 3 to 13 April 1932 Escher joined an archaeological expedition to Gargano, led by the Italian professor Rellini. The Dutch archaeologist mentioned above, H.M.R. Leopold, also went on the expedition. Escher made a great many drawings, but these remained the property of Rellini.

From 22 April to 20 May Escher visited northern Sicily, together with Haas-Triverio. They travelled from Palermo along the coast to Cefalú and Taormina, and then through the neighbourhood of Mount Etna to Randazzo and the fantastic lava formations at Bronte. In Sperlinga the strange cave-dwellings appealed greatly to Escher (cat. no. 221).

In the square in front of the church in Gangi a couple of street urchins asked them if they would like to see some dead priests. The urchins produced a large key, and surrounded by a shouting gang of boys, Escher and Haas descended the steps into the crypt. Almost all the walls were covered with rows of niches containing mummies (cat. no. 217).

They returned to Palermo via the temple of Segesta (cat. no. 218). In Palermo Escher drew the cloister of Monreale (cat. no. 226). He returned from this fruitful journey with twenty-three sketches: plenty of material for the winter months (cat. nos. 217–22 and 224–29).

In Rome his close relationship with the Dutch Historical Institute led to the commission of a lithograph of the Frisian church, San Michele dei Frisoni, with St Peter's, the colonnade and the Vatican in the background. This was a difficult perspective, but Escher succeeded with it. The print (cat. no. 216) was very popular with Frisian priests and high prelates, as Escher's father was happy to note in his diary. The diary also reveals that during 1932 Escher was experimenting with

techniques to achieve more varied effects in his prints. For the woodcut *Carubba Tree* (cat. no. 210) he used different pieces of wood and employed fine shades in the black when he was inking-in. For his lithographs he ordered a device from London for spraying soft tints on the stone.

When the *Emblemata* appeared in the summer of 1932, the art critic G.H. 's-Gravesande visited Escher (who was once again staying with his parents) in The Hague. In subsequent years 's-Gravesande was in regular contact with him and wrote about his work in several periodicals.

ROME BY NIGHT

The year 1933 started well with the sale of twenty-six prints—woodcuts and lithographs—to the printroom of the Rijksmuseum in Amsterdam. The printrooms of Leiden and the Gemeentemuseum in The Hague had acquired prints before. In general the Dutch printrooms bought Escher's works regularly over the years.

Meanwhile Escher was full of plans for a second visit to Corsica. He wandered about there with Haas and Robert Schiess from 2 to 30 May 1933. This time the nineteen drawings he made also led to wood engravings and lithographs (cat. nos. 230, 240–47). The previous trip had only produced woodcuts.

On 22 June the whole family was reunited in the parental home in The Hague. Walch and the publisher Van Dishoeck came to talk about the 'Witch of Oudewater' book, which was to be called *The Terrible Adventures of Scholastica* (cat. nos. 188–205). It was to be printed by Joh. Enschedé in Haarlem. When he went to the printer to discuss the project, Escher took a great interest in finding out about the complicated procedure required for printing banknotes.

During the first months of 1934 Escher worked on a series of prints of Rome by night (cat. nos. 249–60). In each print he experimented with a different shading technique. A drawing done *in situ* by torchlight in the evening was always turned into a woodcut the following day.

AN AMERICAN PRIZE

During July and August Escher and Jetta went to the seaside with their children, renting a house with his brother Eddy and his sister-in-law Irma in Sint-Idesbald, near De Panne, on the Belgian coast. From there Escher visited Ghent and Bruges with Jetta, continuing to Tournai on his own. This trip later produced two woodcuts (cat. nos. 261, 262).

Meanwhile Escher's work was doing well in the United States, which pleased him greatly. He was awarded third prize for his lithograph *Nonza* (cat. no. 247) at the Exhibition of Contemporary Prints, Century of Progress, held at the Art Institute of Chicago. The (sponsored) prize, the sum of twenty-five dollars, was intended to be used for purchase. In this way the Art Institute obtained a print for its own collection. This was the first

Escher's procedure for making a 'composition'. Top left, Escher can be seen making a sketch of a market scene in Kairouan, Tunisia, from a high vantage point, on 20 December 1927.

The drawing is shown above right. Two days earlier Escher sketched the city from outside the walls (drawing above left). In January 1928 he regrouped elements from these two drawings, which resulted in the carefully worked-out composition shown top right

37

Top: Escher drew this woman wearing the local costume in Scanno, Abruzzi, on 17 May 1929. He later used the figure in a lithograph (cat. no. 131)

Above: Escher made this schetch of Pentedattilo on 6 May 1930 (see also cat. no. 137). The grasshopper was later used in the woodcut *Dream* (cat. no. 272)

time an American gallery purchased one of Escher's prints. Encouraged by this success, he was to contribute to exhibitions at the Art Institute on a number of future occasions.

The Arnhem association Artibus Sacrum—Escher's former teacher F. W. van der Haagen was on the board—organized a one-man show for the month of October.

In Rome he had an exhibition in the Dutch Historical Institute, organized by Hoogewerff. He exhibited together with the Dutch painter Otto B. de Kat. The opening on 12 December attracted large numbers. A favourable review appeared in the *Algemeen Handelsblad* of 18 December 1934: 'Escher is an artist who has reached a peak of achievement in both graphic technique and the synthetic treatment of nature. Following an extremely rapid development that would be difficult to carry any further, his talent is now quite mature and very individual.' Later, in *The Graphic Work*, Escher described the majority of these prints as being merely 'finger exercises'.

OFF TO SWITZERLAND

In October 1934 Escher made a strange print of a small aeroplane above a snowy landscape (cat. no. 264). This was intended for the cover of the 1934–35 Winter edition of the Christian weekly *Timotheus*. This journal had published other prints by Escher and they had appealed to its readers. The dark, snowy landscape with its rectangular fields clearly anticipated the famous print *Day and Night* (cat. no. 303) of 1938. Probably a book on aviation that he had borrowed from Hoogewerff provided the inspiration.

Escher's interest in aviation during this period also appears from the fact that he designed a stamp for the Dutch Post Office in aid of the National Aviation Fund. This design was used, though in a slightly altered form.

The stay in Italy came to an end in 1935; but first Escher made a final tour through Sicily with Haas-Triverio. On 9 May they left Rome by train. From Palermo they travelled through Agrigento and Ragusa to Syracuse. On the way Escher made drawings of a windmill at Trapani, the temple ruins of the Greek city of Selinunte, and the weird rocks of Caltabellotta. From Syracuse they took a freighter to Malta, where they stayed for two days. They had plenty of time to draw the harbour at Valletta, with its suburb Senglea and the *Verdi*, a steamer of the Adria company. This provided a coloured woodcut (cat. no. 276; see page 152). The *Verdi* took them back to Palermo, and on 31 May they were back in Rome again.

On 6 June Escher senior heard from his son that an architect had bought ten of his prints for more than 900 lire, almost covering the costs of his travels. Arthur had been tested for tuberculosis and traces of the disease had been discovered. It seemed that a long period of convalescence in mountain air was needed. As this would also be good for George, they had decided to move to Switzerland.

Later it appeared that Escher was prompted to move to

Right: On 7 May 1931 Escher made a sketch of Atrani, near Ravello, from above. It can be clearly seen how he turned this sketch into a preliminary study for a lithograph (cat. no. 148)

Below: The preparatory stage of a woodcut in three colours (cat. no. 230). Squares are drawn on a sketch of Calvi made on 8 May 1933 (for transferring it to the woodblock), which is then elaborated

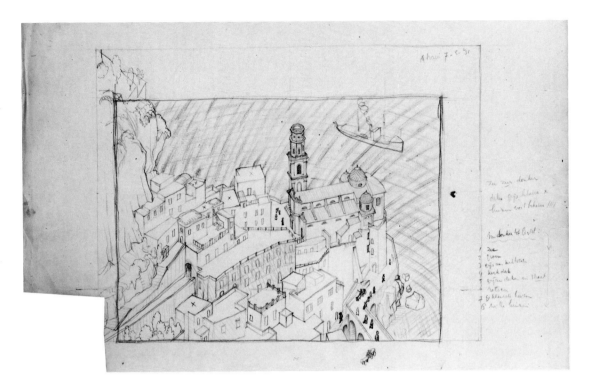

39

Switzerland not only by the health of his children, but also by the political climate in Italy. After many farewells, they left Rome on 4 July 1935. They rented a house in Château-d'Oex from 1 September for nine months.

A SON'S MEMORIES OF HIS FATHER
George especially has vivid memories of life in Rome. In 1978 he talked to J. R. Kist about these years:

'The memories that have stayed with me from that Rome period almost all include Father. Our Sunday walks over many years are the happiest memories I have from that time. After I had gone to church with mother or on my own (until I was sixteen I was a Catholic disciplined by fear), Father would take Arthur and me exploring. Our destination presumably varied according to our age, the season and the weather, and I cannot remember a particular order. The essence of my memory is still the feeling of Father's dry, strong hand holding mine, and the opening up of all sorts of interesting and fascinating aspects of the world.

'Sometimes we would simply walk out of the house and down the hill, where there was a mechanical digger in a gulley— sometimes it was even working—or an impressive steamroller with an exciting smell would rattle by. Or we would walk to the Villa Sciarra, where we climbed an enormously high ridge inside the walls (at least as high as Father's waist) on the way to the gate. Instead of following the ordinary footpaths, Father would take us to quiet, dark places under the fir trees, where we could watch the tadpoles for a long time as they swam around the dark pond. Often we would take the tram—the noisy Roman tram, screeching loudly as it went round bends— right down to the Tiber, where we took the Circolare Esterna or Interna to travel further.

'There were so many possibilities for walks! Our favourites included the Roman Forum, the Palatine and other neighbouring ruins with their sunny, decaying walls—which were perfect for clambering on or playing hide-and-seek—covered with dusty plants and evoking a vague feeling of mystery. Father showed us the acanthus leaves growing there and the capitals of the fallen columns decorated with acanthus motifs, and tried in vain to explain to me that they were the same leaves. We walked through the maze of stone and looked at the banqueting table nearby, which had a channel of water surrounding it so that bowls of food could float past the guests (in the time of the Ancient Romans).

'Often our morning walks would finish on a terrace, dusty and deserted, jutting out from the side of the hill facing the Gianicolo. We would sit down just before noon, Father would take his watch from his pocket and we would carefully scrutinize a particular spot on the hill opposite. At twelve o'clock precisely a white cloud would suddenly appear out of the hill and then we would wait for the explosion of the cannon.

'I could go on like this forever: visits to the zoo, the Pincio, fountains in the city centre, the work on Mussolini's forum, the bocca della verità, Campidoglio, churches, the Via Appia, Castel

Sant' Angelo—all these are quite vivid mental pictures. And all the time, unseen but clearly felt above me, there was Father with his dry, warm hand. (He always complained that we had such clammy little hands.)'

'Father usually kept at a slight distance. He was not very noisy or exuberant. Apart from the ritual of frequent kisses on his cheeks, which were always rather prickly, and the walks while he held my hand, the only memory I have of physical contact was when I sat quietly on his knee, listening to Bach. We had a gramophone (later on an electric one) and occasionally we would listen to it in absolute silence. Yehudi Menuhin, who, in his boy's breeches, had just given a concert in the Augusteo, Wanda Landowska, even Stokowski, they all interpreted Bach in their own way. I listened with pleasure, leaning against Father's stomach until I became too heavy and he would put me down. . . .

'Being ill, as I often was, is crystallized in my memory as listening drowsily in a dimmed light to my father reading to me. He liked to read aloud and did it excellently. In Rome he read Grimm's and Hans Andersen's fairy-tales and, most of all, a book from his own childhood, which contained the story of the Green Magician, the favourite of us all. The woodcut of the floating island [cat. no. 117], with the prince on the tortoise, comes from this story.

'First in Chateau-d'Oex and later in Brussels, we got into the habit of having a bedtime story read to us every evening. In this way we got to know The Jungle Books, Kim, Winnie the Pooh, Nils Holgersson, Jules Verne, and even a few Katjangs, Dik Trom, and other tales of Dutch heroes. During the war, by the light of an oil-lamp, Father read the Odyssey in the translation of Boutens. In this way we also got to know Van Schendel, who was his favourite author for many years.'

'I cannot remember Father playing with us much when we were small, but now and again he would spend a great deal of time and energy on two particular games—mazes and "ball track".

'To make a maze, a room—often the dining-room—was completely turned upside-down. The idea was to build as long a tunnel as possible, through which we, the children, could crawl easily but he could only crawl with difficulty. A good tunnel was dark, winding under upturned chairs and tables put end to end, behind the sofa, turning this way and that and finally opening again into the room.

'The nursery table, the kitchen table, drawing-boards, tea trays were used to create walls, and the large chairs with their rectangular backs were ideal for making an enclosed zigzagging

Opposite page, top: The sea at the mouth of the Ebro; watercolour made on board the *Juno,* on 29 September 1922

Opposite page, bottom: Mural mosaic in the Alhambra; drawing, 20 October 1922

Page 42: Farmhouse, Ravello; drawing, 21 May 1931 (compare cat. no. 207)

CORTE
23-5-'33

path when they were turned on their sides. The whole thing would be covered with travelling-rugs, coverlets and even the Persian carpet which was taken up for the occasion. The fun consisted in crawling fearfully through the dim tunnel, hearing the others scrabbling about nearby, barking like dogs, and then suddenly meeting someone yelling loudly, so that the scary feeling changed all at once to a cosy togetherness, cut off from the world outside.

'Undoubtedly my father enjoyed us having fun, but when I remember my experiences with my own children, I think he must have derived a great deal of his pleasure from designing and building an improvised construction from the materials available at the moment.'

'Another occupation for rainy Sundays or sunny holidays at the seaside was the "ball track". I stil get quite enthusiastic when I think of the fantastic constructions Father would build, pretending they were for our amusement.

'I don't know whether the ball-track principle dated back to his own youth, but I suspect that he gradually developed it himself. My earliest memories are of a very primitive model: Father joined the rails of our toy train together, raised part of the track on a few bricks and put a wooden ball at its beginning. The ball would zigzag down the track, until it rolled off the end, clattering to the tiled floor.

'These small beginnings developed in later years (even to the time when we lived in Brussels) into quite fantastic constructions. The basic principle was always the same: a ball, preferably a heavy, hard one such as a billiard ball, would start rolling at the high point and descend to the floor by way of the longest possible—that is, the slowest possible, and most varied—route.

'The construction was always built from the bottom upwards; it was an exciting and, for us, often frustrating process. The excitement, apart from our shared intense interest, came from the fact that there was always something happening, and that new surprises were added all the time as the work progressed. The frustration was caused by the length of time it took to complete the work.

'The first piece of the ball track, often a set of train rails, was assembled on the floor, because it needed firm support. The slope was then carefully built from the floor upwards, step by step; from time to time we would check to see that the ball would reach the end of the track, and if it rolled too fast, we reduced the incline of the slope. The next section might be a cardboard cylinder, of which Father had a whole collection for sending prints.

'A number of cylinders zigzagging round the room took the ball track to chair height. This might be followed by a length of thick hollow curtain rail, then a plank with slats nailed onto it, then more cardboard cylinders, climbing higher and higher, up to table height. Every time a new piece was added, we had to test and adjust it for minimum speed. The table could be set at a slight incline and a winding path would be laid out on it using books, wooden bricks or a thick piece of rope.

'It would go higher still, with two billiard cues side by side leading to the back of a chair, and so on, until the interest began to wane or the technical problems became insurmountable. One of the charms of these ball tracks was the sound the ball made on different materials, alternately dull, hollow, metallic, and accelerating when there was a nice long stretch, coming almost to a standstill with a click on a new trajectory, and slowly starting again. We would play endlessly with this, picking the ball up at the end of the track and taking it back to the beginning. Some of the most complicated constructions stayed up for days, even weeks.

'On our summer holidays a variation of this was often built in sand. Father would work really hard to build an enormous hill, round which, and through which, the path for the ball would wind down. A different skill was required here because a damp track, down which the ball rolls well, dries out and leads to problems after a while, with miniature avalanches and subsidence.

'His greatest triumph was a large ball track in De Panne, where a small rubber ball was dropped into a hole in the top, appearing at the bottom thirty seconds later. For working on the tunnel he had taken along a special long round wooden stick; after patting the sand firmly around it, he removed the stick, leaving a beautiful tunnel.'

'Once a year at Christmas, Father and Grandfather Umiker, who also lived in Rome, prepared a puppet show. Father had built a small stage with lights, beautiful curtains and wonderful backdrops painted by him and Mother. There were about ten hand puppets, one or two of which he had probably made himself, and now and again Mother would sew a new costume. As far as I know, Grandfather wrote the play; Father and he would rehearse it a few times, and we were always deeply impressed. The play would usually be a fairy-tale or an adventure of Giuppino, an Italian buffoon.'

'The floors in the corridor and the dining-room of the apartment on the Via Alessandro Poerio were covered with ceramic tiles which Father had designed himself. They were white tiles with a simple pattern of coloured lines that ran from one tile to the next, so that every coloured line could be followed zigzagging from one end of the corridor to the other. The tiles had not been properly laid and most of them had worked loose, so that they tipped slightly when you walked on them. For the children it was good fun to race through the house on a tricycle, because the tiles would rattle in a very satisfying way—which was less appreciated by the people living below.'

Page 43: View of Atrani; drawing, 25 May 1931

Opposite page: Corte, Corsica; drawing, 23 May 1933

45

'We lived on the third floor of the Via Alessandro Poerio 122, and Father's studio was on the fourth floor in the attic, built as an extension on the flat roof. I remember the studio as being a large, spacious room, but considering that his worktable appeared so impressively large that I could hardly look over it, I realize that the studio must have been much smaller than it seems in my memory. It can be seen in *Hand with Reflecting Sphere* [cat. no. 268]. When you went in from the landing there was a hard sofa to your left, covered with a colourful bedspread and cushions for leaning against the wall. Next to this stood a large leather armchair with a foot-rest that slid out. Both were "special" for us, and just as to the rest of the studio, our access to them was restricted. Above this corner there were a few bookshelves on the wall. Along the wall to the right of the door there were two cupboards: one with prints and the other with instruments, drawing utensils, etc.

'The studio was connected to the floor below by a "speaking tube" closed at either end with a wooden whistle. To call Father down for dinner, we would take the downstairs whistle out of the pipe, press our mouth against the opening and blow hard, so that the upstairs whistle sounded. When Father took his whistle out of the pipe, we could talk to each other. When he was working, whether drawing or making a woodcut, he would never come down immediately to eat, he always had to "just finish something off"—which sometimes meant that we had started the meal before he had come downstairs.... My strong recollections of Father's love of making woodcuts date from this time, although he always gave this impression, right up to his last years in Baarn. From downstairs we could often hear Father work: he would whistle all sorts of tunes very loudly—from Bach's Double Violin Concerto to popular Dutch folksongs—or he would drum loudly on the worktable with his fingers, so that we could hear the marches through the ceiling when we started our meal in the dining-room.'

Escher's way of seeing.
Above: Photograph of Morano in Calabria, taken on 23 May 1930

Right: Geometrical sketch of the same town, made on the same day, which resulted in a woodcut (cat. no. 136)

46

Switzerland and Belgium   1935–1941

The Schiblers in Steckborn offered the Eschers accommodation until the latter were able to move into the villa Les Clématites in Château-d'Oex in September 1935. However, Escher himself had a lot of unfinished business in Holland: on 27 July he arrived at his parents' house in The Hague, where he stayed for over a month.

During this month he had various consultations. The first was with his cousin Anton Escher, the director of an engineering works. Anton asked him to make a vignette for the works, to be used on stationery. Escher did some preliminary studies and sketches; he used these for a woodcut when he was back in Switzerland.

He talked with the people at the Post Office and with the Enschedé printers about the design for the Aviation Fund stamp. Some alterations were suggested and on 18 August Escher completed the adapted design; all the parties concerned were very pleased with it. Escher went to see the proofs at Enschedé and personally chose the colour. The (brown) stamp was issued on 16 October.

In the middle of August Escher stayed for a few days in Amsterdam with his friend Bas Kist. He visited Artis (the zoo), where he met the man in charge of the insect section, who gave him a large mounted dragonfly. This led to a wood engraving (cat. no. 281) in March 1936.

Between all the visits, Escher spent a great deal of time over a three-week period making an extremely detailed and loving portrait of his father. When he finally completed a satisfactory study, he transferred the portrait to a lithographic stone in a few days. On 25 August the prints were ready. They were not intended to be sold; Escher gave them to members of the family.

In his book *The Graphic Work* Escher later said of this lithograph: 'In the case of the portraiture of someone with strongly asymmetrical features, a good deal of the likeness is lost in the print, for this is the mirror image of the original work. In this instance a contraprint was made; that is to say, while the ink of the first print was still wet on the paper, this was printed on to a second sheet, thereby annulling the mirror image. The "proof" brings out the signature that he himself wrote on the stone with lithographic chalk and which is now to be seen, doubly mirrored, back in its original form.'

SNOW IN SWITZERLAND

On 29 August Escher again left for Steckborn and from there he travelled to Château-d'Oex with his family. His first letters from there were not particularly enthusiastic. Life in Switzerland was far more expensive than they were used to, and George's health was poor. Jetta complained about the silence and isolation. However, Escher threw himself energetically into his work. In the middle of September he finished the woodcut for his cousin; the vignette (cat. no. 275) depicts a welder at work. In October, he made two coloured woodcuts: a large one in three colours of the *Verdi* at anchor in Senglea (cat. no. 276) and a smaller one in two colours of a ruined temple at Selinunte (cat. no. 277), both resulting from his springtime trip with Haas-Triverio. In November he made a painstaking lithograph (cat. no. 278), a copy after Hieronymous Bosch.

Gradually the Eschers became accustomed to their new house and surroundings. The children liked it very much. Jetta practised the piano a great deal and gave lessons to George. Meanwhile Escher had become a member of the local chess club (see cat. no. 284) and played frequently. In the winter they did a lot of skiing.

At the beginning of December Escher started working on a lithograph of a farmer's barn covered in snow. He had it printed on 15 January 1936 but was dissatisfied with it. Later, his son George would remember this vividly; in a letter to C. V. S. Roosevelt in 1975, he wrote: 'It was our first winter in Château-d'Oex and I, as a nine-year-old boy accustomed to Roman winters, was enjoying the snow tremendously. I also liked the lithograph of the shed located a few hundred yards from our house, that he had just finished. I liked its simplicity, and it illustrated many of the features that made me happy in our new surroundings; the clean, soft smoothness of the snowy landscape, the cosy island life of a farmhouse, the mystery of lowhanging clouds. Besides, I was intrigued by the continuity between roof and hill. So I was shocked by father's disgust at the poverty of the print and his sorrow at having lost the wealth and warmth of Italian landscapes. He must have been very upset, for his emotion to come through all these years, and remain imprinted on my memory on the same level as, say, his account of the death of his father or of his passing through the ruins of Rotterdam a few days after the German bombing.'

FAREWELL TO A PASSION

During the winter at Château-d'Oex Escher's thoughts were always on his beloved south. Discussing it with Jetta, he decided to try and make a long trip along the Mediterranean coast in the spring. On 1 February he wrote to the Italian shipping company Adria in Fiume (present-day Rieka), enclosing the woodcut he had made of the *Verdi* the year before.

In his letter he suggested that the shipping company provide a return passage for him from Fiume to Valencia, and for Jetta from Genoa to Valencia. He wished to break the journey as he felt inclined, and be able to continue on the next ship belonging to the company. He had the idea of making a print of every harbour at which the ship would call. By way of payment for the trip, Adria could have a few copies of each print, which they would then be free to use as they wished.

Escher did not really expect the shipping company to 'bite'. To his surprise, however, his letter received a positive response within a few days. The trip, which took more than two months (from the end of April to the end of June), marked an extremely important point in Escher's life, as we shall see later. It was actually a final farewell to his passion for the sunny south and all the things that were so dear to him—the landscape, the architecture and the people.

THE JOURNEY

On 26 April Escher left Château-d'Oex, travelling by express train to Trieste. The weather was beautiful when he arrived, 'after many days of snow and wind in our mountain village', as he noted in his travel diary. He was very happy 'to go back to the familiar land of lemons; like entering a well-loved house'. The following day he arrived in Fiume, and first of all took his baggage on board the *Rossini*. Then he went to Adria's 'splendid administration palace'. He was treated with great respect; he was introduced to 'his' captain and entrusted to his special care, and was given a letter to prevent complications with the police in harbours. Any travelling expenses to places near the harbours were to be reimbursed.

The shipping company had an extensive file of photographs of harbours. Escher spent some hours looking at them and chose those which most appealed to him. Then he went on board and the ship set sail at seven in the evening. The following day they were in Venice. He was admitted to the loggia on the first floor of the Ducal Palace in St Mark's Square. 'From here I drew the Isola di San Giorgio Maggiore through the beautifully carved columns of the loggia.' This produced a woodcut (cat. no. 287).

The next day the *Rossini* called at Ancona. Escher wrote: 'I soon discovered a beautiful little church (Santa Maria della Piazza) with a Romanesque façade, which I am going to draw from the third floor of the house opposite, where the people have been very hospitable to me.' Of this, too, he made a woodcut (cat. no. 288).

The following day they went to Bari. Escher hired a car with five other passengers to visit Alberobello, some thirty miles farther on.

Top: Villa Les Clématites in Château-d'Oex

Above: George and Arthur tobogganing in the garden of Les Clématites

He drew and photographed the 'trulli', curious little houses with round, pointed roofs.

The next harbour would be Catania in Sicily—two days' sailing. Escher took the opportunity of making a drawing of the forecastle of the *Rossini*. This also resulted in a woodcut (cat. no. 286). In Catania he drew and photographed ships in the fishing harbour; he later used this for a wood engraving, with Mount Etna in the background (cat. no. 289).

On 4 May he travelled by train to Giarre with three fellow-passengers, 'to see the same lava stream (of 1928) I had seen and drawn three years before [cat. no. 229]. Here I discovered a very remarkable subject: a house with a beautiful palm tree behind it, itself spared from destruction, but totally surrounded by black lava.' This resulted in one of Escher's most beautiful landscape lithographs (cat. no. 285).

On 5 May the *Rossini* called at Malta, 'nothing new' for Escher, and then returned to Sicily. After two days in Messina, which 'really has nothing beautiful to offer as a city', they sailed along the north coast to Palermo. As they rounded the cape they sailed close to the coast of Calabria. Escher noted: 'I clearly recognize Scilla, where I spent two days with Haas six years ago and did some drawing.'

JETTA'S ARRIVAL

From Palermo the voyage continued to Naples, Livorno and Genoa, where they sailed into the harbour on 11 May. That evening Jetta arrived by train, and the following day they explored the town. Escher found a good subject for a drawing which he wanted to make on the journey back: the Piano di Sant'Andrea, quite close to Columbus' house. The Adria agent arranged for him to draw this from the terrace of the Post Office.

On 13 May they sailed on to Savona but the ship did not stay long enough for the Eschers to disembark. Escher started a drawing of the view from the porthole in their cabin. On 14 May they arrived in Marseilles. They visited the city and Escher decided to draw the view from the Pont Transbordeur on the return journey. The following day they arrived in Barcelona, and from there they visited Montserrat.

On 16 May they arrived in Valencia. They said goodbye to the captain and officers of the *Rossini* and moved in with the Gaffuri family, old acquaintances of Jetta's father. The Gaffuris drove them everywhere they wanted to go. They visited Valencia, Cuenca and Sagunto. On 19 May they went back on board, this time on a Spanish freighter, the *Altube Mendi*, from Bilbao, which was considerably 'less clean and tidy' than the *Rossini*. Escher wrote: 'The hour of departure . . . is obviously quite flexible, like many things in Spain at the moment. . . . In general, the political situation is extremely precarious, and I think this is our last chance during these months to travel around fairly quietly.' He was proved correct; the Spanish Civil War broke out on 18 July.

On 20 May they arrived in Alicante, where they visited Elche by

OLIVARI SAVONA 13-X

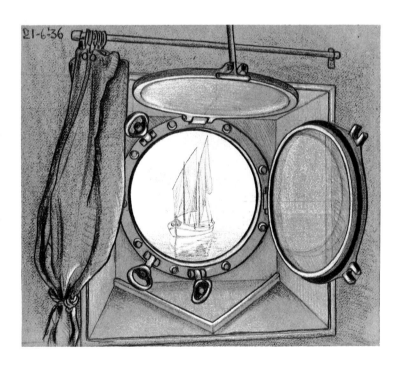

21-6-'36

Top: Escher took this photograph of and through the porthole in his cabin on the *Rossini* on 13 May 1936, in the port of Savona

Above: On the same day Escher started on a drawing of this porthole. He only completed it on 21 June, now using a porthole of the *Paganini* as a model. The circular drawing of the little boat is glued onto the larger drawing

49

Two photographs of the fishing
harbour of Catania, Sicily, made on
3 May 1936. Escher's wood engraving
Catania (cat. no. 289) shows a
combination of these photographs,
with Mount Etna in the foreground

bus. In Cartagena, where they went the following day, Escher
drew a view of the beautiful harbour. This nearly ended badly:
when the drawing was almost completed a policeman approached
and took him to the police station. Cartagena was a naval port,
and drawing was strictly prohibited. The military commander
became involved, but in the end the affair fizzled out, though the
drawing was confiscated. Escher almost missed his boat, but
fortunately the captain was prepared to wait an hour for him.

On 22 May they disembarked again in Almeria. They took the
bus to Granada via Motril, a 'most typical ride'. The next day they
went to the Alhambra and 'thoroughly enjoyed this wonderful
aristocratic work of art'. In the afternoon they started to copy the
ceramic motifs. 'What a contrast: the peaceful, elevated princely
palaces up there, and the filthy, neglected, rotting city below!'
They also spent the next day copying tile and stucco motifs, and in
their hotel room they continued to elaborate their sketches (see
page 53).

On 25 May they took the bus to Guadix and photographed and
drew this area of caves. 'Extremely interesting and strange, all
these dwellings with their white façades, the chimneys protruding
from the rocks, the soil formation in which the caves have been
dug, and the horizon. The whole thing had a very improbable,
dreamlike appearance, rather like a moonscape with moon men.'

The following day was again taken up with copying motifs in
the Alhambra and elaborating the sketches they had made. On 27
May they travelled to Ronda on an ancient, rickety train. They
stayed there for a few days to do some drawing. On the evening of
30 May they left for Córdoba, where they visited the mosque the
next morning. In the afternoon they went to a bullfight.
Fortunately bullfighting was no longer as bloody as it had been on
Escher's previous visit to Spain; the horses were now protected by
mattresses. 'It fascinated me again, just as it had before. The
atmosphere is loaded with passion and it would be unnecessary
and stupid to resist this.' Jetta was also deeply impressed.

Escher spent a day and a half drawing 'the forest of pillars' in
the mosque. Later he went there to copy Moorish brick motifs. On
3 June they travelled on to Seville, where they visited the Alcazar,
but found the palace disappointing after the Alhambra. However,
the garden 'is the most beautiful thing I have seen up till now'.

They had wanted to travel back from Cádiz to Valencia by
freighter, but a dock strike prevented this, so they went by train on
5 June. The 450-mile journey was no fun; their compartment, even
though it was first class, was 'disgustingly filthy'. The next day
they embarked on the *Paganini*, a sister ship of the *Rossini*, in
Valencia. 'After all the squalor in Spain, our ship . . . seems a
miracle of cleanliness.'

On 7 June they were back at sea. They first travelled to
Marseilles, where they arrived the following day. Here, Escher
drew the view of the Notre-Dame-de-la-Garde from the Pont
Transbordeur, which he later turned into a woodcut (cat. no. 290).
They continued to Savona, where they arrived on 10 June. On this

The 'forest of pillars' in the Mosque in
Córdoba; drawing, 2 June 1936

occasion there was enough time to do some drawing. 'I discovered a picturesque old street between high houses, which I drew from the first floor of a shop.' This street later appeared in a 'new-style' woodcut (cat. no. 296).

The same day they sailed on to Genoa—a short distance. On 12 June Jetta left for Château-d'Oex.

'ALMOST THE BEST TIME OF HIS LIFE'

Meanwhile the Adria agent had obtained permission, as he had promised, for Escher to draw 'the beautiful towers, or rather the gateway, of the Piano di Sant'Andrea' from the Post Office terrace. This resulted in another woodcut (cat. no. 295).

From Genoa they sailed on to Livorno, where Escher took the train to Pisa. He climbed the famous Leaning Tower and drew the cathedral from the first tier. This was the basis for another woodcut (cat. no. 294). Later the same day Escher returned to Livorno.

On 15 June he arrived in Naples, and went to visit a nearby Benedictine monastery. As a result of a conversation with a German fellow-passenger, he noted in his travel diary that evening: 'How miserable, confused and stupefying politics are today! European man in general makes me think of someone slowly but surely sinking into a morass. All his attempts to save himself are useless: he sinks in deeper and deeper. Wherever you look in the world there is nothing but hopeless misery and the danger of war, bankruptcy and revolution. To an objective and impartial observer there seems no hope of a better future.... A boat trip such as this is a period of respite.'

On 16 June the ship was in Palermo, where Escher drew a mummy in a catacomb. The following day in Messina he received a congratulatory telegram from Jetta, 'so that I realized it was my birthday'. Meanwhile the *Rossini* had also called at the harbour in Messina. Naturally he went on board to say hello to the captain and officers. He wanted to draw the *Rossini* and include some of the *Paganini* moored next to it, but a *carabiniere* quickly put a stop to that. 'There are obviously no greater idiots than those in Messina,' was Escher's furious comment in his diary.

On 18 June the ship sailed into Malta. Escher drew the harbour with Senglea in the background. They then sailed on to Catania and from there to Bari. On 21 June he finished the drawing of the view through the porthole which he had begun on his outward journey on the *Rossini*. This led to a woodcut (cat. no. 297). On 23 June they dropped anchor in Fiume, where the journey had started. 'In the afternoon I visited Mr Marà [the office chief] in the Adria building, armed with all the work I had done. He seemed very enthusiastic and satisfied with the provisional results, and extremely easy-going regarding my other commitments.' Marà reimbursed Escher's expenses and it was arranged that Adria would receive four copies of each of a total of twelve prints: nine resulting from the trip (cat. nos. 285-90, 294, 295, 297) and three from an earlier date (cat. nos. 211, 226, 276).

The *Paganini* sailed on to Trieste, where Escher bade a 'melancholy' farewell to the ship on 25 June. He then went by train to Venice, where he visited the Biennale. Four of his prints were being exhibited; it 'barely pleased' him. He travelled on to Château-d'Oex, arriving home on 28 June. A dream had ended.

In July Escher and his wife made a walking tour along three Swiss lakes. They then went to stay with Escher's parents in The Hague, taking George with them. They arrived on 4 August, having spent one night on the way with Escher's brother and sister-in-law in Brussels. This was so enjoyable, according to his father's diary, that they were thinking of going to live there too. Château-d'Oex was too expensive, remote and boring.

Escher gave a glowing account of his voyage through the Mediterranean. His father noted that 'it was almost the best time of his life for him, also because of his work'. In The Hague, Escher started on his first print inspired by the journey—the lithograph *House in the Lava* (cat. no. 285). There were problems with the printing so that Escher had to rush to the printer's to make corrections, but finally the results were excellent.

Meanwhile he was also concerned with a problem to which he returned at intervals throughout his life—the transposition of music into graphic representation. He talked about this to his father, who later noted in his diary that his son was so obsessed with the problem that it gave him sleepless nights.

On 1 September the family returned to Switzerland. They travelled via Brussels to look for a house, though as yet without success.

A NEW DIRECTION

After Escher had said goodbye to the south, his work took a direction that was eventually to lead to his becoming famous. From now on he was no longer concerned with expressing his observations—or only rarely—but rather with the construction of the images in his own mind. These images dealt with the regular division of the plane, limitless space, rings and spirals in space, mirror images, inversion, polyhedrons, relativities, the conflict between the flat and the spatial, and impossible constructions. Even in his Haarlem period, and occasionally during his years in Italy, he had made hesitant moves in this direction, but only now did they take shape systematically and start to absorb him. He had the feeling that until then he had merely been doing finger exercises.

The laws that were to fascinate Escher most until his death were those of the regular division of the plane (see also pages 155-73). He had experimented with them already in Haarlem (cat. nos. 65,

Tiles in the Alhambra; drawing,
24 May 1936

52

66, 90). It was then, in October 1922, that he had visited the Alhambra for the first time. 'The fitting together of congruent figures whose shapes evoke in the observer an association with an object or a living creature intrigued me increasingly after that first Spanish visit in 1922,' Escher wrote in 1941, in an article in *De Delver*, an art periodical. 'And although at the time I was mainly interested in free graphic art, I periodically returned to the mental gymnastics of my puzzles. In about 1924 I first printed a piece of fabric with a wood block of a single animal motif which is repeated according to a particular system, always bearing in mind the principle that there may not be any "empty spaces".... I exhibited this piece of printed fabric together with my other work, but it was not successful. This is partly the reason why it was not until 1936, after I had visited the Alhambra a second time, that I spent a large part of my time puzzling with animal shapes.'

Escher's development in this direction after 1936 can be attributed not only to this second visit to the Alhambra, but also to his departure from Italy. In 1959 he wrote about this (in the introduction to *The Graphic Work*): 'In Switzerland, Belgium and Holland where I successively established myself, I found the outward appearance of landscape and architecture less striking than those which are particularly to be seen in the southern part of Italy. Thus I felt compelled to withdraw from the more or less direct and true to life illustrating of my surroundings. No doubt this circumstance was in a high degree responsible for bringing my inner visions into being.' In the same introduction, Escher wrote about his prints dating from after 1936 that they were created 'with a view to communicating a specific line of thought. The ideas that are basic to them often bear witness to my amazement and wonder at the laws of nature which operate in the world around us. He who wonders discovers that this is in itself a wonder. By keenly confronting the enigmas that surround us, and by considering and analyzing the observations that I had made, I ended up in the domain of mathematics. Although I am absolutely without training or knowledge in the exact sciences, I often seem to have more in common with mathematicians than with my fellow-artists.'

An extensive survey of the systematic quality and the partly mathematical background of Escher's mental imagery follows below (pages 135–53).

BRUSSELS

In Château-d'Oex Escher worked hard on his woodcuts and wood engraving for the Adria company. By December 1936 he had finished five of them. He interrupted this work to make a poster, an invitation and an announcement for an exhibition he was

One of Escher's first systematic studies for the division of the plane, October 1936

holding in Château-d'Oex, together with the painter John Paschoud, in the latter's studio (cat. nos. 291–93). The exhibition (from 6 to 14 January 1937) was well reviewed and Escher sold works for a fairly large sum. In his diary his father noted that 'he had not earned so much for a long time'.

In March all the Adria prints were finished. The sketch that Escher had made in Savona on 10 June 1936 was turned into a 'free' woodcut, with an ingenious combination of two different observations (cat. no. 296). The surface of a worktable covered with books and other objects has been put together with a view onto a street in a single perspective, so that it appears as one reality—an impossible reality, which can only exist as an image in the mind. Later Escher gave form to a number of these impossible constructions in his prints.

At the end of March the Eschers made a definite decision to move, and in June Escher and Jetta went to Brussels to look for a house. Meanwhile he was working hard on a new woodcut and completed it at the end of May. He sent his parents a print, curious to hear their reaction. On 5 June Escher's father noted in his diary: 'Enigmatic woodcut. M. calls it Metamorphosis.' He wondered whether his son intended a symbolic significance in the print (cat. no. 298).

However, symbolism did not play a role for Escher, at least as far as this woodcut was concerned. After his sea voyage the previous year he had devoted himself wholeheartedly and imaginatively to the regular division of the plane, and had come up with different ideas for plane-filling motifs. This was by no means all; for Escher the next step was obvious. 'The study of the regular division of the plane on a flat surface led automatically to compositions that expressed a development, a cycle or a metamorphosis,' he wrote in 1941 in the article in *De Delver* mentioned above. In *Metamorphosis* the regular division of the plane and the metamorphosis are combined in an intriguing manner. A motif for filling the plane designed in October 1936 (the 'Oriental' man) changes into a cube motif (that is, from two dimensions to three), and is logically developed to a town by the sea (Atrani).

At the end of July Escher and his wife arrived in the parental home in The Hague. They had come from Brussels, where they had found a house, 31 Avenue Saturne, in the suburb of Ukkel, to the south of the city. They were to move in at the beginning of August. Jetta was pregnant with her third child. Escher was extremely pleased with the school they had found for the children: it was strictly neutral with no religious education, 'though Jetta would have liked this to be different', as Escher's father noted in his diary.

Once the Eschers had settled in Ukkel, they regularly visited Escher's parents, as the entries in 'old Es's' diary show. At the end of August he also noted that George would publish a set of poems 'with a vignette by Mauk' (cat. no. 299). On 30 October in The Hague Escher showed the plane-filling motifs that he had

Top: Escher sketching on the upper deck of the *Paganini*

Above: This street in Savona, drawn by Escher on 10 June 1936, was used in the woodcut *Still Life and Street* (cat. no. 296)

developed up to then to his brother Beer, who was a professor of geology, mineralogy, palaeontology and crystallography in Leiden. Escher's father wrote: 'Beer saw more in this than I thought, in connection with problems that occur in crystallography; this pleased M. a lot.' Two days later, Beer sent his brother a letter with an extensive bibliography on the regular division of the plane. 'It is all very theoretical,' he wrote, 'but the illustrations may be of some use to you.'

Escher did study the literature, but the systems used in crystallography did not satisfy him. He went on to design a whole new system of his own, and in 1942 he put it in writing in a forty-page notebook, with coloured illustrations (see page 149). Later on, he elaborated numerous examples. Finally, in 1965, this led to the book *Symmetry Aspects of M.C. Escher's Periodic Drawings* by Caroline H. MacGillavry (reprinted in 1976 under the title *Fantasy & Symmetry, The Periodic Drawings of M.C. Escher*).

BIRTH AND DEATH

The prints of the division of the plane were now produced in quick succession. In November Escher finished the woodcut *Development I* (cat. no. 300). However, he was not satisfied with the way in which the motif developed inwards, because it allowed too little 'freedom of movement' for the figures. It took him until February 1939 to produce the improved version.

During the winter months Escher continued to experiment with his plane-filling motifs and he used them to good advantage in his prints. A motif of birds flying towards each other, made in February 1938, was incorporated that very month in a woodcut which was to become the most popular of all his prints, *Day and Night* (cat. no. 303). On 6 March Jan was born and Escher's father wrote, 'M. thinks his third son is a beautiful child.'

In May Escher made the first large-size lithographic metamorphosis (cat. no. 305). The woodcut *Sky and Water I* (cat. no. 306), completed a month later, was very favourably received by the press at exhibitions; Escher's 'new style' had begun to stimulate appreciation. G.H. 's-Gravesande was so impressed that he wrote one adulatory article after another (some of them were summarized in a booklet that appeared in May 1940). Escher got to know 's-Gravesande personally and was introduced by him to the architect of the new Town Hall in Leiden. This led to the important commission of designing inlaid panels for the Town Hall.

In December 1938 Escher received a government commission to produce a booklet on Delft, with ten woodcut illustrations. In January 1939 he made a test woodcut (cat. no. 309), whereupon he received the definitive commission. Using his parents' home as a base, he went drawing in Delft day after day in April. He completed the woodcuts in August, but the booklet was never published.

On 14 June Escher's father died. He made a very loving portrait of him on his deathbed. In an interview in the weekly *Vrij*

Nederland, Escher said in 1968: 'I loved my father very much. He always made a great impression on me. I'm very like him. He too was a lonely man and sat in his room most of the time.'

BACK TO HOLLAND

From November 1939 to March 1940 Escher worked on the thirteen-foot-long woodcut *Metamorphosis II* (cat. no. 320), a highpoint in his graphic work. In it, a series of motifs for the regular division of the plane form a continuous pictorial story through metamorphosis and a few associations of ideas, ending in a memory of Italy (the view of Atrani) and one of Château-d'Oex (the chessboard), and finally in a pattern identical to that at the start of the print, thus suggesting a complete cycle. Just before the German invasion of Holland and Belgium on 10 May 1940, Escher carved a beechwood sphere with splashing fish, a three-dimensional elaboration of a motif he had drawn on a flat surface in March. He was extremely fond of this spherical shape until his death: it was an almost perfect symbol of the approach to infinity.

Brussels was occupied by the Germans on 17 May. On the 27th Escher was informed that his mother had died; he was only able to get to The Hague a few days after her funeral. In October, November and December he went up to Holland for stretches of about ten days to settle the estate, execute the commission for the Town Hall in Leiden, re-establish contacts with his numerous Dutch relations, and finally, to look for a school and a house in Holland. There was little reason to stay in Belgium. The Eschers decided to live in the peaceful village of Baarn, where they started by renting a house in the Nicolaas Beetslaan 20. When they moved, on 20 February 1941, George had been a pupil at the Baarns Lyceum for more than a month.

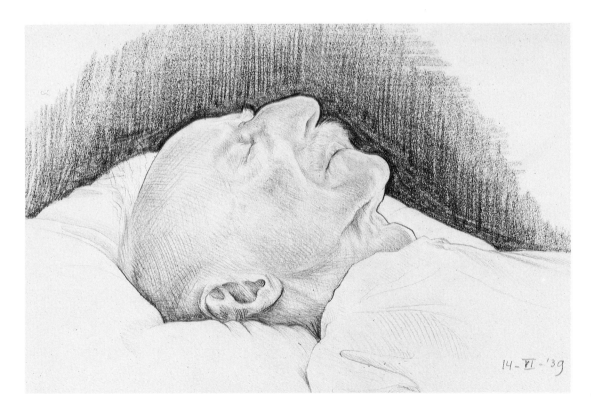

Escher's drawing of his father on his deathbed, 14 June 1939

57

I—'43

Back in Holland 1941–1954

During the war years Escher was fortunate to be able to work in Baarn relatively undisturbed. Nevertheless, the war did not totally pass him by. Some documents remain to show that he, too, came into contact with the horrors of the German occupation, albeit indirectly.

In the night of 31 Januari 1944 Escher's old teacher, Samuel Jessurun de Mesquita, who was a Jew, was taken away by the Germans, never to return. Escher helped to find a safe place for De Mesquita's graphic works and drawings in the Stedelijk Museum in Amsterdam, keeping for himself an etching with the print of a German boot on it. Until Escher's death this etching had its own special place on the door of the cupboard where he kept his drawing utensils.

De Mesquita had meant a great deal to Escher. He had spurred him on to become a graphic artist, and in Haarlem had been a well-loved teacher. Although Escher had later gone his own way, he had kept in contact with De Mesquita and sometimes sent him his work to criticize. A letter of 17 November 1941 gives an impression of this:

'Dear E, Many thanks for the work you sent me. I have been looking at it for many days and have come to the conclusion that you should consider it a milestone. In your letter you seem to pull it down so much that it makes one feel like pulling it up again. I should like to do so, but I'd rather do it in person. My son thinks you have totally succeeded. Please come and see me again sometime, so that we may talk about it; that would be far more satisfactory.'

On 11 January 1944, shortly before being taken away, De Mesquita had sent Escher a note: 'Dear friend, Although I find it very difficult, I cannot help writing to you to wish you strength in preserving your pre-war qualities throughout your life.'

In 1946 Escher helped organize a memorial exhibition for De Mesquita in the Stedelijk Museum, reviewing his life and work in the catalogue.

'He was adverse to any kind of drudgery and liked to discover for himself the value and quality of a procedure that had been used for a long time in a particular way, with materials tested by time and custom. Why should an etching necessarily be made on a metal plate? Could not another material produce surprising results? For a change he even made needle etchings on celluloid and once on a glass plate, of which he made a photographic print. What is the effect if an intaglio printing block is used to make a relief print? Look at the etching he printed as a woodcut. . . .

'By making counterproofs he produced his remarkable woodcuts in which symmetry plays an important part. They were made as follows: a sheet of paper on which a print has just been made, so that the ink is still wet, is covered with a clean sheet and the two are pressed together. This results in the prints becoming partly stuck together with printing-ink. If one sheet is now slowly pulled away from the other, a symmetrical representation is created, half of which is formed by the mirror image on the counterproof. De Mesquita was so exuberant about what he saw when he parted the two prints, like a child about the symmetrical patterns formed by beads and shreds of paper in a kaleidoscope, that he often felt it worthwhile to cut in wood the complete symmetrical picture that was formed.'

Escher also did a great deal of this sort of technical experimenting, especially during the first part of his life. Later, his mathematical mental images took up more and more of his attention, and technique increasingly became merely an aid. However, one example of a technical experiment in the manner of De Mesquita can be seen in the wood engraving *Candle* (cat. no. 330), which Escher engraved in July 1943 and then printed, not only as a relief print, but also as an intaglio print, like an etching (cat. no. 330*a*). Symmetry fascinated him all his life.

NEW ADMIRERS

During the war Escher always refused to participate in public demonstrations or organizations set up by the Germans. When just after the war, in the autumn of 1945, a large exhibition of works by artists who had refused to co-operate with the Nazis was held in the Rijksmuseum in Amsterdam, Escher contributed four prints and one drawing. As a result he gained a few new admirers and buyers.

All kinds of organizations and private people came to him with requests, which he tried to fulfill as helpfully and exactly as possible. For example, B. Merema of the VAEVO (see page 32)

Still Life; scratch drawing, January 1943

asked him for prints to illustrate a publication, and later for four hundred copies of a print to circulate to schools. There was little money available, but Escher did his utmost to find a way of meeting the request within the budget. During the summer of 1948 the four hundred copies (of cat. no. 352) were made, after Escher had agreed to a fee of a thousand guilders, including the cost of materials and printing.

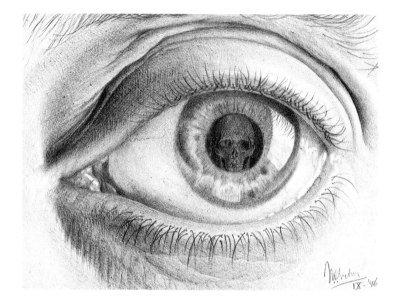

In 1946 Escher became interested in mezzotint, a technique that was new to him and fascinated him because of the possibility of obtaining extremely subtle gradations of light and dark. On 29 December 1947 he wrote to his friends Bas and Len Kist: 'This new mezzotint which I have just finished will serve as a New Year's card and so I am sending one to you too. These things always need a name and I have called it *Crystal* [cat. no. 353] because "Order and Chaos" sounds too ponderous, though that title actually gives a better indication of my intention. Let me add that Chaos is present everywhere in countless ways and forms, while Order remains an unattainable ideal: the magnificent fusion of a cube and an octahedron does not exist. Nevertheless, we can continue to hope for it. Is that not a fine wish for the New Year?'

About this time Escher began to lecture on his work more and more frequently. Bas Kist, who was a member of a group of print collectors, asked him to lecture to this group, and in October 1948 Escher agreed.

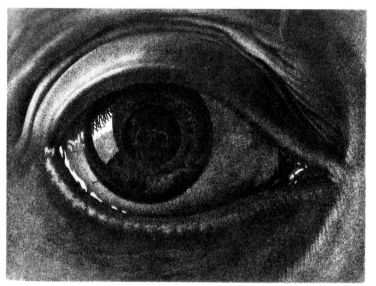

'I have waited to reply to your card until my involvement with the woodcut I am working on has died down a little. I should be happy to speak to your print group about graphic art, but as I think I told you last year, I have no talent whatsoever for public speaking and therefore you will have to put up with a stammering lecturer. Nevertheless I should like to pass on my own enthusiasm for graphic art to others, and particularly to people who are really interested. I hope that by then something will still remain of the intense enthusiasm that has possessed me the past few days while I was making a coloured woodcut [the coloured variation of cat. no. 359]. I am sure there would be a lot to tell you about its technique. I have not done any "black art" (mezzotint) for months, but I will soon start on some now that I have finally acquired a good rocker from England and I have gained some experience, though by no means enough, in doing the five prints I made so far using this technique.'

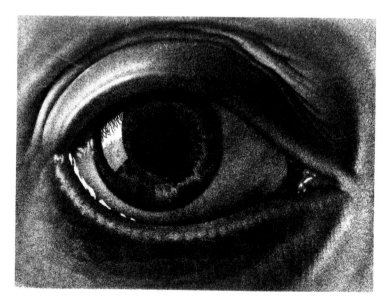

Escher preferred to make his prints on Japanese paper and he did his best to build up an adequate stock. The Enschedé printing office helped him out a number of times. They did so in 1948, this time in exchange for a few prints. On 6 November 1948 Escher wrote to the director, A.D. Huijsman: 'I was delighted to receive today both your letter of the 5th inst. and the parcel containing a hundred sheets of Japanese paper. I am very grateful for your generosity: now, for a while, I can face the future with my mind at rest as far as this essential material is concerned. Of course, I am

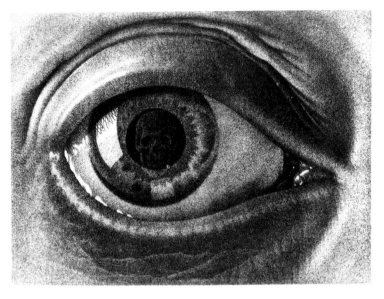

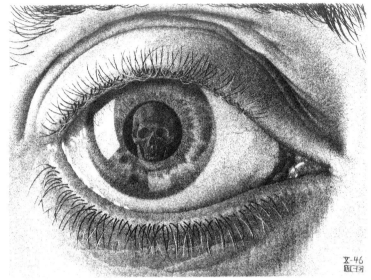

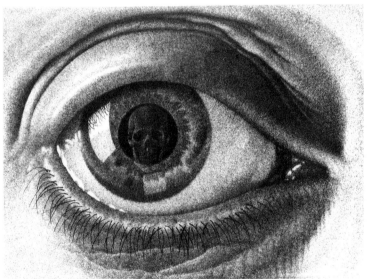

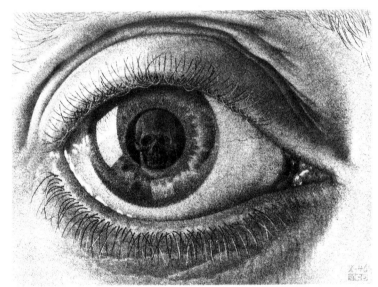

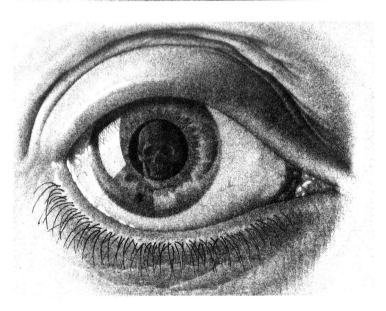

The different stages of *Eye*, October 1946 (cat. no. 344), make clear the laborious and time-consuming mezzotint procedure. *Opposite page, from top to bottom*: Preliminary study (pencil drawing), first state mezzotint, second state. *This page, left, from top to bottom*: Third, fourth and fifth states. *Above*: Sixth state, seventh and final state

more than prepared to add to your collection of my prints those that are missing, in exchange for the paper.'

One of the important collectors of Escher's graphic work was P. Kessler from Arnhem. In addition to prints he acquired a sphere of maple wood carved with a motif of reptiles, filling the entire surface. A number of letters remain showing how pleased Escher was with Kessler's interest, especially as the latter particularly appreciated the mathematical side of his work.

Baarn, 23 November 1949: 'Dear Mr Kessler, The exhibition in Rotterdam was a great success. [Escher had an exhibition in the Boymans Museum with two other graphic artists, Van Heusden and Van Kruiningen.] There were at least two thousand visitors and we gave a demonstration of printing techniques—which was tremendously popular—as well as a chat about our work to an association of print enthusiasts. I sold thirty-two prints, including the four-metre-long metamorphosis. The reviews were many and favourable, so I have no complaints, and the exhibition has been extended by another week.

'The wooden spheres provoked a great deal of interest, but they were understandably more appreciated for the craftsmanship than for being the most consistent application of the regular division of the plane.

'We moved the greater part of the exhibition to Leiden yesterday. It will open there next Saturday in the University printroom. Once again, the three of us will be "beating the drum", and this time in a rather perfectionist way that is new to me: Professor Van der Waal, the director, is prepared to make twelve lantern slides of our choice, form each of our collections. On the evening of 8 December we shall each have a chance to chat about our work in the lecture hall for twenty minutes, illustrating the talks with slides. Thus it will finally be possible to explain it all clearly to a larger audience. I am curious to see how these experiments will succeed. Later in the evening we shall also give a guided tour of the prints themselves.

'However, this is where you come in: would you be prepared to lend your sphere a little longer for this exhibition as well? I would return it to you about mid-December. If you have any objections, do let me know. It has already been installed in a display case, but could still be removed. I think that such "dogmatic" expressions of my art as those spheres will particularly appeal to an intellectual audience of students (if they actually come!). One of my spheres will be projected on a slide . . . .

'Between exhibitions I am very busy; I am working on a new coloured woodcut [cat. no. 365] representing a small (*very* small!) planet, consisting of two inextricably interlocked tetrahedrons of different colours. One of them has triangular pyramid structures with humanoid inhabitants; the other has rocks, strange plants and prehistoric animals. The whole thing is contained in a circular, deep-blue plane, which more or less gives the illusion that the planet is seen through a telescope. As everything feels drawn to the centre because of the force of gravity, the observer must be able to rotate the print around this centre point. The element of movement seems to have taken hold of me here too.'

Baarn, 17 January 1950: 'Dear Mr Kessler, I enclose four different prints; I include the lithograph *Drawing Hands* [cat. no. 355], although you did not mention it, but I have forgotten whether you know it. The prices are shown at the bottom of each print.

'"At the bottom" is in a manner of speaking, and rather arbitrary in the case of my *Double Planet*. For someone who insisted on hanging it on the wall, it would be ideal to be able to rotate it. I have just exhibited it in Amsterdam (at a general exhibition of our group) in a rotating mount. It is a strange thing and from an aesthetic point of view probably monstrous. This does not alter the fact that with it I have succeeded more or less in celebrating or exorcizing my "complex" regarding regular solid figures. No matter how clumsy it is, I am satisfied to some extent. That double tetrahedron has been bothering me for years. I hope to start on a lithograph soon—a sort of repetition and elaboration of the problem I posed in the mezzotint *Crystal* [cat. no. 353].

'*Gallery* [cat. no. 346], dated XII-'46, almost made me despair at the time; I put the finishing touches to it in April 1949. *Other World* [cat. no. 348] is a sequel to it, and the long lithograph *Up and Down* [cat. no. 352] is a sequel to *Other World.*'

Baarn, 15 February 1950: 'Dear Mr Kessler, Thank you for your card and payment. I was delighted that you liked the double planet and that you are able (and wish) to share my personal hobbies so wonderfully well. When I showed the print to my colleagues, their reaction was so minimal—that is, they stood and looked at it without any sign of interest—that it rather discouraged me after all my efforts.

'I do not entirely comprehend the error that you noted (though I appreciate it very much that you *did* note it) but I'm sure it's there. [Kessler had written that in his opinion some of the lines should have converged.] I found the whole question of the intersection of the different planes devilishly difficult. My imagination leaves a lot to be desired, and when one starts a piece of work like this, it leads to constant frustration with one's shortcomings. Besides, the technical execution was particularly laborious this time and, despite my enthusiasm, actually one constant failure.

'If there were no people like you—and fortunately a few others—I might not have the courage to start again every time.'

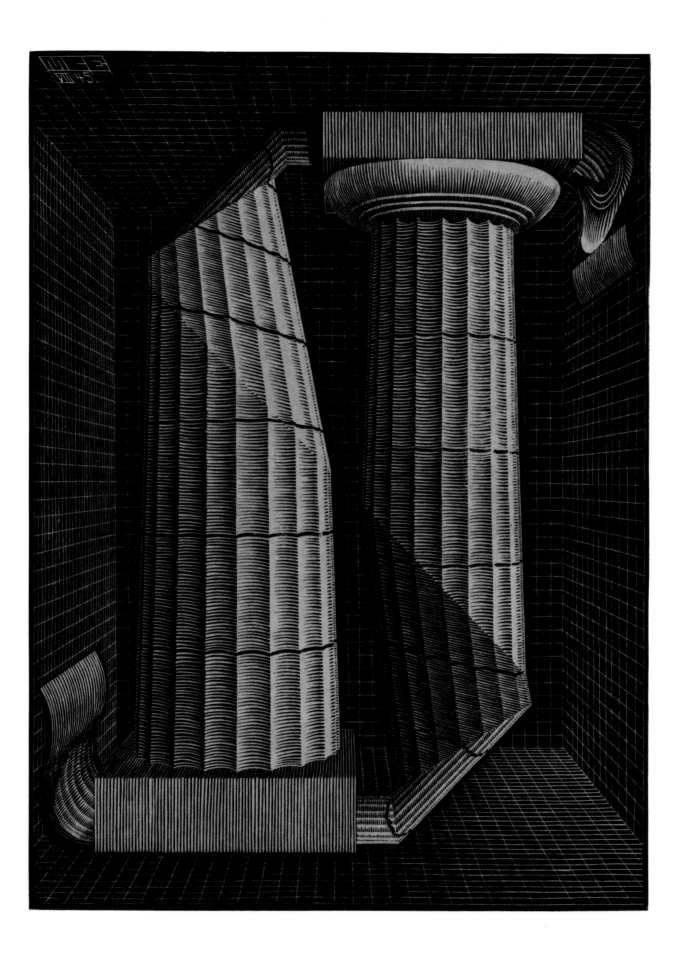

In 1949 Escher did a design which was executed by the weaver Edmond de Cneudt as a tapestry. This tapestry was purchased by the Gemeentemuseum of Arnhem in 1951 (see page 75).

At the end of 1950 Escher started on another non-graphic work. L. C. Kalff of the Philips factory at Eindhoven asked him whether he would be prepared to design a ceiling in a reception area. It would have to be completed before the sixtieth anniversary of Philips, which was to be celebrated in May 1951. Escher accepted the commission and, in close collaboration with Kalff's technical staff, designed a pattern that was executed in 1951 (see page 78).

At the beginning of 1951, the Enschedé printers in Haarlem asked Escher to design a postage stamp for the United Nations. He accepted this too, and the design was entered for an international competition; it did not win, and was never issued.

In 1951 some important articles on Escher's work appeared in influential foreign periodicals. The first was by Mark Severin in the February issue of *The Studio*; Severin had come across Escher's work at an exhibition of Dutch graphic art in Antwerp, in May 1950. Israël Shenker, correspondent of Time-Life, read the article and interviewed Escher in Baarn. The result was an article in *Time* magazine on 2 April 1951, and another in *Life* on 7 May. They were well received and led to a great many reactions and orders. These articles were the beginning of Escher's rapidly increasing fame, especially in the English-speaking world.

When Escher's cousin Lies Bolhuis-Escher bought a print of *Day and Night* (cat. no. 303), he wrote her a letter which tells us something about his family situation at the time, as well as about the beginnings of his fame.

Baarn, 22 May 1951: 'Dear Lies, I enclose the print of D. and N. that you requested. Let us get the business side over with before we go on to other matters: price 50 guilders. . . .

'There is not much change in our general state of health; Jetta is still about the same, terribly heavy going and depressed, but I'm not giving up. George is conscripted until next October; Arthur is enjoying his geology studies in Lausanne; Jan is trying to get into the Lyceum soon.

'I have a lot to do. Two publications in America, *Time* in April and *Life* (American edition of 7 May), have led to all sorts of orders (six of D. and N. since April!) and many letters to answer. I am looking forward to the summer holidays!'

Escher's prints were now being interpreted and used in many different ways. He wrote to Lies Bolhuis that an ophthalmologist in Alkmaar, Dr J. W. Wagenaar, had been using *Day and Night* for some years in lectures, to illustrate one of the laws of perception.

Through him a physician in Deventer, Dr A. W. M. Pompen, had become fascinated by the same print. The latter thought he could detect various symbolic meanings and wrote a letter about it. Escher answered in a friendly way.

Baarn, 3 November 1951: 'Dear Dr Pompen, Thank you very much for your letter of 30 August and for returning my photograph so promptly. I was very pleased to hear what you "see" in the print and I feel honoured that you intend to use it as a slide in your lecture. . . .

'It is fascinating to hear other people's interpretations of my work, especially as the meaning or the symbolism that is sometimes seen in it is completely foreign to me—at least consciously.

'I think I have never yet done any work with the aim of symbolizing a particular idea, but the fact that a symbol is sometimes discovered or remarked upon is valuable for me because it makes it easier to accept the inexplicable nature of my hobbies, which constantly preoccupy me.

'The regular division of the plane into congruent figures evoking an association in the observer with a familiar natural object is one of these hobbies or problems. This is really all there is to say about *Day and Night*. I have embarked on this geometric problem again and again over the years, trying to throw light on different aspects each time. I cannot imagine what my life would be like if this problem had never occurred to me; one might say that I am head over heels in love with it, and I still don't know why.

'It is not my only hobby; there are a few others which intrigue me and sometimes lead me away from the plane and into space. Awareness of the three dimensions, the notion of plasticity, is not as general as one might expect in spatial creatures like ourselves. An understanding of the relationships between plane and space is a source of emotion for me; and emotion is a strong incentive, or at least a stimulus for making a picture.

'It is quite true that "we know only a part", we know only a minute part.'

In April 1952 B. Merema came with another request from the VAEVO for a large edition of a print for distribution to schools. It was decided to print four hundred copies of the lithograph *Contrast* (cat. no. 366) on Dieperink's press. Despite increased costs Escher again agreed to a total fee of one thousand guilders. In addition the VAEVO wanted to make and distribute a filmstrip of about thirty of Escher's prints. They were to be shown in educational institutions, and Merema asked if Escher himself could write an accompanying text. This, too, Escher was pleased to do.

Baarn, 10 May 1952: 'Dear Mr Merema, I cannot but welcome your plan to show young people the products of art by means of filmstrips, for I am aware of the advantages this practical, modern

Page 65: Unfinished block for wood engraving *Balcony* (compare cat. no. 334)

Opposite page: *Doric Columns*; wood engraving in three colours, August 1945 (cat. no. 335)

method of showing art has over the old method. . . . I should therefore be most pleased to contribute to this venture, as far as my own work is concerned. For the last few years I have given a number of lectures about my work, using slides of my prints; while they are being projected I talk about my intentions and what stimulated me to make them. As you know, my intentions are more reasoned, and in many cases more conscious, mathematical and cerebral, than those of most of my fellow-artists, whose directly aesthetic and unconsciously sensitive impulses are sometimes more easily experienced than put into words.'

Being left-handed himself, Escher was always very interested in the problem of left-handedness. Thus, he reacted immediately when, in December 1952, he was sent an article on the subject.

Baarn, 12 December 1952: 'Dear Van der Haagen, It was with a great deal of interest that I read the article on "left-handedness in drawing" in the December issue of the N V T O monthly that you sent me.

'I was particularly struck by the suggestion that left-handed people might be more inclined to draw than to paint; in other words, that shape might be more important to them than colour. As far as I'm concerned, this is perfectly true. I was exclusively left-handed from my earliest childhood (at primary school I found learning to write with my right hand extremely difficult; I should probably have managed far more easily and naturally writing in mirror image with my left hand), and the fact that my feeling for shape is greater than that for colour may also have resulted in my becoming a graphic artist rather than a painter.

'The question posed in this article—"Is left-handedness innate or acquired?"—seems superfluous. If right-handedness is innate, why shouldn't left-handedness be? I do not know of any normal right-handed artists who became left-handed through practice; though I have heard of the reverse. Leonardo may be an example. In the case of the graphic artist S. Jessurun de Mesquita, who died in 1944, I am quite certain. He was proud that, having been born left-handed, he had also learned to draw with his right hand—and, he said, just as easily. For a graphic artist, who is always working with both an image and a mirror image, being ambidextrous is obviously a great advantage.

'It would be interesting to carry out a survey among Dutch graphic artists to find out what percentage is left-handed; perhaps I will actually do this one day.

'I do not know how these traits are passed on; possibly simply from father (or mother) to child. For it can hardly be a coincidence that with a father as left-handed as I am, two of the three sons are also left-handed, at least in their drawing.

'In the spring of 1952 I was on a jury to judge a drawing competition of pupils from five high schools, and the supervising teacher, J. van Ingen, Jr, noted that nine of the fifteen participants were drawing with their left hand. This is sixty percent left-handed

in a pre-selected group—quite remarkable! It is a pity that coincidence is too large a factor in such a small sample; otherwise some very interesting conclusions might be drawn.

'No matter how many left-handed graphic artists there may be, they are apparently still so exceptional and strange that "ordinary" people are immediately struck by it. At least, this was my experience repeatedly in Italy when I used to do a lot of drawing in the open. The curiosity of onlookers was much more about the fact that I was left-handed than about the picture appearing on the paper.'

SUBJECTIVE AND OBJECTIVE
At the end of 1952 a correspondence developed with the above-mentioned Dr J. W. Wagenaar. Escher asked him a great many questions. Dr Wagenaar's extensive reply elicited the following letter.

Baarn, 16 January 1953: 'Dear Dr Wagenaar, Thank you very much for your letter and the copies of your article. I am extremely interested in what you say—as far as I can understand it, for not all of it is clear to me . . . .

'I was very taken by your paragraph on subjective and objective space. You will probably realize from this letter that I know too little about philosophy, and you may even find me unserious, but here it is anyway.

'I should be inclined to say, then, that none of us needs to doubt the existence of an unreal, subjective space. But I for one am not sure of the existence of a real, objective space. Our senses only reveal a subjective world; we may only *think*, and possibly believe, that we can conclude an objective world exists. This reminds me, on the one hand, of a game I used to play with a friend at secondary school, although the parallel does not hold completely (there goes the baker's boy with his cart; he turns the corner and vanishes from sight; now he no longer exists), and, on the other hand, of much more recent thoughts and feelings which sometimes creep over me when, with much interest, I read or listen to astronomers popularizing the theories about the nature of the universe. This wonderful game (for a layman like myself), in which my thoughts penetrate the farthest reaches of so-called real space, farther and farther, with the occasional star or constellation or spiral galaxy as a support or milestone, may suddenly change into the opposite as a result of the question, What is this so-called reality; what is this theory but a beautiful though totally human fantasy? Even if the hypothesis is proved to be correct through observation, that is, through the senses, does this really constitute proof? Why do we have such unshakable faith in our senses? And why should we not be satisfied with the subjective?

'It may seem a bit stupid, but here goes: is that red flower of yours actually there, real, objective and separate from us, even if I see its colour, smell its fragrance, feel its petals with my fingertips, hear a bee buzzing around it, taste its honey (or the bee does)?

Right: Of his 'curl-up' Escher made clay models in various stages of curling up

Below: Preliminary study for the lithograph *House of Stairs* (cat. no. 375)

Does it matter so much if we imagine once in a while that it may not "exist" at all?

'Later, at the end of your letter, you say that you believe in the absolute nature of a concept. So can I, if I wish to. But if I do not wish to, I can also not believe in it. Perhaps the whole question of whether there is, or is not, objective space depends on this.

'I certainly do *not* understand what you say about a pure sphere in objective space and about a solid objectively deviating from the pure sphere, such as an ellipsoid, which could still be perceived as a pure sphere.

'Of course, I should like to talk to you about these matters, but I fear that you will not have time for it.

'I have sent a copy of your article to Dr P.J. Kipp, a biologist in Utrecht, who visited me recently. He was interested in my prints and considers that they might form a means of contact between two varieties of people who increasingly fail to understand each other, because of the growing specialization in these times.

'I am very grateful for your serious attention to the letter I wrote you.'

In March Lies Bolhuis asked Escher to make a bookplate for Dr Pompen. He declined and suggested his colleague Pam Rueter. Escher was too busy himself, partly because of a commission from the Nederlandsche Bank for a design for banknotes. He complained of having too little time for his own work, a complaint that became increasingly common during the following years. He wrote to Lies Bolhuis that his son Jan was now in a children's home in Baarn, since the atmosphere at home was often too oppressive because of Jetta's depressions.

LECTURE IN ALKMAAR

During these years Escher was able to exhibit regularly in museums, art galleries and universities, often together with two or more fellow-members of the Association of Dutch Graphic Artists. Usually he also lectured on his work. Although he had written to Bas Kist in 1947 saying that he was a poor public speaker, it turned out that Escher was able to pack lecture halls. He explained his prints in a clear and fascinating fashion, and increasingly enjoyed doing so. He never gave off-the-cuff lectures but always prepared them thoroughly and wrote down most of what he would say. Some lecture texts have been preserved. A few fragments of a talk he gave on 16 November 1953 to the Friends of the Stedelijk Museum in Alkmaar follow.

'If someone has expressed himself in graphics from his youth; if he has created visual images for many years, always using such graphic means as wood blocks, copper plates and lithographic stones, as well as press, ink, and all sorts of paper for printing on, this technique finally becomes second nature to him. Obviously the technique itself must have been the most important thing for him, at least at the beginning of his career as a graphic artist, or he

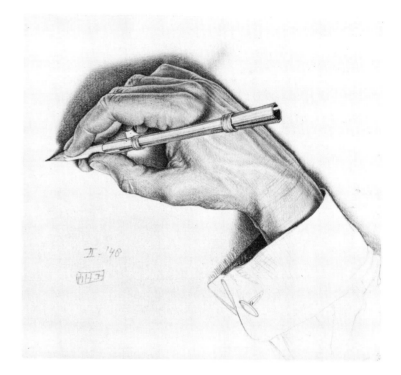

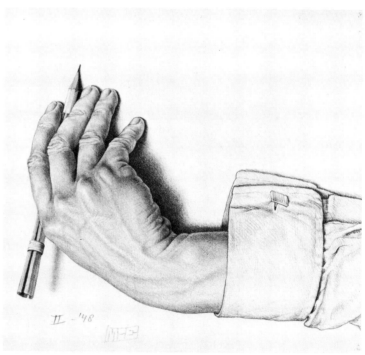

Two preliminary studies for the lithograph *Drawing Hands* (cat. no. 355). It is strange that both drawings are dated 11-'48, while the lithograph is dated 1-'48. Note that Escher used his right hand for both hands

would not have specialized in that direction. In addition, he must continue to use the specific medium he has chosen with unflagging enthusiasm throughout the years, and he will undoubtedly strive all his life for a technical expertise that he will never completely acquire.

'Meanwhile, all this technique is merely a means, not an end in itself. The end he strives for is something else than a perfectly executed print. His aim is to depict dreams, ideas or problems in such a way that other people can observe and consider them. The illusion which an artist wishes to create is much more subjective and far more important than the objective, physical means with which he tries to create it. It is about this very personal matter that I should like to talk tonight.

'Last April I lectured in this same hall to the members of the Physica Society, and what I say today will be an almost exact repetition of what I said then. So I hope that there is nobody present now who was also here then. In a sense I felt more at home in that group of people, whose interest I assume was mainly scientific. This may sound odd coming from someone whom one would rather describe as a "feeling person" because of his profession, but I have often felt closer to people who work scientifically (though I certainly do not do so myself) than to my fellow-artists.

'Soon I want to show you a sort of picture-book in the form of a series of slides, mostly of my prints. In these pictures I shall try to show that they were created as a result of my intense interest in the laws of nature and geometric rhythms in space and on the plane.

'Before I show these slides, however, I should like to make one more effort at explanation, by way of prologue to the picture-book that follows.

'It is human nature to want to exchange ideas and I believe that, at bottom, every artist wants no more than to tell the world what he has to say. I have sometimes heard painters say that they work "for themselves", but I think they would soon have painted their fill if they lived on a desert island. The primary purpose of all art forms, whether music, literature or the visual arts, is to say something to the outside world; in other words, to make a personal thought, a striking idea, an inner emotion perceptible to other people's senses, in such a way that there is no uncertainty about the maker's intentions. The artist's ideal is to produce a crystal-clear reflection of his own self. Thus an artist's talent is not only determined by the quality of the thoughts he wishes to convey—for anyone can have the most beautiful, the most moving images in his head—but also by his ability to express them in such a way that they get through to other people, undistorted. The result of the struggle between the thought and the ability to express it, between dream and reality, is seldom more than a compromise or an approximation. Thus there is little chance that we will succeed in getting through to a large audience, and on the whole we are quite satisfied if we are understood and appreciated by a small number of sensitive, receptive people.

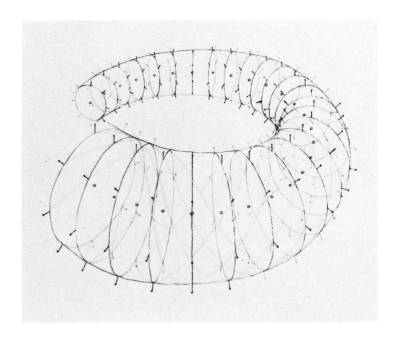

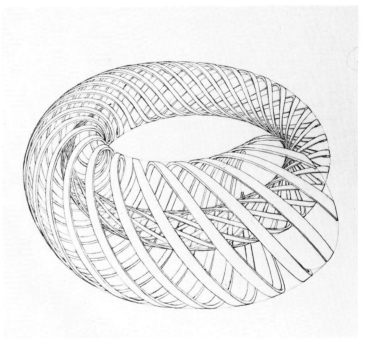

Two preliminary studies for the wood engraving in two colours *Spirals* (cat. no. 390)

71

Top: Study for the division of the plane no. 99; drawing, August 1954. Escher also used this motif for a woodcut vignette (cat. no. 398)

Above: Escher constructed regular spatial figures from all sorts of materials (see also p. 146). This photograph shows a few on his worktable in front of him

'However, we are lacking not only in the clarity of our arguments, but also in unity of purpose. For the time being at least, it is no longer possible for us to build a cathedral together— quite apart from the question whether people were any happier when this was possible. Still, it would be unjust to hold artists' dissension against them. The artist creates a reflection of what he sees around him and in a time of confusion and ferment one should not expect unanimity and a collective vitality from artists when they see only chaos and disharmony. I believe that many people visit museums in the hope of finding peace and a matured beauty which they lack in daily life. They turn to art for relaxation, as a way of drawing breath, because they need something more inspiring than what is usually to be found on the radio or in the cinema. When they see the distorted and cramped pictures hanging on the walls of modern-art museums, they feel cheated and blame modern artists for being less talented than their predecessors in earlier centuries. They forget that the artist's life is just as hectic and tense as their own and do not see that the mirror held up to them is probably a more accurate picture of the world surrounding us than the mirror held up to people by artists in earlier periods. Moreover, few people nowadays attain the peace and concentration necessary for the development of talent.

'Thus there is undoubtedly a rather tense relationship between artists and their audience. But why should we actually separate artists from the mass of their contemporaries, as a small group? Pointing out the differences between other groups of people seems to me more justified.

'There is a noticeable difference between two groups of people which can be distinguished and compared because they have ideas and opinions with an apparently different orientation. I could not think of two names to characterize and distinguish them. The terms "rationalist" and "sentimentalist", for example, do not express what I mean. For want of anything better I have called them "feeling people" and "thinking people", but their real character will become clear only if I describe them.

'By "feeling people" I mean those who, amid everything surrounding them, are most interested in the relationship between themselves and others, and in relationships between people in general. Admittedly they are aware of phenomena in the outside world which are not directly related to people, such as nature, matter and space, but all that does not mean very much to them. They consider it to be of secondary importance and regard it as a stage, a complex of attributes whose purpose is to act as a backdrop for people. On the other hand, they are greatly fascinated by all the problems that face man in society. I call them "feeling people" because I believe that the many ideas which interest them, such as society, the state, religion, justice, trade and, usually, art too, are in the first place related to the feeling relationships between people.

'Most artists belong to this group. This is clear from the preference they have had since time immemorial for depicting the human countenance and the human form; they are fascinated by specifically human qualities, both physical and spiritual. And even if they do not depict man himself, even when a poet is describing a landscape or a painter is doing a still life, they almost always approach their subjects from their interest in man.

'It may seem paradoxical to say that there are similarities between a poetical and a commercial mind, but it is a fact that both a poet and a businessman are constantly dealing with problems that are directly related to people and for which sensitivity is of prime importance. The business-like mind is sometimes described as being cold, sober, calculating, hard, but perhaps these are simply qualities that are necessary for dealing with people if one wants to achieve anything. One is always concerned with the mysterious, incalculable, dark, hidden aspects for which there is no easy formula, but which form essentially the same human element as that which inspires the poet.

'Then there is the other group, which I have rather inadequately described as "thinking people". In this group I include people who consider that they can attribute a specific significance, independent of mankind, to non-human natural phenomena, to the earth on which they live and the rest of the universe around it. This group understands the language of matter, space and the universe. They are receptive towards this outside world, they accept it as something that exists objectively, separate from man, which they can not only see but also observe closely, study and even attempt to understand, bit by bit. In doing this they are able to forget themselves to a greater extent than the feeling person usually can.

'When someone forgets himself, this by no means makes him altruistic; when a thinking person forgets himself, he immediately also forgets his fellow-men, he loses himself and his humanity by becoming engrossed in his subject. Thus he is in a sense more contemplative than a feeling person. Anyone who is profoundly concerned with material things in general, and whose work does not require the involvement of other people, belongs to this group. Factory workers or carpenters may belong to it just as much as chemists or astronomers. They are people for whom the world is so real and tangible that they generally do not take into account how subjective everything is nevertheless. For as far as I know, there is no proof whatever of the existence of an objective reality apart from our senses, and I do not see why we should accept the outside world as such solely by virtue of our senses.

'These reality enthusiasts are possibly playing at hide-and-seek; at any rate they like to hide themselves, though they are not usually aware of it. They simply do it because they happen to have been born with a sense of reality, that is, with a great interest in so-called reality, and because man likes to forget himself. However, it is quite possible that subconscious factors such as a fear of the dark incomprehensible nature of the human condition sometimes play a role, and that "thinking people" are escaping from this. Disillusion, exhaustion, impotence and other inhibitions may have led them to seek peace and respite in dealing with matters that are less complicated and easier to grasp than the enigma of man himself.

'In these descriptions I have tried to highlight the contrast between the characteristics of the two groups. I do indeed believe that there is a certain contrast between, say, people in scientific professions and people working in the arts. Often there is even mutual suspicion and irritation, and in some cases one group greatly undervalues the other.

'Fortunately there is no one who actually has only feeling or only thinking properties. They intermingle like the colours of the rainbow and cannot be sharply divided. Perhaps there is even a transitional group, like the green between the yellow and the blue of the rainbow. This transitional group does not have a particular preference for thinking or feeling, but believes that one cannot do without either the one or the other. At any rate, it is unprejudiced enough to wish for a better understanding between the two parties. . . .

'It is clear that feeling and understanding are not necessarily opposites but that they complement each other. You don't have to be a physicist to experience the miracle of gravity, but with the aid of our intellect, our understanding of a miracle can be enhanced. I do not know if it is true, but I imagine that there are scientists who, by following the paths of the so-called "cold" intellect— possibly without being aware of it—are plumbing the depths of a mystery rather than searching for the solution to a problem. . . .'

EXHIBITIONS

In 1954 Escher made only two prints (cat. nos. 395 and 397), but it was a busy and important year for the spreading of his work. In September a large one-man exhibition was held in the Stedelijk Museum in Amsterdam, on the initiative of the International Mathematical Conference. There was a well-produced catalogue with a preface by the Amsterdam Professor of Mathematics N. G. de Bruijn, who wrote: 'Mathematicians will not only be fascinated by the geometric motifs. Even more important, perhaps, is the same playfulness which one finds everywhere in mathematics and which accounts for the charm that a great many mathematicians find in their profession. The delegates at the conference will be delighted to recognize their own thoughts expressed through entirely different means from those to which they are accustomed.'

Escher gave another lecture on his work at the conference. It led to a number of new buyers, and also to friends among mathematicians. One of the most important was the Canadian professor H. S. M. Coxeter, who was much impressed by Escher's imagery. He maintained contact with Escher and in the following years often suggested new literature, gave his reactions to new prints and sometimes even provided ideas for prints.

Escher's first one-man exhibition in the United States was almost as important. It was held in the Whyte Gallery in Washington, 73

D.C., during October and November and was enormously successful.

The man behind this show was Charles Alldredge, an American who had come to know Escher's work through the articles in *Time* and *Life* magazines in 1951. He began to correspond with Escher and bought his work. In addition, he became a sort of unpaid American agent. He managed to persuade the owner of the Whyte Gallery to hold an exhibition. Escher himself approached the Dutch ambassador in Washington to persuade him to be present at the opening; he also asked him for information about the reliability of the Whyte Gallery. The ambassador reassured Escher that the Whyte Gallery had a good reputation. Originally the exhibition was to be held in the spring, but it was postponed until the autumn. It was opened on 7 October 1954 by H. A. Teixeira de Mattos, first secretary of the Dutch embassy.

Even before it opened, many prints had been sold. On 10 September Alldredge wrote, much surprised: 'By now about one third of your prints have been sold. This is quite remarkable I think. I had been of the opinion that perhaps their appeal would be only to a special group, but I find that interest in your work will be wider than I had thought likely.' In the same letter he advised Escher against a permanent connection with the Whyte Gallery and said he had suggested to *Time* magazine that they should send someone to the exhibition in Amsterdam.

On 26 September Escher set out from Antwerp on the *Giosue Borsi*, a freighter sailing to Naples. From there he travelled overland back to Baarn. It was his first sea voyage since the war and he thoroughly enjoyed it; henceforth he would make a journey like that every year during the summer months. He stopped off at Rome and was met at the Netherlands Institute by correspondents of Time-Life. They interviewed him for an article about his work, which appeared on 25 October in the Atlantic edition of *Time* magazine.

When Escher got home he found enthusiastic reports of the success of the exhibition. More than a hundred prints had been sold and plans were being made for new exhibitions. Escher felt dazed, and apprehensive at the thought of the many copies that would have to be produced, which would leave little time for new prints. He suggested a drastic increase in prices to slow down sales. He was to do this a number of times in subsequent years, though never with much effect—his prints continued to be bought.

He was very pleased that Teixeira de Mattos sent him some very favourable information about his agent Alldredge. In his letter of 18 October 1954 the former wrote: 'At the opening of the exhibition I had the opportunity of becoming better acquainted with Mr Alldredge. He seems a very nice man and gives an excellent impression. He is the advisor to Senator Kefauver and has some very good contacts. His hobby is discovering living artists. One of his discoveries is the well-known writer Rachel Carson, author of *The Sea Around Us*, now a best-seller which has made her a fortune. He is interested in you purely for art's sake

and certainly does not expect any reward. I think you should consider yourself lucky to have Mr Alldredge as an agent and an admirer.'

Escher wrote to Alldredge, in English, on 3 November 1954: 'I am conscious to owe you a great debt of gratitude: in fact the whole success is your work. I feel the necessity to show these notions not only by words, but it seems to me quite impossible to show you my thankfulness clear enough.

'Nevertheless, I will try: I should really be very happy if you would accept at least three of my prints. I pray you to make a choice and to write me the names of those you like best of all. . . .

'Many thanks for the check from Mr . . . of Oklahoma, to whom I shall send tomorrow the four prints you mentioned. I am very glad that you took the initiative to increase already the prices of these four prints: it will be necessary to do the same with all the other prints and specially with the lithographs which are all running short. As for the woodcuts and -engravings: restamping them takes me a lot of time and besides this: I do not intend to pass the rest of my life as a stamping-machine, but I desire to make new work. For the two shows of Amsterdam and Washington I had to spend nearly two months, only by restamping, day after day, the old cuts! The only way to get more freedom seems to be: selling less with higher prices.'

In a letter to Alldredge dated 14 December 1954 Escher mentioned another factor that prevented him from undertaking new work during these months: 'Another reason that makes it difficult to concentrate my thoughts on my work (besides reprinting woodcuts, writing letters and despatching prints) is the fact that we soon will have a new home to live in, a little house that was built for us and which is almost ready, with a greater and better studio than I have in this old house. It will take another two months of hurry before my wife and I will be settled down quietly in our own new one. I am almost certain that, before then, there will be no time to work steadily again and without continuous interruptions.'

LETTERS TO INDONESIA

At the end of 1954 Arthur travelled to Billiton in Indonesia to start working for the Billiton Company, having completed his geology studies at Lausanne. He stayed in Indonesia for four years, during which Escher regularly wrote his son long letters. Many of these have survived because he usually made a copy for himself—as he did with nearly all his correspondence.

One of the last letters he wrote in 1954 was to Arthur.

Opposite page: In 1949 Escher designed this tapestry for the weavers Ed. de Cneudt in Baarn. Left, the working drawing; right, the tapestry, which was woven in 1950 and now belongs to the Gemeentemuseum in Arnhem

Page 76: *Butterflies*; coloured drawing, an 'inverted circle limit' (compare also cat. no. 369)

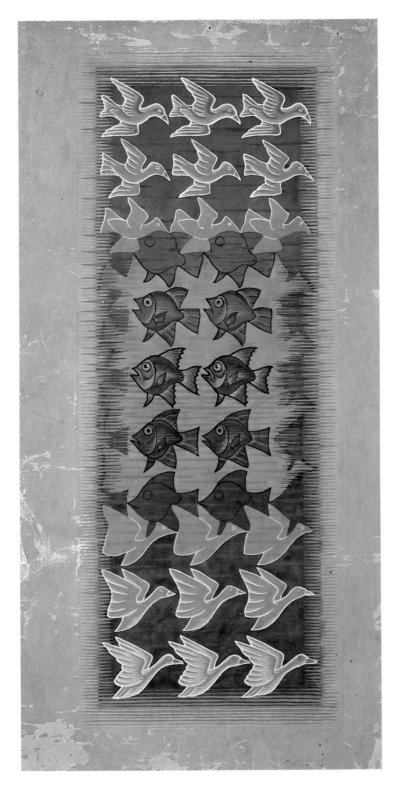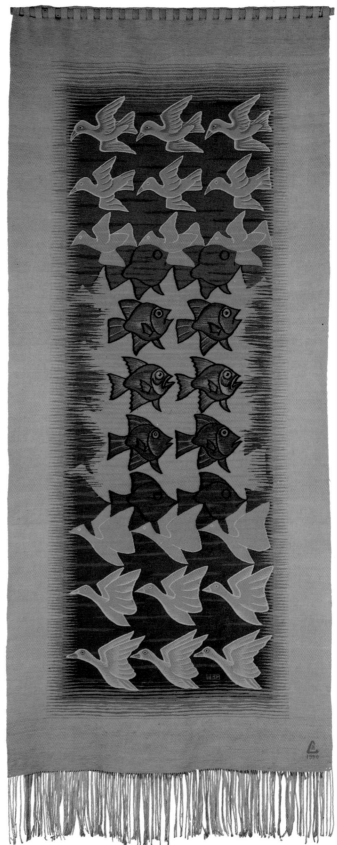

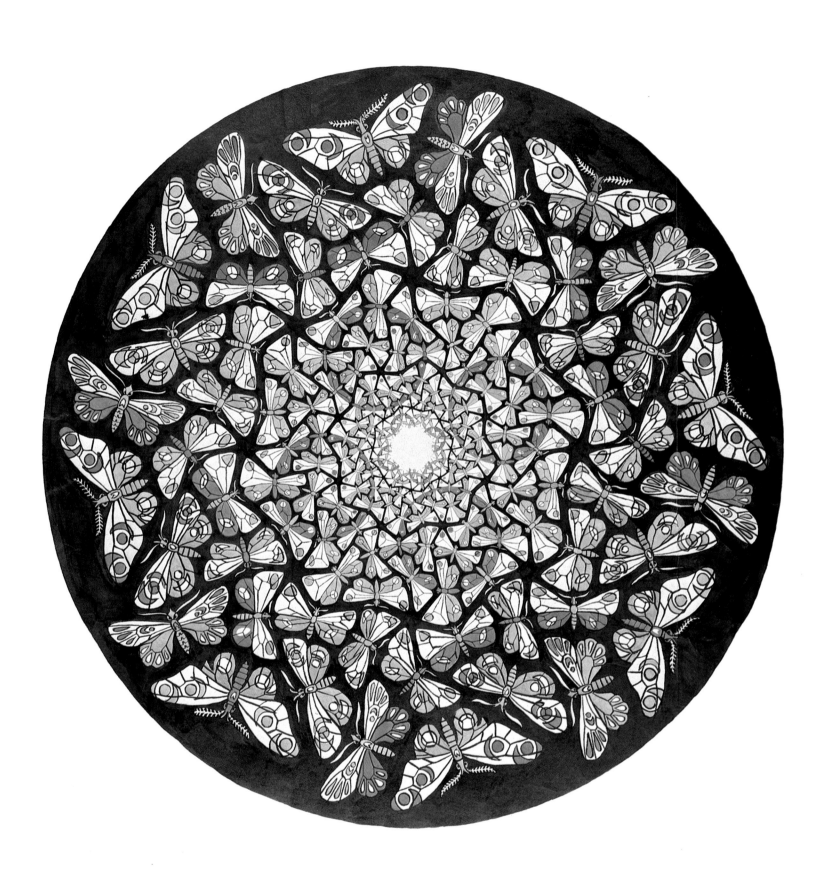

FOND DE GAUME
LES EYZIES
26-VII-50

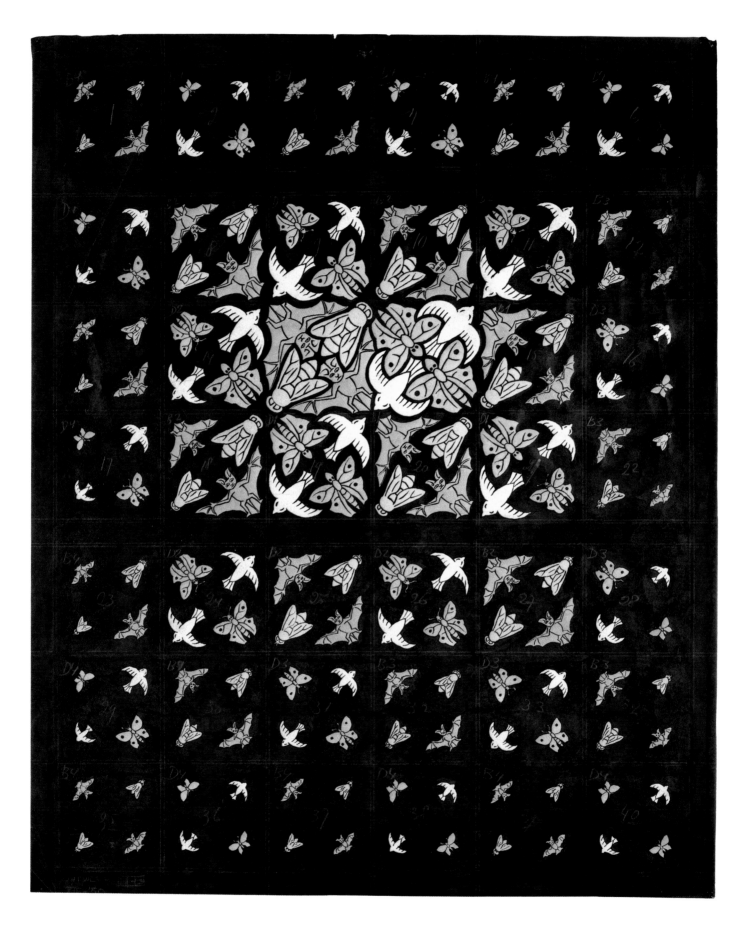

Baarn, 23 December 1954: 'It is time for another installment of news about our ups and downs. Luckily there are more ups than downs; actually there are no downs at all, except for the misplaced a's on this typewriter.

'Things might have been very black by now if our new house had not weathered the rain-and-storm test to which it was subjected quite as well as it did. They (I mean the specialist tilers) had just spent a whole day putting a lorry load of tiles in neat small stacks on the sloping roof, intending to lay them properly the next day; that evening a sort of hurricane blew up. If you remember how the almost horizontal window of my studio happens to be under the roof of the main building, and you also imagine how those loose stacks of eight tiles each could have slid and smashed my windowpanes to smithereens one by one, then you can understand why I took a sleeping pill that night. However, Providence seems to have wished to protect our family personally, for the next morning nothing had broken and not one of the stacks had even moved. Science (George) explains that this

was not a miracle by any means, but as far as I am concerned, the hand of God can be seen in it. Still, it seems advisable to touch wood, for the storm has just started up again after a few hours' respite, and though the tiles have been put into position, they have not yet been nailed down. Who knows what may happen yet?

'The pressure of my affairs in America is abating. It's just as well; after a while all that hustling for dollars becomes a bit tedious. Meanwhile I have started on a new print; I got the idea for it from one of the learned professors of mathematics with whom I got on so well, as *frère et compagnon*, during my Amsterdam exhibition. The title will probably be *Convex and Concave*, and it is concerned with the widely known phenomenon of spatial suggestion which can be imagined as convex or concave, as desired. In the middle of the picture I draw the shapes in such a way that the observer may just as well see them convex as concave; to the right I force him to see things in a convex way (for example, "cube from the outside"); to the left, he has to view things in a concave way ("cube from the inside").'

Page 77: During the summer of 1950 Escher spent a holiday in Les Eyzies, France, where he did this drawing on 26 July

Opposite page: In 1951 Escher designed a ceiling decoration for the Philips company in Eindhoven, a division of the plane in four colours. This is the preliminary drawing

Preliminary study for the mezzotint
Plane Filling I (cat. no. 373); drawing,
March 1951

Letters to Arthur   1955–1957

The worries of the new house, the hectic life that made it difficult for Escher to concentrate on new prints, the books he read, the people he met and also the observations he constantly made about what was happening in the world of nature around him—all this is reflected in his letters to Arthur.

Baarn, 22 January 1955: 'Strange! These weekly missives are rather a relief for me, in contrast with the many tedious and difficult business letters I have to write these days, to my chagrin.... As I might have known, and wrote to you last week, we have still not moved; but at least the removal firm has been warned, and perhaps we shall manage to make the move next Friday.

'For the past week it has been snowing heavily and until yesterday temperatures were below freezing. Now the thaw has suddenly started and the streets are covered with a dirty sludge of mud and snow. I hope that it will drain away before it starts to freeze again.

'This week I had just managed to work a few days in succession on a new print I have had in my mind for months, when yet another spanner was put in the works. This time it was a sort of commission to do a print of the Liberation, in view of the imminent celebration of its tenth anniversary in May. You can hardly call it a "commission"—*if* I accept it, the only decent thing to do would be to do it free of charge. My main concern is whether it will take up too much time, for I am simply not capable of working quickly. There might be an enormous number printed—the plans have not yet been finalized—with free distribution to schoolchildren, for example; so I must certainly watch my step and not "knock up" a print, just like that. I have a month to think it over, so I can still back out, but I am afraid that I shall have to do it' (cat. no. 400).

Baarn, 12 February 1955: 'As much as possible I have been working hard on the design for my new lithograph. This is tremendously difficult when there are constantly all sorts of interruptions, such as: correspondence in that confounded English to my incomparable mentor Alldredge; worries in connection with the house (the extension of a storage room behind the kitchen has just been completed); fights with Mother about what must be kept and what can be thrown away of all the rubbish from Ekeby; helping a Salvation Army "brother" to load a stack of beds,

broken furniture, radio components, old clothes and suchlike on a huge carrier tricycle that is likely to give way; etc., etc., etc. God, I wish I could learn to draw a bit better! It takes so much effort and perseverance to do it well. Sometimes I am close to delirium with pure nerves. It is really only a question of battling on relentlessly with constant and, if possible, merciless self-criticism. I think that making prints the way I do it is almost only a matter of very much wanting to do it well. For the most part, things like talent are mere poppycock. Any schoolboy with a bit of aptitude might draw better than I; but what is usually lacking is the unwavering desire for expression, obstinacy gnashing its teeth and saying, "Even though I know I cannot do it, I still want to do it"....

'On George's advice I have started to read a book by the famous Nobel Prize winner Faulkner. Fortunately it is a Dutch translation, for—Christ!—that gentleman's English is so damned difficult that I shouldn't understand a word of it. Even the Dutch translation is difficult enough. The fellow writes such impossibly long sentences, with subordinate and parenthetic clauses, preferably with as little punctuation as possible.'

Baarn, 27 February 1955: 'As regards my own individual experience: the strongest emotion and impression I had this week was caused by reading a novel by William Faulkner. George says that this author has also had an effect on you. However, his English is so difficult for my limited command of the language that I regret I have to read his books in translation. Still, a good translation is better than an incomprehensible original. The second book of his I am reading at the moment, in an excellent translation, is *Light in August*. Thanks to the good English lessons you had at secondary school you may well understand the original; if you do not know the book, you must see you get hold of it (I can also try and send it to you). I have not read a modern novel that had such an effect on me for many years, probably not since *The Plague* by Camus. It is partly that the psychological treatment of the murderer, comparable to Dostoevski's Raskolnikov, though completely different, is unusually gripping. For that matter, I find the whole Negro problem in the South of the US extremely interesting, and Faulkner has made it clear and comprehensible for the first time (at least to me). He is one of those rare writers with whom one dare not find fault as a layman and who tower over most of their contemporaries.'

Baarn, 23 April 1955: 'Recently I have been working regularly on a new series of prints; I have just started on the third since March. My *Convex and Concave* lithograph [cat. no. 399], in which I broached the problem of "inversion", is not yet exhibited anywhere, though it obviously amuses my visitors, for I have already sold three. Next Tuesday I have to give a short general talk on my work for Professor Schouten's Rotary Club. He used to be chairman of the international conference of mathematicians and gave me the idea for that topsy-turvy print.'

KNIGHTHOOD

Baarn, 1 May 1955: 'Three days ago the town clerk announced that Alderman Ros was coming to visit me the following morning. In view of the warm weather and my being very busy, I had not dressed up in anything special but was working on a woodcut in my old cord trousers and shirt-sleeves, when Mr Ros came into the studio together with the town clerk. I had absolutely no idea why they had come; I thought they might want to buy one of my prints to adorn a wall in the town hall, or I might be given some commission for the municipality. I put on my old jacket, and after shaking hands, I asked them to take a seat. Mr Ros replied that they would rather remain standing. Then he proceeded to tell me that the Mayor was unfortunately indisposed and that he, Ros, was acting in his stead. I wondered why he had to tell me all this standing up, and again asked them to sit down. Ros refused a second time and said they had to remain standing a little longer. I didn't understand it at all. Possibly he had a boil on his backside? Finally he told me the big news: he was honoured to offer me, in the name of our revered Queen, the Knighthood of the Order of Oranje Nassau. As I watched dumbfounded, he took out a beautiful orange box; out came a silver cross inlaid with enamel. He made some unsuccessful attempts to pin this weighty object onto my chest, but he was too nervous—or the safety pin would not go through the material of my lapels. At any rate your dad is a knight, even if it is not of the garter. Why in the world they should want to "decorate" me is a complete mystery. I can only hope it is not a mistake. That evening my name was in the paper along with thousands of others who received a decoration in honour of the Queen's birthday. In fact my knighthood does not really amount to much. At the same time, [the novelist] Vestdijk received an officer decoration of the same Order; a whole class higher. And Van Beinum, the conductor of the famous Concertgebouw Orchestra, was made a knight of the Nederlandse Leeuw—better still.

'But to get back to the point: did you ever imagine that your dad, who lives so far away from the bustle and intrigue of the world, working on his prints day after day like a hermit, would some day be drawn into this sickening scene of vain officialdom, despite himself? However, there is one thing they will never get me to do and that is to wear a decoration in my buttonhole. When I'm tired, I occasionally travel second class on the train [at that time there was still a third class] and I see one of these important gentlemen wearing his decoration. Their deliberate pose and condescending self-satisfied smiles clearly distinguish them from the sad anonymous crowd with empty buttonholes.

'But what on earth can I do about it? Luckily I can swear by God and all his angels that I never moved a finger to get the decoration or licked the boots of any bigwigs.'

Baarn, 28 May 1955: 'Some events have taken place during the past week which are worth recounting to you.

'First of all, I attended the final lecture of your retiring Uncle Beer, as I wrote last week that I intended to. He gave an interesting summary, to a packed hall, of just about all of his thirty-five years' work, illustrating it with beautiful slides. Then a number of learned gentlemen, including Professor Oort, a famous astronomer, as you know, came forward to praise him and his work in the most cordial fashion. It was all truly friendly, simple and sincere (as far as you can tell from their behaviour).

'During the reception afterwards I met your boss, Mr Krol, who was pleased with the way you seem to enjoy your work. One day he might tell me something about the effect your block-diagram instructions for the personnel in The Hague have had.

'Today Schuyff is sending you a box with the first three gramophone records you wanted. He has done this before for people in Indonesia and knows a thing or two about packaging. They will go on the *Willem Ruys*, which is leaving Rotterdam on 1 June. . . .

'I must again air my enthusiasm for the book *The Sea Around Us*, written by that Carson lady. I told you something about it in my last letter. Every day I read a little, with the annoying result that I become quite sick with longing for a sea trip. She describes this liquid element, surveying all the aspects and problems related to it, in such a fascinating, precise and poetic way that it drives me a bit mad. This is exactly the kind of reading-matter I feel the need for most as I get older: a stimulus for my spatial imagination about mother earth, without too many difficult concepts for laymen, but with a mass of facts that together create an extremely clear picture in the mind. It greatly inspires me to make a new print, which admittedly will have no direct connection with the sea, but in which I shall try for the hundredth time to give rein to my sense of suggesting three-dimensional space.

'What she says about the great plasticity of the earth's crust has given me a vision of a gaseous and/or liquid sphere surrounded by a thin crust of solid material which is still subjected to all sorts of transforming influences. This makes me wonder how thick this crust or skin of solidified matter would be in relation to the diameter of the sphere. Thinner than the thin peel of an orange, but thicker than the skin of a soap bubble? Would you write to tell me how many millimetres thick the solidified crust of the earth would be if the earth were a sphere with a diameter of ten centimetres?

Right: Bond of Union; lithograph,
April 1956 (cat. no. 409)

Below: Depth; wood engraving and
woodcut in three colours, October
1955 (cat. no. 403)

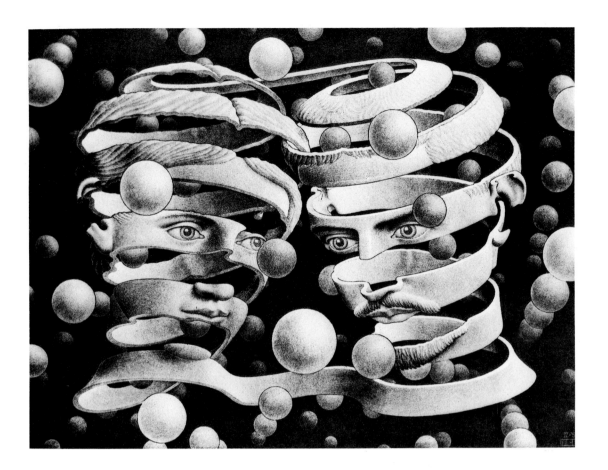

83

'In the chapter I am reading at the moment, she describes the difficulties geologists have in determining the causes that led, for example, to the shrinking of the oceans: apart from the fact that during one of the Ice Ages the polar ice caps took water from the oceans, the eroded material swept down to the sea by the rivers would have filled up the sea bed, were it not that the land had risen and the seabed sunk again because the solid mountain crust became lighter and the sea bed heavier as it filled up. Quite a complicated story!

'All this gives me an almost irresistible urge to go and bob about in one of those liquid pools again, rather than walking on that so-called solid ground all the time. It is such a fantastic feeling to be on a freighter and wake up in your cabin at night, suddenly aware of the contrast with your unmoving bed on land, in which you are accustomed to lie still and horizontal, while at sea your bed constantly rocks around this horizontal.'

Baarn, 5 August 1955: 'I think my last letter dates back more than a month ago. Since then I have been travelling on two freighters for three weeks. I went on the Italian *G. Borsi*, of the Tirrenia company, from Rotterdam direct to Savona. We should have gone into Antwerp but it was closed because of a strike. I came back from Genoa on a Norwegian freighter of ten thousand tons, quite enormous by my standards, and returned to Rotterdam calling at Marseilles, Bilbao and Antwerp, where the strike had ended.

'Both the journey there, Italian style, and the journey back, Norwegian style, were indescribably enjoyable. The contrast between the two trips was very striking and undoubtedly helped to make this—to my taste—an ideal holiday, full of variation and strong impressions.'

Baarn, 18 September 1955: 'Whether it is the influence of your underwater tableaux or a result of my own enthusiasm for the sea and boats, it is a fact that at the moment my work takes me underwater, if only in my mind. I am having fun with a very extensive shoal of fish neatly aligned in "cubic formation", to coin a phrase. Some of them I see in close-up, large and of a bright-red colour. Others I see from a distance, smaller and less brightly coloured. As the distance grows, they become still smaller and hazier, and their red colour gets closer and closer to the bluish-green colour of the water so that finally, in the far distance, they merge completely with the background of water.

'Don't get me wrong: it is all still only in my imagination, like a dream not yet expressed. But this is what it should become. However, it is all so devilishly difficult that often during the last few days I have been close to despair.'

PRINT OF FISH
Baarn, 5 November 1955: 'By Jove, I've really been wanting to sit down quietly at last to write to you. My past few letters have all been so rushed. It is ridiculous, the way we all get excited about

things that are not important. I have seldom felt this so deeply as yesterday afternoon, when I was part of a funeral procession for my very good friend Haasse, who suddenly died of a rupture of the heart muscle. I only met him eighteen months ago and our friendship had grown deeper ever since. Admittedly he was ten years my senior, and superior in wisdom, but I "needed" him all the more for that; he was an answer to my questions and a point of stillness in my immediate neighbourhood. He and his wife formed a double unit, radiating warmth and a love of people. He managed to teach me peace and acceptance in all sorts of preoccupations and uncertainties which often plague me. I miss him terribly.

'And he was barely dead when we were racing at more than sixty miles an hour over the congested main roads of Holland to the place where he was to be cremated, bearing his body with us in a coffin. I had the feeling we were only a hair's breadth from adding a few more dead on this errand of death.

'Now we race on as though Haasse never was. Recently a number of people have died from that small circle for whom I feel affection, and it seems as though life is a school for loneliness. The person who is lucidly aware of the miracles surrounding him, and who has learned to tolerate loneliness, has made a lot of progress on the path to wisdom—or am I wrong?

'Enough of this philosophy. The photographic orders that you asked for in your letter of 20–10 were packaged very cleverly by Jan—the airmail ones, that is—light, solid and shockproof. The rest, including a heavy tin of developing powder, is waiting to be priced by Zandvoort—necessary for the many customs and export papers that have to be filled in. As soon as I know the prices (Z. didn't know them himself), the things will be sent by sea.

'After almost endless problems I finished my new fish print [cat. no. 403]. Although I am by no means satisfied—the simplicity of the "depth" suggestion that I tried to express is one of the most difficult tasks I have ever set myself—I cannot consider it a total failure. The feeling that I did it as best I could is no guarantee of quality, but does give me a sense of peace.

'Next Monday I will send you a copy, let's say as a special birthday present from me; there will be a few other goodies too, by the slow sea route, but a light roll can go by air.

'I am afraid your opinion of the result will not be too high. In case it should be shattering, let me explain the following in extenuation. For the motif I could only use an extremely simplified fish shape, more of a symbol than a real fish, because the thing is repeated about eighty times, each time seen from a slightly different angle. I tried to realize the intended suggestion of depth in all sorts of ways; each way had to be studied as to its woodcutting properties, and had to be possible. At the risk of boring you, let me outline a number of depth-suggestion methods.

'1. Contours. The thickness of the contours decreases as the distance increases.

'2. Network of lines. Each fish is formed in principle from the same number of lines (for example, thirty-two curved lines of shading fill the elliptical body).

'3. Rhythmic positioning of each fish at the intersections of a cubic threefold-rotation-point system. In order to focus extra attention on this system, I emphasized the rotation points in each fish—as a spatial cruciform shape. (At first I made desperate attempts to achieve a less common division of the space, for example the tetra-octahedral possibility as well as others, but these all look too unusual to the untrained observer to evoke any strong suggestion.) In this way you automatically produce attractive series—lots of them—of three or four objects lying diagonally one behind the other; the same foreshortening you can see in the trees of a wood that has been planted in a square, rectangular or other plan.

'4. The colour of the "black" block (it is actually dark brown) is full strength only at the fish in the front; in other words, it is as dark as possible. When pressure is reduced as the distance increases, the colour becomes weaker; the same result is aimed at by increasing the fine shading lines towards the back, by means of engraving rather than printing techniques.

'5. The two colours. Close by, a "warm" colour; far away, a "cold" colour. Thus, as the depth increases, the warm colour decreases and the cold colour increases.

'I could point out other systematicnesses or systematizations, but I think this will do. Can this methodical approach still count as "art"? To answer that you would have to know what art is, and I don't.

'The thin piece of Japanese paper is, of course, meant to be seen against a background of white paper, or it would have absolutely no effect.

'George and Corrie are coming this evening (Saturday) for the weekend again. I have not ventured far enough yet on the path to accepting loneliness, not to look forward to their arrival. They are really excellent fun together.'

All in all, 1955 was a productive year. In his last letter that year to Alldredge, dated 11 December, Escher proudly wrote (in English): 'In the meantime I made two new prints. That means till now five during 1955; more than I did in several years.' In fact there were six, not counting some 'small fry'; he probably did not include a commissioned lithograph (cat. no. 402). Sales continued steadily and interest in his work, especially in scientific circles, kept growing. For example, in the autumn the biochemist Melvin Calvin went to see him. In a letter of 18 October (also written in English), Escher told Alldredge about the visit.

'I wished I had more time to tell you about a very nice visit which payed me a professor Melvin Calvin, bio-chemist of the Radiation Laboratory of the University of California. He worked during some weeks in a room of the dutch Leyden University, where his little daughter of about seven years saw my print *Verbum* [cat. no. 326] hanging on the wall. Her father had not seen anything of it, until his daughter asked him the meaning of that strange drawing, with all these little animals. Then he came near her and saw, that I had been occupied with a similar thought like his own: the creation and more especially his own research about the origin of life and the slow commutation of lifeless in living materials. So he came to Baarn and I was awfully sorry that I could not give him one of the three last copies of *Verbum* I possess. He made me a present of a copy of his recent address to the Amherst College about this very learned and, for a layman, much too difficult subject. I felt touched by the fact that two human beings, living so far away from each other and doing two complete different works in their life, can have a very real contact althesame. And that little girl, who came with her father, looked so strangely intelligent and grave.'

In 1956 Alldredge became involved in Senator Kefauver's election campaign. In a letter to Arthur, Escher told him about it.

Baarn, 12 February 1956: 'I am very pleased with a fat cheque that came from Washington. With this cheque my art dealer paid off everything he owed me at one go, so I can now safely continue to do business with him. The result is not bad at all, selling exactly a hundred and fifty prints since I first established connections in the US. They made me a total of $2,215. There is no doubt that this is entirely thanks to the ever incomparable Alldredge, with whom I still correspond. Sometimes he tells me things about his private life and his work. He earns his living—and a very good one, it would seem—writing speeches which his powerful "boss", Senator Kefauver, has to make more and more frequently now that he is a candidate for the US presidency for the same party as Stevenson— that is, more or less anti-Eisenhower. I doubt whether this Kefauver has much of a chance, but Alldredge wrote to me: "If 'we' succeed, your prints will be hanging in the White House." Alldredge and I also write about all sorts of trivialities. The other day, for instance, he wrote that during the extremely cold weather at the moment, he is feeding the birds in his garden about ten pounds of seed a week. I replied to him yesterday with a long letter about the severe frost we are having here, too—severe by our standards. A few days ago the temperature dropped to nineteen degrees centigrade below zero, and it is still freezing, though fortunately not quite as much (up to about ten degrees). I also feed the birds every day and have identified up to twelve different species (using my bird book). Thanks to my excellent dictionary, I was able to translate all the names into English and tell A. which they were. I am interested to hear from him whether they have exactly the same birds in America. It is very strange to see the thrushes doing their first mating dances out there in the snow, at minus ten degrees. They don't seem to take any notice of the thermometer and just look at the calendar to see whether it is the right time or not.'

The letters to Arthur continued to be frequent and regular.

Baarn, 25 March 1956: 'There is nothing special to say about life here. It goes on—for me at least—with hard work on prints, and I really do not know why I get so involved. At the moment, for example, I am working on another new project which I started about ten days ago. At times, when I feel very enthusiastic, it seems as though no one in the world has ever made anything so beautiful and important. Shortly afterwards—a matter of hours—it suddenly looks useless and I am overcome by the utter pointlessness of all that pitiable fiddling. But having taken it on, I continue the next day as though my very life depended on it. I can even get truly terrified by the possibility of dying before this latest, so-called masterpiece is finished. I do notice every year that about this time I feel tired and I madly start longing for the holidays. I see myself on the boat which I will take in Venice in July and which will take me back to Rotterdam in thirty-five days, via Sicily, London and Hamburg. We shall be in London for seven to nine days; just long enough to have a good look at that place, where I have never been before.'

TOIL
Baarn, 26 May 1956: 'Your last epistle, of 2 May, still requires an answer, all the more because of your philosophical tirade, which needs some discussion.

'The map of Billiton that you sent us some time ago clearly shows where the new drilling area of the T. Brang lies. However, I also noticed that the coast there is marshy; as long as you don't get malaria, it's all right. I can imagine that building a road with bulldozers and a dragline must be an interesting job.

'I can also understand your surprise at the fact that people are after that relatively small amount of tin with a passion and intensity worthy of a better cause. But is it not the same for any work done on earth? Is dredging for tin any crazier than the dealings of a ragman, or making prints like I do? It is all the same in the end; either it is all equally pointless or it is all equally important.

'In any case, it is necessary, not because the world would come to an end if we did *not* do it, but because "toil" happens to be a condition for contentment for present-day Western man; even people in the East are beginning to toil bravely along with us, because they have noticed that, in the end, lazing about leads to unhappiness. I believe that the most important difference between man and other living creatures lies not so much in having or not having a "soul" or a "spirit", but in the astonishing fact that man must "work" as a condition of existence, while a bird does not need to.

'I do not agree with you that you cannot eat the tin which, with so much effort, you have dredged from the ground. Isn't that tin your daily bread and butter, so to speak?

'This it not to say that it would not be nice suddenly to become

aware, from time to time, how mysterious life is. In this way you differ from the majority of your fellow-tin-seekers, who do not even begin to know what a mystery or a miracle is, wherever they are. Now and then I, too, find myself marvelling at something, and the state of clarity in which I seem to be then makes me very happy.

'I think that's enough of these deep thoughts, so I will continue with news of home.

'As for me personally, by far the most important news is that Paul Keller from Münsingen [the husband of one of Jetta's cousins, a good friend of Escher's, with whom he had kept in contact over the years] told me about his ambition to make a sea voyage during his holidays. So we are probably going to Venice together and from there by freighter back to Rotterdam, via Sicily, London and Hamburg. I think I would have difficulty finding a more suitable travelling companion. The only problem is that these freighters never leave on time. The one I had hoped to take in V. at the beginning of July has been delayed for two weeks already now, so that we could take it only at the end of July. Now I am trying to get on the previous sailing, a month earlier, but it may already be booked up. All this has led to endless letters between Baarn, Bern, Rotterdam and Naples, but I do not give up and am still hoping that we shall both end up in deckchairs, getting brown in the Mediterranean sun. He (Paul) and I desperately need to be lazy for a while; after this rotten winter I am suffering from rheumatism, which I want to sweat out, and P. is overworked.

'The odd print I told you about last time is finished, though not yet printed [cat. no. 410]. I don't think I have ever done anything as peculiar in my life. Among other things, it shows a young man looking with interest at a print on the wall of an exhibition that features himself. How can this be? Perhaps I am not far removed from Einstein's curved universe.'

BROTHER ERICH
The sea voyage finally took place from the end of July to the end of August. Just before this Escher visited Ghent, where there was an exhibition of his prints. At the end of August he came into contact with Bruno Ernst, at that time still known as 'Brother Erich', who had been fascinated by Escher's prints for some time and wanted to write about them. This, too, was reported to Arthur.

Baarn, 21 October 1956: 'This time I should like to tell you something about a "Brother" I have met. This Brother, Erich—I only know his Christian name—is a teacher of mathematics at a school.... A remarkable person, who wrote to me out of the blue that my prints fascinated him (and the boys he taught) and that he longed to come and visit me in Baarn. He has now done so. He was much interested in my jokes on perspective, and especially in my "inversion" print *Convex and Concave* (I think I sent you a copy), as well as in my regular divisions of the plane.

'Having seen the *Convex and Concave* print, he demonstrated a method to me of easily "inverting" all sorts of objects and landscapes that meet the eye. It is so completely astonishing that I should like to explain how you do it. You need two good right-angled prisms. You can get them by dismantling an old pair of binoculars. If there is anyone in Billiton who has an old pair he doesn't use any more, you must make sure you get hold of them. I enclose a sketch to show how to hold the prisms to your eyes. Up to now I have borrowed Brother Erich's pair of prisms but I am determined to find my own pair on some flea market, because it would be well worth having some, and if possible mount them in some home-made holder so that they become a two-eyed viewer.

'As you will see from my drawing, everything viewed through them is reversed and appears in mirror image. This in itself is extremely curious—when you look at your own feet, for example. If you step forward with your right foot, you see your left foot move, etc. But this is by no means all. Not only does "left" become "right", but "up" becomes "down", the ceiling becomes the floor. To achieve this, circumstances must be favourable and you must be prepared to practise and look with an open mind. In the woods of Baarn I saw a particularly suitable object a few days ago: a pond covered with dry leaves. When I looked through the prisms, it promptly turned upside-down and gave me quite a fright.

'However, the most interesting thing about all this, what it is really all about, is the "reversal" of stereoscopic reality. More or less the same thing (or perhaps exactly the same thing) happens when you make one image seen with both eyes out of two stereoscopic photographs in reverse, that is, with the left one on the right and the right one on the left. I remember playing this trick when you showed us the geological stereoscopic photographs

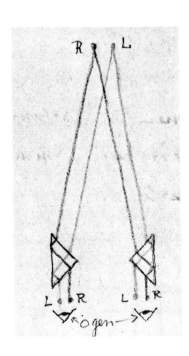

The sketch from Escher's letter, which illustrates the principle of the 'inverted prisms'

of the Swiss mountains; the valleys became "high", swelled out, and the mountains seemed to have depth, like valleys.

'Well now, if you look through Brother Erich's prisms, especially at a web of criss-crossing leafy branches of a number of trees, both near and far away, so that you are seeing countless different distances all at the same time, preferably with different colours—the autumn, as it is now, is very good with red oaks, yellowing trees and misty views—you will be quite dumbfounded and incredulous about what you see. Things that are in reality farthest away seem very close (little pieces of sky shining through the trees become glittering "stars", individual points in space, in front of and nearer than the leaves; I could get quite lyrical) and the thick, leafy branch of a tree nearby is transformed into a deep hole far, far away on the horizon. There is no end to the funny and impressive impossibilities that a patient observer can create for himself in this way.'

Baarn, 18 November 1956: 'Two weeks ago I wrote to you at a time when I was greatly affected by the tensions of the international situation [because of the Russian invasion of Hungary]. Fortunately this has abated a little—not so much "the" situation as "my" situation. I don't know whether the danger of a third world war has diminished since then, but no one can remain permanently conscious of the "state of the nations" (as a learned professor calls his weekly radio broadcast on international affairs). It is not so much cowardice as necessity to engage in ostrich politics, if one doesn't want to die a premature death of fear and helplessness....

'Mother and I have just taken a long walk through the woods, since it has been a sunny and almost windless autumn day. We also sat for a quarter of an hour on two rotten tree-stumps, as the late autumn sun was at its height, still giving out a fair bit of warmth, although I shouldn't think the angle it made with the horizon was much more than twenty degrees. I thought of you with your equatorial sun that rises virtually to the zenith. I should like to see that one day. Although it was lovely in that clearing in the woods, I was tormented by an almost unbearable longing (*par moyen de dire*) for the island of Lipari, which again and again appears in my mind's eye as I saw it this summer. If there is any chance of it, I shall go back there next year, this time to stay a few weeks and to visit Vulcano, which you can reach quickly by boat from Lipari....

'I finished the vignette above [cat. no. 414] a few days ago. It is intended to be a decoration for the invitation card to my next "important" exhibition, together with three fellow-artists, in the Stedelijk Museum in Amsterdam, next February.'

ROOSEVELT
Towards the end of 1956 Escher started working on a private-press edition of a book on his regular divisions of the plane, which would finally be published at the beginning of 1958 by the De

Roos Foundation (see pages 155ff). He had to do six new woodcuts for this and write the text himself. It would take him a great deal of time in 1957.

In America the Kefauver campaign was not successful. Alldredge was kept very busy but he still remained in touch with Escher. By way of a New Year's greeting, he sent a poem he had written himself, as he had done in previous years. Since the Whyte Gallery in Washington, D.C., had passed into other hands and the print gallery was closed, Alldredge temporarily took Escher's prints into his own safekeeping while he looked for a new gallery.

At the end of January 1957 Escher received a letter from Cornelius Van S. Roosevelt, who was to become one of his most important collectors. Roosevelt had come across Escher's work in the *Time* magazine article and the first exhibition at the Whyte Gallery. He had bought prints at that time but wished to enlarge his collection. Escher referred him to Alldredge. In a letter dated 11 February 1957 Alldredge wrote that Roosevelt had visited him and had bought five prints. He also gave some information about him: 'He is a grandson of President Theodore Roosevelt and a nephew of Mrs Nicholas Longworth, a very famous lady here, who owns several of your prints and, I think, brought your work to his attention. He is a pleasant, unassuming person.'

A week later Alldredge wrote that he had found a new gallery: the Sidney Mickelson Gallery in Washington, D.C. He recommended this as being a reputable firm; Escher was pleased when shortly afterwards the gallery was also warmly recommended by Roosevelt, and gladly agreed.

In 1957 Escher continued to correspond with Arthur, though rather less regularly.

Baarn, 24 February 1957: 'George and Corrie are moving fast towards marriage: the wedding is on 9 March.... They are very pleased with the large room in Delft where they will live for a while until G. finishes his studies.

'This afternoon—today is Sunday—I must go to my exhibition in Amsterdam for the last time; we'll close the show tomorrow. I have sold fairly well—thirty-seven pieces up to now. I am glad it is over, because I am getting sick of all the travelling there and back, the letters that have to be written and the prints to be sent, no matter how nice it is to realize I haven't been making prints for nothing. Again I had a most pleasurable contact with some very learned mathematicians, who did their best to explain to me that the print *Print Gallery* has to do with a "Riemann's surface". Despite their lectures, my understanding of it is very incomplete.

'Now that all the fuss about the exhibition is over, I must continue working at full speed on the woodcut illustrations and text for a booklet on the regular division of the plane.'

NATURE UNTAMED

Baarn, 7 April 1957: 'For the past few days, now that the birds are becoming active and singing at the tops of their voices, I have been regularly visited by a beautiful woodpecker that comes—just like the blue tits—to peck at the string of peanuts I hung up in front of my studio window. He is very timid and flies off if I make the slightest movement, but I have been able to observe him very closely a number of times by sitting quite still. He hangs upside down on the string, leaning with his tail, which is at about ninety degrees to his body, against the other peanuts and pecks like a madman, making a hole in the shell between his feet in no time at all. All the while his bright-red rump sticks straight up. What miracles are happening in the world!

'I saw another miracle recently at the "Blauwe Koepeltje"—you know, the open stretch of lawn between the clumps of ornamental trees on the Buitenzorg estate. For the first time in years I saw two deer grazing, at about seven o'clock in the evening. One was quite close, only about thirty feet away. Its snow-white scut was towards me and the wind was in my direction. I must have stood there, absolutely still, watching it for about a minute. Then it obviously noticed me somehow: it turned round, looked me "straight in the eye" for a moment and disappeared like lightning, with great leaps. Its mate, which was grazing a little farther away, followed this example immediately, and seconds later they had both disappeared into the trees and the undergrowth. Thus the Seasnake, who told you about the deer there, was proved to be right in the end. This "untamed nature" in the shape of woodpeckers and deer, in the middle of—or, at least, very close to—that infernal motorway from Amsterdam to Amersfoort where an endless line of those stupid cars chase each other all day long, is extremely valuable to me. It is the presence of these creatures of nature that allows me to accept, if not to understand, the crazy rushing and dashing about in our overpopulated country, patiently and without choking with rage.'

Baarn, 22 April 1957: 'We celebrated Easter here with George, Corrie and Jan.... Tomorrow the party is over and we all resume our daily work. Mine consists of putting the finishing touches to the illustrations for my booklet on the regular division of the plane. I am working on the last woodcut at the moment; then I shall have to review the whole text once more. On 8 May I am going to Groningen, where there is to be an extensive exhibition of my work in the institute of a professor of art history at the university....

'If you should ever become interested in Leonardo da Vinci, whom I find increasingly fascinating, I can recommend all sorts of good books about him. On the sea trip I made last year I met an Italian lady who teaches her own language in Milan. I asked her to find out for me what are the latest and best biographies of Leonardo and editions of his own writings. She in her turn made inquiries at the Leonardo Library in Milan, and finally a most friendly professor wrote me a long letter with a good bibliography. The first book I ordered from this list was a biography by the

French writer Marcel Brion, which I am now reading with much pleasure. I have also ordered Leonardo's complete writings in Italian. What he has to say himself is always the most interesting.

'When you read his short notes, it's just as though he is sitting next to you and you can hear him speaking like a lonely, wise and melancholy great man from fifteenth-century Italy: *"La luna densa e grave, come sta, la luna?"* This is an example of one of those partly melancholy and partly ironic questions which he just jotted down in his notebook and which have a great effect on me, because I seem to recognize—rightly, perhaps, or wrongly—the same silent wondering as my own when I look at the moon. *Densa* is possibly best translated as "compact", and *grave* is "heavy" rather than "serious".'

Baarn, 6 May 1957: 'I am constantly sweating over the text for the booklet on the regular division of the plane. The six woodcuts for it are now finished and the text that has been written already has to be completely rewritten, for a second reading reveals that it is not right at all. Writing is a difficult business for a "visualizer", but it gives me a lot of pleasure.'

Baarn, 6 October 1957: 'I last wrote to you two months ago. In the meantime I travelled for six and a half weeks on the Mediterranean Sea, and I have now been back home for two weeks. . . .

'I have made a voyage on a freighter for the last four years in a row and am definitely becoming addicted to it. I tell all sorts of people about it, but only a seasoned freighter passenger could possibly understand what I am talking about. You never—or very rarely—meet any of them on land.

'Will you come with me next year on a freighter to Mount Athos? We sailed close by it for a few hours and saw the medieval monasteries hanging on the cliffs like eyries. The mountain rises up from the sea a sheer cone, almost seven thousand feet high; you would be able to get up to enough mountaineering tricks while I drew the monasteries.'

Baarn, 2 November 1957: 'The Utrecht town council has invited me to design a mural for the hall of the cemetery. I made a drawing with a scale of 1:20 and it seems that the committee which is supposed to be judging the thing has agreed to it. So, although the matter could still misfire as the commission is not yet official, I am hopeful about it. It will be fun to climb up on a scaffolding once myself, daubing a surface of about twelve by twelve feet for a whole month. I designed a division of the plane consisting solely of fish that "move" in black spirals towards the centre (symbolizing death or dying), while a series of white fish "move" outwards from the same centre (life, birth). The attractive, and at the same time difficult, thing is the diminution of the fish figures into infinity. The outer fish will be about five feet long and I want to try and reduce their size consistently until they are mere specks of about half an inch in length.

'While I am waiting to start this job, I am working on a double spiral in woodcut, in three colours [cat. no. 423], along the same line of thought as that of the mural; I am using a new printing technique based on a very amusing twofold-rotation-point system. It is difficult to explain in words, but what it amounts to is that from each of the blocks (probably three) that I have to cut, I make only half of the surface that they have to fill together; the other half is produced by repeating the blocks after they have been turned a hundred and eighty degrees. I doubt whether "the public" will ever understand, let alone appreciate, what fascinating mental gymnastics are required to compose this sort of print.'

WINGED CREATURES

Baarn, 22 November 1957: 'As I sit here typing, I am constantly distracted from my work by what is going on in front of my large studio window. The other day I put out a horizontal wire with all kinds of titbits for the birds, as I do every year at the beginning of winter—a string of peanuts, two balls of fat and some bacon rind from the butcher. Then there is bird seed and peanuts in a dish. This time the small winged creatures seem particularly keen on it. A few days before I arranged this meal, I had the feeling that the tits in particular were looking at me through the window chirping, "How about it then?" Now they have attacked it greedily; really it's only gourmandizing on their part, since it's not freezing yet and they should easily be able to find food in the wild. However, it is fascinating to see how the tits (so far only three species: coal tits, blue tits and great tits, but when it gets colder, also the crested and long-tailed tits) have to learn every year anew how to peck open the peanut shells and take out the nuts, while hanging upside-down on the string. First they keep trying to perch on the string as though it were a twig. Because they lose their balance in this way, they constantly flap their wings. And apparently they are unable to do two things at once, unlike humming-birds, for example. While flapping their wings, they cannot peck, and while pecking, they cannot flap their wings. As a result they dangle upside-down with their claws holding onto the string as soon as they start pecking, and then they realize it is quite possible to eat upside-down. At the moment, it is like a circus: the string, bacon rind and ball of fat are all occupied by tits. There is a nuthatch on the second ball of fat, a beautiful bird with a yellowish orange front and a blue back, a very short tail and a long woodpecker beak. The line of its beak seems to run on either side of its head with a black stripe, a sort of narrow horizontal band around its head with eyes in it somewhere. This gives it a rather wild, robber-like appearance, and it also seems to have a pirate character: all the tits are afraid of it; it won't allow any other birds to eat near it. In addition, it is messy and rash: it pecks so aggressively and impatiently that pieces of food fly in every direction, to the delight of the blackbirds and finches on the ground below, who are too lazy or too clumsy to do any circus tricks. Now and again the whole lot suddenly fly up with loud cries of alarm when a jay comes near, for these are bloodthirsty bandits. I hope to be visited soon by a woodpecker—another skilled acrobat who can hang upside-down from the string of peanuts, heavy-weight though it is, so that its bright-red rump lights up beautifully. It pecks at a tremendous rate and empties a triple peanut shell in a flash. Luckily the starlings do not come so early in the winter. Once a flock of these blue-black street-urchins has noticed the feed tray, they all sit down on it together and the tray is empty within seconds. They push and shove each other in one big, black mass, screeching loudly.

'There is a great deal of rivalry among all these birds. As far as I have been able to ascertain, only between parents and offspring or between mates is there any question of what human beings call "courtesy", "sacrifice" or "good manners". Apart from these, they begrudge each other literally everything. Of all the birds I watch, the robin is the most defenceless; it does not dare stand up to even the blue tits, and they are much smaller. But among the robins themselves there is again a great deal of merciless rivalry.

'How I go on! I must stop now.'

Baarn, 7 December 1957: 'We are all very well. George telephoned today to tell us that he passed his final examination, which he took this morning. He has also had the last teaching session for his engineering degree with the professor under whom he is studying. Quite probably he will be completely finished in June. It seems possible that you will be here then, so perhaps you can leave for Canada together!

'Today I received the official commission from the Utrecht town council for the mural I wrote about in my last letters.'

Escher did not hear from Alldredge for a long time, but at the end of the year he received another poem. The sales of his prints by the Mickelson Gallery were continuing steadily.

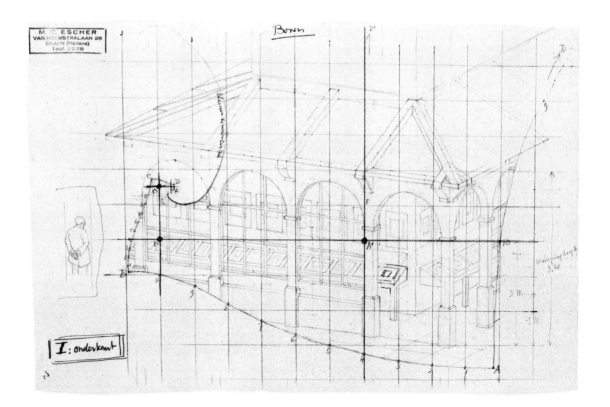

Preliminary study for the lithograph *Print Gallery* (cat. no. 410); drawing, 1956

Crystallographers' Recognition   1958–1960

The correspondence continued between Escher and his son Arthur in Indonesia.

Baarn, 5 January 1958: 'The day after tomorrow I shall finally start daubing the wall of the cemetery hall in Utrecht. In the meantime I have been making various unsuccessful attempts to concentrate on a new print; when that didn't work, I switched to carving a sphere of beechwood, something I used to do occasionally during the war, though I have not done it since. My new work is based on the primitive form of five intersecting tetrahedrons, and the final result is a solid full of deep angles, the surface of which is determined by twelve flower-heads with five petals each. It is a really old-fashioned cabinet-maker's pastime, pure craft work.'

Baarn, 17 March 1958: 'Hooray! I've just received your letter of 10 March, in which you say you are arriving on 1 April.... It's a strange thought that this is most probably the last letter from here to Indonesia. Writing to you like this every fortnight for almost four years has become so much part of me that it will be strange when it is no longer necessary.'

When in October George left for Canada with Corrie to start a new life there, after qualifying as an aeronautical engineer, the regular correspondence started up again. First Escher went on a trip with Jetta, George and Corrie. They sailed from Antwerp on 6 September, arriving in Genoa on the 16th. They travelled around Italy for a time and flew back to Holland from Milan on 24 September.

As soon as George and Corrie had left, Escher started corresponding with them; he continued to do so until his death.

Baarn, 25 October 1958: 'Well, we know quite a bit by now about your journey and your first impressions of Canada. We were fascinated by everything and can imagine quite well what it must be like for you. It doesn't surprise me at all that it hasn't been easy to find work straight away. It would have been a miracle if you had found a job immediately....

'Arthur's prospects of joining the New Guinea Star Mountains expedition, which is leaving in about April 1959, seem to be increasing again....

'Since you left I have been constantly struggling with my sphere-spirals woodcut [cat. no. 428]. After the first proof my high expectations were, as always, greatly disappointed. I am now struggling on—with some feeling of despair—so that I at least achieve a passable result.'

THE COXETER SYSTEM
Baarn, 9 November 1958: 'I've barely finished my sphere spirals (a coloured woodcut) before I'm engrossed again in the study of an illustration which I came across in a publication of the Canadian professor H. S. M. Coxeter, of Ottawa (whom I met in Amsterdam some time ago), *A Symposium on Symmetry*. I am trying to glean from it a method for reducing a plane-filling motif which goes from the centre of a circle out to the edge, where the motifs will be infinitely close together. His hocus-pocus text is no use to me at all, but the picture can probably help me to produce a division of the plane which promises to become an entirely new variation of my series of divisions of the plane. A circular regular division of the plane, logically bordered on all sides by the infinitesimal, is something truly beautiful, almost as beautiful as the regular division of the surface of a sphere. At the same time I get the feeling that I am moving farther and farther away from work that would be a "success" with the "public", but what can I do when this sort of problem fascinates me so much that I cannot leave it alone?'

Baarn, 7 December 1958: 'How wonderful that you've finally succeeded in finding a good job which you enjoy!

'Just a few more words about Marco Polo. During one of my long and boring printing sessions, when I listen to anything on the radio, I heard an enthusiastic review of that book, a new and complete translation which appeared recently. I was so impressed that when Arthur happened to go to The Hague on business, I went up with him in the car, and after looking for a long time in several bookshops, I finally located a copy. I bought it for myself, but gave it to Arthur not an hour later, as he seemed to be interested in it, also from a geological point of view. So I ordered two more copies, one for you and one for myself. Up to now only one has arrived, so I'll have to curb my impatience to read it just a little longer....

'I've forgotten whether I told you anything in my last letter about the nice commission I received to design three regular divisions of the plane for the cylindrical pillars of a new girls' school in The Hague. De Porceleyne Fles in Delft say they can make curved tiles so that six will surround a pillar. Using one type of square tile I succeeded in demonstrating not only three different designs, but also the three systems of dividing the plane—rotation, sliding and glide reflection. . . .

'My woodcut inspired by the Coxeter system is finished [cat. no. 429], and I consider it to be the finest of the "reductions" I have made. The circular limitation of infinitely small motifs, surrounding the whole thing logically and inevitably, is something I cannot take my eyes off. It approaches absolute beauty and purity. I'm curious about Mr. "Cokes-eater's" opinion; I have sent him a print. Wouldn't he be a nice fellow for you to visit? He's a professor at the University of Toronto—perhaps a little bit out of your way.

'Then a printer-publisher from Zwolle has suddenly appeared out of thin air with a proposal to publish an exceptionally finely printed book with beautiful reproductions of my prints, thirty or forty in all (we haven't yet agreed on that). Without definitely committing myself, I agreed in principle, chiefly because these Erven J. J. Tijl have modern offset presses on which they can make perfect reproductions. . . .

'The other day I gave a lecture to a Rotary Club in Hilversum (what a childish fuss with all those little flags and those jovial "friends" being ever so important). The audience included three medics who had made their diagnosis of my "case" by the end of the lecture—obsessional neurosis. I suggested to my publisher that he use this as a title, but he said no. Nor does he want to use "Playful Imaginings", which I like very much. He proposed "Playing with Reality", but that I don't want.'

Baarn, 18 January 1959: 'Arthur recently attended a meeting of all the scientific members of the Star Mountains expedition, which he has now joined officially. He is leaving in mid-March and his luggage goes by sea tomorrow. . . .

'To my surprise, the tiles business for the girls' school in The Hague is also coming along. De Porceleyne Fles fired some tiles as a test and they were wonderful; they pretend to be very enthusiastic but, miser that I am, I must take care they do not steal my plane-filling motifs, and I am no good at all at these things.'

Baarn, 1 February 1959: 'We enjoyed—and I am still enjoying— your series of stereoscopic pictures tremendously! . . . The most spectacular one in this group is the rapids with George in the foreground. I could go on about a picture like this for pages: the low sun touching the flat, wet stone where G. is sitting with a typical snapshot face, but so alive as though the observer were present at the moment the photograph was taken. In fact this is what always strikes me in pictures with a sense of space: the intensity of the observer's involvement. . . .

'When I had delivered the stone [of the lithograph *Flatworms*; cat. no. 431] to Andréa, I returned to printing old prints; these, of course, include both *D. and N.* and *A. and W.* As long as the radio is blaring away, rubbing those spoons periodically is not so bad after all, provided that it doesn't take longer than a week. Mickelson sent me a pleasant check (cheque) for almost $500 for works sold in the past five months. Not bad.'

Baarn, 15 February 1959: 'Yesterday was a long and satisfactory day. In the morning I went to a meeting with my fellow graphic artists in Amsterdam. At three o'clock in the afternoon, the exhibition of the Four Graphic Artists opened in the Boymans Museum in Rotterdam. There were about a hundred and fifty people present, including Beer and Emmy. I was happy to see them, the only members of my family who were there. The whole thing was a great success, although it always leaves me with a hangover. Mr Ebbinge Wubben [the director of the museum] put us on a pedestal as usual and left no stone unturned to ensure our success, notably by means of a splendid catalogue with four reproductions of each of the artists' work. He opened the show himself very elegantly, with a speech in the lecture hal. . . .

'I went to some trouble to explain the disc-shaped print *Smaller and Smaller [Circle Limit I]* to a number of visitors, but it's becoming increasingly clear that on the whole people are not sensitive to the beauty of this infinite world-in-an-enclosed-plane. Most people simply do not understand what it is all about. This is particularly sad as I am working on another print, which should greatly surpass the first. I enclose a cutting from the catalogue. As a first try, I'm certainly not dissatisfied with it, though I now realize that it could be much more fascinating. As you can see, the thing is entirely based on a web of lines which are straight when they run through the centre, and for the rest are all circles whose centres lie outside the disc but increasingly close to the edge, as the circles become smaller. All these circles intersect at angles of either ninety or sixty degrees. In other words: two- and threefold rotation points alternate. Coxeter's letters show that an infinite number of other systems is possible and that, instead of the values two and three, an infinite number of higher values can be used as a basis. He encloses an example of using the values three and seven, of all things! However, this odd seven is no use to me at all; I long for two and four (or four and eight), because I can use these to fill a plane in such a way that all the animal figures whose body axes lie in the same circle also have the same "colour", whereas in the other example, two white ones and two black ones constantly alternate. My great enthusiasm for this sort of picture and my tenacity in pursuing the study will perhaps lead to a satisfactory solution in the end. Although Coxeter could probably help me by saying just one word, I prefer to find it myself for the time being, also because I'm so often at cross-purposes with those theoretical mathematicians, on a variety of points. In addition, it seems to be very difficult for Coxeter to write intelligibly to a layman. Finally, no matter how difficult it is, I feel all the more satisfaction from solving a problem like this in my own bumbling fashion. But the sad and frustrating fact remains that these days I'm starting to speak a language which is understood by very few people. It makes me feel increasingly lonely. After all, I no longer belong anywhere. The mathematicians may be friendly and interested and give me a fatherly pat on the back, but in the end I am only a bungler to them. "Artistic" people mainly become irritated. Yet I might have got hold of the right end of the stick if I get more pleasure from my own prints than from the most beautiful camera in the world, with a lens of one point whatever.

'Yesterday ended with the annual dinner at the Kists' in Amsterdam. It was his sixtieth birthday and therefore extra solemn, but good fun, at it always is. But even he and his family, however full of goodwill, are disinclined to follow me on my lofty circular tours. By way of a speech at dinner I told them Van der Neut's story about the lion who was also so scared of giving a speech. Luckily they enjoyed that.

'Finally, the weather. Today, for the first time in a fortnight it has really thawed, with a westerly wind. The things that have been happening here! Since my last letter, continuous mist and hoar-frost on the trees, such as I've never seen before. A ridiculous topsy-turvy world—not only was everything like a negative film, but because of the ice crystals constantly growing and then breaking off, it snowed only *under* the trees. Where could you find shelter? In the open air!'

Baarn, 28 February 1959: 'I worry dreadfully (sometimes) what Mother and I are going to do this summer. I see hardly any chance of escaping onto a ship on the Mediterranean, no matter how much I long to do so. As usual, and in your absence, God will have to provide a solution. We will go to Canada together sometime, but certainly not yet this year!

'I've absolutely no reason to moan about the "success" of my work, nor about the lack of new ideas, for there are plenty of them. And yet I'm plagued from time to time by an immense feeling of inferiority, a desperate sense of general failure; where do these crazy feelings come from? Meanwhile, on the last day of February, the blackbird is trying out last year's tune again.

'I've now started on a woodcut, another round one, with a circular limit using a system I developed myself, which will have an infinite number of crosses in black, red and white [cat. no. 432]. The Pope will have to buy it from me, for a lot of money. The symbolism is so exaggerated that no one would imagine that I cannot believe in crosses. Amen. If only I could believe in them— that would be something to hold on to.'

Baarn, 19 April 1959: 'I have not been allowed to wear my dear old filthy velvet trousers for over a week now, not because they had to be washed, but because I had to keep visiting, more or less in full regalia, my colleague Hans van Dokkum, who has been seriously ill (varicose-vein operation, four hours on one leg and two more hours on the other; then, having apparently made an over-rapid recovery, embolism and pneumonia so serious that everyone thought he would die; now, back home from hospital again recovering frighteningly quickly, limping around the room); I also went to bury my colleague Alfred Löb, in The Hague, and gave the funeral oration because both chairman and secretary were unable to go; gave a lecture on the regular division of the plane in Utrecht for the annual luncheon of members of the De Roos Foundation, which publishes my book; visited the Katjes in Overveen with Mother, and went to see George and Milie in Bentveld and, it seems, a hundred other things that kept me from my work. . . . So it goes on. Making plans with Paul Keller to sail to Venice from Rotterdam in June, together with a doctor-friend of his from Berne. . . .

'Paul Keller has just recovered from an illness and is longing for the sea in about the same way I long for it. Damn it all, it's the only way of "finding yourself" that's left to us. Isn't that a sad state of affairs?'

Baarn, 12 May 1959: 'Although almost dazed with writing and typing my book day in, day out, in one go (apart from sleeping at night), I realized that I had not written you a single letter since 19 April, and that won't do. I also feel a sense of peace now that I have succeeded today in finishing the short captions for the forty prints to be reproduced. Perhaps this means that the worst of it is over, because you wouldn't believe how much I've been fiddling about, constantly trying to improve those captions! Here and there I think I have written some really good concise descriptions. I regret not being younger, for then it would have been a still more useful exercise, in view of the use I might have made of this skill later (if it is a skill) to express myself succinctly. As I do this work, even though it is fairly enjoyable, I have the sad feeling that I am getting old, for who but an old man would fill his time ruminating about and chewing over things that he made years and years before? It's not a creative pastime, but really digging up forgotten relics. Now I've only an introduction left to write.'

Baarn, 24 May 1959: 'Ha! my writing is over and done with. It's a load off my mind. Now I've just got to put on a bit of a spurt on two urgent commissions (little ones) and, after the holidays, do some serious thinking about a decoration (with motifs for a regular division of the plane, of course) for an outside wall of a new school in The Hague. Before I go on holiday, the matter of the three pillars that have to be decorated with tiles for another school in The Hague has suddenly to be completed in a great hurry, but that isn't giving me too much of a headache. It's extraordinary what you can do with just a single square tile. The "Fles" in Delft is quite amazed. A group exhibition in Amsterdam opening shortly, a private one in Hengelo on 5 June—it's enough to drive me mad.'

Baarn, 21 June 1959: 'Our beautiful house of cards (it was a precarious business from the start) has completely collapsed. Paul naturally had to cancel the trip because of his legal work; Eddy and Irma are coming to Brussels at the end of July, so they can't wait indefinitely for Mother. G. and M. also have other plans.

'So I uttered the medieval saying, "It is God's will". What is God's will? Obviously that Mother and I make the trip together. I wrote to Eddy, went to talk things over in Bentveld, cancelled Mother's K L M ticket and had Paul's boat ticket put in Mother's name. Now we shall have to wait patiently until these sailors stop their strike. As soon as one of the two possible boats sails into Rotterdam or Antwerp, Mother and I will embark and sail to Venice, as planned before. . . . As you have gathered by now, Mother is seldom or ever enthusiastic about anything (except possibly about a little Canadian in the making). She doesn't seem particularly keen on this plan either, but she prefers the idea of sailing over the sea with me to strolling on the boulevard in Menton with Eddy and Irma. . . .

'As far as my work is concerned, and to answer your questions about new prints—for over a month, perhaps even two months (I cannot think properly, because I've brought my typewriter out on the terrace and I'm sitting almost naked to make the most of the sun, which is shining on my back, but not making my thoughts any clearer), I haven't had time for "free work".'

Baarn, 5 July 1959: 'The Erven Tijl book looks promising; I took a whole load of prints over for them to reproduce; they want to publish it by October at the latest. . . . I had a nice visit from a professor from Baltimore and his wife, both ardent crystallographers, who insist I give a speech on my R D in London next summer at an international gathering of crystal-gazers (or sym- and antisymmetrists. Antisymmetry involves using contrasting shades in a design of repeated motifs in space or on a plane. Russian scientists have been interested in this recently, and I myself have not been able to do without it since I started on the regular division of the plane, thirty years ago). When I told them my usual story about not knowing anything about mathematics, they answered: "You obviously know more about it than any of us." Just imagine! Who knows, perhaps something will really come of it, if we aren't in Canada at that time. I had noticed some time ago that old-fashioned crystallographers were quite perplexed by my contrasting shades: old Terpstra, for example, thinks you shouldn't talk in terms of "glide reflection" if the colour changes. And now the Russians say I'm right. As a complete layman in science, I've obviously never been troubled by over-rigid ideas, but I can easily imagine that those old scientific gentlemen find it difficult to let go of colourlessness (contours).'

Baarn, 22 August 1959: 'Now for our four weeks on the Mediterranean Sea and in the Italian ports. The most important thing, closest to everyone's heart, is the question, how did Father and Mother manage to get on? Well, in a word: marvellously. Mother was wonderful. . . . Finally, she even went for a paddle in the shallow tepid seawater on the beach of Brindisi, in the company of the whole group of passengers. We have every reason to be grateful for that Italian sailors' strike, because that was the reason for jumping in at the deep end—if you know what I mean. It was the best conceivable preparation for a trip to Canada next year; we are now quite determined to come.'

SMART LADIES

Baarn, 2 September 1959: 'Next Thursday they are making me a member of the Rotary Club of Baarn; to my delight, my fun-loving friend De Cneudt also joined a short while ago, as well as Klijn, of course, who had been planning on my joining for a long time—for such a long time, indeed, that I was beginning to feel suspicious about the feelings of most of the old fogies of Baarn towards me; but this seems to have been unfounded. Still, I go with some irritation because several of the members are from the coterie of the Queen's court at Soestdijk, and they send shivers down my spine. . . .

'I've just had a call from the Erven Tijl, to say that I shall be receiving some bound sample copies the day after tomorrow. . . .

'I've actually been able to do some Coxetering! The first block [of cat. no. 434] is finished.

'However, the nicest thing to have happened to me recently was a visit yesterday afternoon—which is why I couldn't write to you—from a lady, Professor MacGillavry, who lectures on crystallography at the University of Amsterdam. She came with her sister-in-law, who was also somehow interested in divisions of the plane, and the two of them had their eyes glued to my prints from half past two till after half past five. What a pair of smart ladies! It's such a relief to have visitors at last who don't stare at my creatures uncomprehendingly, but who can chuckle with amusement at anything worth chuckling at. J. Chr.! How they gazed at some of those prints. A few months ago I received a Belgian-American colleague of hers, a Professor Donnay, who lectures somewhere in the US, and apparently she put Mrs MacG. on to me. Obviously she wanted to know what she was letting herself in for, before committing herself. Now that she has seen I'm all right, she will try to have me give a lecture in Cambridge in August 1960, where there is a conference of about seven hundred crystallographers. In fact, that Professor Donnay had also mentioned it and it now looks as though it will really happen. There will be an exhibition of my prints as well, and my travelling and hotel expenses will be reimbursed.

'You'll understand that I don't want to miss this opportunity;

Opposite page: *Whirlpools*; woodcut in three colours, November 1957 (cat. no. 423)

Page 96: *Sphere Surface with Fish*; woodcut in three colours, July 1958 (cat. no. 427)

so *if* Mother and I come to Canada, it will not be until September 1960, but that doesn't seem to be a problem.'

Baarn, 27 December 1959: 'After a good and productive talk with Klijn, I can manage to accept the weekly Rotary lunch parties with more equanimity and less reluctance than a month ago. They might be an excellent medicine for that strange mixture of inferior and superior feelings that plagues me—and not only me, I suspect. If you don't take the noble intentions too seriously, it can be quite amusing—all those strange gentlemen together.'

Baarn, 10 January 1960: 'Two letters from Arthur—one for us and one for Jan—arrived together. He went to great lengths to apologize, but also wrote some interesting news, especially a description of his food-dropping flight to revitalize some starving Frenchmen. . . .

'I read a book by Nevil Shute entitled *On the Beach*. In the end, all of mankind perishes from nuclear poisoning. Weirdly theatrical and sentimental, it fascinated me nonetheless, because I like to see how other people imagine it would be. To some extent, it's comparable with my own work—it doesn't "fly high" or "go deep", but it attests to an ability to imagine situations no one can control.'

In November 1959 one of his customers had sent Escher an article about "impossible objects" by L. S. and Roger Penrose. The article referred to a few of his older prints, but there was also a drawing of an endless staircase, which Escher did not know, and which inspired him to make a new lithograph. He wrote a letter about this to Arthur, who was now in New Guinea.

ASCENDING AND DESCENDING
Baarn, 24 January 1960: 'I'd like to hear more about the work you're doing at the moment; we don't really have any idea what you're getting up to.

'While we wait for your reply, I can tell you I'm busy designing a new print showing a staircase that goes on endlessly ascending— or descending, if you see it that way. This would normally have to be a spiralling thing in which the top would disappear into the clouds and the bottom into hell. Not in my version—it's an enclosed, ring-shaped affair, like a snake eating its own tail. Nevertheless, it's possible to draw it with correct perspective: each step higher (or lower) than the last one. A large number of human figures walk on it, in two directions. One procession climbs wearily up *ad infinitum*; the other descends endlessly. I discovered the principle in a publication that was sent to me, which mentions me

as a maker of a number of so-called "impossible objects". I did not yet know that staircase, which was illustrated by a clear but unskilled drawing. I had used some of the other examples, though.

'That staircase is a rather sad, pessimistic subject, as well as being very profound and absurd. With similar questions on his lips, our own Albert Camus has just smashed into a tree in his friend's car and killed himself. An absurd death, which had rather an effect on me. Yes, yes, we climb up and up, we imagine we are ascending; every step is about ten inches high, terribly tiring—and where does it all get us? Nowhere; we don't get a step farther or higher. And descending, running down with abandon, is not possible either.

'People don't like to talk about falling; they'd much rather talk about ascending. Well then. They have officially invited me to give a lecture and an exhibition in Cambridge next August, during an international conference of crystallographers. Rather a joke: I know nothing about crystallography, scientifically speaking, but they seem to be amused by my fantasies. Well, I'll certainly have to go, don't you think? Immediately afterwards, we'll go and see our grandchild in Canada. I'm working my fingers to the bone, believing I'm ascending. How absurd it all is. Sometimes it makes me feel quite sick.'

Escher started a regular correspondence with the organizer about the practicalities of the Cambridge exhibition, the lecture, accommodation and his participation in various events. Everything was planned in great detail.

Professor Terpstra from Groningen had received very positive responses to Escher's work from Russia, and wrote him a warm letter about it.

Groningen, 1 February 1960: 'Dear Mr Escher, I sent a copy of your *Grafiek en Tekeningen* [the book published by the Erven Tijl] to the academic A. W. Shubnikov in Moscow (one of the top authorities in the field of crystallography). Today I received a letter from him in which he says: "I find Escher's prints extremely interesting, because they are an excellent illustration of the theory of antisymmetry. The picture on the cover of the book, for example, shows that antisymmetry rotation points of the second order exist in the given two-dimensional symmetry group.

'"The print *Day and Night* made a great impression on me. It can be considered as the imaginary antisymmetrical operation of the transformation of our light, left world in the right, dark counter-world of Dirac."

'I presume you will be pleased to hear this. Yours sincerely, P. Terpstra.'

Baarn, 20 March 1960: 'Nothing very exceptional is happening here. I've been working like a madman, first to finish that lithograph at long last (it's now at Andréa's, the old printer, who has just lost his wife; a brave, desperately unhappy old man; I

Page 97: Circle Limit III; woodcut in five colours, December 1959 (cat. no. 434)

Opposite page: Circle Limit IV; woodcut in two colours, July 1960 (cat. no. 436)

haven't yet received the proofs). Then, gritting my teeth, I spent four days making nine more good copies of that extremely laborious circle limit in colours. Every print means printing twenty times in succession—five blocks, each block four times. I do all this with the strange feeling that this piece of work is a "milestone" in my development, but that no one but myself will ever realize it. Nevertheless, the other day I sold a copy of it for the first time, to a young architect for a hundred guilders. In my enthusiasm I obviously talked him round to it. Later I did my utmost to talk him out of it again, but he insisted on having it. . . .

'During the coming days of waiting, I'll spend my time preparing my lecture for Cambridge; the sooner I finish it the better, in case of any last-minute nervous activity.'

Baarn, 27 March 1960: 'I've asked Jim Frater, a Scotsman by birth, as you may know, to give me English conversation lessons. . . . For my own pleasure, I've meanwhile started to read an extremely interesting book entitled *Art and Illusion* [by the art historian E. H. Gombrich], a psychological study of the question: how do human images form in general and works of art in particular? I was given the book as a present by the American publisher, because one of my prints (*Other World*) is used in it.'

MOZART
Baarn, 6 April 1960: 'If you're to be at peace with this strange life; to accept what we don't understand; to await patiently what's in store for us; then you would have to be a wiser man than I am. I occasionally read a chapter in a book by Ortega y Gasset, *Man and People*, recommended to me by Dr Klijn (who owns all Ortega's works). Well, I must say, it's not bad at all, and a lot better than sleeping pills. There's more to Klijn than meets the eye. I visited him and his wife again the other evening, and the main subjects of our conversation were Ortega and Mozart. He has a very good record deck and played me the Sinfonia Concertante in E Flat for violin, viola and orchestra. This happens to be the only work by Mozart that makes me hesitate when I say I don't like him very much, for it moves me deeply. I've heard it live twice, conducted by the late Van Beinum, with Nap de Klijn and Paul Godwin (the latter playing viola). The first and the last movement are quite exuberant in Mozart's usual fashion, "full of *joie de vivre*" according to the connoisseurs. But the middle movement is so infernally sad and beautiful that you have to try hard not to become sentimental. I remember very well how that wonderful violist Godwin laid bare his soul to the audience at the Concertgebouw. It was painfully beautiful. Well, Jan Klijn's record was also beautiful, though it could in no way supersede my memory. I immediately ordered two records and will send you one as soon as they arrive. . . .

'I must go and see Jim for my English lesson. I'm corresponding with a Scottish professor of chemistry who writes long stories about *Alice in Wonderland* and gives chemical formulae for "looking-glass milk". This is all in connection with my glide reflections, about which he is going to write a long article with six reproductions in a journal for brewers in Great Britain. I think he must be retired, for he writes endlessly, page after page. I had to give him detailed information about the sex life of my curl-up creature, which he calls a "twiddle bug".'

Escher wrote in English to father and son L. S. and Roger Penrose in London, enclosing a copy of *Ascending and Descending*.

Baarn, 18 April 1960: 'A Dutch friend of mine sent me some months ago a photo-type of your article. . . .

'Your figures 3 and 4: "continuous flights of steps", were completely new to me and I was so impressed by the idea, that it inspired me recently to a new print, of which I should like to send you, as a homage, an original copy.

'If you should have published, or should know other articles about "impossible objects" or allied subjects with good figures, you should oblige me *very* much by giving me their data.'

The reaction to this letter was very enthusiastic and Escher received a copy of an article on puzzles, which he found fascinating.

On 1 May 1960 he sent a copy of *Circle Limit III* to Coxeter, accompanied by a detailed description in English. 'It is intended as an elaboration of the first black-and-white print which you received before and, though I attained no ideal whatever, I certainly succeeded better this time. The whole area is filled up with series of theoretically an endless number of fishes, swimming head-to-tail in the same colour. The white curved lines through their bodies accentuate the continuity of every series. A minimum of four woodblocks, one for every colour and a fifth for the black lines was needed. Every block has roughly the form of a segment of 90°. This implicates, that the complete print is composed of $4 \times 5 = 20$ printings.

'The central axis is quarternary for the black lines, but binary for the colours. Looking "down-stream" to a series of fishes, every figure has a quarternary axis at the end of its right fin and a ternary axis at the end of its left fin.'

Escher also had a proposal to make to Coxeter. During his visit to George in Canada, he wanted to go to Toronto to repeat the Cambridge lecture. Coxeter was full of admiration for the print, which he immediately used as an illustration in his own lectures, and he agreed to the plan for a lecture in Toronto.

Coxeter also wrote a long mathematical explanation in his letter, which was beyond Escher's comprehension, as he remarked in a letter to George and Corrie.

Baarn, 28 May 1960: 'I had an enthusiastic letter from Coxeter about my coloured fish, which I sent him. Three pages of explanation of what I actually did. . . . It's a pity that I understand nothing, absolutely nothing of it. . . .

'Are you interested in Nevil Shute? I've just read *Requiem for a Wren;* it may be a sentimental story, but it had a great effect on me—a sign of old age? You can have it, if you like. . . .

'In his poor Wren tale, Nevil Shute describes, among other things, a journey that the girl makes from Rotterdam to Seattle, via the Panama Canal, on a Dutch freighter with a good captain. . . . It *could* be that Shute is not making this up and that it would actually be possible to make such a long sea voyage to the West Coast of North America.'

After some detective work, Escher discovered an Italian freighter which sailed from Genoa to the north-west coast via the Panama Canal, and which could take him to Vancouver. From there it would be possible to travel across Canada by train to where George lived. To Escher's delight, he managed to organize the trip so that after the conference in Cambridge—from 17 to 20 August—he could embark in Genoa on 29 August. Jetta was to travel ahead, flying direct to Canada.

There was a great deal to do before leaving. Escher prepared the lecture and accompanying exhibition down to the last detail, while more academics continued to contact him. He received, for example, a letter from Professor C. N. Yang of Princeton with a request for permission to use the study for the division of the plane *Horsemen* as an illustration for his book *Elementary Particles.*

In mid-June Escher also received a letter from Professor Arthur Loeb, who had admired his work for a long time and now wished to visit him. Loeb was a member of the Massachusetts Institute of Technology, in Cambridge, Massachusetts; he was Dutch by birth and was then in Holland with his parents. The visit took place and was a great success; it led to a lasting friendship. Escher wrote about this to George and Corrie.

Baarn, 2 July 1960: 'In addition, it's quite probable that I'll have to repeat my Cambridge lecture in Cambridge, USA, near Boston, at the beginning of October. This is the result of a very nice visit from a young, Jewish, ex-Dutch, naturalized American professor at the university there, a tremendously learned gentleman by the name of Loeb. He lectures on mathematics, designs computers, dabbles in crystallography for fun, and also lectured at C. (England), read my abstract in the collection of lectures which has just been published, and perused my prints for hours, enjoying them enormously. The strangest thing of all is that he told me he was actually a professional musician. He plays the harpsichord, flute and oboe and gives concerts. Aren't there some curious people around? He's rather a shy young man; you'd think he might be an office clerk. He came here from Naarden on his bike, with a briefcase full of perspex models of atom formations—thick sheets that together form a transparent block in which you can see the atoms. All the individual sheets slide over each other, so you

can construct all sorts of formations. He's going to exhibit all this in Cambridge. He hopes that he'll soon be able to buy a little car in his hometown in the US, now that he's almost finished paying off his harpsichord. He says that the university will be happy to pay for my return journey from St Andrews to Boston, for he thinks it is absolutely essential for his students to see my prints and hear me talk about them. I'll be able to stay at his house.'

THE CONFERENCE IN CAMBRIDGE
Baarn, 28 August 1960: 'This afternoon, Jan or Arthur will be taking me by car to Utrecht, where I'll clamber into a sleeper. I'll arrive in Genoa at about midday on Monday and I'm expected aboard the *Paolo Toscanelli* at half past two. The *Toscanelli* is apparently the most modern freighter of that line. . . . It seems as though the boat is really leaving on the 29th, which is three days later than planned. We may make up those days, so it's possible that I'll arrive in Vancouver on 7 October. . . .

'Now I must tell you something about my time in Cambridge. In a word, it was wonderful. They spoilt me enormously for four whole days. The fact that I was the only artist among twelve hundred participants (plus at least three hundred students) was very fortunate. I'd barely arrived when I hastily had to change into my best suit and sit down at a luncheon in St Catherine's College, as a member of the Company of Principal Speakers. In this way I immediately got to know the figureheads of the conference. I was seated between Mr Belov, the leader of the Russian delegation, consisting of forty-seven members, and an American whose name I can't remember. They were both surprisingly friendly and jovial and went to great lengths to praise my exhibition (which I hadn't even seen myself at that point). I gave my lecture the following morning at a quarter past ten in the biggest lecture hall in the place, a dignified structure rather like an amphitheatre, surrounded by gothic arches and pillars and seating about two hundred and twenty. However, the audience was so large that there were people on all the steps. I think there must have been about three hundred people present, and many others later told me how sorry they were that they hadn't been able to get in. . . . It went splendidly; I wasn't even slightly nervous, and, as I later heard, spoke clearly and understandably. Two slides at a time were projected on the white wall when I asked. . . . I enjoyed it all so much that I even ventured to throw in a few jokes that weren't in the written text. At the end I was overwhelmed with deafening applause; I must say it's not unpleasant to experience something like that. . . .

'My exhibition was impeccably arranged on long tables, with printed catalogues. It was in an enormous examination hall where all sorts of technical knick-knacks and strange instruments, such as a whole row of computers, microscopes etc., etc., were displayed, as well as my prints. It looked rather like a hall of a world fair. Next to it there was a conversation hall with easy chairs, tables, a buffet where you could get free coffee, tea or lemonade all day long, and where hundreds of the conference participants walked round, sat down and talked to each other. I, too, had some very pleasant conversations there, including some with a number of Russians, who spoke exceptionally bad English and laughed a great deal.

'I sold twenty-three prints in four days: quite a feat of administration in itself, not getting confused, and noting all the addresses. . . . There was a great deal of interest among the members of MIT in my lecture in Cambridge, Mass. (provisionally arranged for 28 October). I'll have to work hard on it during the boat trip; they'd like longer than forty-five minutes and more prints. It might turn into quite a show. George will have to correct my new text. I'll simply translate the captions from my book.

'There was a beautiful concert in Kings' College Chapel; an interesting excursion to Ely (a Norman cathedral) . . . too much to relate and not a minute for being bored.

'I'm starting this long voyage rather exhausted; I've hardly had time to think about it, but it'll undoubtedly be wonderful.'

Escher and the other members of the board of De Grafische, July 1960. From left to right, standing: Jan Bezemer, Cor Basant, Lou Strik, M.C. Escher; seated: Gerd Arntz, Hans van Dokkum, Pam Rueter

Voyage to Canada 1960

The sea plays an important part in Escher's life; it is always present at significant turning points and highpoints. In 1922 Escher went to Italy by sea, and more or less settled there. When he left Italy and his life took an important turn in Switzerland and Belgium, he made a long and fascinating sea voyage to Spain in the spring of 1936. In 1954, when his exhibition in Amsterdam was held during the International Mathematical Conference, as well as his first exhibition in the United States, he made his first sea trip since the war.

Similarly 1960 formed a highpoint in his life, not only because of his appearances in Cambridge, Toronto and Cambridge, Massachusetts, but also as a result of the seven-week sea trip he made after the summer— his longest yet. In March 1961 he gave a lecture about it to his Rotary Club in Baarn. The text has been kept and follows below in its entirety. It is a summary of his passion for sea voyages and is full of splendid observations, recounted with Escher's typical mixture of intense involvement and detachment.

The order of his tale is also characteristic: it is systematic rather than chronological. After an introduction about the sensation of travelling by sea, he gives his observations of the people, then of the sea and the fauna, then of the starry sky and the moon. Finally, he detaches himself from the earth and life on earth, and takes a look at it from the immense void surrounding it, where he imagines himself to be. This development of the story, which ends with an image of 'pure' emptiness, is very characteristic of his feeling for life.

ESCHER'S LECTURE

I should like to tell you something about my trip to Canada in the autumn of 1960. I travelled to Montreal by freighter in seven weeks, and from there I flew back in seven hours.

My trip had three aims: firstly, I wanted to meet my granddaughter, who was eight months old when I first saw her. (She lives with her parents in St Andrews East, forty-five miles west of Montreal.) Secondly, I promoted 'business' by giving lectures on my work in England, the United States and Canada; and thirdly, I spent six weeks lazing on a boat. It is this holiday trip that I want to talk about here.

To begin with, I want to say something about travelling on a freighter as a passenger in general.

Several times we have heard Wijsmuller speaking about his fascinating and exciting life and adventures as a professional seaman. It might be interesting to try and show what travelling by sea is like from a different point of view, and describe some impressions of a 'landlubber' who would spend his holidays at sea every year, if he had the chance. I am sorry that I shall have to read out my tale, as I really do not consider myself capable of recalling the memories off the cuff. In the past few weeks I have been writing them down in bits and pieces, whenever I had a moment; the whole thing may therefore seem rather fragmentary—but let us see, and hope for the best. This written account has the advantage for me that I have had to put down my impressions before I forget them.

When I ask myself why this sort of sea trip is the best way I can imagine of spending a holiday and why I feel such a strong yearning for the sea every year as summer approaches, I can give various answers.

In the first place, I think it is ridiculous that, living on a globe seventy percent of which is covered with water, we do not seize every available opportunity to find out what it looks like on that water. (On the other hand, I am pleased that by far the greatest number of holidaymakers stay on land, or the sea would soon become unbearable.) Secondly, there is, to my way of thinking, no better method of transport and no better place to stay than a freighter, if you want to rest. No car, no train, no aeroplane and— as a place to stay—no hotel, no mountain hut and no tent is anywhere like as good as a spacious ship with a small number of passengers, when you want to get away and lose contact for a while with the overpopulated land on which we swarm about, tiring ourselves out. Mark you, I said a *spacious* ship with *few* passengers; for a freighter with fifty travellers no longer serves the purpose, not to mention a mailboat.

There are no words to describe the feeling of ecstasy that fills me when I first go into my cabin at the start of a trip. It is a feeling that at last I can have a good rest, with no responsibilities for weeks on end, and no one can contact me by phone, letters, meetings or for daily obligations; there are no newspapers to read, you don't have to listen to the news. (Usually there are plenty of radios on board, though; you can hear them muttering, yammering and yodelling from every officer's cabin that you pass. But you don't have to listen, for you are on holiday, making a trip. For three months I did not listen to a single programme or read a single newspaper except for the cartoons and horror comics in my son's Canadian newspaper in St Andrews. Anyway, reading the newspaper doesn't get you anywhere. When I left, everyone was obsessed with Lumumba, and when I returned, everyone was still obsessed with Lumumba. Even now, another four months later, they are still on about Lumumba.)

On a ship like that, you no longer have to take any decisions yourself. The captain and the steward do it for you. Of course, you know beforehand whereabouts they are taking you, but you can't be sure, for sometimes you get an extra port thrown in, and sometimes they miss one out that was on the list. Where they are taking you is less important anyway than the fact that they just sail you around. If you go on holiday with the idea that you want to visit a particular museum or be present at a particular festival, you would do better to choose some other form of transport, for a freighter is hardly ever on time, and often also changes its route. You have to be satisfied with being looked after in the most excellent way (usually) and try to behave as passively as possible after months of being active. The funny thing is that after a trial period of about a week, you acquire an openness which makes it possible to feel truly surprised again; in other words, to experience the wonders surrounding you—the three dimensions, for example: so-called 'reality'—more intensely than you had dared to hope.

When the sea is calm, the landscape (seascape) seems simple and even monotonous, sometimes with a distant, sometimes with a close coastline, but usually with no land in sight at all. You feel 'free', not only free of care, but also free of the solidity of the earth's crust. It is a wonderful sensation, feeling the liquidity of the water under the ship. This salutary freedom is constantly present, on deck by day, in bed at night. The movements of the ship vary from a gentle rocking to swinging and hurtling; you are never motionless while at sea. Then you start to observe and assimilate all these natural phenomena surrounding you: the infinite variety of the waves and the swell of the sea, and for the first time in ages you look again at the heavenly bodies, the sun, the moon and the stars, and you see the living creatures in and over the sea, the fish and the birds.

Then, for a change, the ship temporarily establishes contact with the mainland, and you really enjoy going into the harbour. You look wide-eyed at the big city full of people, at the loading and unloading, you listen to the noise, and, from your privileged position, you watch all this bustle that—for once—you don't have to join in with, and you think to yourself: Let them go on slogging away, let them tire themselves out; tomorrow I shall sail away from all this noise and stench.

How pleasant it is to stroll into a strange (or sometimes familiar) city and sit down on a bench in a square or park. You

may have a chat with a stranger sitting next to you, if you happen to be in a country where you know the language. Or you just sit drowsily watching the busy traffic, and that familiar, disturbing and frightening feeling of depersonalization creeps over you for the hundredth time: Is this me? What is 'me'? Who is it, sitting here filled with wonder at everything so utterly, so unspeakably? If this all becomes too much, you just get up (and go for a drink in a bar, perhaps, totally lost in the noisy company of a different sort of people, who do know who they are). Then you wander back to the harbour through the balmy night and clamber up the gangplank, and in your neat, convenient cabin you think: Tomorrow we shall be back on the clean, immaculate sea, in the pure, salty air, and it is not nearly time to go home; on the contrary, I am going farther and farther away from home, and it is only now, after a week's holiday, that I am really starting to lose my own preoccupied, active and hurrying self.

Now don't expect a day-by-day account of the sea trip I made from the end of August to mid-October 1960, from Genoa to Vancouver, on an Italian boat. Rather than recounting my impressions chronologically, I would prefer to put my memories in a different order. Let me begin by telling you something about the ship and the people on board.

I THE SHIP AND THE PEOPLE ON BOARD
Two weeks before I embarked, my wife had flown direct to Montreal to see as much as possible of her grandchild, and on 29 August I went on board the *Paolo Toscanelli* in Genoa. This was one of the four freighters of the Italia Line, which has a regular service between Trieste and Vancouver. It was a ship of about nine thousand tons, with accommodation for a maximum of twelve passengers.

The reason that I always sail on Italian ships is not only that I lived in Italy for many years, and consequently am relatively fluent in the language and enjoy the company of Italians, but also that there appears to be more chance of getting a single cabin on board an Italian freighter with passenger accommodation than on the ships of other countries. On the *Toscanelli* I had a beautiful cabin, a room more than ten feet by twelve, with two portholes, a first-class bed, a writing-table, my own bathroom and every possible comfort. You must not underestimate the importance of such a spacious, comfortable private room when you are staying on board for six weeks. The ship also provided plenty of space for the passengers to move about: a snug dining-room, a large conversation room with easy chairs, and three promenade decks, one of which ran the whole width of the ship, about thirty yards.

Sky and Water I; woodcut, June 1938
(cat. no. 306)

There was absolutely no need for passengers to crowd together, and it was easy to get away from each other, even in the open air. In addition, we were free to go on all the other decks, the whole length of the ship, except for the bridge. However, every time there was something particularly worth seeing from the highest possible point, the captain invited us up to the bridge. As far as I was concerned, I was soon on such good terms with the officers that I was nearly always allowed to go up on the bridge whenever I wanted to. Yet my favourite spot on this trip was the deck in the bows. I spent many hours there every day, near the prow. There is no better place on a ship for feasting your eyes on the infinite diversity of fascinating sights around you. I shall try and describe some of these later.

But first I ought to say something about the people with whom I made the trip. The passengers all came together twice a day for hot meals, sitting at three tables, four to a table. The captain and the first engineer joined us at the fourth table.

It seems there are too few diversions for young people on such a long trip on board a freighter, with no dances, swimming-pool or cinema. In fact, almost all the passengers on board were middle-aged. Apart from myself, there were nine Americans, one Belgian lady and one young Swiss, who was a bit of an outsider because of his youth.

When you spend a number of weeks with such a small, enclosed group of people, there is ample opportunity to become acquainted with each other's idiosyncrasies, if not really to get to know each other. I am conscious of my lack of psychological insight in general and I am more interested, especially at sea, in natural objects than in my travelling companions. Yet I must tell you something about some of the people with whom I was in daily contact.

I was fortunate to share my table with three ladies: two unmarried sisters from Philadelphia and a lady from Santa Barbara, on the coast near Los Angeles, who was divorced from her husband and was travelling alone. The two sisters, by the name of Cassidy, were a couple of genial, merry ladies in their early fifties, who were returning from a journey through Europe, where they had spent more than six months. They were by no means well-off and had both worked in an office for years, until they had won a prize of a thousand dollars each for finding the correct solution to some newspaper competition. They thought it was a chance not to be missed and crossed over to Europe by sea, taking their little car. They had travelled around for half a year. They were small and plump, with gentle characters, and both were laden with all sorts of silver ornaments, necklaces, brooches and bracelets made up of a whole collection of minuscule amulet-like charms: saints, crosses and medals which they had collected in all sorts of holy places on their wanderings, such as Rome, Pompeii and Lourdes. This did not prevent them from being violently anti-Kennedy and pro-Nixon, in contrast with Mrs Crockett, the third

lady on my table. An intelligent and intellectual woman, she enormously regretted the fact that Stevenson had no chance of becoming president of the United States. In other ways, too, the third of my 'three graces' contrasted with the two sisters. The only thing they had in common was their age, although I am not quite sure of this, because it is very difficult to estimate the age of a woman who goes to great lengths to look younger than she actually is. But she was slim rather than plump, and both her spirit and her tongue were sharp rather than soft. Nevertheless, of all the passengers, I got on best with her. She could tell very amusing anecdotes of her many travels round the world. After the First World War she had, among other things, spent a few years as an anthropologist in the interior of Dutch New Guinea with her then husband, who was a sort of amateur film-maker. There she had met von Koenigswald, now a professor in Utrecht, whom I had also met. Our boat was taking her back to her house in California, after she had stayed a full year in Majorca. Apparently she had spent most of her time there swimming and sunbathing, for I have seldom seen a so-called 'white' woman who was so thoroughly brown. Despite the domestic atmosphere on our freighter, she would appear for dinner in the most fantastic, colourful décolletés. Her cropped, snow-white hair was anything but natural. Except at meals, she was inseparable from her ancient, greying dog Philip, who followed her about everywhere and was the only living creature on board troubled by sea-sickness.

Mrs Crockett spoke reasonably intelligible English, but the Cassidy sisters rattled on in a terrible Philadelphian accent, often overwhelming me with a flood of largely unintelligible sounds. This could be extremely tiring and I had to keep exhorting them to speak more clearly and slowly so that I should be able to decipher the meaning of their words. I learned a few slang expressions which they warned me never to use in polite company, though I later used them to great effect in Canada.

These descriptions of people are taking up more time than I had thought they would, but there is one other passenger I must mention, with whom I got on extremely well. This was Mr Alway, a seventy-three-year-old ex-bulb-cultivator from Tacoma. When competition from Dutch bulb-growers became too great, he switched to growing rhubarb with great success. With his fun-loving, just as elderly wife, he too had made a long trip through Europe. He was a quiet man with a shy smile, and the sea fascinated him just as it does me. He also spent hours watching and waiting to observe the fish in the water. When the ship was tied up at the quay in a harbour, I would often find him sitting on a crate on the quayside, watching the loading and unloading and usually wearing a garish shirt and a cap with an enormous peak. He looked a 'softie', but nothing could be further from the truth.

Once or twice he would tell me fascinating stories about his youth. For example, when he was twelve years old, he had made a three-month trip in a rowing-boat, quite alone, all the way from

Tacoma, through the fjord-like inland seas, to Vancouver Island, a distance of over a hundred and twenty miles, making two hundred and fifty miles there and back. During that summer he lived largely on fish he caught himself, which he grilled over a woodfire, and he slept in his boat. One evening when he was tying up at a beach on Vancouver Island, he heard shouting and screaming from a little way inland. He walked towards the noise and found an Indian woman lying on a heap of straw in a delapidated hut. She told him that her husband was away and that she could feel she was on the point of giving birth. 'Well, I helped her as best I could,' said Alway. He put the child next to her when it was born, and gave her some water to drink, which he found in an earthenware jar in the corner of the hut. He waited until the husband came home and then returned to his rowing-boat. But he did row a little farther on to the next suitable place to spend the night. He told me the whole story in an offhand sort of way, hesitating slightly and completely without trying to impress me.

There is really so much to tell about my travelling companions. About Joe Tucker, for example, a rich ex-Italian cook who owned a restaurant in Seattle, a corpulent, loud-mouthed guy of about sixty-five, who came from a poor family in the Abruzzi. When he was sixteen he emigrated to the United States. At that time he was called Giuseppe Galletti, and in a confidential mood he once told me that he had felt ashamed about changing his name. He was travelling with his wife, an American born in Seattle. She was quiet and modest; it seemed to me that life was not easy for her, with that thundering husband incapable of speaking at a normal volume. Perhaps he was a tyrant at home, but it was obvious that the two of them were very fond of each other.

Now I must mention the officers with whom I had some contact every day. The captain and the first mate both came from Trieste, where many officers in the Italian Merchant Navy and the Marines come from. They were both tall and thin, like many people from Trieste and unlike most of their other compatriots.

My experience as a passenger on Italian freighters is that there is a great contrast between the captain's job and that of the first mate. This may seem surprising, since every captain is an ex-first mate. I have often heard that Italians are lazy, but I think it would be more correct to say that an Italian becomes lazy when he can leave the work to someone else. You can hardly imagine anyone with more to do and who has to work harder than the first mate of a freighter just before, during and just after calling at a port. When there are a number of ports in succession for a few days, the poor man gets hardly any sleep at night.

It is not really surprising that such an overworked man looks forward to the time when he can take it easy, as a captain. I should not like to say that all Italian captains are lazy; I have come across some hard-working ones, but the captain of the *Toscanelli* made no bones about it and admitted himself, '*Ah si, caro Signore, sono un uomo pigro*'—'Yes, dear sir, I am a lazybones.'

In the course of the years I have experienced at least ten different crews of Italian freighters and I have formed the impression that an officer is busier and busier as he goes up in rank, until the moment when he becomes captain. Obviously the weight of responsibility is in itself a burden, which can sometimes be extremely heavy. As soon as a situation arises that is outside normal routine, for example when there is mist and heavy traffic at sea, or during a storm, the lazy captain suddenly wakes up and his feeling of responsibility is clear. But during a summer voyage when the weather is fine and the sea calm, he has ample opportunity to spend his time on activities totally unrelated to his profession. I once travelled on a ship in the Mediterranean, where the captain seemed to be interested in nothing but the charms of a young Englishwoman. This had advantages for the other passengers, for when we passed by Stromboli, on our way from Messina to Naples, he had the ship sail right round the island so that he could show the lady as much as possible of the magnificent views of the fire-spitting volcano. The next day he said to me: 'If the company in Naples hears about this, I'll be in deep water, but I don't care, I'm retiring in three months.' I regret I never made another trip with him, for he died shortly afterwards. He was a great fellow.

As I have said, not only the captain ate with us, but the first engineer as well. On an Italian boat his official title is 'Direttore delle machine' or simply 'Direttore'. He was a very nice man— kind-hearted, merry, and with a great sense of humour. Whenever there was some friction between our indolent captain and the American passengers, the Direttore very tactfully managed to calm everyone down and get them all laughing by making jokes. He was small with a big paunch, and a pale, puffy clown's face.

In the evening, when the passengers would be lying in deckchairs on the rear deck under a starry sky, recovering from the huge meal, he would walk up and down the promenade deck for an hour with the second engineer, to compensate for his lack of movement and fresh air. His stomach swaying rhythmically in front of him, his left arm round the shoulder of his young companion in a fatherly fashion, and his right hand gesticulating wildly, he would walk to and fro seriously discussing professional matters.

Italian seamen are so much fun to sail with! They have a naturally cultivated manner, an inborn courtesy and a spontaneous way of getting along with strangers, which always has a liberating effect on me on a holiday trip.

There is, no doubt, a good reason why the Dutch are renowned for being particularly skilled and experienced navigators, but no matter how able and tough they may be, I always prefer an Italian freighter for an enjoyable voyage. A Dutchman is naturally more inhibited than an Italian, but in addition there is that dreadful class-consciousness in the Dutch population, expressed more strongly than anywhere else in the pronunciation of the language, which often hinders an easy contact between the passengers and the crew on a Dutch ship. I have found that in the enclosed community of a small Dutch ship there is often a terrible pettymindedness, which sometimes manifests itself in an undisguised intolerance towards everyone who does not comply exactly with the conventional Dutch middle-class norms and ideas. However, this petty-mindedness and intolerance is a consequence of being inhibited.

A few years ago I spent some days in Hamburg harbour on an Italian boat. (On a freighter you simply have to accept the harbours you're offered.) One evening I was ferried to the town in a roomy boat belonging to the harbour service. It stopped at a whole series of places where crews from all sorts of freighters embarked, so that finally there were about a hundred people on board, in groups of different nationalities. There were Italians from my own ship, there were Russians, Americans, Japanese and . . . a group of Dutch sailors. It seemed that most of them were going on shore leave to the celebrated entertainment centre Sankt Pauli (what a name!) and they sat in their best clothes silently looking round or quietly talking. They all had the expectant, assured manner of men who know what they are going to do— except for the Dutchmen. They obviously had to fire each other to conquer their inhibitions, and were preparing loudly for the pleasures awaiting them. They seemed to have drunk themselves tipsy on board their own ship in anticipation and were hanging around shouting and babbling in their dreadful language, waving half empty bottles of beer in their hands. I have seldom seen a more striking contrast than that between the dignified, cool reserve of the representatives of the other nationalities and the unpleasant, offensive lack of manners of my compatriots, and I have seldom been so glad that no one could tell from my face that they *were* my compatriots.

Finally, let me mention one of the sailors of the *Toscanelli's* crew. Just as the navigation officers on Italian freighters often come from Trieste, the sailors are frequently from southern Italy. With us, Sicilians and Neapolitans do not have a very good reputation. They are thought to be untrustworthy, and it is a fact that in Naples or in the provinces farther south tourists are often tricked or robbed. This is not surprising when one knows how terribly poor the population is and how careless and unsuspecting tourists sometimes are. But when you understand the language a little, and you can thus show that you are not prepared to be squeezed like a lemon even though you're a stranger, these small gesticulating people with their dark skins turn out to be friendly, hospitable, childlike and polite, and above all, very sensitive to any praise of the land of their birth.

Apart from the boatswain, called 'Nostromo' or 'our man', I particularly had contact with one of the sailors because he was the ship's barber. He cut everyone's hair, even the lady passengers'. When you saw him dangling high up in the air against the mast he was painting, standing on a little plank tied by a rope, in his dirty sweater and torn trousers, it was difficult to imagine that this was

Top: Don Pantaleone in front of his cliff-top church

Above: In February 1932 Escher made the lithograph *San Cosimo* (cat. no. 208) of Don Pantaleone's church

the same man who had come to your cabin the day before, washed, neat and tidy, wearing a snow-white shirt, to style your hair, a full-fledged Figaro. He handled the barber's scissors and the barber's razor with refined delicacy and would talk softly in the sing-song dialect of his region about his wife and his daughter who was so good at school with the nuns; and about his father who was a barber in Torre dei Greci. When he was only five years old, he had helped his father to lather the clients while standing on a stool to enable him to reach.

In the evening you would see him doing the hair of his fellow-sailors. It was interesting to watch—a wonderful pantomime. On the rear deck, under the bright light of a lamp in the pitch-black night, the client would sit upright on a kitchen chair, stock-still as a display figure, and the barber would style the black curls of the motionless back of his head, scissors snipping away, his little finger in the air, like a priest performing a sacred dance in honour of an idol.

I have just remembered another open-air barber scene. Admittedly it has nothing to do with my trip to Canada, but I should just like to mention it while I think of it. Thirty years ago I used to stay in a village on the Amalfi coast. I would often visit Don Pantaleone, the old priest of a church that is perched like an eagle's nest against a cliff, a thousand feet above the water. In front of the church there is a tiny little square with an incredibly wide view over the dark-blue Mediterranean. Once when I had climbed the long stairs and arrived at the little square, I saw Don Pantaleone having a shave in an armchair placed in the cool shadow of the cliff face, just in front of the open door of his church. This was another of those scenes one never forgets—the way that old man in his grubby surplice was having his white stubbly beard shaved, his head leaning right back. The silence of the warm spring afternoon was only broken by the rasping of the razor and the chirping of crickets, and the air was heavy with the scent of orange blossom. The only other present was a little boy who stood patiently waiting like a choirboy, with a bowl of clean water in his hands and a clean white towel over his arm.

2 THE SEA AND ITS WILDLIFE

But now I will finally stop talking about all those people and try to tell you something about the sea itself and the wildlife there that swims in it and flies over it.

I should like to advise anyone going to sea as a passenger to take three things: firstly, good large-scale maps so that you do not have to keep bothering the officers with the usual passenger questions, 'What is the name of that island?' 'What mountain is that?' When land is sighted, it simply gives me a sense of satisfaction to find out straight away on a map what it is. When we crossed the Atlantic Ocean and there was no coast to be seen for seven days, between Madeira and the Caribbean Islands, the captain gave me a copy of the noon bulletin every day. This showed our speed, the atmospheric pressure, the temperature, the direction of the wind and the ocean current, as well as giving information about the location of the ship, so that I could plot our route fairly accurately on my map.

Secondly, it is a good idea to have a star map when you are at sea, for there is no better place for star-gazing in comfort than a ship sailing through warm southern seas.

Thirdly, a good pair of binoculars is almost essential at sea. Preferably they should be lightweight and small enough to keep in your pocket, because you should really always have them with you when you are on deck. At any time something can come up which you would miss with the naked eye.

The Sea I have looked at the sea for many hours and tried to take in the infinite variety of movement of the waves. Where the sea is most open—on our trip this was on the Pacific Ocean, after coming out of the Panama Canal and sailing up the West Coast of Central and North America—the waves are not only the most impressive, but also the easiest to analyze. In her beautiful book *The Sea Around Us*, Rachel Carson described them better than I can, but that should be no reason for me to be silent on the subject.

Somewhere on the other side of the Pacific, near Japan or Australia, a storm may have raged, and a ship like ours sailing along the West Coast of America in beautiful, calm weather, only notices the slow swell of incredibly wide waves, coming from the west. You see them coming towards you in straight bands, parellel to the horizon. The troughs are so wide and the crests so slight that you hardly feel them on the ship, but you can estimate their height when, except for the masts, a distant boat completely disappears into one of these troughs. Sometimes a local wind would be blowing from the east, chasing short angry-looking waves in the opposite direction, over the long ocean ridges, so that there was a combination of two movements opposing each other, in which the shorter waves would clamber up the slopes of the long ones like mountaineers.

One windless day we dropped anchor half a mile out to sea off San José in Guatemala. We lay there all day to unload heavy sacks—I can't remember what was in them—into broad, flat barges. The passengers had the opportunity of going ashore by motorboat, but this turned out to be more complicated than it looked. Now that our boat was lying still, the long waves were creating a swell that made the little motorboat alongside rise and fall rhythmically at least six feet. Standing on the accommodation ladder down the ship's side, you had to jump across at the exact moment that the motorboat was at your level. Admittedly this was no impossible task, but still a number of passengers refused to jump.

The surf on that coast was so violent that a construction of planks had been built from the beach into the sea for loading and unloading. It was rather like the old pier at Scheveningen, only much more rickety and not as long. The whole structure was 109 supported by iron posts that looked rusty and unreliable, as the sea boomed and thundered against them. We were ingeniously hoisted onto the pier from the motorboat one by one—in a solid armchair hanging from a rope, which was lifted by a grinding steam engine. Once safely arrived on the planks at the end of the pier, we walked to the beach while the sea foamed and seethed underneath and on either side.

I have never in my life seen such monumental surf. We all know how the waves on our North Sea coast become steeper and steeper as they approach the beach, how they curl round and smash down in a waterfall of swirling foam.

As I walked towards the beach over that pier in San José, I came to a place halfway where you were at exactly the right spot to see through one of those tubes of light blue-green water, just before it destroyed itself with thundering force and collapsed. The waves moved in such straight lines, parallel to the coast, and so evenly, that they all curled along their entire length at exactly the same place each time, forming a transparent cylinder nearly four feet in diameter and with an estimated length of at least fifty yards. I kept on looking through the hearts of these amazing blue-green tunnels of water, and just couldn't get enough of the spectacle as it was repeated again and again.

There was a beautiful, steeply sloping beach of fine-grained grey sand, but no one was having a swim. This was obviously too dangerous because of the strong suction of the water, which would wash back with tremendous speed after each wave had broken. It was a pity, for it must be a wonderful sensation to see one of those crystal-clear arches curve over you and feel it breaking on you.

[*The Wildlife*]   As regards the marine life, the only whales I saw on the whole trip was a pair playing together (to put it anthropomorphically) just in front of the harbour of Marseilles, of all places, when I had been on board for just a day. I was watching the landing-pier as we were entering the harbour, when suddenly, about a hundred yards away, something like a plume of smoke spurted up from the calm sea, immediately followed by another. Fortunately I had my binoculars with me, and I soon saw two rounded, black backs appearing one by one, like segments of turning wheels, followed by the tails, only to disappear again. This was repeated a few times with intervals of several minutes. It was not the first time that I had seen examples of this comparatively small type of whale in the Mediterranean. They grow to a length of thirty or forty feet and the Italians call them *capo d'olio*, or 'oil heads'. I don't know their proper name. I regret that I have never seen a larger species.

Of all the creatures in the sea, the dolphins are the easiest for a ship's passenger to observe. There are many of them in the Mediterranean, especially around the Straits of Gibraltar, but I watched them a number of times throughout the trip, right up to Vancouver.

As soon as they notice a ship, they hasten towards it, dozens of them, preferably swimming just in front of the bows. If you lean over the railings on the forecastle and look straight down where the bows cleave through the water, you see them slipping through the clear sea like a flock, swimming close together. If one could ever use the term 'sporting playfulness' in connection with animals, it certainly applies to these creatures. They give an impression of being obsessed with racing the ship. Sometimes it seems as though they deliberately allow the ship to catch up, only to shoot ahead again. Again and again they jump into the air to take breath, lifting their whole bodies out of the water in a beautiful arc, and then dive back into the sea nose first, or do a belly-flop on the surface of the water; they turn round, showing their white bellies, and you can almost hear them laughing with pleasure. They swim mainly using their tail fins, but these move to and fro so fast that you cannot see them at all and it is as though an invisible screw were propelling them forwards. I have also seen them a number of times playing in front of the bows at night in a phosphorescent sea. They look like firework rockets, trailing long, snake-like, criss-crossing ribbons of light behind them.

It is said that they can swim at great speeds and can even keep up with a destroyer doing thirty knots. However, my observations suggest that they prefer slower boats. When I was once sailing on an old steamship that could barely do ten knots, a school of dolphins managed to play in front of the bows for ten minutes, whereas they would let us go after only a few minutes on the *Toscanelli*, which could do fourteen to sixteen knots.

Flying fish, which I have seen only occasionally in the Mediterranean, become more numerous as the sea gets warmer. I momentarily mistook the first one I saw for a bird skimming just above the sea. But when it suddenly vanished without a trace I realized that it must have been a fish. Later on I had ample opportunity to watch them closely. In the Caribbean there were schools of hundreds together, all shooting up out of the water at the same time. When a whole school flies up together out of the mirror-like smoothness of the sea, the water surface seems to arch up in a system of long, parallel or radiating lines which end abruptly where the fish fall back into the sea. Sometimes our approaching ship seemed to frighten an invisible school underwater, and they would appear like the fragments of an exploding bomb, of which the bows formed the centre, radiating outwards. But it was only really possible to study their flight properly when one of them happened to fly alongside the ship. These small creatures of only seven to sixteen inches must have gathered an enormous speed underwater by the time they jump out. Apparently they can glide up to two hundred yards through the air, and I have often followed them with my binoculars as they skimmed the tops of the waves or through the troughs, getting a bit farther each time by pushing off from the water surface with short, vibrating movements of the tail. Their long and beautifully iridescent blue pectoral fins remain stiff and spread out, stretched as taut as the wings of a glider.

Just after coming out of the Panama Canal, I saw the first sea turtles as we sailed north along the coast of Costa Rica. The forecastle was again the best place to observe them properly. The specimens I saw swam just below the surface of the water, sometimes with their shells sticking out, like very small islands. It was only when they were very close that you could see the whole creature properly for a moment. They give the impression of being slow and rather helpless; I can hardly imagine that they eat fish and must therefore be able to swim fast in order to catch their prey. Once, when I was watching the foaming, blinding white spray by the bows, we bore straight down on a floating log. On either side a sea turtle was gnawing contentedly. It was only when we had nearly reached them and almost sailed over them, that they became aware of the danger and tried to find a safe way out. Later, in the famous and truly spectacular Marineland Aquarium near Los Angeles, I was able to observe them longer and better, but even so it is more satisfying to watch them in their natural environment.

One afternoon, as I was sitting on one of the mushroom-shaped bollards on the forecastle and had almost forgotten the sea because I was engrossed in the wild sky, full of ribbons of cloud in incredible shades and colours, the telephone rang. They sometimes phoned me from the bridge when they saw me sitting on the bows, to point out something worth seeing. So I quickly opened the cupboard and took the phone off the hook. The thoughtful voice of the captain said: 'Have a look, starboard. There's a school of tuna fish half a mile away—there must be hundreds of them.' Being a layman, I could not tell they were tuna fish at that distance, let alone with the naked eye, but I could see that a long stretch of the calm sea was turbulent and covered in foam. However, through my binoculars I saw the long, elegant fish with their pointed tapering tails and sharp-pointed caudal fins, close together and jumping out of the water like madmen. All together they looked like a tangled web of fast, arching lines and they had obviously caught an enormous amount of food consisting of smaller fish.

That same afternoon I also saw sharks, and twice, very close, a swordfish jumping completely out of the water, at least ten feet long. It had a sword sticking out from the front of its head which looked all of five feet long, and its wet body was a fiery red, reflecting the setting sun.

As for the birds, the seagulls were obviously the most prolific. When we sailed through the Juan de Fuca Strait south of Vancouver Island, at the end of the journey, the ship was surrounded by a flock of hundreds of screeching seagulls, splattering the whole deck with their white droppings, to the great annoyance of the crew. Sometimes a whole row of them would perch on the railings, resting, bent forward in the blustery wind. You could get to within a few yards before they would slowly spread their wings, were lifted by the wind and swept away.

It's a pity that I don't know enough about sea birds to be able to identify the different species that we saw. In addition, most of the birds of North America are different from those on our continent, so that my European bird book was of little use.

I saw some beautiful black duck-like birds flying in a long line over the wild sea, just skimming the crests of the waves and then flying down into the troughs in a curious fashion so that ten together formed another wave line.

On the north coast of Vancouver Island we spent a day in a fjord-like inlet of the Strait of Georgia, by the quay of an enormous cellulose factory. We had to load hundreds of tons of cellulose, packaged in white, cube-shaped bales.

Here I saw a whole flock of water birds that were entirely unfamiliar. They were bobbing about on the short, rippling waves, just alongside the moored ship, in groups of three to six. They were just like miniature swans, with grey bodies, eight or ten inches long; with a long, slender neck, white in front and black at the back, a sharp beak and bright-red beady eyes. They were exactly the same shape as swans, scaled down to half the size. When, say, a group of four seemed to be drifting aimlessly about, one of them would suddenly be missing, for I would see only three. Obviously one had dived underwater, but with such lightning speed that I had not seen it actually doing so, though I did catch the moment at which four had suddenly become three. I observed them that day for a few hours, noting on my watch how long they remained invisible. This always appeared to be between forty and forty-five seconds. They never finished their underwater activities in half a minute for example, and their mysterious absence never lasted longer than forty-five seconds. After forty seconds the bird would pop up again a few feet away from its group, and then swim hurriedly back to its companions.

Naturally I asked the officers on the ship, who visited these parts regularly a few times every year, whether they knew the birds. They called them *tuffini*, 'little divers'. An American passenger told me they were 'carmorans'. According to my European bird book, these are cormorants, but they certainly weren't cormorants, which do not have such long necks, like question marks. They were more likely to be grebe, a special American variety of grebe, with a swan's neck.

At any rate, I thought they were exceptionally beautiful and graceful, as you must have gathered from the time I am taking to describe them now. However, in a more critical mood, I have wondered why I thought they were so beautiful. Surely they were no more beautiful than the white swans in the pond at Groeneveld? Could anyone imagine anything more graceful and charming than two white swans in a sylvan pond? The exceptional attraction I felt to these American birds was probably based on novelty and the unknown quality of their appearance. When a blue tit appears outside my window in the winter in search of the string of peanuts hanging there, I hardly give it a second look, although it is no less fascinating a creature than a woodpecker.

However, the latter seldom appears, so that I am quite fascinated when it occasionally does pluck up the courage to come and peck at my peanuts so amazingly quickly and efficiently that it eats more of them in half a minute than a blue tit does in half an hour.

While we lay at anchor off the coast of El Salvador, I also had the opportunity to watch carefully the flight of grey pelicans as groups of them flew around us in wide arcs. As a pelican flies, its extremely long beak with its dangling yellow pouch is stretched horizontally straight in front of it, at the end of its S-shaped neck. A row of pelicans could always be seen sitting on our ship's mooring posts, just like the little old men of the Salvation Army sitting on their benches on the Wilhelminalaan.

Just once I saw an enormous bird; I imagined it to be a condor It came towards us out of the distance, flying in front of the wind; we sailed underneath it and it disappeared into the mist behind us. I did not see it make a single movement of its wings as it continually circled through the air, wings outspread and quite rigid.

[3   THE SUN, THE MOON AND THE STARS]

The sunsets on our voyage were often tremendously colourful and beautiful and I frequently watched them, quite breathless with excitement. I did this systematically every day when there was a chance of a cloudless sunset, and then I would wait expectantly, hoping just once to see the 'Green Flash'. Fantastic tales are told about this phenomenon. For a long time many people considered it to be a myth. But a few years ago a reputable book appeared on the subject, written by an Italian astronomer, who described the phenomenon and captured it in a series of beautiful colour photographs, so that there is now no more room for doubt.

When the horizon is totally cloudless at the point where the sun sets, it is possible, in certain favourable atmospheric conditions, for the last visible part of the edge of the sun to flash with a bright green light. Apparently the atmosphere above the Red Sea is particularly suitable for the appearance of the 'Green Flash', but it has also often been observed in the Mediterranean. The descriptions of eye-witnesses vary enormously and this is not surprising, since the phenomenon lasts only for a fraction of a second. Some people have tried to convey their impression in a coloured drawing. I once saw a picture in which the artist had drawn a semi-elliptical green mark, wide at the horizon and tapering upwards more or less to a point; the shape he had drawn did look rather like a 'flash'. However, nothing of this is seen in the photographs in the Italian book that I mentioned.

My own impression is based on the one and only time I was fortunate enough to see the phenomenon myself. I should never be able to draw it, though it was certainly a striking experience.

I had stood and waited so often in vain on my travels through the Mediterranean in years gone by. But on 24 September 1960, as we sailed along the entrance to the Gulf of California, I finally had the chance.

The sky was by no means totally cloudless that evening, but there was a completely clear and open stretch at the horizon, where the sun was setting. When three quarters of the elliptical disc of the sun had disappeared below the horizon, I put my trusty binoculars to my eyes and (for the hundredth time) excitedly followed the fast-shrinking segment of the sun. As usual when there is little water vapour in the atmosphere, it was a blinding orange-red colour, almost up to the end. But for a fraction of a second the colour of the last visible luminous line of the sun changed to a bright green. The change in colour happened so suddenly and so quickly, that in my memory it seems like a sort of green explosion that quite dazed me. Immediately afterwards I wondered what I had actually seen. Perhaps I could answer that question more accurately if I were able to see the 'Flash' a second time. For the time being I cannot express the experience better than by saying that it was like a soundless green bang.

The sunset and the 'Green Flash' form a suitable introduction to the stars in the night sky.

We reached the southernmost point of our voyage when we came out of the Panama Canal, at about five degrees north latitude. For the next few days the sun set at about a quarter past six. It dived under the horizon at a fairly steep angle, so dusk only lasted half an hour. Before sitting down to dinner at seven o'clock, I had thus plenty of time to be present at the entire gradual transition from day to night. When there was no moon, the first lights in the sky became visible while the glowing sun had hardly disappeared behind the horizon. Three bright planets would appear one by one: first Venus, just behind the sun; then Jupiter, a lot farther and higher in the sky; and finally Saturn, still a bit farther away. Every day it was very satisfying—with the help of those first three points of light, and sometimes the moon as a fourth—to follow the arc of the ecliptic along the span of the heavens, before the constellations of the zodiac became visible. While the blue sky became gradually darker and blacker, the fixed stars would appear one by one, until the whole sky was covered with them.

There is no better opportunity of enjoying the starry sky in peace than on the pitch-black foredeck of a ship sailing through southern waters. In the balmy night you can stretch out on your back on a tarpaulin, and if you have a torch and a star map, you can quite leisurely fix the eternal figures of the constellations in your memory and identify them. The Milky Way spans the sky above your head like a luminous arch from horizon to horizon. Almost at the zenith, Cygnus flies with its long neck and wings spread wide. Deneb shines on its tail and forms a beautiful triangle together with Vega and Altair.

At first I had some difficulty getting to know my way around near the southern horizon; for when you are near the Equator, Scorpio and Sagittarius shine higher in the sky than where you are used to seeing them in Holland. Recognizing their characteristic figures was made even more difficult last year by Jupiter and

Saturn, which were right in the middle of it all, like intruders, and it took me some time before I had separated these two planets from their environment. However, when you can study the star map in reality night after night, you finally become familiar even with such unusual combinations, and the whole sky becomes a landscape in which you learn to recognize every figure.

It has always irked me as improper that there are still so many people for whom the sky is no more than a mass of random points of light. I do not see why we should recognize a house, a tree or a flower here below and not, for example, the red Arcturus up there in the heavens as it hangs from its constellation Boötes, like a basket hanging from a balloon.

All this has nothing to do with an understanding of astronomy (and even less of astrology!). It is quite possible for a layman in the field of astronomy like myself, to enjoy recognizing all those noble, striking figures, which become all the more real as you get to know them better.

I should like to end this description of the stars with the Pleiades, which I once saw rising up out of the sea. When and where in Holland is the atmosphere ever so free from dust and mist that you can see the stars clearly right down to the horizon? One evening I saw a point of light appearing on the horizon, followed a moment later by another one. I thought they were the lights of a ship sailing by in the distance. But then a third light appeared, and a fourth, and finally there were seven altogether; it was then that I recognized the Pleiades, making for the heavens in full sail, like a ghost ship.

So much for the stars. Now for the moon. But what is there to say about the moon that everyone doesn't know already? We all know her and you certainly don't have to make a sea voyage to see her more clearly than you can in Holland. However, I did have a better chance to marvel at her during those long, lazy warm nights at sea, in more peaceful surroundings than in daily life, and to wonder what she means to us.

I philosophized on this question, lying in my deckchair as she looked down on me like a huge lamp, high above the sea. Then I started to imagine the significance she might have for four different categories of people.

First of all, for the *poet*. How does a poet see the moon? I am not particularly poetically inclined myself, so I apologize in advance to any poets or poetically-minded people present, if I misjudge them.

I imagine that a poet, as a feeling person, projects himself into the moon and that she becomes an attribute of his own self, for a poet often talks and likes to talk about how he experiences things. The quality and the colour of moonlight influence or accentuate his mood. He uses the moon as a symbol, as a means of suggesting a particular mood or indicating a certain atmosphere. Depending on his requirements, he will describe her as 'a blood-red moon' or speak of 'the cool moonlight' or 'the moon's silvery light'. And in

an expression such as 'the astonished face of the moon', she has even become a direct mirror of the human countenance.

Second question: What does the moon mean to an *astronomer*? If he has a scientific approach, he sees her, quite independently from himself as an observer, as an object of study situated in the universe. The object he is interested in is a virtually spherical, dark lump of matter; he wishes to understand her relation to the earth and her significance with regard to the other heavenly bodies, and express these in precise terms and figures. By means of observation and calculation he assembles a host of data, of which he is certain that they accord with reality, or at least as certain as it is possible to be at a given moment in human evolution.

Third question: How does an *indifferent person* see the moon? Of course he knows, or has learned at school, that it is a ball which constantly rotates round the earth, but this means nothing at all to him. It is much too 'ordinary' to get excited about, just as ordinary as a street lamp, only less practical. The moon does not arouse his interest at all; he finds it impossible to marvel at her. In fact he probably rarely marvels at anything. To him it is a disc of light, a round, flat, white cake from which someone occasionally takes a bigger or smaller bite.

Lastly, there are people who would like to use their intellect in a sensitive way. When they look at the moon, they first of all try to experience her solidity. They enjoy and gain satisfaction from testing her spherical shape with their eyes. They love to become engrossed in the transition from light to shadow on her curved surface, preferably during the first and last quarter, when the sun illuminates her from the side. It does not matter much to them to know exactly how many miles separate her from the earth, for it is possible to experience the concept of 'distance' quite strongly without any idea of measurement. In fact one can philosophize endlessly on the concept of 'distance', which, in itself, is incomprehensible.

Closer to home for a moment, and leaving the moon altogether, let us take a look at the enigma of distance.

Actually, I am rather reluctant to offer broad theories about sensory observation while there are a physiologist and two doctors present, but I will take a chance. If I get it wrong, they will have to explain it to me later.

Suppose I am strolling through my garden and I stop by a flowering shrub. With a bit of luck it is possible to perceive the shrub with four of my senses. I can *see* its shape, and the colours of its leaves and flowers; I can *smell* the fragrance; when I stretch out my hand, I can *feel* the leaves and twigs; and finally, I can *hear* these rustling in the wind. However, none of these four methods of perception brings me a step closer to the answer to the question: What is the distance between the shrub and myself?

Let me just return to the moon for a moment. When I was sitting on my ship, marvelling at the distance between the moon and myself to such an extent that it almost frightened me, my gaze travelled towards her, as it were, along a long, straight line: I shot the arrow of my imagination at her. Breathless with wonder, I experienced her silence, her apparent immobility, her perfect equilibrium in space. She became a symbol for me, or, rather, a demonstration of gravity, which is not a boring, cerebral concept, but another living and thrilling incomprehensible phenomenon.

It seems to me that feeling and analysis are not incompatible, and ought to be complementary. You do not have to be a physicist to experience the miracle of gravity, but with the help of the intellect, your awareness of the wonder may be deeper. I do not know if it is true, but I imagine that there are scientists who are plumbing the depths of a mystery rather than seeking the solution to a problem, using the paths of the so-called 'cold' intellect.

The routine of daily life makes it impossible for anyone to remain constantly in a state of innocent openness. Most of the time we are meekly sleepwalking on a treadmill. But now and again it suddenly seems possible to shake off this lethargy. During one of these bright moments it is as though all the things we have had to learn in order to fit into society—sometimes with a great deal of trouble—fall away. We suddenly feel like carefree children playing an absorbing game, with no heaviness, erudite theories or affectations.

For that matter, we do not need the moon to play an absorbing game. The earth itself, our mighty clod of earth, is sometimes sufficient for our imagination.

I believe that people nowadays vilify the 'good name' of the earth more than they used to do. They travel around her in their irritating aeroplanes and insult her by suggesting that she is smaller than she used to be. 'The world has become small' is the stupid, arrogant phrase of the businessman sitting in his aeroplane. He flies so high above the clouds that he sees and experiences nothing. In Montreal he gets into a sort of hollow cigar, sits down in an armchair, and as he is shot into the air like a projectile and hurtled forward by roaring jet engines above the invisible sea, he is bored to death if he does not eat or sleep. Less than seven hours later they put him back down on the ground at Schiphol. Seven hours is still far too long for this journey, even though you have crossed the whole Atlantic Ocean. It is all a waste of time for someone who is busy. I think it's about time KLM started flying a bit faster.

Sometimes, just before I fall asleep at night, I have a beautiful vision. In my imagination I see the earth floating like an enormous orange, stately and still, in the pure emptiness surrounding her. I see her slowly rotating, always lit up and warmed on one side by her mother, the sun. Ribbons and shreds of cloud float around her, and between these the seas and the multi-coloured continents, with their humid plains and snowy mountaintops, sparkle and shimmer. And I see the hot, yellow deserts and the frozen polar icecaps.

I am so far removed from the beautiful earth that the people scurrying around in their cities are of course no longer visible. Whether this is such a good thing as it seems to be at the time is open to question. But it is a fact that my vision is so beautiful, so restful and so full of peace that I usually fall asleep soon afterwards.

That is why this also seems to be the right moment to end my story, at least for today.

Opposite page: In 1960 Escher designed this tiled façade for the hall of a school in The Hague. It was executed in concrete in two colours

Page 116: *Möbius Strip I*; woodcut in four colours, March 1961 (cat. no. 437)

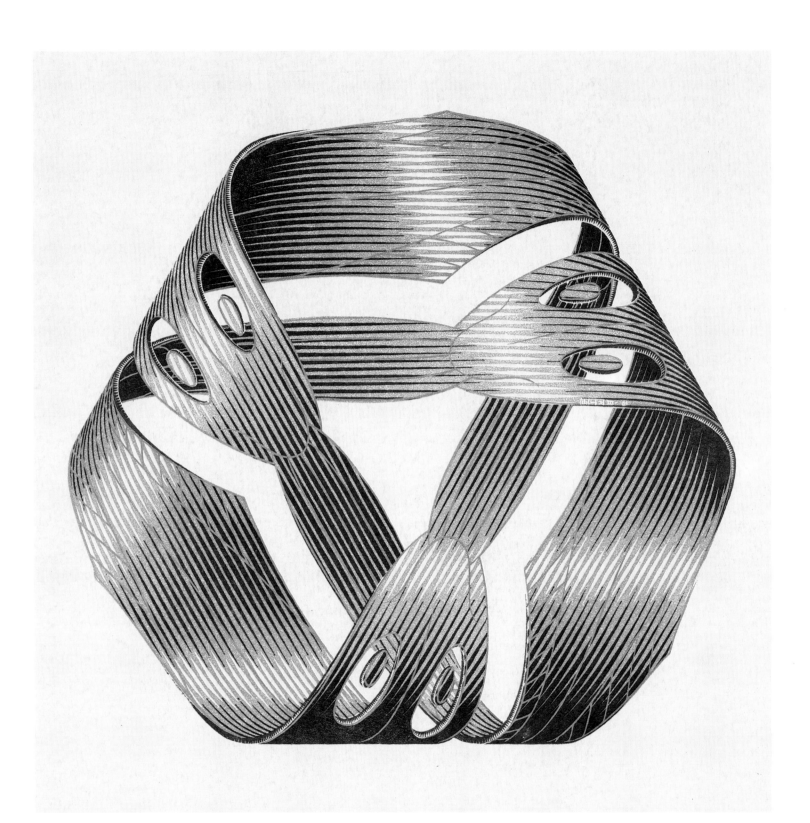

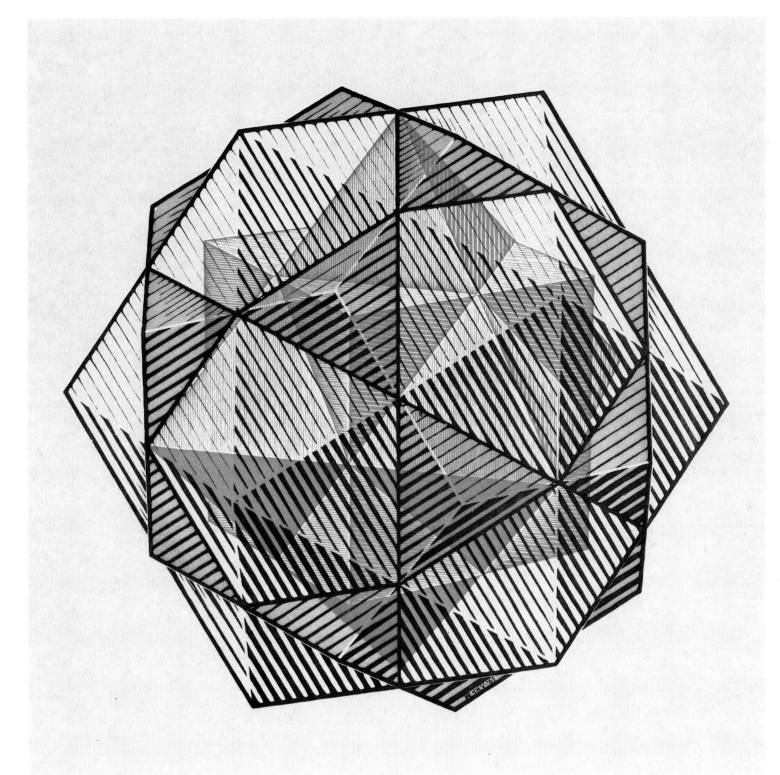

The Final Years   1961–1972

During the very successful year 1960 Escher sold a large number of prints, including some to the distinguished collector Lessing J. Rosenwald, of Jenkintown, Pennsylvania. He also made countless new friends, among them Professor Caroline H. MacGillavry, mentioned above, who was so impressed by Escher's studies for the division of the plane that she set out to have them published under the auspices of the International Union of Crystallography. Escher was very enthusiastic, for, as he wrote to her on 2 January 1961, 'it would crown this work, which I consider to be basically more important than my graphic prints, which are aimed at a non-specialized public'. In 1965 Professor MacGillavry's efforts bore fruit in the publication of her book *Symmetry Aspects of M. C. Escher's Periodic Drawings*.

Among his many New Year's letters in 1961 there was one from Professor von Hippel, a leading scholar and head of a department at MIT, where Loeb was also working. Since his visit to Cambridge, Massachusetts, Escher had been calling Loeb by his Christian name, Arthur. He had become a close friend of Loeb and his wife, Lotje, and corresponded regularly with them. Escher occasionally made profitable use of Loeb's many contacts, for example, when a new art dealer appeared on the scene.

Baarn, 21 February 1961: 'How's life with you? I heard about your tremendously severe winter and heavy snow on the East Coast of the US. Are you having that too? Our winter has been exceptionally mild and wet.

'Do you mind my asking you for some information about Mr Paul Schuster? He wrote to me at the beginning of the month about his art gallery and the loss of his entire collection of paintings and prints in a fire last December. As part of his plan to build up a business again by purchasing new works, he asked me for prices and gave you as a reference, as well as von Hippel and Fletcher.

'I sent him a list of prices (which I increased recently or I would have no time left at all for doing any new work, and from which he won't get any reduction, so he's free to determine his own profit margin). However, I didn't think it would all happen as quickly as it has. Today I received a second letter, with an order for ten prints. . . .

'I've also been corresponding, with some pleasure, with Martin Gardner, a columnist for the *Scientific American* (and author of some very interesting notes on Lewis Carroll's *Alice* books, which he recently edited). He is a friend of H. S. M. Coxeter in Toronto (whom I have a lot to thank for) and is publishing an article in the April edition of the magazine about the latter's work as a mathematician. It is illustrated with two of my symmetrical divisions of the plane, one of which is on the cover, in colour. All this just fell into my lap! (And then I have the nerve to complain about lack of time for new work, because of all the correspondence.)'

Loeb replied that Schuster had a good reputation, and that Escher had meanwhile become so popular that the ten prints would no doubt be sold very quickly.

Escher also continued to correspond regularly with George and Corrie.

Baarn, 26 February 1961: 'It surprises me that you've not had much snow, after all the stories about the East Coast of the US. I had a nice, chatty letter from the two Cassidy sisters, who shared my table on the *Toscanelli* and who are interested in my exhibition in Philadelphia at the Art Alliance. They managed to get there with much difficulty, because of the heavy snowfalls. "It is the worst winter in more than seventy-five years. We have already had about fifty inches of snow. Transportation has been at a standstill for many days, and heaven only knows when it will return to normal," they wrote to me on 9 February.

'Apparently I've not yet written to you about this exhibition. Rosenwald arranged it all for me. It involves no worries for me at all and can only lead to sales. All the prints exhibited, about forty of them, belong to R., so he has to deal with all the fuss. Or rather, his secretaries, for he is "quite famous not only as an art patron but also as a philanthropist; we laughed when you asked if we knew his name," as the Cassidy sisters wrote.

'My busy correspondence is finally decreasing, so I am free to do more work on the Möbius strip [cat. no. 437]. However, three

Page 117: Four Regular Solids; woodcut in three colours, May 1961 (cat. no. 438)

Opposite page: *Square Limit*; woodcut in two colours, April 1964 (cat. no. 443)

119

days ago Arthur arrived quite unexpectedly and we are travelling to Geneva with him by K L M next Wednesday. His car will be waiting at the airport to take us on to Barboleusaz. [Arthur had rented a chalet in the Swiss hamlet of La Barboleusaz.] It should be a pleasant and comfortable journey with just the three of us. He's now busy packing large trunks, because he's going to spend a few years in a flat in Lausanne working for his doctorate.

'Jan is doing a course at the Berlitz School in Lausanne. It seems to be the best way of learning reasonable French in a short period. [Jan was also going to study geology in Lausanne.] . . .

'Fiet [de Willebois] is dying. I heard that she has cancer and there is nothing that can be done. . . . I am deeply affected, for she is such a dear old friend, and her courage and cheerfulness have always seemed so wonderful to me. . . .

'Every now and then I write a few lines for the story of my voyage on the *Toscanelli*. . . . I'm relating my enjoyment as a freighter passenger in general. It's the first time I've done this.'

Baarn, 26 March 1961: 'The day after we came back from Switzerland I heard that Fiet had died. . . . Her death leaves me with a terrible sense of emptiness. I must have loved her very much, as I have always known, more or less. . . .

'I've been busy "talking" since coming home, but I'm beginning to feel sick of all that gabbling about my work. . . .

'One is never really satisfied. The uselessness, hollowness, impotence at the end of it all, feeling flattered, hating yourself when you feel like a lemon squeezed dry. I've always known that silence is golden and speech is lead, yet I'm talking more and more.

'All the birds are chasing each other in our garden. The long-tailed tits are hanging upside-down from the weeping willow, which is full of buds, fat enough to burst. The woodpeckers are laughing in every corner of the wood.'

In June and July 1961 Escher went on a boat trip in the Mediterranean with Paul Keller; it was to be his last. Jetta stayed in Switzerland during that time. Back home in Baarn, Escher found a big pile of mail waiting for him. It included an article by the eminent art historian E. H. Gombrich.

Baarn, 30 July 1961: 'I am much pleased with an article by a certain Professor E. H. Gombrich, an art historian at the University of London, in *The Saturday Evening Post* of 29 July 1961, entitled "How to Read a Painting (Adventures of the Mind)". After an introduction in which he mentions several well-known artists, he explains at great length how you should look at my prints, using three reproductions by way of illustration. He seems to be impressed by my work, for he goes on about it for more than three columns, though he does have some criticism of its (possible) aesthetic value. And the publishers actually paid a hundred and forty dollars reproduction rights for those three simple prints! This, too, could lead to greater things. And so I'm

afraid that I'll never get away from all the correspondence and the printing of more copies of old prints. Perhaps this is just as well—for all I know I may have been bled dry already and have nothing left to say. Perhaps I'll never do any more new work that's worthwhile.'

Baarn, 3 November 1961: 'On the radio I heard that the Nobel Prize for Chemistry went to Melvin Calvin, who visited me a few years ago and is wildly enthusiastic about my print *Verbum*; at the time . . . he couldn't afford the relatively low price, but recently he bought one of the latest prints for two hundred and fifty dollars. It's rather nice, that he just couldn't put it out of his mind.'

NEW PLANS

In mid-October 1961 Escher received an invitation from Professor von Hippel to lecture again in Cambridge, Massachusetts, in the autumn of 1962. There was also to be an exhibition of his prints. Escher readily agreed; as in 1960, he wanted to combine the trip with a visit to George and Corrie in Canada. While in the United States, he would again stay with Arthur and Lotje Loeb, his regular correspondents.

Baarn, 5 January 1962: 'Do you know Professor Herbert L. Beckwith, Director of Exhibitions at MIT? Von Hippel has engaged his services for my exhibition next autumn. Beckwith recently wrote me a nice letter: they would be pleased (he says) to exhibit my bits and pieces from 10 September to 2 October 1962. . . .

'Do you also happen to know Professor Cyril Stanley Smith, of the Department of Humanities at MIT? . . . He bought my thirteen-foot-long print *Metamorphosis*. So did von Hippel, for that matter.

'Just now, as I was writing this letter, the post brought me a copy of *Elementary Particles* by Chen Ning Yang. He asked me a while ago if he might reproduce my "horsemen" in it. They are also shown on the cover. Those horsemen are riding all over the world, and all sorts of very learned minds seem to see something in them, though what it is, I can't for the life of me understand. It's a pity, though I do feel flattered and honoured, and in the meantime I bumble calmly on, if they leave me enough time. Fortunately I have a new print in my head at the moment, which wants to get out. Title: *Red Ants*. I'm burning to tell you more about it, but my lips are sealed—with superstition.'

Apart from writing letters and reprinting old prints, Escher spent a great deal of time working on new commissions, among them a design for a pillar in the new building of the Ministry of Transport in Haarlem, and reading Pepys' *Diaries*, *The Wind in the Willows*, and a number of works by Teilhard de Chardin. He was so enthusiastic about these books that he decided to sent them to George and Corrie.

Baarn, 4 February 1962: 'So, with Pepys III, you will get a whole lot. I don't think I'll even wait for your reply, for you're short of new books anyway, aren't you?...

'We're all just like squirrels. The other day I spied on one with my binoculars for over an hour. The little creature seemed to be a bundle of nerves, building a nest in the hollow of a knotted tree in the middle of winter, of all times. He scampered to and fro, constantly gnawing off twigs to take to his nest. Most of the time he would find them quite a way off, and would then have to pull them to the unfinished nest by a long, tiring route, often holding a long branch between his teeth, so that it became stuck again and again. Then he would have to pull it free, go back and find a better way. Trying to arrange all that stuff into the nest, without a moment's rest for a whole hour, he worked like an obsessed madman, seemingly without any other thought. Until suddenly the obsession disappeared without a trace. Since that day, two weeks ago, I have never seen him so much as look round at his nest; sometimes he goes quite near, but he doesn't see it or smell it, it no longer seems to exist for him....

'One stage removed, I am just the same. I too work on something like a madman for a while, as though my life and my happiness depend on it. A year later I've forgotten all about it and I can't for a moment remember what it was that so fascinated me.

'We are all pieces of Evolution (to quote Teilhard), and if he's right, this evolution will end in millions of years at the mysterious "point Oméga".'

Baarn, 18 February 1962: 'Professor von Hippel, the "big man" of the MIT Insulation Research Department, overwhelms me with kindness. Loeb calls him "the patriarch".... He is now buying several very expensive prints, which are virtually sold out....

'Mickelson has also gone overboard again buying prints. Sometimes he is so impetuous that I cross my fingers, but up to now he pays regularly. Then there is Mr Roosevelt, who also continues to show interest. His latest idea is to have my beechwood sphere with twelve fish copied on a reduced scale in ivory, by a Japanese netsuke sculptor. To give me confidence in the latter's skill, he sent me photographs of amazing examples of small sculptures. If I give my permission for the reproduction, I'll be rewarded with one of the only two copies that are to be made. They'll be spheres with a diameter of about two inches. Naturally I'm looking forward to it tremendously!'

A TRIP MISFIRES

Among the many orders was one for a copy of the print *Day and Night* which von Hippel wished to give to his friend Niels Bohr.

The plans for the second American trip became increasingly detailed and extensive, but despite all the extra work involved, Escher looked forward to it enormously. However, at the end of April he was suddenly admitted to hospital for a serious operation, and on his behalf Arthur had to cancel all the arrangements that had been made. He would need a long time to recuperate and never fully recovered physically.

At the end of September he wrote to his friends Arthur and Lotje Loeb.

Baarn, 23 September 1962: 'Thank you very much for your kind letter of 11 September. My diary, too, is full of the many pleasant engagements that I should have enjoyed in Canada and the United States during these months: staying with you, the exhibition and lecture for the MIT, a visit to von Hippel's log cabin in the White Mountains, an exhibition in Middletown, Conn., etc. It all misfired, but I hope it will be possible another year.

'It's just as well I cancelled the whole thing in time, before I even knew how terribly long this illness would continue. True, I have been home now for three and a half weeks, but the first time I was discharged from hospital, at the end of July, I was readmitted only a week later for another operation on my stomach—not as serious as the first, but nevertheless it took three hours to remove a large number of fistulas, as they call the thin channels which caused the inflammation and prevented the wound from healing. Now, at last, things have improved a lot, at least as far as surgical matters are concerned: the wound seems to have definitely closed and I no longer have to wear a bandage. However, becoming strong and fit again leaves much to be desired: I feel as weak as a kitten and lie dozing on the sofa for hours on end every day. I'm writing this letter sitting on a straight-backed chair, by way of daily training; for next week I'll have to stand the test of attending the wedding of my son Arthur in Wassenaar....

'So far, nothing has come of working on new prints like in the good old days, nor of reprinting old ones—which is becoming very urgent. Much too tiring. It's a strange feeling to be so weak when you've been healthy almost all your life, as I have.'

Escher attended the wedding without difficulty and even made a speech. He was planning to go to Canada the following year, although he was often not at all sure that he would be able to make it.

Baarn, 30 October 1962: 'I'm still as skinny as a rake, with no appetite at all, despite Mother's efforts to cook delicious meals for me. It's strange suddenly to become such a worn-out old man.

'I must stop moaning and be happy with the satisfaction I get from my work....

'However, my greatest satisfaction came from the decision of the International Union of Crystallography to publish my coloured regular divisions of the plane for students of crystallography. They agreed unanimously at the last international conference in Munich. My friend MacGillavry is coming soon to make the final selection. It took them three years to arrive at this decision, but the authorities are spread over the whole world.

'And now, in the near future, I see the possibility of resuming my free work at last. How wonderful it would be to make a new print!'

Baarn, 16 December 1962: 'Slowly the life of the old couple on the Van Heemstralaan is getting back to normal. I work as much as I can and so does Mother. A very self-centred existence: I begrudge almost every minute that is not spent making woodcuts, eating or resting. . . .

'We'll probably come and stay in the autumn. I still feel so unsure of myself (close to death, you might say, as I am constantly reminded of that damned carcass) that I dare not move far away from the safe refuge of the hospital in Baarn this spring.'

Baarn, 17 February 1963: 'It was wonderful in Groningen. I was cosseted and pampered in the comfortable house of my friends the Dekkings, and in the evening at least three hundred and fifty people came to see my slides, despite mud and snow. How friendly and interested the people of Groningen are, or at least the members of the Physics Society. It all went very well, also thanks to Arthur's new slides (mostly of old prints). Afterwards there were long discussions in the board room, and I sat and listened with a sense of inexpressible gratitude that I was still alive.

'My old friend Jan Willebois is also getting back on his feet. He must be closer to me than I had realized for years, and it's a curious thought that we looked so deep into the eyes of Death more or less at the same time, and are still doing so.

'The visit to Groningen has given me hope for the future, and next week I'll be going to Amsterdam twice: for a meeting of the board of De Grafische (the first time in a year) and to celebrate the birthday of my friend Bas Kist. It's madness to go really, but they insist, so I shall have to. This wild behaviour takes its toll later on and it will take two days for me to "recover".

'Meanwhile I really must make some proofs of my *Red Ants* [cat. no. 441]. Who knows how they will turn out?'

OLD FRIENDS DIE
At the beginning of April 1963 Escher received word from the United States that his first American agent, Charles Alldredge, had died on 18 March after a long illness. Escher himself was feeling gradually better, but Jan de Willebois continued to be very ill, as Escher wrote to George and Corrie.

Baarn, 14 April 1963: 'He keeps getting close to death and then struggles back to life a little. . . . How many months have his wife and daughter been nursing him now? The tragedies in the lives of so many of my friends affect me more deeply than they used to.

'Now that I've finished the *Red Ants*, I'm working on reviewing the forty regular divisions of the plane which will be reproduced in the crystallography publication. It's quite a job and strangely enjoyable; "strange" because there's no creativity involved. It's a

laborious chewing over of drawings made years ago. It must be the rhythm which fascinates me so much. But there are some new ones too: MacGillavry pointed out that a few systems are missing and for these I invent new birds, fish or reptiles. The nightmare of doddery old age (if that is to be my lot) is softened by the hope that I'll be able to continue making new divisions of the plane—for ever and ever.

'Some of the people I correspond with from the Bell Laboratories have asked me to come and lecture to them. So you see I'm thinking ahead to the autumn of 1964.'

It was decided that Escher would not travel to Canada in 1963 but would spend the summer holidays in La Barboleusaz with his children, including those from Canada.

On 24 September, shortly after his return from Switzerland, his old friend Jan de Willebois died. Escher himself was getting stronger. He was making many new copies of old prints and gave a number of lectures. Whenever he fell into a sombre mood, he would try to exorcize it through work.

Baarn, 16 November 1963: 'When I think of old age (obviously because of my own future and Mother's) I become very sombre. Getting weaker, with reduced capacity for work—it's dreadful. Therefore I'm trying to do as much as possible at the moment; and as I'm constantly being asked for copies of my prints, I go on printing. There are always people coming to see me, including many Americans. I've put up all my prices but it doesn't seem to make much difference. Meanwhile I am very slowly getting used to my physical infirmity and it seems as though my intestines are getting better and also getting used to the purges of strong medicines. There shouldn't be any time left over for worrying; and for the last few weeks there hasn't been. I've often told you: the most difficult thing of all is contentment and acceptance.'

Baarn, 5 January 1964: 'I too have to admit, whether I like it or not, that I feel much better. As a result, the plans for next autumn are becoming increasingly complicated: in an optimistic mood I decided in principle that I would go on tour through the US from Canada after all, because I have had six invitations to give lectures. . . . I must therefore soon start intensive correspondence to organize everything. Perhaps nothing will come of it at all, and that wouldn't matter, since it's all so very tiring and I don't even know whether I'll be able to cope at that time.'

Escher did start his correspondence and an impressive series of events was arranged. He was also working on a new print, as he wrote (in English) to Coxeter.

Baarn, 25 March 1964: 'Actually I am busy with a new woodcut, filled with fish-figures, getting smaller and smaller infinitely from the centre towards the edges and having the shape of a square. So

its title could be "square limit". I fear that it will be far less
interesting, seen from your theoretical point of view, than my
former Circle limit-prints, but from my own practical point of
view, it is at least one first solution of a problem which engaged me
since long. As soon as I am ready with this work (in a month
perhaps), I shall send you a copy.'

Escher wrote to George and Corrie that his half-brother Eddy was
in a very bad way.

Baarn, 23 May 1964: 'Uncle George and I have had another talk
with the neurologist who is treating Uncle Eddy. He explained his
hopeless condition, so we now understand it a bit better. . . .
  'I'm going to post this letter and then go for a walk in the
woods. Yesterday at about six o'clock in the evening I was in the
"tulip-tree woods" and two song thrushes were well and truly
singing at the tops of their voices. I stood by and listened,
speechless with wonder. What a duet! The wild duck trailing long
lines of ducklings have been and gone, but the tame geese from
Castle Groeneveld still come and stand round me, honking loudly
and pulling at my trouser-legs when I happen to have some bread
with me. These are my happiest moments. But the foliage is getting
thicker and the first weeks of spring have already passed. All those
dark leaves have a charm of their own, though. Actually the wood
is always beautiful in every season, provided that you aren't too
tired. Strange, incomprehensible, cruel and beautiful world.'

Baarn, 5 July 1964: 'On the train to Utrecht I was suddenly
overwhelmed and enormously moved by a sky full of clouds at
different levels. I experienced a sense of space and three-
dimensionality such as I'd not experienced for a long time. It's
possible to become suddenly aware of these things, even in an
overpopulated country like Holland. Provided that you are
looking up, you'll suddenly see that timeless and unbounded
eternity. Do you think it silly, or can you imagine what I mean?'

On 1 October Escher left for Canada with Jetta, bravely looking
forward to the busy programme ahead. However, shortly after
their arrival he fell ill again and had to be admitted to a hospital in
Toronto for another operation. Once again, all the arrangements
for lectures and exhibitions had to be cancelled. This time he was
able to leave the hospital fairly quickly. At the beginning of
November they were back in Holland and Escher picked up his
activities straight away, as his letters to Canada show.

Baarn, 14 November 1964: 'We're both very well; I sometimes
hear Mother humming and I'm terribly busy myself. . . . The only
unfortunate thing is the increasing attention my body demands
every day, but apart from that, I definitely feel much better than I
did before MacDonald pricked a hole in my stomach. . . . Perhaps
I should go for a check-up but at the moment I'm not planning to.

What an obstinate affair life is, and the lust for life. You can think about death as much as you like, but it doesn't get you any further, and you go on with your daily activities, no matter how stupid and unimportant they may be....

'I've just paid a visit to Jan Klijn; it was pleasant and comforting (although I don't need that) to the extent that MacDonald's report doesn't give any indication that he found dangerous growths. Something is growing in there, but it is relatively harmless . . . as far as they could see. (Nevertheless, MacD. told me that he thought it really was cancer, and from Klijn too I get the feeling that he suspects it.) He thinks I am quite right to stay out of the doctor's way; make sure that everything continues "running smoothly" and don't take notice of anything else. When it hurts I'll obviously start screaming anyway.

'I am sending you *The Wallet of Kai Lung* by Ernest Bramah, which I enjoyed very much: the humour is curious and mannered, quasi-Chinese, though it's actually typically European and over-civilized.'

CONCERT
Baarn, 13 December 1964: 'It's stormy and raining. Since the day we came home from Canada, when it was two degrees below zero, it's been very mild. Yesterday evening I went up to the Concertgebouw in Amsterdam with my friends the Klijns, in their car, through buffeting wind and rain. We heard the Dutch String Quartet playing Beethoven, Schubert and Mendelssohn. It was the first of a series of five concerts to which they'll take me this winter. I thoroughly enjoyed the live music, and the old-fashioned atmosphere of a concert was wonderful, though it was rather tiring. It seems that I still belong in that strange hustle and bustle of all those hungry music-lovers. They played Opus 132 by Beethoven, which he completed two years before his death, when he was fifty-five. This quartet is difficult to understand, full of unexpected turns and—most probably—very deep thoughts. At times I was fascinated, and the rest of the time I simply enjoyed that curious oval room with its stucco mouldings, full of attentive people, and the four musicians trying so hard to make the music as perfect as possible. How is it possible, in an age so full of canned music, that there is still so much attention for first-hand, direct music, that on a set date, at half past eight in the evening, four musicians can suddenly muster the concentration that enraptures a room full of people? Beads of perspiration stood on their foreheads; they seemed to be in a trance and, damn it, they managed to do it again. What happened there was a true miracle. Nap de Klijn and Carel van Leeuwen Boomkamp and the old, worn-out Paul Godwin with his beautiful viola. It's simply incredible; a hundred and fifty years later, old Beethoven must be turning in his grave with all his problems, his deafness, his loneliness and his grief.

'So you see, it did something for me—that first concert in I don't know how many years. An evening like that is really fascinating

from beginning to end. So are the talks in the interval with people you haven't seen for ages, old concert fans, aficionados who have come to dream to music for an evening, and a lot of young people for whom Schubert and Mendelssohn may be a new experience. Despite all the snobbery and showiness, there's so much enjoyment in an evening like that. It's such a shame that Mother cannot conquer her loneliness and share the experience with me.'

CULTURAL PRIZE
Baarn, 14 February 1965: 'There are some tiring days ahead. The municipality of Hilversum have awarded me their annual cultural prize and it's being presented to me with a lot of pomp and circumstance on 5 March.... What pleased me even more was that I was allowed to choose who would play the accompanying music. Without a moment's hesitation, I chose Janny van Wering to play her harpsichord. She is actually willing to carry out my dearest wish and play the twenty-fifth of the Goldberg Variations for me—in my opinion, the most beautiful of them all. She will be playing three or four times during the event, nothing but Bach, all at my request! The actual prize is nothing to me, compared with all this....

'That's on 5 March. On the ninth I'm flying to Paris, ten minutes before Mother flies to Copenhagen. Thirty of my prints are being exhibited for a month at the Institute [Institut Néerlandais] and on the eleventh I'll give my lecture. On the thirteenth I'm flying to Copenhagen as well.... We'll be back home on 17 or 18 March.'

In his speech of acceptance of the Hilversum prize, Escher again discussed the nature of his prints, and questioned the definition of 'art'.

'In my prints I try to show that we live in a beautiful and orderly world and not in a chaos without norms, as we sometimes seem to.

'My subjects are also often playful. I cannot help mocking all our unwavering certainties. It is, for example, great fun deliberately to confuse two and three dimensions, the plane and space, or to poke fun at gravity.

'Are you sure that a floor cannot also be a ceiling?

'Are you absolutely certain that you go up when you walk up a staircase?

'Can you be definite that it is impossible to eat your cake and have it?

'I ask these seemingly crazy questions first of all of myself (for I am my own first viewer) and then of others who are so good as to come and see my work. It's pleasing to realize that quite a few people enjoy this sort of playfulness and that they are not afraid to look at the relative nature of rock-hard reality.

'Above all, I am happy about the contact and friendship of mathematicians that resulted from it all. They have often given me new ideas, and sometimes there even is an interaction between us. How playful they can be, those learned ladies and gentlemen!

'To tell you the truth, I am rather perplexed about the concept of "art". What one person considers to be "art" is often not "art" to another. "Beautiful" and "ugly" are old-fashioned concepts which are seldom applied these days; perhaps justifiably, who knows? Something repulsive, which gives you a moral hangover, and hurts your ears or eyes, may well be art.

'Only "kitsch" is not art—we're all agreed about that. Indeed, but what is "kitsch"? If only I knew!

'This emotional valuation is too subjective and too vague for me. If I am not mistaken, the words "art" and "artist" did not exist during the Renaissance and before: there were simply architects, sculptors and painters, practising a trade.

'Print-making is another of these honest trades, and I consider it a privilege to be a member of the Guild of Graphic Artists. Using a gouge, engraving with a burin in an absolutely smooth block of polished wood, is not something to pride yourself on—it's simply nice work. Only as you get older, it's slower and more difficult, and the chips don't fly around the workroom quite so wildly as they used to.

'Thus I am a graphic artist heart and soul, though I find the term "artist" rather embarrassing.'

Baarn, 7 March 1965: 'Meanwhile life is crumbling away around us. Another dear old friend died suddenly: old Andréa, aged seventy-nine. He fell over in his hall and died on the spot. He'd just printed four lithographs for me, two hundred and sixty prints altogether. He'd been working on these for some months, for it was very slow work and there was no rush.'

FLOCON
Baarn, 25 April 1965: 'Did I mention my enthusiasm about a topological knot which my *frère spirituel* Albert Flocon included in his book of engravings—though it's not well enough done? (By the way, what is topology? It's not in my dictionary of unusual words; I only know that *topo* means place, and of course I know "topography". Flocon introduced me when I gave my lecture in Paris and presented me with that extremely curious book of his. Now he's written an article about my work in *Jardin des Arts*. Perhaps it will be published one day.) A thick knot-without-end, in a cable for instance, which displays the three co-ordinates in a most interesting way. I should definitely like to make a print of this, since I appear to see more in it than he does. There's a large painting in his studio—he paints as well as engraves, and teaches at the Académie des Beaux-Arts—of one of my perspective tricks, with the caption: "Hommage à M.C. Escher." So now I should do a print of his (?) knot as a homage to Albert Flocon. I hope I manage to organize a lecture and an exhibition for him in the Maison Descartes in Amsterdam, but my letter to the director of that institute remains unanswered and I fear that there will be too little interest among French-minded Amsterdammers for such an expert in spherical perspective.'

Baarn, 13 June 1965: 'Oh dear, that knot! In the evening I sometimes feel dizzy with the effort. Can you imagine how difficult it is? I've finally arrived at a relatively definite plan: three pictures, together in one coloured woodcut, with a square, a cruciform and a circular profile of the sausage. A tour-de-force of perspective. Am I so stupid that it seems so difficult? Perhaps I'm suffering from old age. It's strange that people often think I'm so "clever".'

Baarn, 8 August 1965: 'At last our journey has been booked. The week of 12–18 September was already completely booked up. Sold out that long in advance! So I have had to book for Tuesday 21 September. Arrival in Toronto will be at the same time as last year, for nothing has changed between Schiphol and Montreal. We can stay until the evening of Monday 11 October....

'The book *Symmetry Aspects...* has been published. It looks very elegant but I was a bit disappointed nevertheless, after looking forward to it so much.'

Baarn, 7 September 1965: 'I feel as though I have never been so busy as now; everyone seems to have gone mad; there's no end to the orders, and of course the effect on me is writing, writing, printing, printing. Paris has also started now: a dealer in prints [Prouté], *"le plus sérieux de Paris"*, according to my friend Flocon, ordered six. I'm constantly being visited by Americans and keep having to send them prints. So at present there is no chance of studying the knot again.... Still, I am more determined than ever to carry it out; for the first coloured woodcut, which I consider to be inadequately executed [cat. no. 444], was remarkably successful.'

Baarn, 16 January 1966: 'This month I have to give three lectures, two of which within the next week. Thus I follow Mussolini's advice: *vivere pericolosamente*, for these days I can never be quite sure I won't suddenly spring a leak. Still, if you don't take a few chances, you might just as well stay in bed. I look at people differently nowadays. In the packed concert hall last night, for example: how many of those apparently unconcerned music-lovers might be in circumstances like my own?'

Baarn, 30 January 1966: 'Yesterday I spent a large part of the day answering a letter from Martin Gardner, who intends to devote one of his *Scientific American* columns to me this spring. I find it a commendable intention not to be despised, and I had to write him a detailed letter, for the fellow is ever so friendly. He's going to choose the necessary illustrations at Cornelius Roosevelt's in Washington. R. has about eighty of my prints and is always immediately prepared to loan them to anyone who wants them.'

Baarn, 24 April 1966: 'I'm planning our itinerary.... Isn't more than a month a bit much for you? Don't you think I might get bored and turn into an undesirable guest if I'm idle for a whole month?

'As far as that consideration goes, I've had a wonderful idea—I'll simply bring some work along with me! A week ago I started work on a project that has been in my head for over a year—a "Möbius knot", of the cruciform-profile type, top left in the first "Knot" print....

'I'm working as if on fire, and can't get over the joy of it, for there's nothing more wonderful than turning a vision into reality. But I'm also working in a rage and gnashing my teeth, for there's nothing more irritating than constantly being disturbed by Americans who are either coming or going, by more and more correspondence, and by always being handicapped by my health, which makes such daily demands on me. But anyway, at least I've made a start! I've been mulling it over in my mind for a whole year and at last I think I've found a satisfactory solution to the problem.'

Baarn, 11 September 1966: 'One of these days two people from *The Observer* will visit me, a science correspondent and an art critic, who wish to write about me in their illustrious paper. I also received official notification from the Gemeentemuseum in The Hague about a large retrospective exhibition in 1968.... For the first time, a lot of early sketches and drawings will also be shown.'

Baarn, 29 January 1967: 'This will be just a short letter, because two Americans are arriving at eleven o'clock. Life rushes on like a young horse out of control and I puff alongside trying to keep up. It's all very tiring....

I've had a few problems again, both with my stomach and with sleeping. Now and then I feel I've had quite enough of a life that's become a constant fight. If not fighting people, then fighting circumstances; I never seem to get away from it. Always rigid and tense. Lying lazily on the pulsing body of a freighter, that's the real thing, but for me it's over forever.'

AN EXTRA LONG METAMORPHOSIS
Baarn, 11 June 1967: 'The annoying thing is that my head cannot cope at all with these affairs [financial arrangements] because I'm thinking about a very attractive commission which the Post Office might offer me.... A new and enormous post office in The Hague has an empty wall above the counters, about a hundred and fifty feet long. This is to be decorated with a sort of frieze about five feet high. The aesthetic consultant of the Post Office would like to use my old *Metamorphosis*, photographically enlarged and then painted onto the wall (not by me!—by a skilled craftsman). However, my *Metamorphosis* is eight inches high and thirteen feet long. Thus, for a height of five feet, the length is only a hundred feet. I therefore have to add an extra fifty feet—that is, add or insert six feet of new metamorphoses to the original woodcut strip. That is perfectly possible, but it's quite a job. I'm curious to see whether it'll turn out as I can visualize it now, vaguely, in my mind's eye.'

Baarn, 19 May 1968: 'The other day I was again in the post office in The Hague. They've not got very far, but the young painter's apprentice (he's twenty-one) is doing it extremely well and with a great deal of enjoyment. It'll take another six months before it's completed.

'The opening of the exhibition is very soon. It will take place on the evening of 7 June, for an invited public. I'm expected to give a short lecture....

'On Sunday the ninth Roosevelt is coming to dinner; it may be rather nice with all those people, just as it was good to have dinner with von Hippel recently....

'It's a great relief to me that, between other matters, I've also been able to design the motifs for the two pillars at the new school in Baarn. The actual-size drawings of the tiles to be fired by De Porceleyne Fles are to be sent tomorrow.'

Baarn, 13 June 1968: 'The opening [of the exhibition in The Hague] was a great success (if I may say so). The biggest hall available in the museum, the lecture hall which seats three hundred and twenty, was packed, and more than a hundred people who couldn't get in were standing outside. Both directors (of the museum and the printroom) made speeches, then I put on my own airs and graces, as well as giving a short lecture with slides, which was quite successful. I felt completely at ease, and it all took just over an hour....

'Roosevelt's visit was great fun!... Of course he bought a dozen old prints and ordered forty copies of the catalogue to give to friends and other interested people in the US.'

LIVING ON HIS OWN
At the end of 1968 Jetta left Baarn; she could bear it there no longer and went to Switzerland, where her son Jan took care of her. Escher now lived on his own with a housekeeper.

Baarn, 12 January 1969: 'My life without Mother goes peacefully on. Hans Taets [the housekeeper] looks after me very well (at my suggestion we've been on Christian-name terms since the beginning of the year—she finds it difficult, I do not at all). It's peaceful to the extent that I try to do all the work required of me as well as I can without overtiring myself. This is not easy, because printing woodcuts is a matter of working out a daily quota,

Opposite page: Escher keeping his records, 1963

Page 128: *Knots*; woodcut in three colours, August 1965 (cat. no. 444)

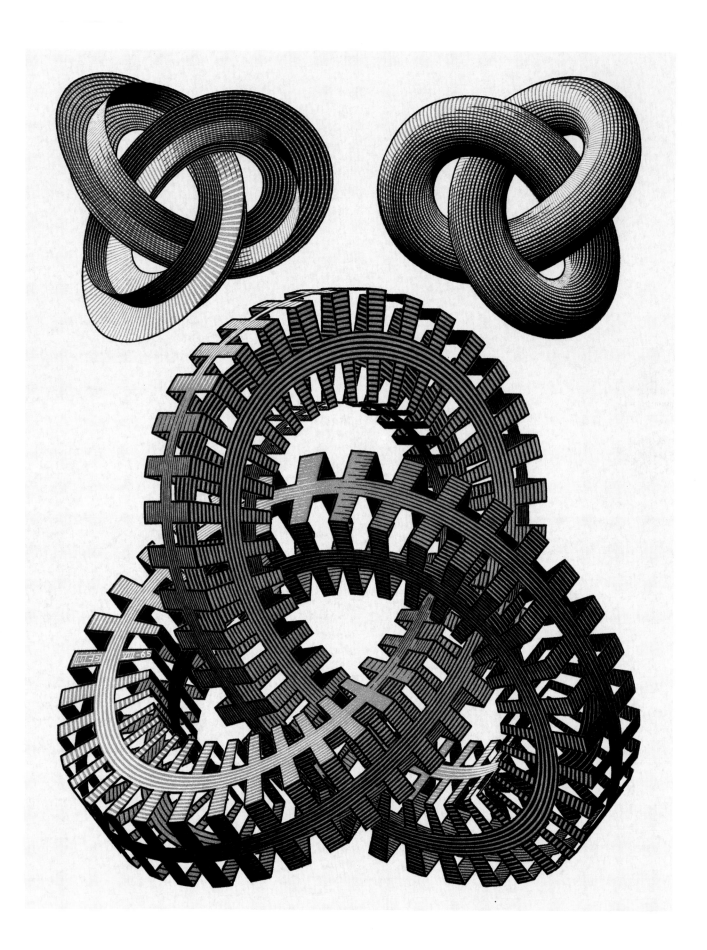

making up the correct amount of printing-ink, etc. Each time I pick up an old block, often a year or even two years after the last printing, it's a dicey business, because in most cases I've forgotten the special difficulties and tricks inherent in that particular problem. But these problems, or, rather, the satisfaction you get from realizing that it does work again, are the main spice of my life at present.'

Baarn, 16 March 1969: 'I'll quickly run through the Sunday morning gossip; it's quite late already and at one o'clock the Klijns are picking me up to go to the last-but-one concert of the season in Amsterdam, together with Hans Taets. I do so hope that they will be prepared to take tickets again next season—or, rather, that they will allow me to take tickets for them, and I may go with them in their car; now that I'm alone and stronger than I have been for the past few years, I really enjoy music and their friendship. However, I can't be sure; Rie Klijn's health is not getting any better and we're all afraid that she'll not be with us next winter—she herself, most of all. Perhaps "afraid" is not the right word; being a doctor's wife and an ex-medical student must help—I don't think she has a great fear of death. But it is a pity, a terrible pity. . . .

'A quarter past five and I'm home from the concert already! Plenty of time for a cup of tea and a postscript to this letter. During the music as I sat in that large room full of attentive people, behind a stage with over a hundred musicians bowing and blowing away, it struck me that we are much further developed than chimpanzees or dolphins, after all. Good Lord, how complicated human society is! I must have thought of chimpanzees because of a book I've been reading in short bursts for over a month now—*The Naked Ape* by Desmond Morris, "a zoological study of the human animal". This morning I heard a programme about dolphins on the radio. The zoologist who's in charge of the dolphinarium at Harderwijk, where they train dolphins as at Marineland near Los Angeles (which I visited in 1960), had some interesting things to say. Apparently those creatures are more intelligent than chimpanzees, and the zoologist regretted that they do not have hands and fingers; then they would really show you a thing or two! Still, I can hardly imagine a dolphin playing the violin. This evening I'll again have some time to read my naked ape, since there's no newspaper on Sundays.

'This afternoon a famous Russian pianist played the first piano concerto by Chopin; a miracle of virtuosity, both of the composer and the pianist. I used rather to despise Chopin; when you're young it's often all or nothing. Perhaps old age has made me "mellower", as they say. There's a lot to admire in that spectacular work and speculating about the romantic feelings of all those

elderly ladies with their grey permanent waves is really also tremendously fascinating. You can almost see them melting whenever there is a piano solo. Sitting there during the concert enjoying all sorts of things, you wonder how long this will still be possible in our mechanized world. For how long will over a hundred flesh-and-blood musicians be prepared to make such enormous efforts for two hours in a hall full of people? (I recently read in the paper that during rehearsals and performances, the members of the orchestra are under such tension—if only because of the common rhythm—that their pulse speeds up unnaturally.) Surely this can't go on for much longer? Wouldn't it be easy to imitate all that blowing and bowing on a few electronic instruments? For that matter, it's already too expensive for the State to subsidize. The theatre is also disappearing. Perhaps very small theatres and little orchestras will be able to survive for a while.'

Baarn, 20 April 1969: 'The hippies of San Francisco continue to print my work illegally. I received some of the grisly results through a friendly customer over there. Among other things, such as virulently coloured posters, I was sent a forty-eight-page programme or catalogue of the so-called "Midpeninsula Free University", Menlo Park, California. It included three reproductions of my prints alternating with photographs of seductive naked girls.'

Baarn, 6 July 1969: 'My flight to you has now been definitely booked for 19 August. There's a good chance that I'll finish my woodcut before that time; the second block is nearing completion.'

Escher also wrote to Arthur and Lotje Loeb about this woodcut (*Snakes*, cat. no. 448), which was to be his last print.

Baarn, 13 July 1969: 'I don't imagine that this will be a "masterpiece" (although we should really pretend to believe this of each new piece of work), but I'm extremely satisfied because my hand doesn't shake at all, and my eyes are still good enough for such precision work, thanks to a magnifying glass lit up by a circular neon tube (which doesn't heat the wood!). I've been doing this kind of work for over fifty years now and nothing in this strange and frightening world seems more pleasant to me. What more could a person want? Meanwhile I have to stop my ears as my American clients are constantly clamouring for faster service, but this time I'll just let them wait for once.'

ROSA SPIER HOUSE
In the spring of 1970 Escher was re-admitted to hospital for another major operation. When he was home again, he wrote to Canada that he was going to move into a service flat in Laren.

Baarn, 6 May 1970: 'The matter of the Rosa Spier House is finally

Page 129: Two sections from the three-colour woodcut *Metamorphosis III*, 1967–68 (cat. no. 446)

Opposite page: *Snakes*; woodcut in three colours, July 1969 (cat. no. 448)

settled! From 1 June I'm renting a bed-sitting-room (very small—twelve feet square) with a studio opposite, twenty-five by twelve feet, about half of which I need for my work, so I can use the rest as a living-room. (Very important: I have only to cross the corridor to get to the studio; at first I was offered a combination of rooms with a hundred and sixty feet of corridor between them.)

'I don't intend to move until August. My trip to Canada will therefore not be happening this year. I hope Jan and Liesbeth will have time to come and help me move during that month, as they offered to. . . .'

Baarn, 24 May 1970: 'Yesterday I visited my surgeon at the hospital. He was very satisfied with my "condition", more satisfied than I am myself, for I feel weak and am easily tired. . . .

'The day after tomorrow the members of the board of the "Escher Foundation" are again coming to a meeting here. It'll be quite a day. We'll have to have a serious discussion about the new book which Meulenhoff are going to publish at the end of the year, and about putting a stop to the pirate reproductions of my prints, now in Sweden as well.'

Escher also wrote that Bruno Ernst was to visit him. 'This will be the fourth Sunday afternoon, from four o'clock to half past six, that he is coming to see me in order to collect information for a book on my work, seen especially from the point of view of a mathematician. He told me that if he didn't try now and get as much information out of me as he could to clarify his theoretical understanding, I might be dead, and then the book would never happen. He has great hopes for the book, even if it will only be published in the distant future. It's also very amusing for me to see how he tries to express my intuitive approach clearly in words I have never used myself, or even understood.'

Meanwhile, Escher wrote (in English) to Roosevelt about his move.

Baarn, 10 June 1970: 'Dear Mr Roosevelt, . . . It is time indeed to tell about my moving from here, Baarn, to Laren, a village not far from here. At the end of next August I shall be living in the "Rosa Spier House" (Rosa Spier was a famous harp-player). It is a home for aged artists (about 60 in all: writers, musicians and painters). There are 12 fine studios for painters (or graphic artists) and I shall have one of them, as well as a little living-bed-room. There is a modern kitchen where our hot meals are made, a doctor and a nurse are present for sick people. All the artists-inhabitants live individually; there is no need to see other people if you don't want to.

'My wife lives, since $1\frac{1}{2}$ year, in Switzerland (she is Swiss originally) and our house in Baarn is much too large for one man alone. . . .

'Yesterday I received a very nice visit of Miss Kefauver, daughter of the late senator Estes Kefauver, who was a good friend (and boss) of Charles Alldredge, who died in 1963. . . . He was indeed a wonderful man. I never met him personally but we wrote each other many letters and now and then he sent me one of his famous poems. . . .

'Would you also be so good to tell prof. Servos about my moving-intentions, as well as Sidney Mickelson? I have no time to write them a letter, but I hope not to forget to send them a removal-card in due time.'

Escher was quite happy in the Rosa Spier House, but his health continued to deteriorate. From the beginning of 1971 he was no longer able to make new prints or to print old ones, but whenever possible he wrote to his children and countless friends and relations—for example, to his old friend Bas Kist:

Laren, 15 March 1971: 'Dear Bas, You must think: out of sight, out of mind. I know that you've had a birthday since your enjoyable visit of 11 February, and that you celebrated it, if not in style, at least in the mood, finishing with a concert in Musis. I didn't contact you at all, but let me make the excuse that I was "suffering", to a greater degree. However, I don't want to go on about that and will only say that my very considerate and (I think) competent doctor in Laren put me on an intensive course of antibiotics while the surgeon who carried out my last operation was away on holiday. The treatment tired me out, but it did completely get rid of my fever and at least some of the other frightening symptoms.

'At this moment I'm lying (as usual) on my sofa, trying to write in a rather awkward position, for it's still a relief to be horizontal after I've been forced to sit up for a while. Just now I had to sit up for a shearing session with the barber. The fact that the five-week-old locks of hair like a beatnik's have been removed makes me feel quite content.

'I also have the feeling that I'm continually rounding off some of the activities of my life. Hans Locher came the other day to fetch an enormous pile of prints, so now they must have two copies in the printroom of the Gemeentemuseum of every piece of work that I've ever produced. This was his express wish. I'm quite unable to print any woodcuts again—it's far too tiring. Thus my stock of woodcuts is steadily diminishing, for I continue to sell both here and abroad as long as the prints are available, which will not be much longer. As regards the lithographs: yesterday my printer brought me the last hundred and fifty prints of three different "best-sellers". Thus it will be a year or more before they're all gone (if an old wreck like me can manage to package and send them). But I've also put a stop to all this lithograph printing now. We (almost) brushed away a tear: the good old printer and I may meet again in the hereafter.

'I'm preparing for permanent residence in this perfect Rosa Spier House, with no regrets whatsoever. It'll no longer be possible to travel to Canada or Denmark—unless my doctors perform miracles, and I don't think they're capable of that; it's probably just as well. Imagine how it would be if they could cure any illness. No one would ever die. I can't even see myself making shorter trips (to Velp, for example), unless I hire an ambulance.

'It's only when one is sometimes in pain that one realizes how wonderful it is not to be in pain. In this vale of tears, could anything be more wonderful than falling asleep in a soft bed? So I'm not at all scared of death, provided it comes painlessly in an almost imperceptible transition to Nirvana. Kind-hearted doctors are quite capable of arranging this nowadays, if they aren't trapped in stupid dogma. . . .

'Rather than continually moaning about my own ailments, I should have asked how you are. I hope you're well.'

During 1971 Escher managed to visit Bas by taxi after all, and was even able to visit Arthur briefly in Denmark. The Meulenhoff book, *De Werelden van M.C. Escher* (*The World of M.C. Escher*), was published on 10 December, and Escher lived long enough to see it become very successful. Personally he considered the book by Bruno Ernst to be more important, but he did not live to see this. He died on 27 March 1972 in the hospital in Hilversum, at the age of seventy-three.

George Escher described his father's last days in a letter to Bruno Ernst, dated 5 January 1978.

'About 15 March [1972] Vermeulen telephoned to say that Father was deteriorating rapidly. I arrived in Hilversum some days later; Arthur and Jan had been there for a few days. Father was very weak, often sedated and hardly eating at all. For the first time in his life he was partly bald. He slept a little, woke up again, chatted a bit, and then fell asleep again. It was obvious that the doctor did not believe the end was close at hand, and as three sons at a time in a sick-room is rather busy, Jan and Arthur decided to take turns in going back to work for a few days. . . .

'The first few days were a bit strange. We tried to move Father and get him to eat something, on the nurses' insistence, but without success. He had no wish to extend this senseless time in bed and wanted to finish it as soon as possible. After a few days he was fed only intravenously, which diminished the problems and made him calmer.

'It was the beginning of a very pleasant and peaceful period. There was no drama. Arthur and I or Jan and I would sit in Father's room until midday, at his feet or by the window, with a book or writing-paper to write home. Then we would go out for a meal and return later, until it was time to go back to the hotel for that day. It was very pleasant and Father obviously enjoyed having us near, although he complained the first few days about the waste of time. From time to time he would open his eyes, and we would chat or he would joke about the hereafter, philosophizing about it occasionally. He knew very well that he had only a few days left to live, and he would have preferred to have made an end of it sooner, but apart from the occasional friendly request that the doctor should stop trying to do his best, he accepted the necessity of allowing the doctors and nurses to do their jobs.

'So the days went by. Through the window, I watched the trees, the gusts of wind and rain or the spring sun, with Father's breathing in the background, sometimes soft, sometimes louder, stopping when he woke up. Now and then I would hand him some orange juice or help him to move to a different position. I would have a chat with Jan or Arthur, or read a little in some book by Dorothy Sayers or Agatha Christie. There seemed to be little change in his condition. Jan decided to return to Copenhagen on the 24th or 25th, Arthur planned to come to Hilversum a few days later (for Easter?).

'On the 27th I spent the morning with him as usual. We had a little chat and he made a joke about the ridiculousness of his situation, which left me smiling for a while. When I returned to the hospital after lunch I was met by a nurse who took me to Dr Glazenburg. He told me that Father had died early in the afternoon. The period of being close and together was over.'

The official unveiling of the *Metamorphosis* mural behind the counter at the post office on the Kerkplein in The Hague, 20 February 1969 (Escher second from the left)

134

The Vision of a Mathematician

In 1956 Escher met the mathematics teacher Bruno Ernst (see page 86), who was intrigued by the mathematical quality of Escher's work. By means of an extensive analysis of his prints and preliminary studies, long conversations with Escher himself and a detailed correspondence, Bruno Ernst eventually developed a system which covered all this 'mathematical' work.

The following pages discuss the basic principles underlying Escher's work as described by Ernst in the light of the system developed by him, which is outlined below.

Bruno Ernst's contribution concludes with a word on Escher's hobby of astronomy.

THE ANALYSIS

Two separate periods can readily be distinguished in Escher's work: pre 1937, in which landscapes predominate, and post 1937, which is characterized by a marked mathematical tendency. My aim was to discover some structure and coherence in the work from this 'mathematical period'. Escher himself could not give me any information about it.

An analysis of the prints on the basis of their subject matter and aim produced surprising results. It appeared not only clearly to demarcate a number of periods, but also to provide an instrument to discover unity, coherence and evolution in the work and to arrive at a characterization of Escher's field of exploration.

The first step was to make an inventory of the pictorial content of the prints. This produced categories such as mirrors, regular polyhedrons, spirals, Möbius strips, buildings and animals. This result still did not lead to any great insights; I could only make progress if I also included the intentional content, the 'meaning' of the print, in the inventory. In order to avoid subjectivity as far as possible, I had many consultations with Escher himself.

THE CATEGORIES

After some unsatisfactory attempts with more extensive lists, I arrived at a list of eleven categories of pictorial content and/or intention:

1   regular spatial figures;
2   regular division of the plane;
3   spirals;
4   Möbius strips;
5   perspective;
6   metamorphoses and cycles;
7   approaches to infinity;
8   the conflict between depicting something on a plane and the three-dimensional reality which is depicted;
9   the penetration of more worlds;
10   spatial anomalies (impossible figures);
11   relativities.

I made a list of a large number of Escher's prints and drawings, in chronological order (for the sake of completeness I included work from 1920 onwards), and I noted which of these eleven categories applied to each print or drawing. Upon studying this inventory it appeared that the landscape period was clearly followed by three successive, distinct periods in which Escher was intrigued by at least two categories:

c. 1937–c. 1946, categories 6, 8 and 9;
c. 1946–c. 1955, categories 1, 5 and 9;
c. 1955–1969, categories 7 and 10.

Category 2 (regular division of the plane) did not appear to be restricted to a particular period; in fact Escher had worked on this from 1922 and continued to do so until almost the end of his life. On second thoughts, categories 3, 4 and 11 did not seem sufficiently distinctive to warrant a separate place in the system.

THE SEVEN THEMES

On the basis of the system described above, I arrived at a total of seven themes with which Escher was concerned in his 'mathematical' prints; these themes will be further elaborated in the following pages.

1   Penetration of worlds. See category 9 above.
2   The illusion of space. See category 8.
3   The regular division of the plane. See categories 2 and 6.
4   Perspective. See categories 5 and 11.
5   Regular solids and spirals. See categories 1, 3 and 4.
6   The impossible. See category 10.
7   The infinite. See category 7.

SOURCES OF INSPIRATION

On the basis of my analysis of the themes occurring in Escher's work, it is possible to draw some clear conclusions about the sources that inspired him. These were:

the structure of the plane;
the structure of space;
the relationship between these two.

A child who looks into a mirror for the first time is surprised when he notices that the world behind the mirror, which looks so real, is actually 'intangible'; however, he soon ceases to consider this false reality as being strange. In the course of time the surprise disappears, at least for most people. For them a mirror is merely a tool, used to help them to see themselves as others see them.

To Escher, however, the mirror image was no ordinary matter. He was particularly fascinated by the mixture of the one reality (the mirror itself and everything surrounding it) with the other reality (the reflection in the mirror). Examples of this can be seen even in his early work. For instance, in 1920 he made a large pen-and-ink drawing of the interior of the St Bavo church in Haarlem. Roughly in the centre of the drawing there is the reflecting sphere of a chandelier (see opposite page). Most of the interior of the church is reflected in this sphere; even Escher himself and his easel with drawing-paper can be seen in the reflection. Thus the St Bavo church and the sphere are in the same place here; they interpenetrate, as it were.

This theme of penetration plays a central role in the lithograph *Still Life with Mirror* of 1934 (cat. no. 248). The frame of the mirror and the objects surrounding it emphasize the reality of the mirror itself. At the same time the lithograph shows another reality, namely that of the street, which has become part of the room by being reflected. But this is by no means all: the objects standing or hanging in front of the mirror are also reflected and thus, in their turn, become part of the street scene. Thus the reality of the room and that of the street are combined in an ingenious way.

Spherical-Mirror Prints   A similar situation can be seen in a number of Escher's spherical-mirror prints. In *Still Life with Spherical Mirror* of 1934 (cat. no. 267), a reflecting spherical bottle is lying on a newspaper and a book. Next to the bottle there is a Persian 'man-bird', a present from Escher's father-in-law. The 'second reality' can be seen in the same place as the bottle: Escher in his studio, drawing on a lithographic stone. Here too, the two worlds are connected by means of the reflection of objects close by (man-bird, newspaper and book), so that they are seen twice.

In the lithograph *Hand with Reflecting Sphere* of 1935 (cat. no. 268), Escher is holding the sphere in his hand (which is itself reflected) so that he also has himself and his studio 'in hand'. It could hardly be more concise! In fact, he used the spherical-mirror theme only once more for a 'large' print, the lithograph *Three Spheres II* of 1946 (cat. no. 339). Here the reflecting sphere is part

of a 'comparative study'; two equally large spheres are shown next to it, one opaque, the other transparent and filled with water. Escher was interested in the sphere filled with water because it acts both as a lens (with an inverted image) and as a spherical mirror. All three spheres are reflected in the polished surface of a table; the spheres at left and right are reflected in the middle one; and to crown it all, the whole scene can again be seen as a reflection of the sheet of paper on which the artist is drawing!

Escher realized that the natural world, too, contains examples of the apparent interpenetration of worlds. Prints based on this idea include the mezzotint *Dewdrop* of 1948 (cat. no. 356), the linocut *Rippled Surface* of 1950 (cat. no. 367) and the woodcut *Puddle* of 1952 (cat. no. 378; see also page 139). However, the most successful example is the lithograph *Three Worlds* of 1955 (cat. no. 405). Here the real world is formed by the floating leaves which mark the surface of the water. The world under the water is embodied in the fish, and what is above the water (the trees) is seen as a reflection. It is all interwoven in such a completely natural way that the superficial observer may not even grasp Escher's intention.

Magic Mirror   The lithograph *Magic Mirror* of 1946 (cat. no. 338) is a singular case. In this print Escher plays with the whole mirror idea *à la* Lewis Carroll. The fabulous creatures behind the mirror appear to be just as real (or just as unreal) as those in front of it. Both categories are 'born' from the mirror: the creatures end their short lives as interlocking plane-filling motifs, first black, then white, on the 'floor' where the mirror is standing. Escher emphasizes the unreal character of the fabulous creatures by not giving the 'real' sphere lying in front of the mirror a real reflected counterpart; the second 'real' sphere is simply lying behind the mirror and bears no relation to the first.

Other Penetrations   In some prints Escher also tried to achieve an interpenetration of two worlds without using mirror effects. One obvious example is the woodcut *Porthole* of 1937 (cat. no. 297), in which the porthole itself—perceived as a 'reality' because its immediate surroundings are depicted—coincides with the freighter sailing in the distance. In another woodcut of the same year, *Still Life and Street* (cat. no. 296), the enclosed space of the room where the observer is seated is projected into the street which he is observing. The grotesque distortion becomes clear when the top and bottom edges of the print are cut away (see the picture opposite): the books become structures two storeys high, and the jar of tobacco turns into an enormous pillar.

Right: Detail of the pen-and-ink drawing of the interior of the St Bavo church, dating from 1920

Below: The distortion in the woodcut *Still Life and Street* (cat. no. 296) is particularly striking when the top and bottom edges are 'cut away'

The attraction of many of Escher's prints lies in the fact that they suggest things which do not actually exist and sometimes even cannot exist. In contrast with the irrationality of the Surrealists, Escher's context is strictly rational; every illusion that is created is the result of a totally reasoned construction.

Every spatial picture on a plane is based on illusion. The surface used for the drawing is flat, two-dimensional; however, we perceive what is depicted as spatial, three-dimensional. This can be explained quite simply: the retina in our eye can be regarded as a plane. Thus the image of the (three-dimensional) space around us that is projected onto the retina through the lens in our eye is also flat—that is, two-dimensional. Whether we are looking at a white cardboard cube or at a drawing consisting of nine lines (see below) makes no difference to us: the image on the retina remains the same. (The question of stereoscopic vision—with both eyes—is not considered here; we perceive the world around us as being spatial even when we are looking with one eye.) From an early age we become used to interpreting the two-dimensional image on the retina as being three-dimensional.

Escher was fascinated by the fact that the human brain absolutely insists on making two-dimensional pictures spatial. For some time he made playful attempts in his prints to 'break through' this illusion of space; he seemed to be saying to the observer, 'Look at it—it's flat and will always be flat!' In vain, as he himself realized full well. The illusion persists, in spite of opposition.

In the woodcut *Doric Columns* of 1945 (cat. no. 335; see also page 66), two drawings of pillars have been folded and bent a number of times; the result is then drawn in a cell-shaped space. Despite the folds, we still see the columns as three-dimensional objects.

In the woodcut *Three Spheres I*, also of 1945 (cat. no. 336)—which incidentally is a masterpiece of woodcutting skill—no spheres are depicted, but flat planes. The network of white ellipses suggests a spherical shape. In the top figure we see a frontal view of the flat plane; the three-dimensional suggestion is obvious here. The central figure has been cut from a sheet of drawing-paper on which the top figure is shown, and then folded over. The fold should hinder the illusion of space; but no, we immediately turn it into a three-dimensional object. At the bottom Escher put another copy of the top figure, now lying 'on the floor', but we refuse to believe this and see it as an elongated egg.

In the woodcut *Dragon* of 1952 (cat. no. 379), a dragon is putting its head straight through a wing, and its tail through its body. This is quite possible, for the dragon is only a flat object, as anyone can see. 'But the dragon itself does not seem to agree,' said Escher, 'for it is biting its tail in a way that would only be possible in three dimensions. It is mocking my attempts.'

In the lithograph *Drawing Hands* of 1948 (cat. no. 355), too, the conflict between the plane and space is expressed in a striking manner. For either of the three-dimensional, drawing hands, the other, drawn hand is flat.

In a number of prints Escher makes apparently three-dimensional creatures free themselves from the plane and/or return to it. The lithograph *Reptiles* of 1943 (cat. no. 327) is a fine example. The spatial quality of the reptiles is merely illusory: they may have crawled out of the plane of the *drawing* but they are still in the plane of the *print;* their return to the sketchbook is therefore not an essential loss.

Escher's metamorphoses also sometimes take place as a move from the plane into space, and vice versa; thus, in the woodcut *Day and Night* of 1938 (cat. no. 303) geometrical planes change into flying birds.

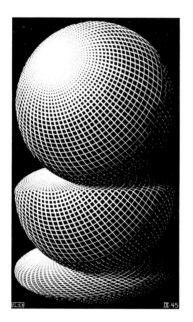

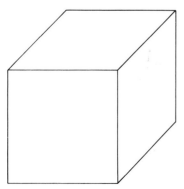

Above: The wood engraving *Three Spheres I* and a photograph illustrating the 'intention' of this print

Left: these nine lines suggest a spatial object, a cube

Opposite page: *Puddle*; woodcut in three colours, February 1952 (cat. no. 378)

Escher repeatedly emphasized, both in lectures and in his writings, that the regular division of the plane interested him more than any other subject that he dealt with in his work. The text of his essay *The Regular Division of the Plane* (see pages 155–74), which was published in 1958, attests to this. We shall now take a closer look at the background of Escher's greatest hobby.

In principle a regular division of the plane is a jigsaw puzzle with identical pieces—not particularly interesting, on the face of it. Figure 1 on the next page shows some of the more obvious examples: squared paper (*a*), stone walls (*b* and *c*), parallelograms (*d*), triangles (*e*), a honeycomb (*f*). Pentagons cannot be used; nor can polygons with more than six angles.

Let us examine the possibilities of a rectangle. The rectangles in figure 1*a* are not particularly interesting, but if you cut a piece off one side of each rectangle and stick it onto the other side (figure 2), the picture becomes livelier. If you then move a semi-circle from the bottom to the top (figure 3), it becomes even more attractive. In this way one could go on endlessly creating all sorts of fascinating patterns.

In the years following 1936—when he had become truly obsessed with the regular division of the plane after his second visit to the Alhambra—Escher developed his own system to incorporate all the possibilities in this field. He described it in 1941 and 1942 in a workbook of about forty pages, now in the Gemeentemuseum in The Hague (see page 149); he later used this as a guide for designing new divisions of the plane. Broadly speaking, his system is as follows:

I   *Rectangles:* a one motif and two colours; *b* one motif and three colours; *c* two motifs and three colours.

II   *Triangles:* a with threefold rotation points; *b* with sixfold rotation points; *c* with three- and sixfold rotation points.

Escher's system is not particularly satisfactory from a logical point of view because different vantage points are used for each subdivision. However, the mathematical system that is used in crystallography is logical, and some parts of this were adopted by Escher (he had made a study of some of the literature on crystallography before formulating his own system). A brief description of the mathematical system follows:

Imagine a regular division of the plane extending to infinity in every direction. A thin sheet of glass or tracing-paper is laid on top of this. The regular division of the plane is traced onto it. There is now an original and a duplicate, which cover each other entirely. Moving the duplicate over the original usually results in a confused double image, but in the case of a few particular movements of the duplicate, it can again cover the original in such

a way that it looks as though it has not been moved at all. It is possible to distinguish four different ways in which the duplicate can be moved:

1   sliding (translation);
2   reflection;
3   slide reflection (glide reflection);
4   turning (rotation).

I shall discuss each of these movements individually and, to keep things as simple as possible, use a virtually rectangular motif as an example in each case.

Sliding   See figure 4. The motif is shown top left. When the duplicate of the regular division of the plane is slid to the right across the length of the rectangle, the original is again covered in such a way that only the original regular division of the plane can be seen. The same effect can be achieved by sliding it up across the height of the rectangle, or obviously also by sliding it, for example, three times the length to the right and then twice the height down. Exactly the same applies to the distorted rectangles in figure 5.

Reflection   If you draw some letters or a figure on a sheet of glass with a felt-tip pen and then turn it over (figure 6), you will see a mirror image of what was originally drawn. In the same way it is possible to turn over the duplicate of a regular division of the plane in such a way that the original and the mirror image are one on top of the other. If you do this to figure 4, the duplicate can no longer cover the original in any position; this regular division of the plane does not permit reflection. However, in the case of figure 7, it does. If a line s is drawn on the original and the duplicate of the rectangle at the top left, and the duplicate is turned over at the line s, it will cover the original without requiring any further sliding movement; s is known as a *mirror line*. The same can be done for the whole regular division of the plane in figure 7. It seems that there is even another sort of mirror line (s¹) in the figure: this is an 'added bonus'. Thus figure 7 can be repeated not only by sliding but also by means of reflection around the lines s and s¹.

Slide Reflection   Figure 8 is derived from the stone-wall grid in figure 1*c*. It is immediately obvious that the rows of fish are always each other's mirror images. Nevertheless it is not possible to draw a mirror line anywhere in such a way that the duplicate will cover the original if it were to be turned over at this line. However, one can draw in the lines g_1 and g_2, which have certain special characteristics. If the duplicate is turned around one of these lines and if it is then slid *along this line* one row up or down, the duplicate again completely covers the original. As the regular division of the plane is in this case repeated by reflection, followed by being slid along the mirror line, this movement is known as slide reflection (or glide reflection, hence the notation g for the mirror line).

Detail of a textile print (kakemono), one of Escher's early attempts at the regular division of the plane

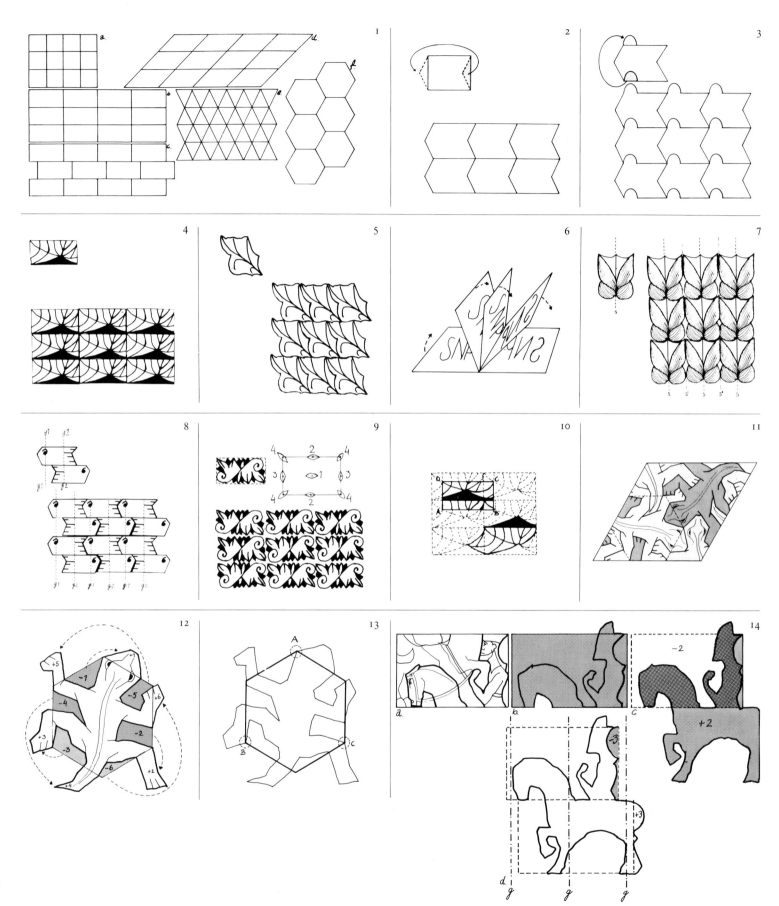

In figure 8 ordinary sliding movements are also possible: sideways over one fish, but vertically over *two* fish! This not only demonstrates that slide reflection is something special (it required a vertical movement over only one fish), but also that the unit from which this division of the plane is composed (the sliding cell; see below) contains two fish—the image as well as the mirror image, like the little figure top left in figure 8.

Rotation If, in figure 4, you stick a pin vertically through both the regular division of the plane and the duplicate, and you then turn the duplicate through a complete circle (360 degrees), the duplicate once again covers the original. However, this is nothing special; it would be possible to do this with any arbitrary figure, even a portrait or a landscape. But if you do it with the motif in figure 9, putting the pin exactly in the centre of the motif (top left), the duplicate again covers the original after being rotated through a semi-circle (180 degrees); if the motif is rotated through a whole circle, the duplicate covers the original twice. The centre of the motif is therefore called a *twofold rotation point*.

The regular division of the plane shown in figure 9 has twofold rotation points in the centre of the motifs. It is not only the motif that has the pin stuck in it, which is repeated when rotated through a semi-circle, but the whole of the regular division of the plane. As an added bonus there are three other groups of rotation points— the mid-points of the long sides of the motif, the mid-points of the short sides, and the corner points (scheme shown top right in figure 9).

The four different possible ways of movement described above form the basis of the mathematical classification of the regular division of the plane. Before elaborating on this I should like to introduce the concept *sliding cell*. This is the piece of the jigsaw puzzle which is *only* repeated by sliding (that is, not by rotation or reflection). All regular divisions of the plane are composed of sliding cells. However, in the case of certain regular divisions of the plane the *shape* of the sliding cell is by no means fixed. In figure 4, a sliding cell can be seen top left, but there are many other possibilities. Thus the rectangle ABCD drawn in figure 10 may equally well be considered to be the sliding cell of figure 4. It does not even have to be a rectangle; the small figure to the bottom right of that rectangle can function as a sliding cell. However, the area and the 'pictorial content' of a sliding cell are fixed. What is chosen in any particular case as a sliding cell depends on personal preference.

The sliding cell can sometimes contain several (similar or different) motifs. For example, a fish from the bottom row of figure 8 can never be repeated as a fish from the row above it by means of sliding. Here the sliding cell contains a fish as well as its mirror image, as shown top left in figure 8, for example.

If, when analyzing a particular division of the plane, you first find the sliding cell and then the possible mirror lines, slide-reflection lines and rotation points, you will have a fairly comprehensive insight in the structure of the division of the plane concerned.

The unique quality of Escher's regular divisions of the plane lies in the fact that from the very beginning he attempted to compose them from recognizable images (see also pages 158 ff.). He created his motifs in a systematic way, by distorting triangles, quadrangles or hexagons. In 'The Regular Division of the Plane' he illustrates this by transforming in three stages a plane filled with parallelograms into a plane filled with birds, in which only sliding can take place (woodcut I, page 159, sections 4–10). When parts are added on the right, they are taken away on the left, and vice versa; this is also happening at the bottom and the top. It is a very gradual process, but eventually the originally abstract figures assume definite bird shapes.

This procedure led to Escher's metamorphoses and cyclical prints in which one shape gradually changes into another, from undifferentiated to differentiated shapes and (in the case of cycles) back again.

I shall discuss two prints of a division of the plane in greater detail.

Reptiles In this lithograph of 1943 (cat. no. 327), a reptile crawls out from the flat surface of a sketchbook and eventually returns to it by a long detour. The division of the plane shown in the sketchbook only has threefold rotation points. The sliding cell contains three reptiles; if a diamond is chosen as the sliding cell (figure 11), this contains two almost perfect reptiles, while the third one is found spread around them in bits and pieces. When he created the reptile, Escher used a hexagon as the basis; he cut out six pieces and stuck them back on in the correct places on the outside (figure 12). The (threefold) rotation points are at three corners of the hexagon (figure 13); at A three heads come together, at B three legs, and at C three knees.

Horseman A study of a division of the plane of 1946 forms the basis of this three-coloured woodcut of the same year (cat. no. 342; see also page 150). The division of the plane is derived from a stone-wall grid in which the stones have been slightly staggered left to right (figure 1c), as indicated in figure 14d. Two of these 'stones' together form the sliding cell, which contains a horseman with his horse *and* their mirror image. One rectangle contains exactly one (cut up) horseman with his horse. Figure 14 shows how Escher arrived at the shape of the horseman by means of three congruent indentations and bulges—a tour-de-force of the imagination, within the great restrictions imposed by the shape of a rectangle. This division of the plane only has glide-reflection lines; these are shown in figure 14d.

Escher occupied himself for many years with the peculiar problems of depicting perspective. At an early stage he used the laws of classical perspective in an original way. In the woodcut *Tower of Babel* of 1928 (cat. no. 118) and in the wood engraving *St Peter's* of 1935 (cat. no. 270), he focused the attention on the *nadir*, a point directly below the feet of a standing observer; he did this by choosing an unusual, extreme vantage point. Thus the nadir becomes the *vanishing point*, a function which in 'normal' pictures is fulfilled by one or more *distance points* lying on the horizon. Another unusual way of drawing is achieved if the artist chooses a point directly above his head (the *zenith*) as a vanishing point.

In a few astonishing prints Escher showed that zenith, nadir and distance point are only relative concepts. These prints are the mezzotint *Gallery* of 1946 (cat. no. 346), the wood engraving *Other World* of 1947 (cat. no. 348) and the lithograph *Relativity* of 1953 (cat. no. 389), in which these concepts prove to be interchangeable. In two other prints, the lithograph *Up and Down* of 1947 (cat. no. 352) and the lithograph *House of Stairs* of 1951 (cat. no. 375), he also used *curved lines of perspective* which he had developed himself, an extremely interesting discovery. Escher described the considerations which led him to introduce curved lines of perspective in a lecture. I shall summarize it here.

First, Escher explained classical perspective using vanishing points on the horizon. He then gave examples of situations in which the vanishing point is at the zenith or the nadir. On the subject of the latter he said: 'We see this when we are looking down from a window in the twentieth floor of a skyscraper.' There is a sketch of this in his notes (see opposite page, sketch 1).

Escher then talked about curved lines of perspective. 'Imagine that as we are looking down from our window on the twentieth floor, there is a building forty floors high opposite. We might now wish to do a drawing of that whole skyscraper, from the bottom right to the top. If we look down, we can see the street and the base of the building; if we look straight up, we can see the edge of the flat roof. How could we reproduce such a dynamic, cinematographic image, in which the eye passes from the zenith to the nadir through one hundred and eighty degrees, as a static image on the flat surface of a sheet of paper? Let us do it in three stages to begin with. Firstly, looking *downwards:* this produces an image very similar to the picture that has already been drawn. Secondly, looking *at the horizon:* that is, at the level of the twentieth floor opposite. The perpendicular lines now run truly vertically across our paper. Thirdly, looking straight *up* at the edge of the roof: now the verticals are again seen to converge on the zenith vanishing point.

'In order to produce a single continuous picture from these three separate ones, we draw curved lines from zenith to nadir, which touch the corresponding lines of the three stages.'

Escher made another sketch illustrating this (2).

Other World   We are in a strange room in which up, down, left, right, front and back can be substituted arbitrarily, depending on whether we wish to look out through one window or another. The centre of the picture is always the vanishing point; it is the distance point when we look through the windows on the left and in the middle. This is also the view we should expect normally.

If we look through the window at the top and the adjacent one on the right, the same vanishing point has become the nadir; we now see the moonscape from above. The central window has suddenly turned into the floor of the room.

If we look through both windows bottom right, the vanishing point has become the zenith: we are now standing on the moon looking up at the starry sky above. The central window has also changed its function: it is now the ceiling.

In this work Escher thought of a very clever way to give the single vanishing point a triple function, while drawing three pairs of virtually identical windows in the room.

In the mezzotint *Gallery* he had not yet succeeded in doing this. Here the same, normal moonscape is seen when we look through the two opposite walls of the room. The top window faces down and the bottom window faces up, leaving a long dark tunnel in the centre, which is not very logical, and with which Escher was not satisfied at all.

Up and Down   If you want to study this print thoroughly, it is best to cover the top half with a sheet of white paper. We are standing between a tower (right) and a house. The house is connected to the tower by two arcades at the top. Straight in front of us there is a sunny square which might be somewhere in southern Italy. On the left there are two staircases which go up to the first floor of the house, where a girl is looking down out of a window, having a wordless conversation with the boy on the stairs. The house is obviously on the corner of a street and is joined to another house to the left, not shown in the print. At the top of the part of the print that is not covered over, there is a tiled area which is seen as a ceiling, the middle of which is the zenith. All the verticals bend towards this point.

If the covering sheet is moved in such a way that only the top half of the print is visible, exactly the same scene can be seen again: the square, the palm tree, the corner house, the boy and the girl, the staircase and the tower. But this time it is as though we are looking down on the scene from a great height. The tiles at the bottom of the visible part of the print are now on the floor. Their centre is right below our feet. What was first the ceiling is now the floor: the zenith has become the nadir and all the verticals are curved lines to this nadir.

Only now we look at the print in its entirety. The tiled area occurs three times: at the bottom as a floor, at the top as a ceiling, and in the middle with a double function as both a floor and a ceiling.

The tension between top and bottom is greatest in the tower on the right, when we see it as a single object. Just above the centre there is a window that faces down, and right next to it, just below the centre, there is a window facing up. This gives the corner room very peculiar qualities. There must be a diagonal across this room which cannot safely be crossed. Top and bottom, floor and ceiling alternate along this diagonal. Anyone who thinks he is standing squarely on the floor will find that with one step over the diagonal he will suddenly be hanging down from the ceiling! Escher did not draw this happening, but he consciously suggested it with the two corner windows. It is all suggested by the double function of the central vanishing point, which simultaneously functions as zenith and as nadir.

There is more happening in the centre of the print. Imagine going down the steps to the entrance of the tower. If this staircase runs on inside, we walk to the top of the tower upside down; but what do we find there if we look out through the top window? Do we see the roofs of the square on the bottom half or are we somehow looking at the bottom of the square from below? Are we high up in the air or under the ground?

Up and Down is a print full of surprises. Imagine how dizzy you would feel at the top of the stairs where the boy is sitting. It is not only possible to look down (at the tiled floor in the middle), but also to look down-down. Are you now hanging or standing up? How does the boy in the top half feel when he leans over the railing and looks at himself at the bottom of the stairs? Can the girl at the top also see the boy at the bottom?

House of Stairs After 1947 the problem of the relative nature of vanishing points and curved lines of perspective continued to intrigue Escher. In 1951 he came to the general conclusion that you could choose a number of vanishing points and connect them alternately with bundles of curved lines. This gives a network for spatial pictures in which top, bottom and straight ahead cannot be distinguished. An application is shown in the lithograph *House of Stairs*, in which an arbitrary number of these spatial pictures can be stuck together in a long vertical strip. The network drawn by Escher for *House of Stairs* is shown below; it has three vanishing points.

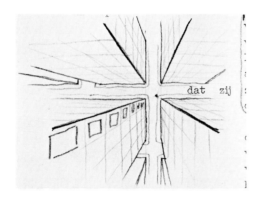

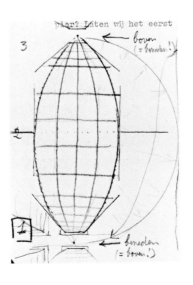

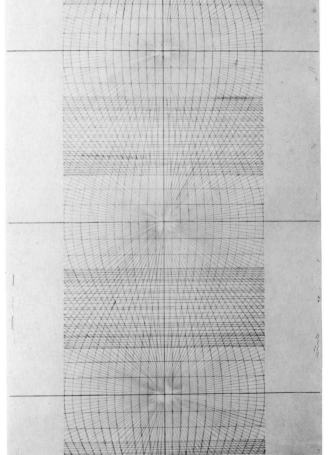

Above: Sketch 1

Right: Sketch 2

Far right: The network for *House of Stairs*

145

Escher was greatly interested in crystals. He was not so much intrigued by the crystals themselves, as by the endless number of possibilities for composing regular spatial figures, such as can be found in the shapes of crystals. He saw nature as a sort of professional colleague, for whom he had the greatest admiration.

He did not restrict himself to crystal forms that occur in nature, nor to the classical regular (so-called 'platonic') solids. He was also interested in all sorts of star-shaped solids. These can occur, for example, when two or more simple forms (cubes, octahedrons, etc.) interpenetrate. He constructed models in wood and thick paper. The Verblifa tin which he made in 1963 (see page 151) was also a result of this hobby.

Escher wanted to express his enthusiasm in his prints, but realized that he could not expect any great interest in this subject from the average print collector. The letter he wrote to his son George on 21 May 1961 about the woodcut *Four Regular Solids* (cat. no. 438; see also page 117) illustrates this: 'Certainly a print which will hardly appeal to the general public and will therefore not be easily sold. However, I am really satisfied with it myself. If you ask me why I make such crazy things, such absolutely objective objects with no personal touch at all, I can only answer that I can't help myself.'

Earlier on Escher had used regular solids (whether or not interpenetrating) in prints such as the mezzotint *Crystal* of 1947 (cat. no. 353), the wood engraving *Stars* of 1948 (cat. no. 359), the wood engraving *Double Planetoid* of 1949 (cat. no. 365), the lithograph *Contrast* of 1950 (cat. no. 366), the lithograph *Gravity* of 1952 (cat. no. 380), the woodcut *Tetrahedral Planetoid* of 1954 (cat. no. 395) and the lithograph *Flatworms* of 1959 (cat. no. 431). In the lithograph *Waterfall* of 1961 (cat. no. 439) he used regular solids as ornaments.

Gravity The lithograph *Gravity* shows an interesting regular solid, a star dodecahedron. A careful study of the print shows that this solid can be composed of five-pointed stars (made out of cardboard, for example) which have pieces cut out of them in an ingenious way so that they may interlock. It is then possible to populate the star dodecahedron with twelve four-legged tailless creatures (the pyramids in which the creatures live are always formed by the five points of a star; they have five sides and thus have only five openings for the parts of the body which protrude). Escher called this print 'Gravity' because each of the heavily built monsters is so obviously pulled towards the centre of the 'planet'.

Flatworms Escher discovered that tetrahedrons and octahedrons can be stacked in certain combinations in such a way that they totally fill up a space. In the lithograph *Flatworms* he plays with these building blocks. The resulting structure has mainly angles of 60 degrees, which produces an extremely odd architecture. For in more 'down-to-earth' architecture, angles of 90 degrees are by far the most common.

Spirals Escher's interest in special spatial constructions is also apparent in a number of prints with spatial spirals. The first of these, the wood engraving *Spirals* of 1953 (cat. no. 390), is particularly successful. Escher had been inspired by a picture of a spiral ring in a sixteenth-century Italian book, though it was ugly and the perspective was incorrect. It was a challenge for him to produce a construction with the correct perspective which was also aesthetically pleasing; in addition, he made the task even more difficult. He let the 'tube' formed by the spirals grow thinner and thinner so that instead of a ring, he created a spiral turning in on itself. The result, which required a dozen very exact preliminary studies (see page 71 for two of them), is thus a spiral composed of spirals—a 'super spiral'.

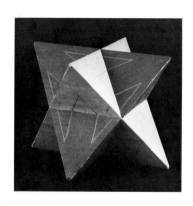   

Four models of star-shaped solids made by Escher. See also the photograph on page 72

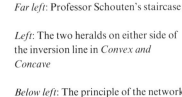

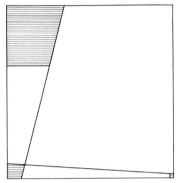

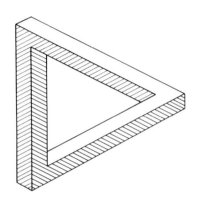

Far left: Professor Schouten's staircase

Left: The two heralds on either side of the inversion line in *Convex and Concave*

Below left: The principle of the network for *Print Gallery*

Below: Roger Penrose's triangle

6 THE IMPOSSIBLE

In 1963 Escher gave a lecture in Hilversum devoted entirely to 'the impossible'; he illustrated his ideas with his own prints. In his introduction he described what had inspired him to make them.

'Sometimes it seems as though we are all obsessed with a longing for the impossible. The reality around us, the three-dimensional world surrounding us, is too ordinary, too boring, too common. We yearn for the unnatural or the supernatural, the impossible, the miraculous. . . .

'If you want to express something impossible, you must keep to certain rules. . . . The element of mystery to which you want to draw attention should be surrounded and veiled by a quite obvious, readily recognizable commonness.'

During a lecture in Amsterdam, also in 1963, Escher said: 'In my opinion an impossible situation only really stands out when the impossibility is not immediately obvious. If you want to draw attention to something impossible, you must try to deceive first yourself and then your audience, by presenting your work in such a way that the impossible element is veiled and a superficial observer would not even notice it. There should be a certain mysteriousness that does not immediately hit the eye.'

That Escher's 'impossible figures' completely meet this requirement is obvious from the popularity of this group of prints in particular. The impossibilities with which we are concerned here are of a specific nature—they are 'quasi-spatial'. They seem to be three-dimensional structures; they can be drawn on a flat surface, but could not possibly exist as spatial figures.

The potential for making these prints is limited; they depend on fairly rare geometric configurations. Escher borrowed most of the basic figures from other people, re-creating them in concrete form. The prints have such a sophisticated structure and choice of detail that they come across as pictures of situations which could really exist.

Convex and Concave   Professor J. A. Schouten gave Escher a small metal staircase painted white, which strikingly demonstrates the phenomenon of 'seeing things inside out' (photograph top left). When it is viewed with one eye, the image conjured up in the brain constantly changes. We see something that completely accords with tangible reality, and the next instant all the inwards-pointing angles point outwards, and vice versa, so that we seem to observe an object that is not there at all. This phenomenon inspired Escher to make the lithograph *Convex and Concave* (1955, cat. no. 399).

When carefully studied, this print is a visual nightmare. At first glance, it seems to be a symmetrical structure: the left half is an approximate mirror image of the right half and the transition from left to right is gradual and very natural. Nevertheless something terrible happens at the transition in the centre: everything is literally turned inside out. The top becomes the bottom, the front

147

becomes the back. People, lizards and flowerpots rebel against the inversion; we identify them too clearly with tangible realities of which we do not know the inside-out form. But they, too, have to pay the price when they cross the borderline: their relation to the environment becomes so strange that looking at them makes you feel dizzy. For example, at the bottom left a man is climbing onto a platform by a ladder. He sees a small temple in front of him. He could stand next to the sleeping man and wake him up to ask why the shell-shaped pool in the middle is empty. Then he could go to the stairs on the right with the intention of walking up them. But it is already too late! What looked like stairs seen from the left, has suddenly turned into part of an arched vault. He would notice that the platform, which was once firm ground under his feet, is now a ceiling, and he would crash down with a terrified scream. The borderline between the left and the right half cannot be crossed without danger.

This visual shock is probably felt most intensely when you look at the two heralds on either side of the borderline. The herald on the left is looking down from the window onto the crossed vault of a temple (see detail on previous page). He can climb out, stand on the vault and jump onto the platform from there. Now look at the herald a little lower down on the right: he is seeing an overhanging vault above him. He would certainly not consider jumping onto the platform, for he is looking down into an abyss. The platform is invisible to him, for in his half of the print it is pointing backwards.

Print Gallery This strangely distorted lithograph of 1956 (cat. no. 410) reproduces to a great extent an older print—the coloured woodcut *Senglea* of 1935 (see page 152). Bottom right, we see the entrance to a gallery where an exhibition of prints is being held. At the extreme left we see a young man who is looking at one of the prints on the wall. This print shows a ship, and further on, top left, the houses of Senglea along the quay. If he allows his eyes to wander to the right, he can see the row of houses continuing to the right of the print. If he then lets his eyes wander down, he can see a house on a corner. At the bottom of this house he can see the entrance to a gallery where an exhibition of prints is being held; at the extreme left he can see a young man who is looking at one of the prints on the wall . . . thus the young man is himself in the print he is looking at!

The whole trick depends on a network that Escher has developed for this print, which marks out an enclosed circular expansion of the plane. By means of the diagram on the previous page this clever network can easily be explained. In the bottom right-hand corner of the large square a very small 'square' has been drawn. This small square constantly increases in size along the bottom edge towards the left; at the left side it has grown to four times its size. Along the left side upwards it again increases four times in size, so that a square which was originally 1×1 mm is now 16×16 mm. This expansion continues along the top edge

towards the right and then along the right edge down, where the total multiplication factor has become 256. In the figure only two steps are represented. In fact Escher also does this in the print: we see the gallery growing larger from the bottom right to the top left. The last two steps cannot possibly be carried out within the square, due to lack of space. It is most ingenious now, for the last two steps, to focus the attention on one of the prints in the gallery; within the square this can be enlarged two more times. Finally Escher had the entrance gate in the print, now enlarged 256 times, coincide with the starting point. Thus the original entrance to the gallery is included in the print of the print; the circle is complete.

Belvedere The belvedere in this lithograph of 1958 (cat. no. 426) is partly used as a prison. Thus it is quite possible that the turret is part of a royal palace. The attire of the visitors could also be an indication of this. The structure on top of the prison is architecturally unusual; it looks like the *projection* of a building, a three-dimensional reality, but it could not exist in our three-dimensional world, any more than the cube-like shape being studied by the young man on the seat.

It looks as though the top floor of the belvedere is straight on top of the floor below. This impression is reinforced by the woman and the man on the right. They are exactly one above the other, but they are looking in different directions, at right angles to each other. There is something strange about the eight pillars joining the floors. Only those at the extreme right and the extreme left behave in a normal fashion; the other six join the front to the back and must therefore run diagonally across the middle storey.

The sturdy ladder looks quite straight, and yet the top is clearly leaning against the outside of the building, while the bottom is standing inside it. If you were standing in the middle of the ladder, you would not be able to say whether you were inside or outside the building: looking down, you would say 'inside'; looking up, you would have to say 'outside'.

If we cut the print horizontally across where the pillars seem to cross over, the two halves would be perfectly normal: it is a matter of making impossible connections, as in the case of the cuboid which the young man is holding in his hands contemplatively.

Waterfall This lithograph of 1961 (cat. no. 439) is based on Penrose's triangle (see previous page). Three bars at right angles to each other seem together to form a spatial object. At the corners nothing is wrong, but going from one corner to another, you notice that there is something wrong with the connection. In this picture Escher used a combination of three of these forms. The water continues to flow forever!

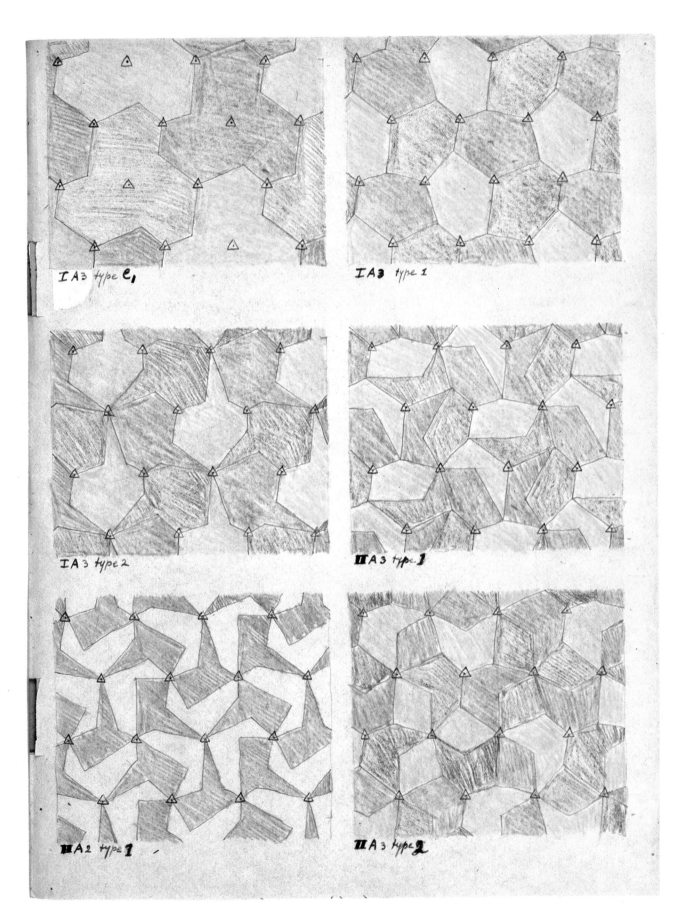

I A3 type e₁

I A3 type 1

I A3 type 2

II A3 type 1

II A2 type 1

II A3 type 2

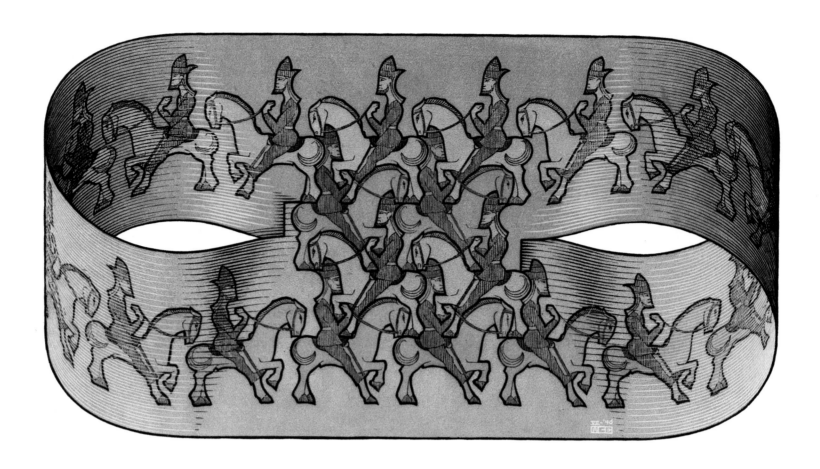

During the same period that he was taking any opportunity to create figures that could not exist in space, Escher was also working on expressing the infinite. He had felt an interest in the infinite in space or time for a long while. When he talked about his need to express the infinite he referred to his regular divisions of the plane and the wooden spheres in which and on which he carved his congruent figures. But neither the divisions of the plane nor the spheres were primarily aimed at expressing the infinite.

After 1955 he used another mathematical principle to approach the infinite: he changed from congruent figures to similar ones. It was now possible to make the figures smaller and smaller, until they had reached the limit of what could still be seen with the naked eye; in this way an infinite number of figures could still be shown on a limited surface.

Initially the results were unsatisfactory. In the woodcuts *Division* (cat. no. 411) and *Smaller and Smaller* (cat. no. 413), both of 1956, he was annoyed by the fact that the edge of the print permitted an expansion of ever larger figures; the infinite had not yet been captured within the frame of a print. In the woodcut *Whirlpools* of 1957 (cat. no. 423; see also page 95) he used a better solution. But in 1958, in a book by the mathematician Professor H. S. M. Coxeter, Escher saw a figure that delighted him. Without understanding the relevance of the figure in the context of Coxeter's book he immediately saw in it what he was looking for to depict infinity. He discovered how to construct the figure himself, and filled it with fish, an infinite number of fish. This was the woodcut *Circle Limit I* (cat. no. 429). In *De wereld van het zwart en wit* ('The World of the Black and White', Amsterdam, 1959) he wrote about it: '[The print] shows the application of a method, a way which could lead to the creation of a perfect two-dimensional universe, but it is not for me to say that perfection has been achieved in this specific example. This rudimentary basic motif of fish, as shown in the centre of the print at its largest, three times in white and three times in black, leaves a lot to be desired as far as the expression is concerned. Nevertheless I am satisfied with the result because it is something I have been searching for in vain for years. The size of my fish patterns, at its largest in the centre, gradually decreases outwards, reaching the limit of the infinitely small size, and at the same time of the infinitely large number, in a circle which encloses everything.'

Later in the year in which his article was published, Escher completed a coloured woodcut that expressed his intentions in a much better form—*Circle Limit III* (cat. no. 434; see also page 97).

This work was not based on the scheme he had discovered in Coxeter's book, but on a network he had derived from this scheme; the three lines through the centre have disappeared. He described it in 1968, in the catalogue for his big exhibition in The Hague: 'In the coloured woodcut *Circle Limit III* the . . . limitations [of *Circle Limit I*] have to a large extent been overcome. There are now only series composed of "through traffic": all the fish of the same series have the same colour and swim head to tail on a circular course from edge to edge. The closer they get to the centre, the larger they grow. Four colours are needed so that each row contrasts in its entirety with its surroundings. No single component in all these rows, which, from infinitely far away, rise straight up out of the limit like rockets, and return to it, ever reaches the border.'

In 1964 Escher made *Square Limit* (cat. no. 443; see also page 118), a coloured woodcut in which the same idea, with a different scheme, is elaborated in a square. He was happy with the result and sent Coxeter a copy of the print. The latter's comment was rather disappointing: 'Very nice, but merely Euclidian, not very interesting. The circle limits are more interesting, being non-Euclidian.'

In all the prints that he titled . . . *Limit* or *Path of Life*, Escher used his skill in the regular division of the plane to fill the print with similar, recognizable figures. In the print that concluded his work, the woodcut *Snakes* of 1969 (cat. no. 448; see also page 130), he solved the problem of expressing the infinite in a yet more elegant way, even without using one of his regular division of the plane patterns.

In the preliminary sketches, the scheme of the 'Coxeter prints' can be seen on the outer edge of the circle. However, the centre does not show the motif—the ring of a coat of chainmail—at its largest, but is again a limit of the print towards the infinitely small. The network for this tour-de-force is an invention of Escher's own, far more complicated than the one he used in the drawing after Coxeter. The three snakes which take the print from pure abstraction resulted from Escher's study of a number of photographs of snakes in books he bought for the purpose.

A striking feature of this print, which takes us to the limit of the infinite both at the edge and at the centre, is that Escher made no attempt—as he had in previous works aimed at approaching the infinite—to depict the smallest circles visible to the naked eye. He felt that just the suggestion of an infinite decrease in size was sufficient.

Opposite page: Most of the three-colour woodcut *Senglea* of October 1935 (cat. no. 276) can be found in the lithograph *Print Gallery* of May 1956 (cat. no. 410)

Page 151: The tin designed by Escher in 1963 for the Verblifa company

Lastly, a word on Escher's hobby of astronomy. When he moved back to Holland in 1941, he became a member of the Dutch Association for Meteorology and Astronomy, which organized lectures and published a magazine—*Hemel en Dampkring* (The Sky and the Atmosphere). His interest in astronomical and meteorological phenomena gradually increased, and at some point he started to make precise notes of his observations (he had a 60-mm telescope). One of the notebooks of his observations during the summer of 1944 has been kept. On 17 July he noted the following: 'The clear sky last night . . . persuaded me to get out the telescope again, for the first time in a long while. . . . I have been waiting for a suitable evening for weeks because I drew a detailed star map last month with George's help, and I had also made lists of all kinds of objects and general information about the fixed stars that are of interest to amateurs.'

That night he observed some binary stars and constellations. 'The famous Andromeda spiral nebula, which I observed a number of times in the past, and which can be seen with the naked eye as a faint light blur, does not look any better through a telescope: it is still a formless haze, though it produces a mysterious sensation because of its immense distance from us.'

The following night he continued his observations. 'There was not a single cloud to be seen; it promised to be a splendid night for observation. . . . I started at about midnight and went on without a break until about a quarter to four, when the first light of dawn . . . made the sky distinctly lighter. Of the fifteen binaries on my programme, I managed to separate fourteen, including the five I had separated two days previously, as well as three which I had tried to separate in vain. I will list them individually in the order of the distance between the components.' Part of Escher's list of these fifteen observations is given below. Any amateur astronomer will consider this list impressive; the double stars are spread throughout the sky and the fact that Escher was capable of observing all these objects through a telescope in the course of a few hours is proof of a great familiarity with the constellations. In fact he had even more on his programme. 'In addition to these fifteen binaries I tried once again to find the ring nebula in Lyra . . . and succeeded immediately, probably because the atmosphere was so clear. It is between β and γ Lyrae, slightly closer to β, and looks like a fairly sharply outlined grey disc, barely contrasting with the sky. . . . It reminded me of an indistinct fingerprint on the dome of the heavens (not a thumb, rather a middle finger).'

In later years, when Escher was no longer such a fanatical observer, he was still interested in astronomical phenomena, as we can see from his lecture to the Rotary Club about his voyage to Canada (see pages 111–13).

Part of a page from Escher's notebook, concerning his observations of binary stars

The Regular Division of the Plane

In 1957 the De Roos Foundation, a private press producing limited editions for members only, commissioned Escher to write an essay on his hobby of the regular division of the plane. A year later the essay was published in book form under the title of Regelmatige vlakverdeling; *it was illustrated by woodcuts which Escher had especially made for it (cat. nos. 416–21; see also the catalogue, page 342).*

The text that follows is the first English translation of this essay. All references to 'this book' are to the original Dutch edition of 1958.

The printmaker has something of the minstrel spirit; he sings, and in every print that is made from a single block of wood, copper plate or lithographic stone he repeats his song, over and over again. It does not really matter if the occasional sheet gets lost or stained or torn; there are copies enough to convey his thoughts, and if there are not sufficient available he can print a new series, in which each individual work is equally perfect, original and complete, as long as the plate from which it is printed is not worn.

How different this is from the principle of uniqueness inherent in painting! We can well understand that a painter often finds it difficult to part with his spiritual creation, his unique work of art. The best he can hope is that it will be lovingly cared for by its foster parents.

The graphic artist, however, is like a blackbird singing at the top of a tree. He repeats his song over and over again, and it is complete in each print that he makes. The more that are required, the better he is pleased. He wishes that the wind would scatter his leaves over the earth, the farther the better; not like the dry leaves of autumn, but rather like seeds ready to germinate and light as a feather.

Is it not remarkable—and, at first glance, perhaps also surprising—that the graphic artist attempts to achieve his purely spiritual aim of a fruitful transfer of thoughts from one person to as many others as possible by means of techniques that require the most down-to-earth craft work? His painstaking craft absorbs him to such an extent and makes such demands on his time and attention that he sometimes forgets it is only a means or a medium, and not an end in itself. This explains the tendency shared by many people who make or collect prints to ascribe an exaggerated value to the pure methods and characteristic qualities of the old and respected, even venerated graphic techniques. In this way undue emphasis is laid on the material quality; the actual aim of all this toil is barely taken into consideration any longer. No matter how much joy can be gained from following a noble craft, it should not be forgotten that it is a means of repetition and multiplication.

Repetition and multiplication—two simple words. However, the whole world of the senses would collapse into chaos without these two concepts. As soon as we lose sight of them, the world seems hopeless and merciless. Everything we love, learn, recognize, accept and put into order we owe to them. The marvellous and mysterious natural laws surrounding us depend on them. The whole world is kept going by them; if they ceased, the universe would fall apart at once. (I have not forgotten mutations; these will be discussed later, in the sense of metamorphosis.)

Repetition and multiplication. In a narrower sense they lead us to the subject of this essay, 'the regular division of the plane'. I am filled with a feeling of helplessness, now that I am faced with the need to define this phrase. In this book it is the images and not the words that come first. (As its designer, for his part, wishes to emphasize the visual element by his imaginative use of type, the thoughts expressed by the words are not of primary significance for him either. He joins his personal need for the division of planes to my own, and expresses it, as I do, in images, using the letters themselves as figures, as signs of recognition, without worrying about their literary function. In the same way, I use the shapes of animals as beacons, without worrying about their biological significance.) It is outside my scope to use letter symbols, but in this instance I am forced to use them. However, I have not been trained in this, as I have in the use of images, which convey thoughts more directly than the descriptive word. Yet my images require an explanation, because without one they are too hermetic, too much a formula, for the uninitiated. At the same time the play of thoughts they express, though essentially quite factual and impersonal, seems to my constant amazement to be so unusual and, in a sense, so new that I could not find an 'expert' with sufficient understanding to write about it, apart from myself.

For me it remains an open question whether the play of white and black figures as shown in the six woodcuts of this book pertains to the realm of mathematics or to that of art.

Een raficus

heeft in zijn wezen iets van een troubadour;

On the first text page of *Regelmatige vlakverdeling* (The Regular Division of the Plane) the designer Aldert Witte 'emphasized the visual element by his imaginative use of type' (printed in black and red)

If it counts as art, why has no artist—as far as I have been able to discover—ever engaged in it? Why am I the only one fascinated by it? I have never read anything about the subject by any artist, art critic or art historian; no encyclopedia of art history mentions it, no fellow-artist or predecessor has ever been involved in it. There have been a few sporadic instances of decorative art that share the same roots, which I shall mention later, but these are rudimentary and embryonic. They do not arise from profound reflection and therefore do not penetrate to what I consider to be the heart of the matter.

In mathematical quarters, the regular division of the plane has been considered theoretically, since it forms part of crystallography. Does this mean that it is an exclusively mathematical question? In my opinion, it does not. Crystallographers have put forward a definition of the idea, they have ascertained which and how many systems or ways there are of dividing a plane in a regular manner. In doing so, they have opened the gate leading to an extensive domain, but they have not entered this domain themselves. By their very nature they are more interested in the way in which the gate is opened than in the garden lying behind it. To develop this metaphor: a long time ago I chanced upon this domain in one of my wanderings; I saw a high wall and as I had a premonition of an enigma, something that might be hidden behind the wall, I climbed over it with some difficulty. However, on the other side I landed in a wilderness and had to cut my way through with a great effort until—by a circuitous route—I came to the open gate, the open gate of mathematics. From there, well-trodden paths lead in every direction, and since then I have often spent time there. Sometimes I think I have covered the whole area; I think I have trodden all the paths and admired all the views; and then I suddenly discover a new path and experience fresh delights.

I walk around all alone in this beautiful garden, which certainly does not belong only to me, but whose gate is open to everyone. I feel a revitalizing yet oppressive sense of loneliness. That is why I have been extolling the existence of this paradise for many years and why I am now compiling this book from words and images—even though I do not expect many people to wander through. For what fascinates *me*, what provides *my* experience of beauty, often seems to be considered dry and tedious by others.

The expression 'regular division of the plane' is, as I have said before, not one that renders further explanation superfluous. To the artistically inclined reader—if I may indeed be so bold as to assert some connection with art—it does not suggest anything with which he might feel familiar, as might such words as 'expressionism', 'still life' or 'palette knife', to mention only a few quite disparate and arbitrary terms.

I must therefore attempt an explanation, and offer the following:

A plane, which should be considered limitless on all sides, can be filled with or divided into similar geometric figures that border each other on all sides without leaving any 'empty spaces'. This can be carried on to infinity according to a limited number of systems.

This description may be clarified by some simple examples.

A floor can be covered, or its area be filled, with tiles that are all the same shape and size. In the most common case the tiles are square. This is also the simplest conceivable way of dividing a plane regularly: two identical systems of straight, parallel lines intersecting at right angles. Starting from this example, one can imagine a series of systems for dividing a plane, progressing from simple to complicated by using square, rectangular, diamond-shaped, triangular and hexagonal elements successively. It is obvious that filling a plane with hexagons is more complicated and is based on a less straightforward system than a composition consisting of squares. But all these figures meet the requirement put forward above: they can be fitted together in such a way that no space remains between them; that is, the strip of 'filler' separating the tiles for practical reasons can theoretically be reduced to nil.

This explanation does not aim to acquaint the reader with all the systems; crystallographers, who have specialized in these systems, have studied and recorded their number and characteristics. I do not consider it necessary to be familiar with all the ins and outs of graphic art in order to be a collector of prints; no more do I think one should struggle through all the theoretical principles of the division of the plane in order to appreciate it and to accept that it can act as an inspiration, as it does for me.

At this point the first woodcut can supplement and clarify my description. Woodcut I incorporates a process of development. The observer is invited to follow this by going through the stages one by one, starting at the top left of a strip of pictures that fills the sheet in a zigzag fashion, through twelve stages of growth and metamorphosis, which I shall describe in order.

[1]   The beginning is grey. The method of printing used when no colours are included is generally to print from a block with black ink on white or off-white paper. I have serious objections to this method, even though I have used it myself for as long as I can remember. This is because of the inconsistency of the presence—even before we start—of one of the two contrasting elements, namely white, though we pretend to be creating both black *and* white. The latter is even continued in the margin of the sheet of paper. As a result, the balance between the two components of the contrast white *versus* black is disturbed. This is a nuisance in any print, but it becomes quite unacceptable in one concerned with the regular division of the plane. For here the white and the black portions are completely equal in value, as I will show below. It would be so much more logical, at least in theory, to print grey paper with both white and black ink. Unfortunately there are too many practical problems; not only are there technical difficulties in covering dark paper with a light ink, making it almost impossible

to obtain a clear white, but in addition the whole procedure requires twice as much time and effort, because two blocks have to be cut instead of one—one for the white portions and one for the black.

In making the six woodcuts for this book the usual method was employed. For each print a single block was cut, and prints were made with black ink on white paper. But at my express wish, the edges around the prints were printed with a grey tone as nearly as possible half-way between black and white. In my opinion this considerably enhances the balance of the contrast.

As soon as one can see that something is developing, that there is action—as in woodcut I—one may ask whether there was anything there before 'the story' began. Is it not feasible to accept 'grey' not merely in a static sense, as above, but also in a dynamic sense, as the origin of the contrast between white and black developing from it? In this way I consider the indeterminate, misty grey plane as a means of expressing static peace, of rendering the absence of time and the absence of dimension that preceded life and that will follow it; as a formless element into which all contrasts will dissolve again, 'after death'. For this reason, too, it is good that all the black-and-white prints in this book are surrounded by a neutral grey.

[2]   Two systems of straight, parallel lines emerge from the indeterminate grey mists. They form the guidelines for the division of the plane. The distance between them and the angles at which they intersect reveal something of the character of the figures that will grow out of them later. The surface area of each of these, in particular, is henceforth totally determined by the area of each parallelogram and will remain constant during the succeeding metamorphoses.

[3 and 4]   The two intersecting systems of straight lines that emerged in the previous stage are in a sense a 'fiction'. Visual delimitation or bordering is not achieved with 'lines' but by the effect of the contrast between planes of different shades. Thus the figures bordering on each other have to be separated factually before developing any further. We are already certain that the minimum of two contrasting shades is sufficient in this case, since each time there are four figures meeting at a single point. This is not always the case. On a floor filled with hexagonal tiles, not four but six hexagons meet at one point. In that case a minimum of three shades is needed to distinguish them visually. Here, however, white and black suffice, and grow to maximum contrast by the end of section 4.

[5 and 6]   At the start of section 2 there was an infinite range of possibilities, from which we chose a particular division into parallelograms. Now, at the start of section 5, we again find ourselves at a crossroads. From three available principles of dividing a plane we have to choose one. For the sake of brevity the   157

three principles can be characterized as 'sliding', 'rotation' and 'glide reflection'. I shall describe the characteristics of these types of division as opportunity arises in the course of the text. In the present instance I chose sliding as being the simplest of the three.

The straight lines of the borders between white and black in section 4 change gradually in section 5 and 6. They become increasingly bent and broken; where 'white' advances, 'black' automatically recedes.

[7] In this section the gradual growth of the figures has come to an end. They have achieved their definitive form and will retain it to the end of the strip. Although nothing seems to remain of the original parallelogram, its characteristics are nevertheless incorporated in the completed figure or 'motif'. Thus the area of every motif is still the same as that of the earlier parallelogram, and the points where four figures meet are still in the same place in relation to one another.

The principle of sliding that is used in this division of the plane can now be described as follows. If one imagines that each of the white and black motifs is a piece cut from cardboard or wood, like the pieces of a jigsaw puzzle, it would be possible carefully to lift one out and, by moving it in a straight line parallel to the plane of the 'puzzle', simply by 'sliding', position it on top of any other piece so that it covers the other completely. In sliding, therefore, the position of the figures in the picture in relation to one another always remains the same.

The white and the black silhouettes have assumed a particular and not an arbitrary shape, since the process of their development was consciously directed to creating these now definitive figures. As far as the strict discipline and the extreme limitations of the present system for dividing the plane allowed, an attempt was made to create a form in which the observer can recognize familiar elements. I assume that he will have a vague impression of something floating, with a body and two partially overlapping wings or fins; probably, therefore, a bird or a fish.

[8] This uncertainty ends as soon as the black silhouettes are filled with a few detail lines. It leaves no room for doubt: there are black birds flying against a white background.

[9] Obviously this can be done the other way round just as well. When we move the detail lines from the black to the white motifs, the representation appears in reverse and white birds can be seen against a black background.

Thus something remarkable has happened in 8 and 9: by the drawing of a few simple lines one has evoked the ideas of relief, depth, 'near' and 'far', foreground and background. These ideas were totally lacking in the first four sections; at most the idea of a 'floor' or a 'wall' could perhaps have occurred to us, but the two-dimensional nature of the plane was not disturbed. Propelled by associations, we can even go one step farther and arrive at 'day' by

way of the sequence background–white–air in section 8, and at 'night' in section 9.

[10] A completely regular division of the plane in the sense I mean comes about only when the function of an 'object' can be attributed to *each* of the congruent figures. The question whether there is then still a 'background' will be dealt with when this strip has been followed to its conclusion.

[11] The white and the black marks that we read as birds can also be seen as something else. If we shift the eye and the mouth from right to left and turn the wing into a fin, the birds become fish.

[12] Finally it is of course also possible to unite the two types of animals in a single division of the plane. In the solution put forward here, black birds fly to the right and white fish swim to the left, but they can be made to change places at discretion.

This concludes my description of the first woodcut. It showed clearly that a succession of gradually changing figures can result in the creation of a story in pictures. In a similar way the artists of the Middle Ages depicted the lives of saints in a series of static tableaux, each showing an important moment and together telling their story, either in separate sections or in a continuous landscape, within a single frame. The observer was expected to view each stage in sequence. The series of static representations acquired a dynamic character by reason of the space of time needed to follow the whole story. Cinematic projection provides a contrast with this. Images appear, *one after the other*, on a still screen and the eye of the observer remains fixed and unmoving. Both in the medieval pictorial story and in the developing pattern of a regular division of the plane the images are *side by side* and the time factor is shifted to the movement the observer's eye makes in following the sequence from picture to picture. It is possible to look at a film strip in the same way when it is held in the hand. Books are also read in more or less the same manner.

Now that we have seen that a plane can be completely filled with or built up of figures each of which depicts a recognizable object, the question arises whether they can all be an 'object' at the same time. Is it possible to create a picture of recognizable figures without a background? After years of training in the composition of lines dividing equal units, I thought I could answer this question affirmatively, until I encountered some doubts through a correspondence with the ophthalmologist Dr J. W. Wagenaar. He is better qualified than I to judge this matter from a scientific point of view. I quote the following extract from his letter:

'In my opinion you do not in fact create pictures without a background. They are compositions in which background and figure change functions alternately; there is a constant competition between them and it is actually not even possible to go on seeing

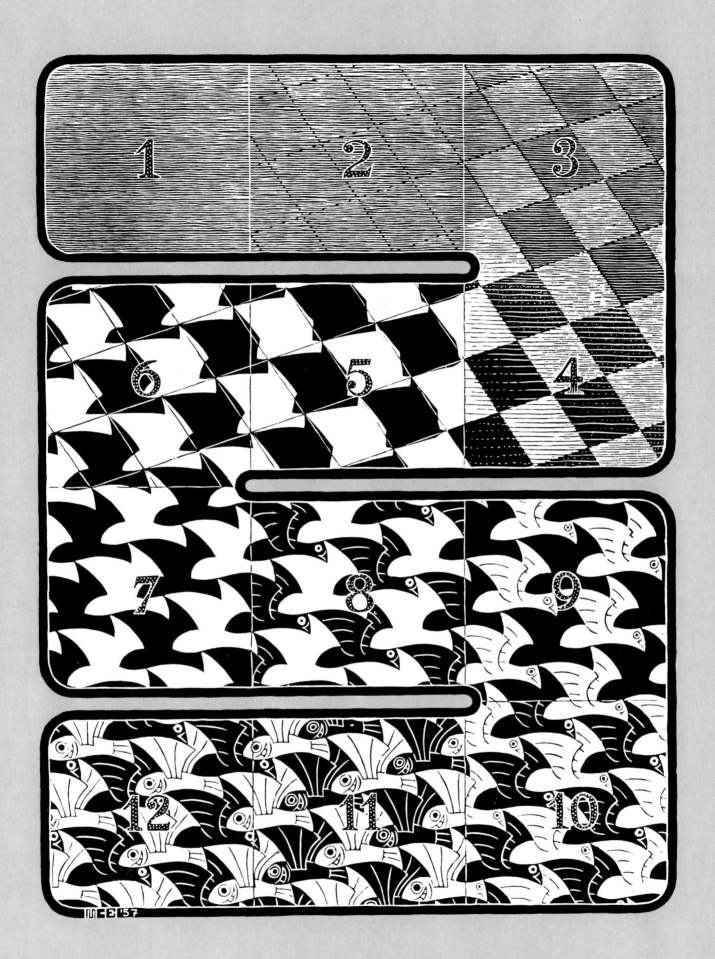

one of the elements as the figure. Irresistibly the elements initially functioning as background present themselves, in a cyclical way, as figures. Your compositions do not have a visual static balance but a dynamic balance, in which, however, there is a relationship between figure and background at every stage. It is like seeing the world with a red glass in front of one eye and a green glass in front of the other: in that case the world does not look either red or green but constantly changes from one to the other and back again (at least if both eyes have equal strength and one is not distinctly dominant!). A static balance is possible only if the whole figure is seen as a pattern, separate from the representation "bird" or "fish".

'It is not conceivable to see only a "figure", because anything that manifests itself as a figure, as a "seen object", is limited, whether in reality or not. A limitation means a demarcation with regard to something else; this "something else" is the background from which the figure (or object sensation) detaches itself. On the other hand, it *is* possible to see only background, for instance when standing in a fog, or when placed in an Ulbrich sphere. This is a piece of equipment made for physiological experiments on sensory phenomena. It consists of a large sphere in which the subject can sit. Inside, it is painted mat white all over, so that the lighting is diffuse and the eye has nothing upon which to focus.'

My correspondent's clear explanation contributed a great deal to my understanding of the regular division of the plane, and it is therefore appropriate to include it here.

Thus it seems that two units bordering on each other cannot simultaneously function as 'figure' in our mind; nevertheless, a single dividing line determines the shape and character of both units, serving a double function. In this unusual and strange manner of drawing, there is understandably a complete absence of impulse and spontaneity. After a great deal of patience and deliberation, and usually a seemingly endless series of failures, a line is finally drawn, and it looks so simple that an outsider cannot imagine how difficult it was to obtain.

In this kind of work fantasy and imagination are essential, not to mention tenacity. These qualities take us over from somewhere 'outside ourselves', but we can make ourselves more accessible to them and encourage and stimulate them by various methods. I discovered one example in the writings of Leonardo da Vinci, and I have translated the passage as best I can:

'If you have to depict a scene, look at some walls daubed with marks or built from stones of different kinds. In them you will see a resemblance to a diversity of mountainous landscapes, rivers, rocks, trees, sweeping plains and hills. You can also see battles and human figures, strange facial expressions, garments and countless other things, whose shapes you could straighten and improve. These crumbling walls are like the peals of church bells in which you can hear any name or word you choose.'

Leonardo's advice is useful in stimulating imagination and fantasy in general. But experience has taught me that it is

particularly valuable in designing regular patterns to fill planes, since one is then largely concerned with putting chaotic shapes into order and making abstract forms concrete.

Despite this conscious effort the artist still has the feeling that moving his pencil over the paper is a kind of magic art. It is not he who determines his shapes; it seems rather that the stupid flat shape at which he painstakingly toils has its own will (or lack of will), that it is this shape which decides or hinders the movements of the drawing hand, as though the artist were a spiritualist medium. In fact he feels quite amazed, dazed even, by the work that he sees appearing under his hand, and experiences a submissive feeling of gratitude or resignation towards his creations, depending on whether they behave helpfully or rebelliously.

In the pages above we have looked at the problem of the regular division of the plane from various angles in relation to woodcut I. Now we shall consider the other illustrations, in which other aspects of the subject will be emphasized. I realize that this will give the essay an improvised character, without a systematic structure or headings, but what else can one expect from a graphic artist to whom words are of secondary importance compared with images? Visual thinking is of a different order from literary thinking. Therefore a more or less arbitrary succession of thoughts, written down in the order in which they arise as I look at the prints one by one, will have to suffice.

Woodcut II is divided into four horizontal strips, the top strip of which is divided again into three square sections, A, B and C.

I copied A and C in the Alhambra at Granada. They are mural decorations composed of similar, adjacent ceramic tiles that together form a colourful mosaic. I chose these two from the great diversity of patterns that gleam and glitter on the walls and floors, not only because they are good examples of what may be considered the 'primitive' stages of the regular division of the plane, but also because it was perfectly possible to translate the range of colours in which they are executed into white and black; this is by no means true of all the Alhambra patterns.

I discovered pattern B as a woodcut in a Japanese booklet. I do not know whether it is an original Japanese design; it could equally well be Chinese. It is very well known and is often found, reproduced as line, without any division by contrasting colours. The particular character of 'primitive' plane-filling can be seen more clearly if the patterns are alternately white and black.

The primitive stage represented by these three regular divisions of the plane—by which I mean their abstract mathematical character—makes it difficult to find in them the characteristics of any particular culture. B possibly has an even more Eastern feeling than A or C, and it seems probable that B arose from observation of wicker-work, because it gives an impression of plasticity.

I have often wondered why, in their decorative zeal, the

designers of patterns such as these never, as far as I know, went beyond abstract motifs to recognizable representation. This does not detract from the beauty and ingenuity of their creations, in which more and less complicated systems can already be distinguished. The principle of 'rotation' appears in C even more clearly then in B, as will be described more fully below. But why did they never elaborate on associations, even though these must surely have arisen? The figure in C, in particular, reminds me of 'something I know'—a hammer, a bird or an aeroplane.

As it is precisely this crossing of the divide between abstract and concrete representations, between 'mute' and 'speaking' figures, which leads to the heart of what fascinates me above all in the regular division of the plane, it is important to discover whether there are actually reasons why figurative representations are not found anywhere.

I know of two cultures, the Jewish and the Islamic, which for religious reasons do not allow the making of 'images'.

In the second of the Ten Commandments, Moses forbade his people to make images (Exodus 20:4): 'Thou shalt not make unto thee any graven image, or any likeness of any thing that is in heaven above, or that is in the earth beneath, or that is in the water under the earth.' I find the emphasis upon what is 'in the water under the earth' particularly striking, because fish make such suitable motifs for filling my planes. 'Anything that is in heaven above' less obviously refers to birds—or perhaps it does not refer to birds at all; it may rather refer to the sun, moon, stars or clouds.

As far as I know, practising orthodox Jews have generally kept this commandment. Jewish artists must therefore find it difficult to be practising believers.

Regarding the Muslims, I gained my information from someone who is more familiar with the subject than I. The following is an extract from his letter:

'I have found an article by the great Islamic scholar Professor C. Snouck Hurgronje (in his *Miscellaneous Writings* II, pp. 453 ff.), from which I gather that there is *no* prohibition in the Koran concerning the depiction of living creatures, but that it is based on the sacred text (*hadith*), which reads: "He who makes images will suffer the most severe punishment on the Last Day." This refers to the makers of images, while a text about the presence of images in houses reads that "the angels of mercy do not enter dwellings where there are images".

'The orthodox writings completely confirm these texts. They describe the creation of images of well-loved or respected people as an abomination, because they see it as the root of idolatry. Moreover, depicting anything that has been created is an imitation of the work of Creation and can therefore only be a caricature. This kind of presumption is wrongful in the eyes of God, and on the Last Day the wretched image-makers will be required to blow life into their creations. This is the theory; in practice, however, it is different and even the various books of law make concessions, which in general terms boil down to the idea that if an image is made or put in such a place that it will be treated or touched without respect—for instance, pictures on carpets that are trodden underfoot or cushions that are sat upon, or in corridors or places where it would be impossible for them to lead to idolatry—the use of images is not forbidden. This applies to the user, *not* to the maker; for the maker, the letter of the law applies.

'In countries like Persia and India these commandments were set aside on a large scale; however, I do not know what the situation was in countries where the law was adhered to more strictly, in Arabia for example, and presumably also in Moorish Spain. In Persia and India not only were animals depicted quite freely, but also people, and even the Prophet, not to mention the rulers, military leaders, important officials, etc., although this was mainly in miniaturist art.

'Thus there was a prohibition, not in the Koran but in the religious tradition, for the maker and the user with regard to the representation of *living* creatures. It was thought to conflict with the ideas on the work of the Creator, which cannot be equalled by mortal man, any such attempt only leading to caricature.'

I do not believe that there are prohibitions against making images for any other people besides Jews and Muslims. The Japanese and the Chinese were not hindered at all by their religion in crossing this threshold and transcending the first stages of the regular division of the plane illustrated in A, B and C. And yet, as far as I know, neither they nor any other peoples keen on decoration have ever done so. In fact, most have not even reached this primitive stage. Possibly they never attempted the division of a plane exclusively into similar figures, except for the embryonic patterns of regular polygons, squares and triangles that are often seen on our own floors and walls. Altogether it is doubly unfortunate that the only people obviously intrigued by this possibility—the Moors—was not allowed to proceed beyond abstractions, quite apart from the question whether they would have wanted to.

As I wrote at the beginning of this essay, I wander through the garden of the regular division of the plane all alone. No matter how much satisfaction can be gained from being lord of one's own domain, the loneliness is not easy; in this case it really seems impossible. Every artist—or rather, everyone, to avoid referring to 'art' as much as possible—has all sorts of highly personal characteristics and idiosyncrasies. However, filling up a plane with regular shapes is not a nervous tic, bad habit or hobby. It is not a subjective pursuit but an objective one. Try as I will, I cannot accept that something as obvious as making adjacent figures recognizable and giving them a meaning, function or significance has never occurred to anyone but myself. It is only when we advance beyond the primitive stage that the game becomes more than simple decoration.

Long before I discovered in the Alhambra an affinity with the Moors in the regular division of the plane, I had recognized this

III

interest in myself. At first I had no idea at all of the possibility of systemetically building up my figures. I did not know any 'ground rules' and tried, almost without knowing what I was doing, to fit together congruent shapes that I attempted to give the form of animals. Gradually, designing new motifs became easier as a result of my study of the literature on the subject, as far as this was possible for someone untrained in mathematics, and especially as a result of my putting forward my own layman's theory, which forced me to think through the possibilities. It remains an extremely absorbing activity, a real mania to which I have become addicted, and from which I sometimes find it hard to tear myself away.

How slowly one moves in a boat that is not floating with the current! How much easier it is to continue the work of illustrious predecessors whose worth is accepted by everyone. A personal experiment, an edifice where one has to dig the foundations and build the walls oneself stands a good chance of turning into a ramshackle shed, and yet one might choose to live there rather than in a palace built by someone else.

Before going on to discuss each of the illustrations, I should like to indicate the method used in all of them except woodcut VI to represent the different systems. In each case there are three stages to be distinguished. The first stage is the reverse of the final stage, that is, a white object on a black background as against a black object on a white background. The second stage is intermediary between the two, and is the true, complete division of the plane, in which the opposing elements are equal. In I, 2 and 3 of woodcut II these three stages run horizontally, while in woodcuts III, IV and V the transition takes place vertically for the sake of variety.

I continue with woodcut II and consider the three strips in sequence.

The beetle in strip I is another example of sliding, and as such it is similar to the fish and birds in woodcut I. But the beetles are symmetrical laterally, and are seen from above, whereas the figures in woodcut I are asymmetrical and are viewed from the side.

The vertical and horizontal directions of observation raise the question of the types of recognizable objects that are most suitable for use as motifs in the regular division of the plane.

Firstly, they should be enclosed forms; it should be possible to enclose the whole figure with an unbroken outline—they should be separate objects. This considerably limits the choice among the infinite number of shapes surrounding us. For example, plants, which are joined to the earth more obviously than animals, do not make good objects for use in the regular division of the plane, since they can hardly be depicted without giving an indication of what they are joined to. Similarly, parts of plants, flowers or leaves, are not obvious figures for the division of the plane (unless they have become detached).

Secondly, the outline should be as characteristic as possible. It should clearly identify the nature of the object; preferably the effect of the silhouette should be so striking that the object can be recognized even without any internal detail, which always has a disturbing effect on the figure as a unit.

Thirdly, there should be no excessively deep or shallow indentations or bulges in the outline. These, too, make the figure difficult to grasp in its entirety. The adjacent black and white shapes should be easy to distinguish, without straining the observer's eye. The beetle in strip I is a borderline case: the succession of white and black legs would turn into a grey arched plane if they were thinner or longer, and each individual leg would be difficult to recognize as part of the body of a beetle.

The motifs for the division of the plane that satisfy these three conditions are less common than one might think.

Inanimate objects that can be recognized as familiar things almost always belong to the category of man-made tools. Their silhouettes are usually too simple and too straight, and lack sufficient indentation. Their profiles are often symmetrical, and although this need not in itself be an objection, as the beetle motif has shown, in most cases their shapes are unsuitable for the game of dividing the plane because of it.

The most usual shapes are those of living creatures. However, for animals the question immediately arises, from what angle should they be viewed so that their silhouettes are as characteristic as possible? Quadruped mammals are usually most easily recognized when viewed from the side, while reptiles and insects appear most typical from above and the human form is most characteristic when seen from the front.

My experience has taught me that the silhouettes of birds and fish are the most gratifying shapes of all for use in the game of dividing the plane. The silhouette of a flying bird has just the necessary angularity, while the bulges and indentations in the outline are neither too pronounced nor too subtle. In addition, it has a characteristic shape, from above and below, from the front and the side. A fish is almost equally suitable; its silhouette can be used when viewed from any direction but the front.

The dragonfly motif in strip 2 shows the second of the three principles for the division of the plane, which I termed 'rotation' above.

Whereas all the beetles in strip I—both the black and the white ones—were shown in the same position, climbing vertically, the dragonflies behave differently. At the left of the strip they are facing alternately to the left and to the right, as black objects on a white background, their longitudinal axis being horizontal. At the right of the strip they appear in a vertical position as white figures, with their heads alternately pointing up and down. They have turned 90 degrees in relation to the black ones, but in addition both the white and the black ones have themselves turned 180 degrees.

IV

To help us to understand these two rotating movements we can imagine two identical photographic transparencies of the middle section placed one on top of the other on a lighted screen. Initially they are placed so that the white area of the top one completely coincides with the white of the lower one, and the black area covers the black. At a point where four dragonfly wings meet, we insert a needle through the two films and, keeping the bottom transparency still, rotate the top one, using the needle as a pivot. At first this gives a kaleidoscopic effect of white and black shapes multiplying and continually changing shape, with the proportion of black continually increasing and the proportion of white decreasing until we have gone through a quarter circle. In other words, when the upper transparency has rotated exactly 90 degrees in relation to the lower, all the white shapes have disappeared, obscured by the black. After rotating through another quarter circle, white and black are equal again, as in our starting point. In this way the motifs cover each other four times during a full rotation of 360 degrees; this is known as a fourfold rotation. On the other hand, if we prick the needle through the films at a point where two heads and two tails come together, there are only two moments where the figures cover each other during a full rotation, and these are positioned diametrically opposite one another—a twofold rotation point.

The flying fish of strip 3 also fill the plane by a system of rotation, though this is different and more complicated. The original figure in the dragonfly design was a square, but in this case it is an equilateral triangle. Instead of two different rotation points, there are now three—a twofold, a threefold and a sixfold. The way in which they change round on the plane is easier to illustrate (fig. 1) than to describe. Three series of parallel lines have been drawn, intersecting at angles of 60 degrees and thus dividing the plane into equilateral triangles. The twofold rotation points are indicated by elliptical symbols in the middle of one side of each triangle. Small triangles indicate the threefold points and little hexagons show where the sixfold points are. So there are two threefold points, one twofold and one sixfold in each fish. After my description of the rotations of the dragonfly pattern, it should not be difficult for the reader to imagine putting the needle pivot again on the different rotation points and describing arcs of 180, 120 and 60 degrees respectively.

Although the pattern dividing the plane in strip 3 is created in a manner following no less stringent laws than those governing the patterns in strips 1 and 2, there seems to be a greater freedom, a spontaneity and playfulness in the six positions of these flying fish. This is not only because of the absence of right angles, but also because the figures themselves are no longer laterally symmetrical. Anyone with a feeling for the strange beauty of the regular division of the plane will derive more pleasure from this last example than from the preceding ones.

Woodcut III embodies the third principle of dividing a plane, glide reflection. Again the figures that constitute the pattern are all similar, but the black horsemen and the white horsemen are each congruent only among themselves, that is, only the black can cover black, and white, the white, without moving off the plane. (Just as a right and a left hand are not congruent, though they are similar.) Examples of congruency are seen in strips 1, 2 and 3 of woodcut II, in which the figures could be made to cover each other by being shifted or rotated without disturbing the two-dimensionality. If, however—as in the case of the horsemen—motifs are repeated in mirror image, one of them has to move through the third dimension for covering to be possible. It must leave the plane and be turned upside down before being slid to cover its former reflection. This is the movement summarized in the term 'glide reflection'.

Another instance of glide reflection can be seen in woodcut IV. Yet the system by which the dogs adjoin and reflect each other is basically different from that used in woodcut III. The black horsemen all ride from right to left, in rows one above the other, and the white ones all ride from left to right; here, white is always a mirror image of black. However, in woodcut IV each horizontal procession of congruent dogs consists of alternating black and white dogs, so that motifs of the *same* colour can also be each other's mirror images.

Finally, woodcut V is an example of glide reflection combined with rotation, while at the same time two figures of different shapes are repeated in the pattern. Both are reptilian with a head, a tail and four legs. But the black ones are squat, broad and short, while the white ones are long and thin. Another example of dividing the plane with two dissimilar motifs was used in the decorative pattern on the spine of this book [see page 169]: a light and a dark bird are repeated according to the principle of sliding. In woodcut V, however, the reptiles adjoin in a complicated way which again is more easily illustrated (fig. 2) than described. The basic shapes are diamonds. The reptiles seem to be laterally symmetrical. (However, this symmetry is illusory, as can be observed by comparing the left and right hind legs of the white creatures.) The long diagonals of the diamonds form the longitudinal axes of the white reptiles, the short ones those of the black reptiles. Pairs of horizontal rows of diamonds are repeated over and over again glide-reflected. The rotation points are exclusively twofold and are again indicated by a small elliptical symbol. They can be found at the intersections in the middle of each pair of two glide-reflecting rows.

Before continuing with the discussion of the remaining illustrations, I should say something about the application of the division of the plane to horizontal and vertical surfaces.

Horizontal and vertical are concepts so inherent to life on earth

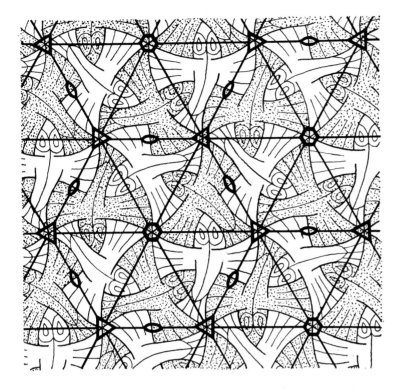

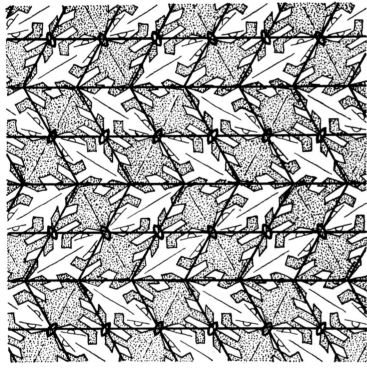

that we are hardly aware of them. The force of gravity controls all our activity on the spherical surface of the earth. Natural phenomena around us continually show us vertical lines, for instance in trees thrusting upwards perpendicularly, or in the thread of a spider as it lets itself down; horizontal lines can be seen in the surface of the sea or pools. When man builds he is no more than a servant or a slave of gravity, and the artist interested in architectural decoration and filling planes is inevitably confronted with the choice between vertical, rectangular walls and horizontal floors and ceilings on which to express his ideas. Consequently, he must ask himself what would look better depicted vertically and what horizontally.

I already mentioned the directions—from above and below, from the front and the side—in which animals' silhouettes appear most characteristic. It is obvious that a bird seen from below outlined against a background of clouds or blue sky is a more appropriate subject for the ceiling than for the floor of a room. On the other hand, a fish seen as if in water from the balustrade of a bridge or the side of a ship would be more suitable for a floor than a ceiling. Both examples suggest the horizontal, though these images of the heights and the depths can also be depicted on walls, as they often are; our imagination is versatile enough for this to be acceptable. It is different with animals seen from the side or the front. A vertical surface is definitely preferable for representing these. The horsemen pattern in woodcut III and the dogs pattern in woodcut IV would be decidedly less suitable as a floor or ceiling decoration than as a wall decoration, because the concepts 'above' and 'below', which are inextricably linked to their appearance, are not interchangeable. Thus we may say that, on the whole, glide-reflection motifs are suitable for walls, rotation motifs for floors and ceilings, and sliding figures for both.

In general, and not particularly in connection with the regular division of the plane, our own verticality is the reason why the walls of rooms are covered with pictures and patterns more often than the floors and ceilings. We happen to look towards the horizon more readily and with less strain on our neck muscles than we look up or down. Only when we are lying down flat do our eyes turn automatically towards the heavens. It is therefore understandable that since time immemorial artists have had a marked preference for subjects with a horizon, whether visible or not, and that they usually paint pictures designed to be seen on the vertical plane.

Thinking about all this reminds me of the tours through the Sistine Chapel I made with an expert guide a number of times when I was living in Rome. No matter how fascinating Michelangelo's ceiling is, the effort of staring upwards while standing is my predominant memory. A less exalted example, but one that was easier and more pleasant to look at, was the spectacle that presented itself to my eyes as I was being shaved by my Roman barber, whose premises were in one of the rooms of an old palazzo. I often think of those flourishes and pink cherubs with

Top: Figure 1   *Above*: Figure 2

167

nostalgia when I am sitting back in my Dutch barber's chair and see nothing but a bare, unimaginative ceiling.

Just as I started in woodcut I with a 'story' in pictures, I now end in woodcut VI with another example of what may be considered as dynamic progression. In this case there is no developmental process of contrast and shape, but a halving or a doubling, a diminution or an enlargement, a division or a multiplication depending on whether the print is read from the top downwards or from the foot upwards. Whichever description we choose, it is the case that 'something happens' in a vertical direction. Two limits can clearly be distinguished: at the top the plane is limited by the 'singleness' of one reptilian creature, which spans the entire width of the print like a roof; at the bottom the design is concluded in a horizontal line by the 'multiplicity' of a theoretically infinite number of infinitely small creatures.

This process is represented diagrammatically in figure 3. The creatures have been simplified to their initial basic form of right-angled isosceles triangles; the limit of diminution is attained in the base line rs.

The progression from top to bottom goes as follows: the triangles O, A1 and B1 together make a square, in which the line pq is one of the diagonals. The surface A1 is the same as B1, and together they are equal to O. But A1, C1 and E1 also form a square; so that C1 and E1 are each half of A1. This demonstrates how the surfaces are constantly halved: $0 = 2 \times A1 = 4 \times E1 = 8 \times A2 = 16 \times E2 = 32 \times A3$, and so on, *ad infinitum*.

Superficially all the reptiles in woodcut VI seem to be similar. But in fact the pattern is built up of six figures which are neither similar nor congruent but, as six together, constitute a group or block that is repeated as a unit.

If we again substitute the triangles shown in the figure for the reptilian creatures, the rectangle pqut is one of these blocks of six. It is repeated in a similar block, four times smaller, in the rectangle tvxw. All the individual reptiles indicated by the same capital letter, for example E1, E2, E3, etc., are similar.

As we are concerned here with a system of dividing the plane in which three figures touch at one point, white and black alone are insufficient to distinguish them: a third shade should really have been used to distinguish the third figure. I have deliberately not done this. The only other shade I could have used would have been grey. However, in this woodcut grey has a specific function as the colour of the background. When white and black shapes become smaller and smaller and get closer and closer, becoming in theory infinitely small, the ideal grey described at the beginning of this essay is created automatically. Therefore not only is the surround of the woodcut grey, as in all the other prints, but an attempt is made within the print to achieve the ideal grey, which results when black and white coalesce.

168   Woodcut VI is the only example in this series in which the division

of the plane requires more than two shades. A complete survey of the possibilities of the regular division of the plane would need to contain at least twenty illustrations in three colours in addition to black and white. I have designed numerous patterns with a rhythmic repetition of two different shapes, as shown in woodcut V, and even of three or more dissimilar figures, for which it is advisable to use three or even four colours. The equivalence of three motifs requires three equivalent colours. White, grey and black are unsuitable for this; they are not equivalent because they form a progression, expressing an increasing intensity.

The fact that I have restricted myself in this essay to white and black accords very well with my propensity for a 'dualistic' outlook. I have hardly ever experienced the pleasure of the artist who uses colour for its own sake; I use colour only when the nature of my shapes makes it necessary or when I am forced to do so by the fact that there are more than two motifs.

The idea of infinite extension inherent in the regular division of the plane does not lead to logical enclosure in any of the woodcuts we have been discussing, not even in the last, which lends itself to unlimited extension to left and right. Yet the urge for enclosure and bordering is one of the motives that have stimulated me to make quite a number of closed compositions inspired by the division of the plane.

Even though it is unfortunately impossible to reproduce these works here, I should still like to say something about the most important of the ideas that I have tried to express in them. These I can divide into five sections:

I   TWO-DIMENSIONALITY

The question is to what extent we are aware of space and the miracle that we call 'reality'. Our whole existence is so closely tied up with the concept of three-dimensionality that we can no more truly imagine two dimensions than four. The perfectly flat plane exists for us no more than anything beyond space. If an element in the division of the plane suggests the shape of an animal to me, it immediately makes me think of volume. The flat shape irritates me—I feel like telling my objects, you are too fictitious, lying there next to each other static and frozen: *do* something, come off the paper and show me what you are capable of!

So I make them come out of the plane. Not, of course, in reality. On the contrary, I am deliberately inconsistent, suggesting a plasticity in the plane by means of light and shade. In this way I enter dangerous territory, quicksands on which I prefer not to venture too far. Words, at least my words, are not adequate to approach it; pictures do so much better.

My objects, given life in a fictitious way, are now able to proceed as independent plastic creatures, and they may finally return to the plane and disappear into their place of origin. This cycle then forms a complete subject to be used in a print.

If the plane-filling design that served as a starting point consists

of the repetition of two motifs differing in form and character, these can express any opposite quality by consuming each other, or, if a more peaceful solution is preferred, by reconciliation in an embrace. Obviously there are all kinds of possible variations on this theme, and I have let myself be tempted to use a different solution in each case.

2 CURVED SURFACES

Instead of leaving the plane only in the imagination, as described above, it is possible to do so in reality. I do not mean that the figures should step out of the plane completely as separate individuals, for instance by being modelled in clay, for the result would be ambivalent, half flat and half spatial. What I have in mind is the possibility of bending and folding the picture plane itself. Why should not the surface of a cylinder or a cone, an egg or a sphere be as suitable as a plane for rhythmical division? This appeared to be the case when I tried it: for example, the surface of a sphere can be divided into 2, 4, 6, 8, 12, 20, 24 or more equivalent and similar spherical triangles, which are either congruent or each other's mirror image. As an object in itself, such a sphere covered with a finite number of repeated motifs forms a beautiful symbol of infinity in an enclosed form. If you take it in your hand and slowly rotate it, the figures covering it form an infinite progression, and yet they are always the same figures repeating themselves. I have made a number of such spheres in wood with the motifs carved in bas-relief; an effect of contrast was obtained by staining the wood in two or more shades.

However, such a leap into space remains exceptional for someone who is not a sculptor. A graphic artist can rarely afford this sort of excursion into reality, and he likes to return to the flat surface and the illusionism in which he feels more at home. Moreover, these offer him a wider field in which to develop his fantasies. Nevertheless, a graphic artist can use the cylinder, if he so wishes, without abandoning his métier, by bending the paper on which he has made the print into a tube, so that the top and the bottom—or the right and the left—of his design join up. But the division of the plane would still be arbitrarily limited in the direction of the cylinder's axis. He could never shape his plane into a sphere without creasing the paper.

3 THE DYNAMIC EQUILIBRIUM BETWEEN THE MOTIFS

This most fascinating aspect of the division of the plane, already described above, has led to the creation of numerous prints. It is here that the representation of opposites of all kinds arises. For is not one led naturally to a subject such as *Day and Night* by the double function of the black and the white motifs? It is night when the white, as an object, shows up against the black as a background, and day when the black figures show up against the white. Likewise, the idea of a duality such as air and water can be expressed in a picture by starting from a plane-filling design of birds and fish; the birds are 'water' for the fish, and the fish are

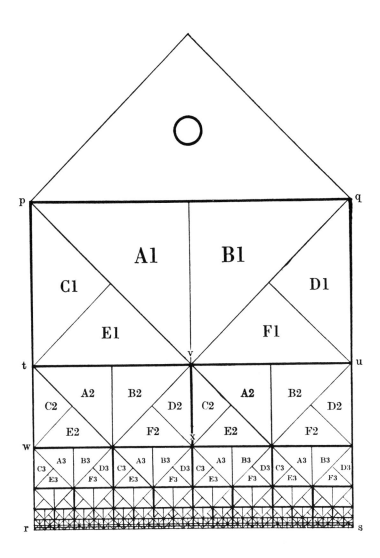

Top: Detail of the design for the cover   *Above*: Figure 3

169

'air' for the birds. Heaven and Hell can be symbolized by an interplay of angels and devils. There are many other possible pairs of dynamic subjects—at least in theory, for in most cases their realization meets with insuperable difficulties.

4 THE PICTURE STORY, THE ACTION

The dynamic character of the regular division of the plane was discussed in the description of woodcuts I and VI, as well as in the preceding paragraph. I once tried reducing the elements in size as far as possible, as in woodcut VI, but with the 'limit' of the smallest in the centre of the design, that is, at a point instead of in a line. The material I chose was a cube of palmwood of the best quality available, and on this I engraved figures of animals starting from the edges and reducing towards the centre. As I came to the centre, my hand had to be steadier, my eyes sharper, and the demands I made on my burin and my material became higher and higher. When the space was reduced to one square centimetre, I needed a system of three magnifying glasses, one on top of the other, to see clearly what I was doing. The smallest figure recognizable as a complete animal—with a head, tail and four legs—had an overall length of about two millimetres. In the course of this extremely precise job—precise by my standards, but what is our Western skill compared with the expertise of the craftsmen of the East?—I found again that the human hand is capable of minute yet utterly controlled movements, as long as the eye can see clearly enough what the hand is doing. When the hand becomes unsteady, this can almost always be attributed to the inadequacy of the artist's sight. When one thinks one has reached the limits of one's dexterity, increased dexterity is often possible if a stronger magnifying glass is used.

I have also often depicted the developmental processes of shapes and of intensity of contrast (as in woodcut I) in strip form, sometimes in a closed circle, or moving inwards towards a centre, or radiating outwards from a centre. It is even possible to turn this evolutionary process into the story of the Creation. Primitive forms emerge from a misty indeterminate greyness, developing in progressively contrasting shades into animal figures—creatures of the earth, sea and sky, outlined, in the final stage of their development, against the background of the element in which they live. I made a print like this many years ago.

5 METAMORPHOSIS

It is difficult to describe the metamorphoses of the motifs, so that an example is given in figure 4. It shows a fragment, greatly reduced in scale, of a series of metamorphoses—associations of images and ideas united in a woodcut, printed from 16 different blocks on a strip of paper four metres long. The fragment reproduced here shows just one metamorphosis, namely, from left to right, the transition from 'insect' to 'bird'. First the black insect silhouettes join; at the moment when they touch, their white background has become the shape of a fish. Then figures and background change places and white fish can be seen swimming against a black background. Thus the fish function as a catalyst; their shape hardly changes but their position vis-à-vis each other does: their ranks change. When they have joined, the spaces between them have turned into birds.

Figure 4 shows again that a succession of figures with a number of metamorphoses acquires a dynamic character. Above I pointed out the difference between a series of cinematographic images projected on a screen and the series of figures in the regular division of a plane. Although in the latter the figures are shown all at once, side by side, in both cases the time factor plays a part.

Here I should like to venture still further and point out comparisons, possibly even analogies, between the regular division of the plane and music. Not that I consider them equal in magnitude, for music may be seen as equal to the whole range of the visual arts, in which the regular division of the plane plays only an extremely small part—even when it is an artistic manifestation; it is, of course, possible to regard it as an objective matter quite apart from any thought of art.

Before I mention what I see as correspondences, I should question whether it is meaningful to compare image and sound. I should say straight away that I am aware of their different natures. Music exists only as it is heard—from the time it starts to the time it ends, not before or after; whereas a series of pictures is static and does not have to be re-created continually once it has been made. I also realize that the arts can be divided into two groups: on the one hand, those in which duration is fixed, such as music, the theatre, film and dance; on the other hand, the visual arts with their material products, including architecture.

Despite these differences in their natures, I believe that the series of images in the division of a plane and the succession of sounds in a piece of music can be seen as if they were rungs of a single ladder, linked by intermediate rungs as follows: first, the visual perception of images placed side by side on a plane: second, the silent reading of text, that is, the mental interpretation of word symbols placed side by side; third, the reading aloud of text, so that the words are now a sequence of sound vibrations; fourth, the singing of words, the creation of a song; fifth, the singing of a wordless melody; sixth, instrumental music.

Now to point out the correspondences I have noticed, most tentatively, and leaving it to the reader to decide whether or not they have any validity.

Just as music has different types of rhythmic organization, indicated by two, three, four and six beats to the bar, the division of a plane can be composed using two-, three-, four- and sixfold rotation points, each representing a particular method of rhythmic repetition of the motifs on the plane.

It seems an indisputable fact that 5/4 time is less popular with the average music-lover than the other time signatures mentioned above. I believe that it was not used at all until the beginning of the

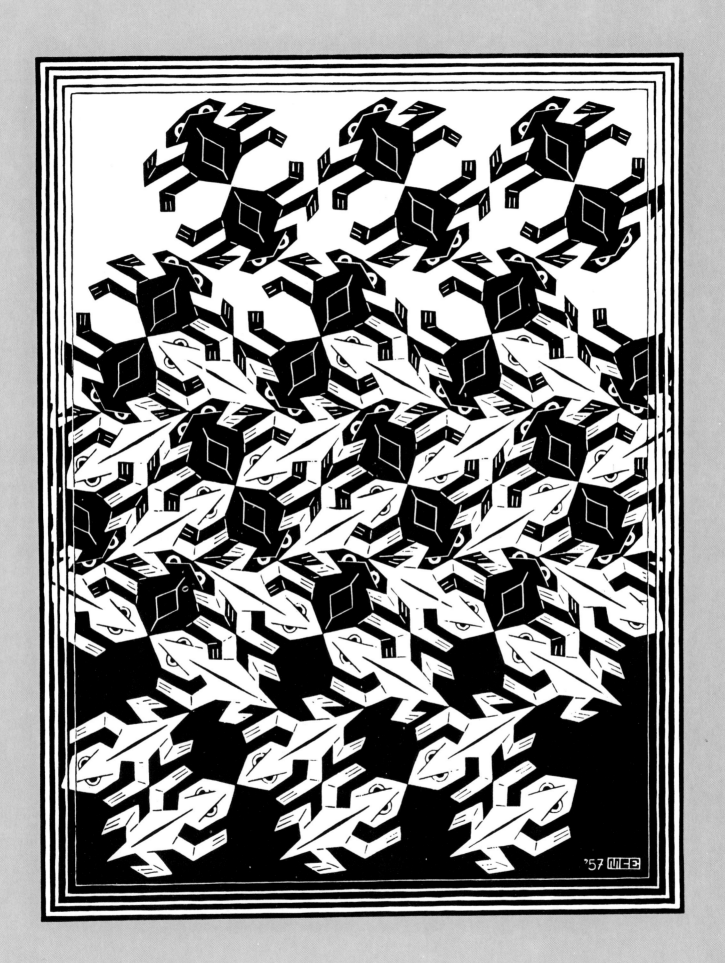

nineteenth century, and then only sporadically compared with the old, tried and tested time signatures. It would be going too far to suggest a direct analogy with the absence of a fivefold rotation point on the flat plane—which is only possible on a spherical surface—but it is worth remarking on as a curious coincidence.

That general elements such as rhythm and repetition play an important role both for the ears in music and for the eyes in the division of the plane also indicates some relationship between them. I have often noticed that 'counting the beat' does not become possible only with the static figures on the plane, but begins before this, when, drawing on paper or engraving in wood, the hand makes repeated rhythmic movements as in a dance, which the artist feels the urge to emphasize with his voice, by singing.

More particularly, it seems that musical canons incorporate concepts such as augmentation, diminution, retrogression and even mirroring. These are visually indicated in the score in a way directly comparable with the figures of the regular division of a plane.

To conclude, let me mention the influence of Bach's music on my work. His rationality, his mathematical order and the strictness of his rules probably have much to do with this, though not directly. As far as I can observe, hearing his music influences my feelings, yet despite or perhaps because of this, the flow of his sounds has an inspiring effect, evoking particular images or flashes of inspiration, and also, more generally, stimulating an unquenchable desire for expression. His music, more than any other classical or modern composer's, reveals something self-evident to me, something I expected without being aware of it, just as one sometimes 'recognizes' a landscape that one sees for the first time. In the middle of a sterile period, I am sometimes filled with a vague feeling of expectancy and sudden hope during a concert. The desire for creativity precedes the desire to create something specific, and is the spark to set the process of expression in motion. In my periods of weakness and spiritual emptiness and lethargy, I reach out to Bach's music to revive and fire my desire for creativity.

Figure 4

Catalogue

Compiled by   F.H. Bool   J.L. Locher   F. Wierda

This catalogue of prints provides a complete survey of Escher's etchings, wood engravings, woodcuts, linoleum cuts, lithographs and mezzotints. Woodcuts that have been printed exclusively on textiles have not been included, but where these are printed on textiles as well as on paper, this is stated.

Descriptions of the prints are based on the archives of the Gemeente-museum in The Hague, unless otherwise stated.

CONTENTS

The catalogue consists of two parts. Pages 178–328 contain the illustrations with short descriptions. Pages 329–43 give further information about the prints.

ORDER OF CONTENTS

In principle the prints are arranged in chronological order. The following five criteria were used:

1 Where the year and the month are known, this order is followed.

2 Where the month is not known, but the period in the year is ('between March and July'), the print is put after the last month of this period.

3 Where only the year is known, it is put at the end of that year.

4 Where only a period of two years is known ('1919 or 1920'), it is put after the first year.

5 Where the date is between square brackets (for their significance see below), the print is put after the prints with the same date without square brackets.

Six prints of unknown date (cat. nos. 233–38) have been put after a similar print which can be dated.

Prints from books illustrated by Escher (with woodcuts from the original blocks) have been entered in the order in which they are found in these books. The group of prints from each book has been located using similar criteria to those which apply to individual prints; see above.

The books are:

Flor de Pascua (1921). The woodcuts were completed in October 1921 and are therefore listed under that year (cat. nos. 68–83).

XXIV Emblemata (1932). The woodcuts were made in 1931 and 1932, and are therefore listed between these two years (cat. nos. 159–86).

De vreeselijke avonturen van Scholastica (The Terrible Adventures of Scholastica) (1932). The woodcuts were also made in 1931 and 1932, though mainly after those for *Emblemata*, and are therefore listed after them (cat. nos. 188–205).

Regelmatige vlakverdeling (The Regular Division of the Plane) (1958). The woodcuts were completed in June 1957, and are therefore listed under that year (cat. nos. 416–21).

Escher made woodcuts for *Emblemata* and *Scholastica* which were not used in the books. In both cases these woodcuts are listed immediately in front of the book group.

Pages 178–328

Prints and Descriptions

PRINTS

Only the image area of the print is shown, omitting margin with pencilled signature, information about editions, etc.

CATALOGUE NUMBER

Each print is numbered individually. Variations are indicated by an 'A' number. Cat. no 68 appears as A, B, C and D, since the four images formed a group in the booklet *Flor de Pascua*.

Posthumous prints (see below) are indicated by the letters PP after the catalogue number.

TITLE

Round brackets are used for parenthesis where two or more titles used by Escher himself are known. The less commonly used variant is given in parenthesis.

Square brackets are used for parenthesis to enclose a descriptive title where no title given by Escher is known.

For many of his early prints (up to c. 1940) Escher gave a descriptive Italian title. These titles are not used here.

DATE

Dates shown between square brackets are approximate, while often derived from reliable sources. These sources are to be found listed under 'Notes on the Illustrations' (pages 329–43). Where no source is given, the date has been estimated on the basis of stylistic characteristics, etc.

TECHNIQUE

Prints include linoleum cuts, woodcuts, wood engravings, lithographs, mezzotints, etchings. If more than one state is known, the state of the print shown is given. If the print shown is a counterproof, this is indicated.

COLOURING

Most of the originals of the prints shown in this catalogue are printed in black or grey on white paper. Where this is not the case, details are given after the technique used.

DIMENSIONS

Dimensions of the prints are given in millimetres and inches, height preceding width.

Notes on the Illustrations

Posthumous Prints

GENERAL

This second part of the catalogue supplements the particulars given in the captions on pages 178–328. Where no further information is available, the print is not listed.

ORDER OF INFORMATION

1 Catalogue number
2 Title (often abbreviated)
3 Collection (see below)
4 Note on date (where applicable)
5 Location within the print of signature and/or date
6 Location in margin of added signature and/or date
7 Other additions
8 Text incorporated in the print
9 Other information

N.B.   6 and 7 refer only to the particular example of the print illustrated. This information may not apply to other copies of the same print.

The edition printed is not given, since it is not possible to be certain about this, especially as regards the woodcuts and engravings.

COLLECTION

Unless otherwise indicated, prints are in the collection of the Gemeentemuseum in The Hague. Most of the other collections indicated as holding prints are open to the public. The Beels collection is housed in the Meermanno-Westreenianum Museum in The Hague; the Roosevelt and Schwartz collections can be found in the National Gallery of Art in Washington, D.C.

The A numbers reproduced (variations) are in some cases in private collections (which are not named).

The blocks used to print many of Escher's woodcuts and engravings, linoleum cuts and mezzotints have been preserved. They have been rendered unusable, mostly by being drilled, to prevent pirate copies.

When this collection of blocks was examined, it appeared that there were six of which no prints were known. These were three early prints (dating from 1917, 1920 and 1921), a basic block for wrapping-paper, a variation of the black block that was never printed for a multi-coloured woodcut dating from 1939, and an unfinished woodcut variation of cat. no. 334 (see page 65).

This last unfinished block could not be printed, because the design on it would then have been lost. The other five (one linoleum block and four wood blocks), however, have been reproduced. These posthumous prints—all with drilled holes—are shown in chronological order in the first part of the catalogue with only their catalogue number (followed by the letters PP) and the title.

1
[Escher's Father, G. A. Escher]. 1916
Linoleum cut in purple
$210 \times 157 \, (8^1/_4 \times 6^1/_8'')$

2
[Bookplate Bastiaan Kist]. [1916]
Linoleum cut in red and black, printed
from two blocks
$103 \times 123 \, (4 \times 4^7/_8'')$

3
[Chrysanthemum]. [1916]
Linoleum cut in green
$164 \times 131 \, (6^1/_2 \times 5^1/_8'')$

4
[Head of a Child]. [1916]
Linoleum cut in green
$114 \times 89 \, (4^1/_2 \times 3^1/_2'')$

5
[Skull]. January 1917
Linoleum cut in two tones of grey,
touched up by hand
$211 \times 174 \, (8^1/_4 \times 6^7/_8'')$

6
[Railway Bridge across the Rhine at
Oosterbeek]. [January 1917]
Etching, first state
$86 \times 123 \, (3^3/_8 \times 4^7/_8'')$

7
[Mascot]. [January 1917]
Etching, second state
$76 \times 60 \, (3 \times 2^3/_8'')$

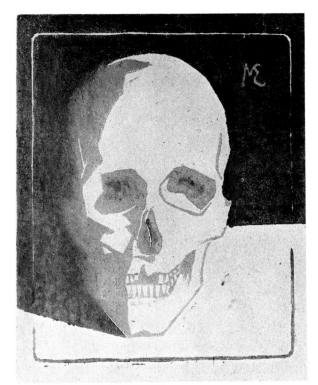

1 2   4 5
3   6 7

8
[Portrait of a Man]. February 1917
Linoleum cut
$188 \times 137 \, (7^3/_8 \times 5^3/_8'')$

9 PP
[Self-Portrait]
Described on page 343

10
[Hen with Egg]. August 1917
Linoleum cut, second state
$113 \times 115 \, (4^1/_2 \times 4^1/_2'')$

11
[Still Life]. December 1917
Linoleum cut
$234 \times 163 \, (9^1/_4 \times 6^3/_8'')$

12
[Baby]. 1917
Linoleum cut
$93 \times 110 \, (3^5/_8 \times 4^3/_8'')$

13
Young Thrush. 1917
Linoleum cut
$96 \times 86 \, (3^3/_4 \times 3^3/_8'')$

14
[Monogram MCE]. 1917
Linoleum cut in red
$51 \times 51 \, (2 \times 2'')$

8   9   12   14
10   11   13

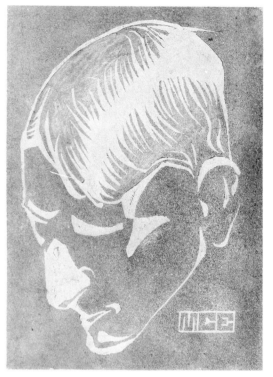

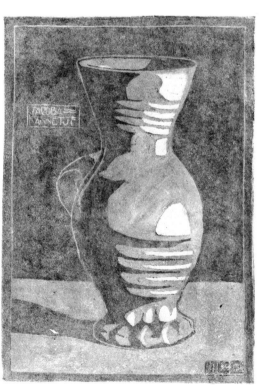

15
Bookplate M.C. Escher. 1917
Linoleum cut in green
106 × 71 (4^1/$_8$ × 2^3/$_4$")

16
Bookplate Heleen van Thienen. 1917
Linoleum cut
107 × 80 (4^1/$_4$ × 3^1/$_8$")

17
[Self-Portrait]. 1917
Linoleum cut in green and brown,
printed from one block
147 × 104 (5^3/$_4$ × 4^1/$_8$")

18
Jug. [1917]
Linoleum cut in two tones of brown,
printed from two blocks
216 × 152 (8^1/$_2$ × 6")

19
The Rag Pickers. [January] 1918
Linoleum cut in black, wine-red and
purple, printed from three blocks
200 × 160 (7^7/$_8$ × 6^1/$_4$")

20
[Sunflowers]. [August] 1918
Linoleum cut
165 × 151 (6^1/$_2$ × 6")

21
[Fiet van Stolk-Van der Does de
Willebois]. August 1918
Linoleum cut, second state
146 × 108 (5^3/$_4$ × 4^1/$_4$")

22   25 26 27
23 24

22
[Waves]. 1918
Linoleum cut and watercolour in grey
and red
71 × 172 (2³/₄ × 6³/₄″)

23
[Two Bells]. 1918
Linoleum cut in brown
86 × 63 (3³/₈ × 2¹/₂″)

24
[Self-Portrait]. 1918
Linoleum cut in light blue and dark
blue, printed from two blocks
143 × 113 (5⁵/₈ × 4¹/₂″)

25
[Bookplate T. de Ridder]. 1918
Linoleum cut
Diameter 90 (3¹/₂″)
Compare cat. no. 26

26
[Bookplate Tony de Ridder]. [1918]
Linoleum cut in grey green
Diameter 50 (2″)
Compare cat. no. 25

27
Bookplate R. I. H. [Roosje Ingen
Housz]. March 1919
Woodcut
52 × 33 (2 × 1¹/₄″)

28
[White Cat]. [October or November]
1919
Woodcut
166 × 166 (6¹/₂ × 6¹/₂″)

29
[The Borger Oak, Oosterbeek]. 1919
Linoleum cut
98 × 83 (3⁷/₈ × 3¹/₄″)

30
[Portrait]. 1919
Linoleum cut
243 × 161 (9⁵/₈ × 6³/₈″)

31
[Portrait of a Bearded Man]. 1919
Woodcut
c. 120 × 90 (4³/₄ × 3¹/₂″)

32
[Seated Man with a Cat on His Lap].
1919
Woodcut
117 × 90 (4⁵/₈ × 3¹/₂″)

33
[Blocks of Basalt along the Sea]. 1919
Woodcut
165 × 165 (6¹/₂ × 6¹/₂″)
Compare cat. no. 84

34
[Tree]. 1919
Woodcut
392 × 313 (15¹/₂ × 12³/₈″)

187

28 30   32 34
29 31   33

188

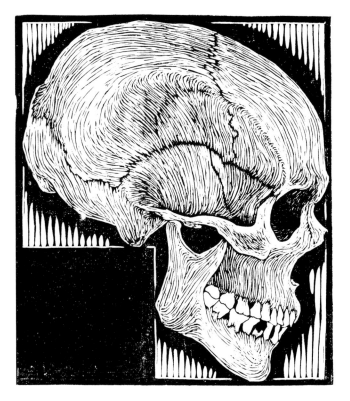

35
Life Force. 1919
Linoleum cut
428 × 426 (16⁷/₈ × 16³/₄")

36
[Self-Portrait]. 1919
Woodcut
175 × 131 (6⁷/₈ × 5¹/₈")

37
[Parrot]. [1919]
Linoleum cut
275 × 166 (10⁷/₈ × 6¹/₂")

38
[White Cat]. [1919]
Woodcut
163 × 251 (6³/₈ × 9⁷/₈")

39
[Skull]. [1919 or 1920]
Woodcut, second state; counterproof
199 × 172 (7⁷/₈ × 6³/₄")

40
[Wayang Puppet]. [1919 or 1920]
Woodcut
180 × 140 (7¹/₈ × 5¹/₂")

41
[Clouds above the Coast]. [1919 or
1920]
Linoleum cut
520 × 287 (20¹/₂ × 11¹/₄")

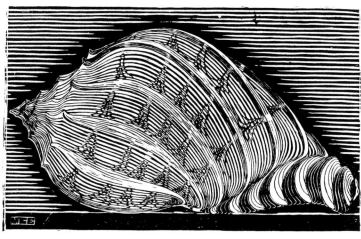

42
[Sea-shell]. [1919 or 1920]
Woodcut
165 × 251 (6^1/$_2$ × 9^7/$_8$″)

43
[Sea-shell]. [1919 or 1920]
Woodcut
138 × 230 (5^3/$_8$ × 9″)

44
[Self-Portrait in a Chair]. February
1920
Woodcut
195 × 168 (7^5/$_8$ × 6^5/$_8$″)

45 PP
[Rabbits]
Described on page 343

46
[Female Nude in a Landscape]. 1920
Woodcut; counterproof
180 × 265 (7^1/$_8$ × 10^3/$_8$″)

47
Fairy-tale. 1920
Woodcut
462 × 369 (18^1/$_4$ × 14^1/$_2$″)

48
Wild West. 1920
Woodcut
357 × 175 (14 × 6^7/$_8$″)

49
[The Fall of Man]. 1920
Woodcut; counterproof
347 × 347 (13^5/$_8$ × 13^5/$_8$″)

50
[Escher's Father with Magnifying
Glass]. [1920]
Linoleum cut
255 × 335 (10 × 13^1/$_4$″)

51
[Portrait of a Man]. [1920]
Woodcut
345 × 350 (13^5/$_8$ × 13^3/$_4$″)

52
[Man Standing]. [1920]
Woodcut
366 × 179 (14^1/$_2$ × 7″)

53
[Seated Old Woman]. [1920]
Woodcut
250 × 180 (9^7/$_8$ × 7^1/$_8$″)

54
[Flower]. [1920]
Etching
234 × 188 (9^1/$_4$ × 7^3/$_8$″)

55
[Seated Female Nude with Flowers].
[1920 or 1921]
Woodcut, second state, with pencil
corrections; counterproof
107 × 142 (4^1/$_4$ × 5^5/$_8$″)

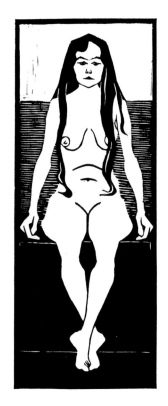

56
[Seated Female Nude]. [1920 or 1921]
Woodcut
186×74 ($7^3/_8 \times 2^7/_8''$)

57
[Female Nude in a Chair] [1920 or 1921]
Linoleum cut
544×306 ($21^3/_8 \times 12''$)

58
[Seated Female Nude]. [1920 or 1921]
Woodcut
228×205 ($9 \times 8^1/_8''$)

59
[Seated Female Nude]. [1920 or 1921]
Woodcut
340×204 ($13^3/_8 \times 8''$)

60
[In Mesquita's Classroom]. [1920 or 1921]
Woodcut
310×232 ($12^1/_4 \times 9^1/_8''$)

61
[Sea-shells]. [1920 or 1921]
Woodcut
330×602 ($13 \times 23^3/_4''$)

56 57   59 60
58   61

62
[Reclining Female Nude]. [1920 or 1921]
Lithograph
160 × 312 (6¹/₄ × 12¹/₄″)

63
[Roosje Ingen Housz]. [1920 or 1921]
Lithograph
173 × 150 (6³/₄ × 5⁷/₈″)

64
[Poster]. [1920 or 1921]
Lithograph in orange, purple, yellow and green
231 × 179 (9¹/₈ × 7″)

65
[Plane-filling Motif with Human Figures]. [1920 or 1921]
Woodcut
370 × 427 (14⁵/₈ × 16³/₄″)
Compare cat. no. 66

66
[Plane-filling Motif with Human Figures]. [1920 or 1921]
Lithograph in blue, green and red
432 × 312 (17 × 12¹/₄″)
Compare cat. no. 65

67
[Paradise]. [February] 1921
Woodcut, second state, printed on strawboard; counterproof
257 × 494 (10¹/₈ × 19¹/₂″)

197

62 63   65 66
    64   67

Flor de Pascua

68A
[Sunflower], page 5. 1921
Woodcut
18 × 18 (³/₄ × ³/₄″)

68B
[Heart], page 5. 1921
Woodcut
18 × 18 (³/₄ × ³/₄″)

68C
[Bluebells], page 5. 1921
Woodcut
18 × 18 (³/₄ × ³/₄″)

68D
[Alarm Clock], page 5. 1921
Woodcut
18 × 18 (³/₄ × ³/₄″)

69
[The Scapegoat], page 19. 1921
Woodcut
120 × 92 (4³/₄ × 3⁵/₈″)

70
[Convention], page 26. 1921
Woodcut
120 × 90 (4³/₄ × 3¹/₂″)

71
[Fulfilment?], page 35. 1921
Woodcut
120 × 92 (4³/₄ × 3⁵/₈″)

72
[Madonna], page 46. 1921
Woodcut
119 × 92 (4⁵/₈ × 3⁵/₈″)

73
[?], page 55. 1921
Woodcut
120 × 90 (4³/₄ × 3¹/₂″)

74
[The Ghost], page 70. 1921
Woodcut
120 × 90 (4³/₄ × 3¹/₂″)

75
[La Pensée], page 83. 1921
Woodcut
120 × 90 (4³/₄ × 3¹/₂″)

76
[Theosophy], page 95. 1921
Woodcut
120 × 91 (4³/₄ × 3⁵/₈″)

77
[The Weathercock], page 104. 1921
Woodcut
117 × 91 (4⁵/₈ × 3⁵/₈″)

78
[Perfume], page 122. 1921
Woodcut
120 × 90 (4³/₄ × 3¹/₂″)

79
[Whore's Superstition], page 134. 1921
Woodcut
120 × 90 (4³/₄ × 3¹/₂″)

80
[The Sphere], page 147. 1921
Woodcut
120 × 90 (4³/₄ × 3¹/₂″)
Compare cat. nos. 267, 268, 339 and
368

81
['Never Think before You Act'], page
156. 1921
Woodcut
120 × 90 (4³/₄ × 3¹/₂″)

82
[Beautiful], page 162. 1921
Woodcut
120 × 90 (4³/₄ × 3¹/₂″)

83
[Love], page 167. 1921
Woodcut
118 × 90 (4⁵/₈ × 3¹/₂″)

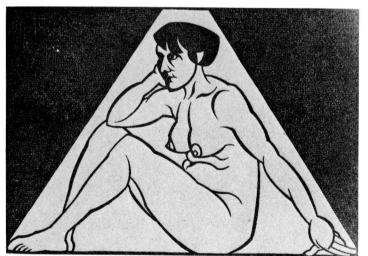

200

84
[Blocks of Basalt along the Sea]. 1921
Woodcut
139 × 180 (5¹/₂ × 7¹/₈″)
Compare cat. no. 33

85
[Seated Female Nude]. 1921
Woodcut, printed on blue paper
179 × 264 (7 × 10³/₈″)
Compare cat. no. 86

86
[Seated Female Nude]. [1921]
Linoleum cut
236 × 351 (9¹/₄ × 13⁷/₈″)
Compare cat. no. 85

87 PP
[Wood near Menton]
Described on page 343

88
[Hand with Fir Cone]. [1921]
Woodcut
278 × 166 (11 × 6¹/₂″)

89
St Francis (Preaching to the Birds).
[January] 1922
Woodcut
509 × 307 (20 × 12¹/₈″)

90A
[Eight Heads, basic block]. [January,
February or March] 1922
Woodcut
189 × 294 (7¹/₂ × 11⁵/₈″)

90
[Eight Heads]. [January, February or
March] 1922
Woodcut, printed once from the whole
block and eight times from different
parts
325 × 340 (12³/₄ × 13³/₈″)

91
Bookplate B. G. Escher [Beer]. [1922]
Woodcut
50 × 50 (2 × 2″)

92
[Eagle, vignette]. [1922]
[Woodcut]
50 × 50 (2 × 2″)

93
San Gimignano. July 1922
Woodcut
247 × 321 (9³/4 × 12⁵/8")

94
(Roofs of) Siena. December 1922
Woodcut
323 × 219 (12³/4 × 8⁵/8")

95
Serenade in Siena. [January or February] 1923
Woodcut
324 × 159 (12³/4 × 6¹/4")

96
San Gimignano. [January or February] 1923
Woodcut
289 × 493 (11³/8 × 19³/8")

97
Dolphins. February 1923
Woodcut
291 × 492 (11¹/2 × 19³/8")

98
[Palm Tree]. July 1923
Woodcut
379 × 280 (14⁷/8 × 11")
Compare cat. no. 109

99
[Announcement card for Exhibition M. C. Escher, Siena]. [1923]
Woodcut
235 × 157 (9¹/4 × 6¹/8")

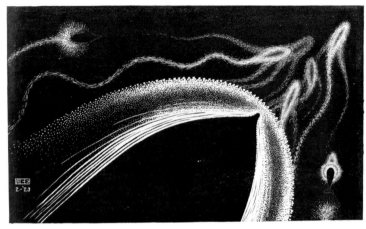

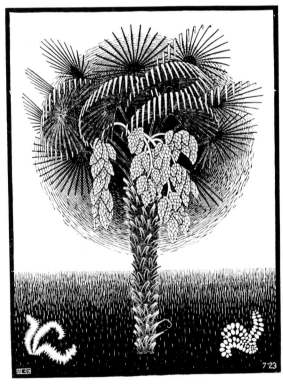

93 94
95

96 97
98 99

100
[Self-Portrait]. November 1923
Woodcut
$324 \times 160 \, (12^3/4 \times 6^1/4'')$
101
Portrait of G. Escher-Umiker [Jetta].
February 1925
Woodcut
$492 \times 278 \, (19^3/8 \times 11'')$

101A
[Portrait of Jetta, shortened version]
Height 286 $(11^1/4'')$
102
Vitorchiano nel Cimino. February
1925
Woodcut
$390 \times 570 \, (15^3/8 \times 22^1/2'')$
103
St Vincent Martyr. July 1925
Woodcut
$209 \times 283 \, (8^1/4 \times 11^1/8'')$

104
The First Day of the Creation.
December 1925
Woodcut
280 × 377 (11 × 14⁷/₈″)

105
The Second Day of the Creation (The Division of the Waters). December 1925
Woodcut
279 × 374 (11 × 14³/₄″)

106
The Third Day of the Creation.
January 1926
Woodcut
373 × 278 (14⁵/₈ × 11″)

107
The Fourth Day of the Creation.
February 1926
Woodcut
278 × 375 (11 × 14³/₄″)

108
The Fifth Day of the Creation.
February 1926
Woodcut
375 × 284 (14³/₄ × 11¹/₈″)

109
The Sixth Day of the Creation. March 1926
Woodcut
375 × 280 (14³/₄ × 11″)
Compare cat. no. 98

110
[Announcement card for Exhibition M. C. Escher, Venice]. 1926
Woodcut in blue, printed on grey cardboard
415 × 174 (16³/₈ × 6⁷/₈″)

PRIMO GIORNO ~ GEN.1:1·5
CREAZIONE DELLA TERRA E
DELLA LUCE · LO SPIRITO DI
DIO SOPRA LE ACQUE ~

SECONDO GIORNO GEN.1:6/8
SEPARAZIONE DELLE ACQUE

TERZO GIORNO GEN.1:9/13
CREAZIONE DELLE PIANTE!

QUARTO GIORNO GEN.1:14/19
CREAZIONE DEL SOLE E DELLA
LUNA ✳✳✳✳✳✳✳✳✳✳ ✳

QUINTO GIORNO GEN.1:20/23
CREAZIONE   UCCELLI E
DEI PESCI ✕—✕—✕

SESTO GIORNO GEN.1:24/31
CREAZIONE   ANIMALI E
DELL'UOMO ✕ 🐘 ✕ 🐘 ✕ 🐘

111
[Tree]. 1926
Wood engraving
120 × 97 (4³/₄ × 3⁷/₈″)

112
[Birds]. 1926
Woodcut
63 × 83 (2¹/₂ × 3¹/₄″)
Compare cat. no. 113

113
[The Six Days of the Creation]. 1926
Woodcut, printed from two blocks;
counterproof
179 × 83 (7 × 3¹/₄″)
Compare cat. no. 112

114
The Fall of Man. March 1927
Woodcut
375 × 276 (14³/₄ × 10⁷/₈″)

115
Procession in Crypt. July 1927
Woodcut
604 × 442 (23³/₄ × 17³/₈″)

116
Rome (and the Griffin of Borghese).
December 1927
Woodcut in grey and black, printed
from two blocks
445 × 438 (17¹/₂ × 17¹/₄″)

117
Castle in the Air. January 1928
Woodcut
624 × 388 (24⁵/₈ × 15¹/₄″)

118
Tower of Babel. February 1928
Woodcut
$621 \times 386 \,(24^{1}/_{2} \times 15^{1}/_{4}'')$

119
Fara San Martino, Abruzzi. May 1928
Woodcut, printed on two sheets
$446 \times 582 \,(17^{1}/_{2} \times 22^{7}/_{8}'')$

120
Bonifacio, Corsica. October 1928
Woodcut
$710 \times 413 \,(28 \times 16^{1}/_{4}'')$

121
Citadel of Calvi, Corsica. October 1928
Woodcut
$445 \times 577 \,(17^{1}/_{2} \times 22^{3}/_{4}'')$

122
[Birth announcement card of Arthur
Escher]. December 1928
Woodcut in bronze, gold, green and
blue, printed from one block, and
stamping in blue
$138 \times 76 \,(5^{3}/_{8} \times 3'')$

123
Corte, Corsica. January 1929
Woodcut in grey and black, printed
from two blocks
568 × 436 (22³/₈ × 17¹/₈″)

124
La Cathédrale engloutie (The
Drowned Cathedral). January 1929
Woodcut
721 × 416 (28³/₈ × 16³/₈″)

125
Infant (A[rthur]. E. Escher). February
1929
Woodcut in reddish brown and two
tones of pink, printed from three
blocks
410 × 365 (16¹/₈ × 14³/₈″)

126
Goriano Sicoli, Abruzzi. July 1929
Lithograph
238 × 287 (9³/₈ × 11¹/₄″)

127
Genazzano, Abruzzi. November 1929
Lithograph, second state
268 × 196 (10¹/₂ × 7³/₄″)

128
Self-Portrait. November 1929
Lithograph
264 × 203 (10³/₈ × 8″)

129
Barbarano, Cimino. December 1929
Lithograph
176 × 236 (6⁷/₈ × 9¹/₄″)

215

130
Cerro al Volturno, Abruzzi. January
1930
Woodcut
653 × 483 (25³/₄ × 19″)

131
Street in Scanno, Abruzzi. January
1930
Lithograph
627 × 431 (24⁵/₈ × 17″)

132
Castrovalva, [Abruzzi]. February 1930
Lithograph
530 × 421 (20⁷/₈ × 16⁵/₈″)

133
Aragno. [February] 1930
Lithograph
212 × 106 (8³/₈ × 4¹/₈″)

134
The Bridge. March 1930
Lithograph
536 × 377 (21¹/₈ × 14⁷/₈″)

135
Palizzi, Calabria. October 1930
Woodcut
241 × 320 (9¹/₂ × 12⁵/₈″)

136
Morano, Calabria. October 1930
Woodcut
240 × 321 (9¹/₂ × 12⁵/₈″)

137
Pentedattilo, Calabria. October 1930
Lithograph
197 × 255 (7³/₄ × 10″)

138
Fiumara (of Stilo), Calabria. October
1930
Lithograph
227 × 299 (8⁷/₈ × 11³/₄″)

139
Cattolica of Stilo, Calabria. November
1930
Lithograph
226 × 297 (8⁷/₈ × 11³/₄″)

218

140
Pentedattilo, Calabria. December 1930
Woodcut
323 × 236 (12³/₄ × 9¹/₄")

141
Pentedattilo (Panorama), Calabria.
January 1931
Woodcut
321 × 232 (12⁵/₈ × 9¹/₈")

142
Scilla, Calabria. January 1931
Lithograph
297 × 226 (11³/₄ × 8⁷/₈")

143
Tropea, Calabria. January 1931
Lithograph
313 × 235 (12³/₈ × 9¹/₄")

144
Santa Severina, Calabria. February
1931
Lithograph
232 × 310 (9¹/₈ × 12¹/₄")

145
(Cloister near) Rocca Imperiale,
Calabria. February 1931
Lithograph
231 × 307 (9¹/₈ × 12¹/₈")

146
Rossano, Calabria. February 1931
Woodcut
240 × 309 (9¹/₂ × 12¹/₈")

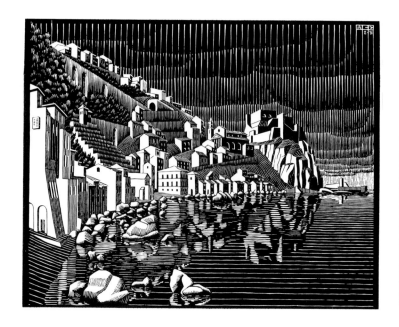

147 147A
Scilla, [Calabria]. February 1931
Woodcut
240 × 308 (9¹/₂ × 12¹/₈″)
148
Atrani, Coast of Amalfi. August 1931
Lithograph
275 × 379 (10⁷/₈ × 14⁷/₈″)
Compare cat. nos. 298, 320 and 446

149
[Invitation]. September 1931
Wood engraving
120 × 90 (4³/₄ × 3¹/₂″)
Compare cat. no. 214
150
Covered Alley in Atrani, [Coast of
Amalfi]. November 1931
Wood engraving
180 × 129 (7¹/₈ × 5¹/₈″)
151
(Dilapidated Houses in) Atrani, [Coast
of Amalfi]. November 1931
Lithograph
308 × 226 (12¹/₈ × 8⁷/₈″)

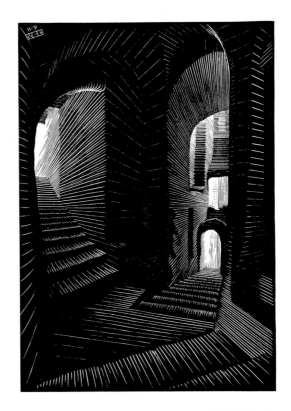

147   147A   150
148   149   151

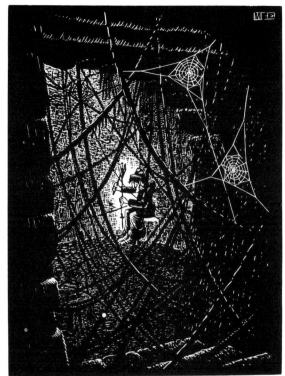

155
[Kite]. Between March and June 1931
Woodcut
180 × 96 (7^1/$_8$ × 3^3/$_4$")
Compare cat. no. 165

156
[Flowers]. Between March and June
1931
Woodcut
180 × 135 (7^1/$_8$ × 5^3/$_8$")
Compare cat. no. 162

157
[Sundial]. Between March and June
1931
Woodcut
180 × 140 (7^1/$_8$ × 5^1/$_2$")
Compare cat. no. 169

158
[Squirrel]. Between March and June
1931
Woodcut
179 × 140 (7 × 5^1/$_2$")
Compare cat. no. 176

XXIV Emblemata

159
First title-page. [1932]
Woodcut
180 × 140 (7^1/$_8$ × 5^1/$_2$")

160
Second title-page. [Between April and
June 1931]
Woodcut
177 × 138 (7 × 5^3/$_8$")

161
Table of contents. Between March and
June 1931
Woodcut
180 × 140 (7^1/$_8$ × 5^1/$_2$")

227

162

I, Vase. Between March and June 1931
Woodcut
180 × 140 (7¹/₈ × 5¹/₂″)
Compare cat. no. 156

163

II, Anvil. Between March and June
1931
Woodcut
180 × 140 (7¹/₈ × 5¹/₂″)

164

III, Lute. Between March and June
1931
Woodcut
180 × 140 (7¹/₈ × 5¹/₂″)

165

IV, Kite. Between March and June
1931
Woodcut
180 × 140 (7¹/₈ × 5¹/₂″)
Compare cat. no. 155

166

V, Buoy. Between March and June
1931
Woodcut
180 × 140 (7¹/₈ × 5¹/₂″)

167

VI, Palm Tree. Between March and
June 1931
Woodcut
180 × 140 (7¹/₈ × 5¹/₂″)

168

VII, Weather Vane. Between March
and June 1931
Woodcut
180 × 140 (7¹/₈ × 5¹/₂″)

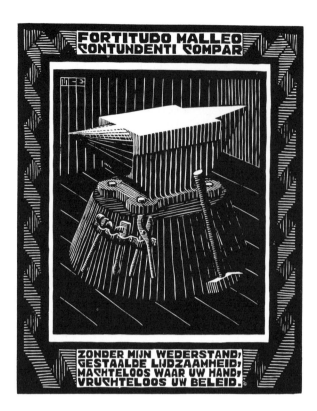

AD SUMMA NITENS NIHIL CONSEQUOR

STUWT MIJ EEN KRACHT OMHOOG,
EEN KRACHT MIJ NEERWAARTS BINDT:
EEN DOELLOOS DING VOOR 'T OOG,
FIER SPEELGOED VAN EEN KIND.

NE MISERE IN VADA
IMPACTUS PEREAS

VOLHARDEND, MACHTELOOS
GETEISTERD DOOR DEN VLOED,
WEERSTREEF IK VRUCHTELOOS:-
ZOO BLIJFT UW VAART BEHOED.

PROCERA EX GRAMINE SURGENS MIRABILIS

Van den grond vervreemde
zonderlinge boom,
Sta ik rank en neem de
wereld op in mijn droom.

Officium meum stabile agitari

Standvastig in mijn willoosheid
wend ik mij,'t wenden nimmer moe.
Gij smaalt mijn wispelturigheid?
Dus is mijn taak, mijn trouw, zie toe!

PATET QUAELIBET ULTIMA LATET

EEN SCHADUW MEET HET SCHEIDEND UUR
AAN MIJN ONWRIKBAARHEID VOORBIJ;
ZOO WIJST HET WENTELEND GETIJ
ZONDER RESPIJT UW EIGEN DUUR.

Vias pondere perseveranter exaequo.

Wanstaltig en gezeuld,
grommelend, afgebeuld,
plet ik met norsch gedruisch
mijn weg in 't gruis.

Percute me, et eversione tenus, percute!

Inwendig ben ik hard en koud,
daar is in mij geen gloed noch vier,
doch slaat mij 't lot, zoo men igvoud
spatten de gensters ginds en hier.

XXIV Emblemata

169
VIII, Sundial. Between March and
June 1931
Woodcut
180 × 140 (7¹/₈ × 5¹/₂″)
Compare cat. no. 157

170
IX, Steamroller. Between March and
June 1931
Woodcut
180 × 140 (7¹/₈ × 5¹/₂″)

171
X, Flint. Between March and June 1931
Woodcut
180 × 140 (7¹/₈ × 5¹/₂″)

172
XI, Candle Flame. Between March and
June 1931
Woodcut
180 × 140 (7¹/₈ × 5¹/₂″)
Compare cat. no. 407

173
XII, Signpost. Between March and
June 1931
Woodcut
180 × 140 (7¹/₈ × 5¹/₂″)

174
XIII, Beehive. Between March and
June 1931
Woodcut
180 × 140 (7¹/₈ × 5¹/₂″)

175
XIV, Frog. Between March and June
1931
Woodcut
180 × 140 (7¹/₈ × 5¹/₂″)

Vivo! Anima trepidans in me absumitur.

Ik ben mij zelf: een licht. Gij vindt
in mij uw eigen lot bepaald.
Blijf aldus niet voor't wezen blind,
dat in mijn schijn U tegenstraalt.

Omnes praeter unam praeclusae.

Bedachtzaam, —achteloos, —
neem vrij uw weg : U werd,
welk pad ge straks verkoos,
elk ander pad versperd.

IN ADVERSIS SEDULITAS INEPTA

BEDRIJVIGHEID GETROOST,
ARBEIDZAAM, ONVERPOOSD,
MITS HET GEWELD VAN'T ZWERK
NIET WOEDT OVER ONS WERK.

SILENTIUM OMNI STREPITU MAIUS

DE KWAKERSCHAAR DOORRIJT
DEN ZOMERNACHT OM'T ZEERST;
TOCH WELFT DE STILTE WIJD,
ROERLOOS—EN OVERHEERSCHT.

silva motum arcano continens silet

Het kraakt; er raakt
iets los in 't bosch;-
het rept,-dan staat
het woud weer stil, in stilte. MEE

Dissolutionis ex humore speciose praefloresco

Wasdom van geheimenis,
nabloei van de nacht,
voos is mijn verrijzenis:
een verwezen pracht.

ARBITRIUM PARI MOMENTO TEMPERANS

VERWILDERING ONTSTAAT,
WAAR IK GEEN VREDE STICHT,
HOE VOND DE WERELD BAAT,
HIELD IK GEEN EVENWICHT!

NEMINEM NISI STULTUM SUBMITTIMUS

ONS SCHONK MEN 'T VOOS GEZAG,
DE WILLEKEUR VAN 'T LOT
TE RICHTEN BIJ BEJAG,
TE STIEREN TOT EEN SPOT.

176

XV, Squirrel. Between March and June 1931

Woodcut

180 × 140 (7^1/$_8$ × 5^1/$_2$″)

Compare cat. no. 158

177

XVI, Toadstool. Between March and June 1931

Woodcut

180 × 140 (7^1/$_8$ × 5^1/$_2$″)

178

XVII, Balance. Between March and June 1931

Woodcut

180 × 140 (7^1/$_8$ × 5^1/$_2$″)

179

XVIII, Dice. Between March and June 1931

Woodcut

180 × 140 (7^1/$_8$ × 5^1/$_2$″)

180

XIX, Butterfly. Between March and June 1931

Woodcut

180 × 140 (7^1/$_8$ × 5^1/$_2$″)

181

XX, Cactus. Between March and June 1931

Woodcut

180 × 140 (7^1/$_8$ × 5^1/$_2$″)

182

XXI, Well. Between March and June 1931

Woodcut

180 × 140 (7^1/$_8$ × 5^1/$_2$″)

176 177   **181**
178 179   180 **182**

LATEBRA TUTA DEPRAVATIO ANIMI

EEN TOEVLUCHT OP ZIJN SCHOONST,
ONTAARDING OP ZIJN BEST;
EEN HALF KUNSTMATIG NEST;
NAAR MENSCHENAARD EEN WOONST.

Copiam non abunde
redundans effundo

Een lafenis verstrekt
met mate,-op haar tijd
het leven kweekt,en rekt,
één regendrop verblijdt.

REPULSAE SUSPICIOSAE TORVA SUBOLES

VAN KWADE TROUW HET BEELD,
VERSPERREND NAAR VERMOGEN;
IN ONMIN EENS GETEELD,
IN ACHTERDOCHT GETOGEN.

VAN DIT BOEK, GEHEEL VAN DE OOR=
SPRONKELIJKE HOUTBLOKKEN GEDRUKT
DOOR G.J. VAN AMERONGEN & C₂ TE
AMERSFOORT, OP SIMILI JAPON VAN
VAN GELDER, IN EEN OPLAGE VAN 300
GENUMMERDE EXEMPLAREN, WERDEN
DE EXEMPLAREN, GENUMMERD I-XXV,
DOOR DEN HOUTSNIJDER GETEEKEND.
N₂ 32

JAN WALCH
DE VREESELIJKE
AVONTUREN
VAN SCHOLASTICA
HOUTSNEDEN VAN
M.C.ESCHER

XXIV Emblemata

183
XXII, Retreat. Between March and
June 1931
Woodcut
$180 \times 140 \, (7^1/8 \times 5^1/2'')$

184
XXIII, Watering-can. Between March
and June 1931
Woodcut
$180 \times 140 \, (7^1/8 \times 5^1/2'')$

185
XXIV, Padlock. Between March and
June 1931
Woodcut
$180 \times 140 \, (7^1/8 \times 5^1/2'')$

186
Colophon. [1932]
Woodcut
$45 \times 60 \, (1^3/4 \times 2^3/8'')$

187
[Initial A]. [1932]
Woodcut
$80 \times 60 \, (3^1/8 \times 2^3/8'')$

Scholastica

188
Front of cover. [1932]
Woodcut
$101 \times 150 \, (4 \times 5^7/8'')$

235

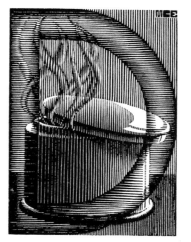
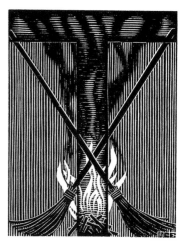

Scholastica

189
Initial S, page 3. [1932]
Woodcut
80 × 60 (3¹/₈ × 2³/₈″)

190
Initial S, page 4. [1932]
Woodcut
80 × 60 (3¹/₈ × 2³/₈″)

191
Illustration, page 5. October 1931
Woodcut
229 × 168 (9 × 6⁵/₈″)

192
Initial D, page 7. [1932]
Woodcut
80 × 60 (3¹/₈ × 2³/₈″)

193
Initial T, page 10. [1932]
Woodcut
80 × 60 (3¹/₈ × 2³/₈″)

194
Illustration, page 11. October 1931
Woodcut
229 × 168 (9 × 6⁵/₈″)

195
Initial H, page 12. [1932]
Woodcut
80 × 60 (3¹/₈ × 2³/₈″)

196
Initial H, page 13. [1932]
Woodcut
80 × 60 (3¹/₈ × 2³/₈″)

197
Illustration, page 15. November 1931
Woodcut
229 × 168 (9 × 6⁵/₈″)

198
Initial V, page 17. [1932]
Woodcut
80 × 60 (3¹/₈ × 2³/₈″)

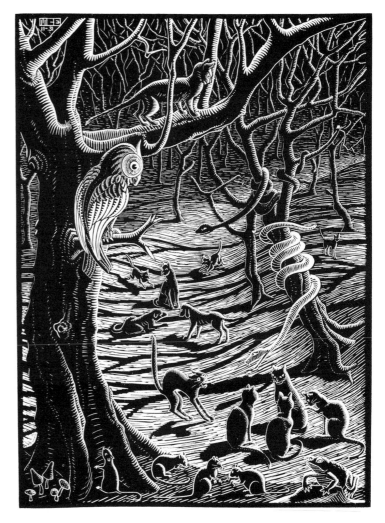

189   190   191   194   197
      192   193   195   196   198

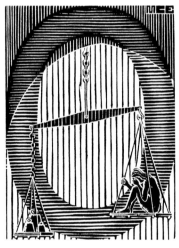

206
San Cosimo, [Ravello]. January 1932
Wood engraving
280 × 210 (11 × 8¼″)

207
Farmhouse, Ravello. January 1932
Lithograph
233 × 311 (9⅛ × 12¼″)

208
San Cosimo, Ravello. February 1932
Lithograph
313 × 222 (12⅜ × 8¾″)

209
(The Hamlet of) Turello, Southern
Italy. March 1932
Lithograph
311 × 225 (12¼ × 8⅞″)

210
Carubba Tree, [Ravello]. February
1932
Woodcut in black and grey, printed
from two blocks
319 × 239 (12¹/₂ × 9³/₈″)

211
Atrani (Seen from Pontone), Coast of
Amalfi. February 1932
Woodcut
316 × 238 (12¹/₂ × 9³/₈″)

212
Porta Maria dell'Ospidale, Ravello
(Old Church, Ravello). February 1932
Wood engraving
269 × 211 (10⁵/₈ × 8¹/₄″)

213
San Giovanni (in Campidoglio),
Ravello. February 1932
Wood engraving
280 × 210 (11 × 8¹/₄″)

214
Lion of the Fountain in the Piazza at
Ravello. March 1932
Wood engraving
213 × 232 (8³/₈ × 9¹/₈″)
Compare cat. no. 149

215
[Design for Dutch Peace postage stamp
of 12¹/₂ cents]. March 1932
Woodcut and pencil
138 × 171 (5³/₈ × 6³/₄″)

216
San Michele dei Frisoni, Rome (Tenth Century). June 1932
Lithograph
435 × 491 (17^1/$_8$ × 19^3/$_8$″)

217
Mummified Priests in Gangi, Sicily. June 1932
Lithograph
204 × 274 (8 × 10^3/$_4$″)

218
Temple of Segesta, Sicily. December 1932
Wood engraving
322 × 242 (12^5/$_8$ × 9^1/$_2$″)

219
Castel Mola (and Mount Etna), Sicily. December 1932
Lithograph
225 × 310 (8^7/$_8$ × 12^1/$_4$″)

220
Cathedral of Cefalú, Sicily. December 1932
Lithograph
227 × 283 (8^7/$_8$ × 11^1/$_8$″)

221
Cave Dwellings (near Sperlinga), Sicily. January 1933
Woodcut
241 × 318 (9^1/$_2$ × 12^1/$_2$″)

217

216

218 219

220 221

222
Randazzo and Mount Etna, Sicily.
January 1933
Wood engraving
240 × 318 (9¹/₂ × 12¹/₂″)
223
Palm. February 1933
Wood engraving in black and grey-
green, printed from two blocks
397 × 397 (15⁵/₈ × 15⁵/₈″)
224
(Old Lava from) Mount Etna near
Bronte, Sicily. February 1933
Lithograph
217 × 307 (8¹/₂ × 12¹/₈″)

225
Caltavuturo in the Madonie
Mountains (C. in the Madonie), Sicily.
February 1933
Lithograph
229 × 308 (9 × 12¹/₈″)
226
Cloister (of) Monreale, Sicily. March
1933
Wood engraving
320 × 241 (12⁵/₈ × 9¹/₂″)
227
Scláfani, Sicily. April 1933
Woodcut
240 × 320 (9¹/₂ × 12⁵/₈″)
228
(Cesarò and Mount Etna), Sicily. April
1933
Wood engraving
190 × 320 (7¹/₂ × 12⁵/₈″)

222	223		225	227
	224		226	228

229
Lava Flow of 1928 from Mount Etna,
Sicily (Fresh Lava (1928) near
Nunziata, Sicily). April 1933
Lithograph
212 × 313 (8³/₈ × 12³/₈″)

230
Pineta of Calvi, Corsica. June 1933
Woodcut in light grey, dark grey and
black, printed from three blocks
357 × 468 (14 × 18³/₈″)
248   Compare cat. no. 378

231
Phosphorescent Sea. July 1933
Lithograph
327 × 245 (12⁷/₈ × 9⁵/₈″)

230   231
229

249

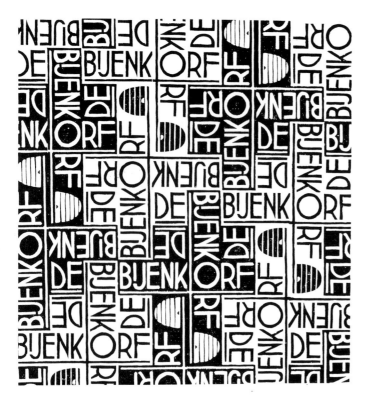

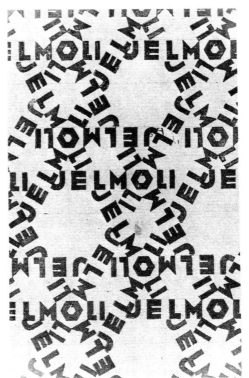

239
Fireworks. November 1933
Lithograph
$424 \times 227 \, (16^3/_4 \times 8^7/_8'')$

240
(Church at) Corte, Corsica. December
1933
Wood engraving
$319 \times 240 \, (12^1/_2 \times 9^1/_2'')$

241
Calvi (: the Fishing Town [Seen] from
the Citadel), Corsica. December 1933
Wood engraving
$320 \times 241 \, (12^5/_8 \times 9^1/_2'')$

242
Gulf of Porto, Corsica. December 1933
Lithograph
$235 \times 323 \, (9^1/_4 \times 12^3/_4'')$

243
Old Olive Tree, Corsica. January 1934
Wood engraving
$320 \times 240 \, (12^5/_8 \times 9^1/_2'')$

244
Tugboat (Old Harbour of Bastia,
Corsica). January 1934
Wood engraving
$278 \times 208 \, (11 \times 8^1/_4'')$

253

245
Corsica, Calanche (Calanche of Piana, Corsica). January 1934
Lithograph
308 × 207 (12^1/$_8$ × 8^1/$_8$″)

246
Calanche of Piana, Corsica. February 1934
Wood engraving
238 × 317 (9^5/$_8$ × 12^1/$_2$″)

247
Nonza, Corsica. February 1934
Lithograph
313 × 232 (12^3/$_8$ × 9^1/$_8$″)

248
Still Life with Mirror. March 1934
Lithograph
394 × 287 (15^1/$_2$ × 11^1/$_4$″)

249
Nocturnal Rome: Church Domes
(Domes of Santa Maria di Monte
Santo and Santa Maria dei Miracoli,
Seen from the Pincio). March 1934
Woodcut
234 × 309 (9¹/₄ × 12¹/₈″)

250
Nocturnal Rome: Colonnade of St
Peter's (Portico of Bernini). March
1934
Woodcut
311 × 229 (12¹/₄ × 9″)

251
Nocturnal Rome: San Nicola in
Carcere (at the Via del Mare). March
1934
Woodcut
237 × 314 (9³/₈ × 12³/₈″)

252
Nocturnal Rome: Small Churches,
Piazza Venezia [also described by
Escher as S. M. di Loreto and
S. S. Noma di Maria, Piazza di
Traiano]. March 1934
Wood engraving
242 × 320 (9¹/₂ × 12⁵/₈″)

253
Nocturnal Rome: Santa Francesca
Romana (Seen from the Basilica of
Constantine). March 1934
Woodcut
195 × 304 (7⁵/₈ × 12″)

254
Nocturnal Rome: Santa Maria del
Popolo (Piazza del Popolo). April 1934
Woodcut
241 × 285 (9¹/₂ × 11¹/₄″)

255
Nocturnal Rome: San Giorgio in
Vellabro (Seen from the Arch of
Giano). April 1934
Woodcut
299 × 211 (11³/₄ × 8¹/₄″)

257

256
Nocturnal Rome: the 'Dioscuro'
Pollux (Piazza del Campidoglio). April
1934
Woodcut
298 × 238 (11³/₄ × 9³/₈")

257
Nocturnal Rome: Trajan's Column.
April 1934
Woodcut
334 × 185 (13¹/₈ × 7¹/₄")

258
Nocturnal Rome: Basilica of
Constantine (at the Via dell'Impero)
[also described by Escher as Basilica di
Massenzio]. April 1934
Woodcut
210 × 310 (8¹/₄ × 12¹/₄")

259
Nocturnal Rome: Castel Sant'Angelo.
April 1934
Woodcut
223 × 318 (8³/₄ × 12¹/₂")

260
Nocturnal Rome: Colosseum. May
1934
Woodcut
230 × 294 (9 × 11⁵/₈")

261
St Bavo's, Ghent. July 1934
Woodcut
317 × 240 (12¹/₂ × 9¹/₂")

262
Tournai Cathedral. August 1934
Woodcut
409 × 364 (16¹/₈ × 14³/₈")

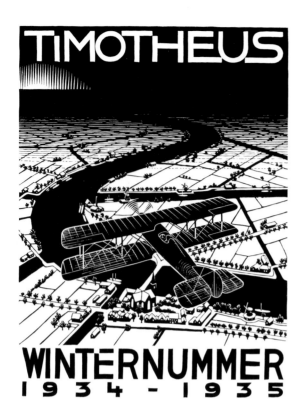

263
(Old) Houses in Positano. August 1934
Lithograph
245 × 286 (9⁵/₈ × 11¹/₄″)
264 264A
Aeroplane above a Snowy Landscape
(cover of *Timotheus*, Winter issue
1934–35). October 1934
Woodcut; proof
300 × 220 (11³/₄ × 8⁵/₈″)
Compare cat. no. 303

265
Bookplate A. Rooseboom. October
1934
Wood engraving
80 × 29 (3¹/₈ × 1¹/₈″)
266
Coast of Amalfi (composition).
November 1934
Woodcut
697 × 408 (27¹/₂ × 16¹/₈″)
267
Still Life with Spherical Mirror.
November 1934
Lithograph
286 × 326 (11¹/₄ × 12⁷/₈″)
Compare cat. nos. 80, 268, 339 and 368

268
Hand with Reflecting Sphere (Self-Portrait in Spherical Mirror). January 1935
Lithograph
318 × 213 (12^1/$_2$ × 8^3/$_8$″)
Compare cat. nos. 80, 267, 339 and 368

269
St Peter's [Seen] from the Gianicolo [Rome]. February 1935
Wood engraving
241 × 321 (9^1/$_2$ × 12^5/$_8$″)

270
Inside St Peter's. March 1935
Wood engraving
237 × 316 (9^3/$_8$ × 12^1/$_2$″)

271
Grasshopper. March 1935
Wood engraving
181 × 242 (7^1/$_8$ × 9^1/$_2$″)

272
Dream (Mantis Religiosa). April 1935
Wood engraving
322 × 241 (12^5/$_8$ × 9^1/$_2$″)

273
Scarabs. April 1935
Wood engraving
180 × 240 (7^1/$_8$ × 9^1/$_2$″)

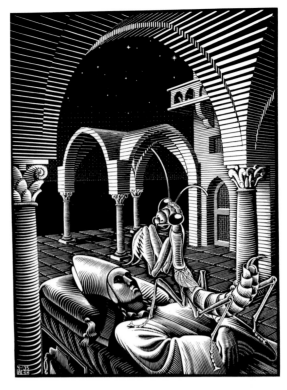

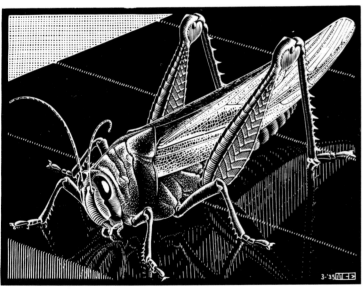

274
Portrait of G. A. Escher. August 1935
Lithograph; counterproof
262 × 208 (10³/₈ × 8¹/₄″)

275
Trademark (Welder). September 1935
Woodcut
155 × 105 (6¹/₈ × 4¹/₈″)

276
Senglea, Malta. October 1935
Woodcut in black, grey and grey-
green, printed from three blocks
310 × 460 (12¹/₄ × 18¹/₈″)
Compare cat. nos. 334 and 410

277
Selinunte [Sicily]. October 1935
Woodcut in grey and black, printed
from two blocks
224 × 305 (8⁷/₈ × 12″)

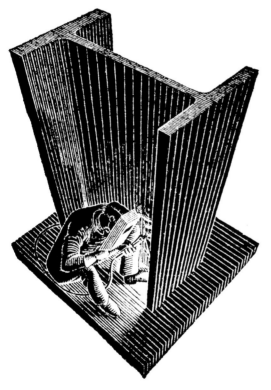

265

274　　　　　　　　276
　　　　　275　277

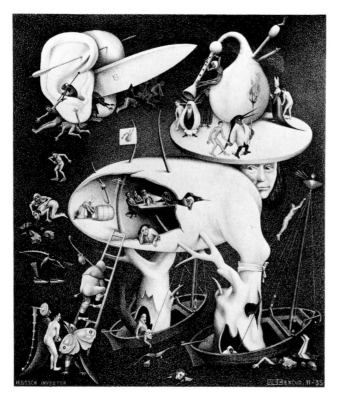

281
Libellula (Dragonfly). March 1936
Wood engraving
210 × 280 (8¹/₄ × 11″)

282
Between St Peter's and the Sistine
Chapel. March 1936
Lithograph
311 × 220 (12¹/₄ × 8⁵/₈″)

283
SS. Giovanni e Paolo, Rome. May 1936
Lithograph
117 × 98 (4⁵/₈ × 3⁷/₈″)
Compare cat. no. 340

284
Advertisement Chess Club Château-
d'Oex. July 1936
Woodcut
310 × 240 (12¹/₄ × 9¹/₂″)

278
'Hell', copy after [a scene by]
Hieronymus Bosch. November 1935
Lithograph
251 × 214 (9⁷/₈ × 8³/₈″)

279
Snow. January 1936
Lithograph
325 × 273 (12³/₄ × 10³/₄″)

280
Prickly Flower. February 1936
Wood engraving, third state
277 × 207 (10⁷/₈ × 8¹/₈″)

285
House in the Lava near Nunziata,
Sicily. August 1936
Lithograph
270 × 355 (10⁵/₈ × 14″)

286
Freighter. September 1936
Woodcut
505 × 370 (19⁷/₈ × 14⁵/₈″)

287
Venice. October 1936
Woodcut
247 × 323 (9³/₄ × 12³/₄″)

288
Ancona. November 1936
Woodcut
310 × 240 (12¹/₄ × 9¹/₂″)

289
Catania, Sicily. November 1936
Wood engraving
240 × 321 (9¹/₂ × 12⁵/₈″)

290
Marseilles. December 1936
Wood engraving
305 × 240 (12 × 9¹/₂″)

286
285
287 288
289 290

270

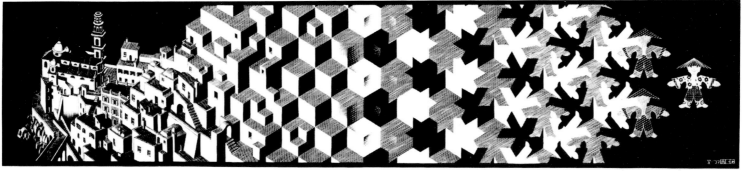

291
[Poster for Exhibition John Paschoud
and M.C. Escher]. [December 1936]
[Linoleum cut]
433 × 296 (17 × 11⁵/₈″)

292
[Invitation card for Exhibition John
Paschoud and M.C. Escher].
[December 1936]
Woodcut
70 × 93 (2³/₄ × 3⁵/₈″)

293
[Announcement card for Exhibition
John Paschoud and M.C. Escher].
[December 1936]
Woodcut
60 × 79 (2³/₈ × 3¹/₈″)

294
Leaning Tower, Pisa. January 1937
Woodcut
309 × 229 (12¹/₈ × 9″)

295
Piano di Sant'Andrea, Genoa.
February 1937
Woodcut
298 × 249 (11³/₄ × 9³/₄″)

296
Still Life and Street. March 1937
Woodcut
487 × 490 (19¹/₈ × 19¹/₄″)

297
Porthole. March 1937
Woodcut
258 × 277 (10¹/₈ × 10⁷/₈″)

298
Metamorphosis [I]. May 1937
Woodcut, printed on two sheets
195 × 908 (7⁵/₈ × 35³/₄″)
Compare cat. nos. 148, 320 and 446

HET BEZWAARDE HART

GEDICHTEN
J.G.ESCHER

299
Het Bezwaarde Hart: vignette for cover
and page 3. September 1937
Woodcut; proof
$82 \times 63 \,(3^1/_4 \times 2^1/_2'')$

300
Development I. November 1937
Woodcut
$437 \times 446 \,(17^1/_4 \times 17^1/_2'')$
Compare cat. nos. 320 and 446

301
[Study for cover of programme *St
Matthew Passion*]. [February 1938]
Woodcut
$205 \times 129 \,(8^1/_8 \times 5^1/_8'')$

302
Programme *St Matthew Passion*.
February 1938
Woodcut
$153 \times 104 \,(6 \times 4^1/_8'')$

303
Day and Night. February 1938
Woodcut in black and grey, printed
from two blocks
$391 \times 677 \,(15^3/_8 \times 26^5/_8'')$
Compare cat. nos. 264 and 264A

304
[Birth announcement card of Jan Escher]. March 1938
Woodcut in blue
$117 \times 77 (4^5/_8 \times 3'')$

305
Cycle. May 1938
Lithograph
$475 \times 279 (18^3/_4 \times 11'')$

306
Sky and Water I. June 1938
Woodcut
$435 \times 439 (17^1/_8 \times 17^1/_4'')$

307
Birthday card for J. Greshoff.
November 1938
Woodcut in black and grey-green,
printed from two blocks
$180 \times 140 (7^1/_8 \times 5^1/_2'')$

308
Sky and Water II. December 1938
Woodcut
$623 \times 407 (24^1/_2 \times 16'')$

274

309
Delft: Entrance to the Oude Kerk.
January 1939
Woodcut
266 × 179 (10¹/₂ × 7″)

310
Development II. February 1939
Woodcut in brown, grey-green and
black, printed from three blocks
455 × 455 (17⁷/₈ × 17⁷/₈″)
Compare cat. nos. 310A, 320, 327 and
446

310A PP
Development II, first version
Described on page 343

311
Delft: Grote Markt (Marketplace
[Seen] from the Tower of the Nieuwe
Kerk). May 1939
Woodcut
323 × 218 (12³/₄ × 8⁵/₈″)

312
Delft: Nieuwe Kerk. May 1939
Woodcut
237 × 319 (9³/₈ × 12¹/₂″)

313
Delft: Voldersgracht. June 1939
Woodcut
350 × 232 (13³/₄ × 9¹/₈″)

314
Delft: Oostpoort. June 1939
Woodcut
322 × 217 (12⁵/₈ × 8¹/₂″)

315
Delft: (Interior) Nieuwe Kerk. July
1939
Woodcut
314 × 209 (12³/₈ × 8¹/₄″)
316
Delft: Town Hall. July 1939
Woodcut
334 × 224 (13¹/₈ × 8⁷/₈″)

317
Delft: Voldersgracht (detail). August
1939
Woodcut
314 × 210 (12³/₈ × 8¹/₄″)
318
Delft: ([Seen] from the Tower of the)
Oude Kerk. August 1939
Woodcut
292 × 193 (11¹/₂ × 7⁵/₈″)
319
Delft: Roofs. August 1939
Woodcut
196 × 204 (7³/₄ × 8″)

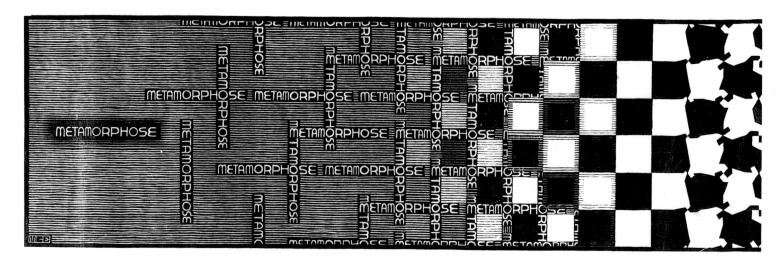

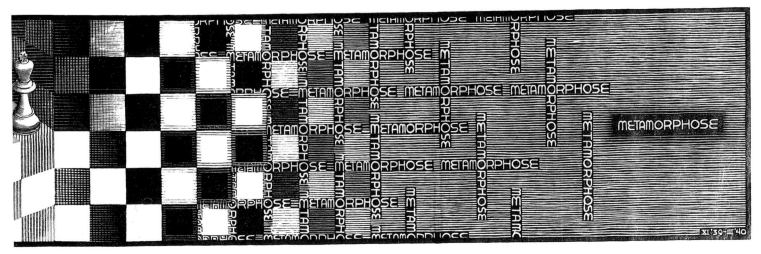

320
Metamorphosis II. November
1939–March 1940
Woodcut in black, green and brown,
printed from twenty blocks on three
combined sheets
192 × 3895 (7¹/₂ × 153³/₈″)

Compare cat. nos. 148, 298, 300, 310,
327 and 446

321
Bookplate Dr P. H. M. Travaglino.
April 1940
Wood engraving, second state
60 × 80 (2³/₈ × 3¹/₈″)

322
Bookplate G. H. 's-Gravesande.
December 1940
Wood engraving
61 × 61 (2³/₈ × 2³/₈″)

323
Fish. October 1941
Woodcut in three tones of grey-green,
printed from three blocks
507 × 384 (20 × 15¹/₈″)

324
[Plane-filling Motif with Reptiles].
[1941]
Woodcut
124 × 154 (4⁷/₈ × 6¹/₈″)

325
Bookplate D. H. Roodhuyzen de Vries-
Van Dishoeck. June 1942
Wood engraving
80 × 60 (3¹/₈ × 2³/₈″)

326
Verbum (Earth, Sky and Water). July
1942
Lithograph, second state
332 × 386 (13¹/₈ × 15¹/₄″)
Compare cat. no. 364

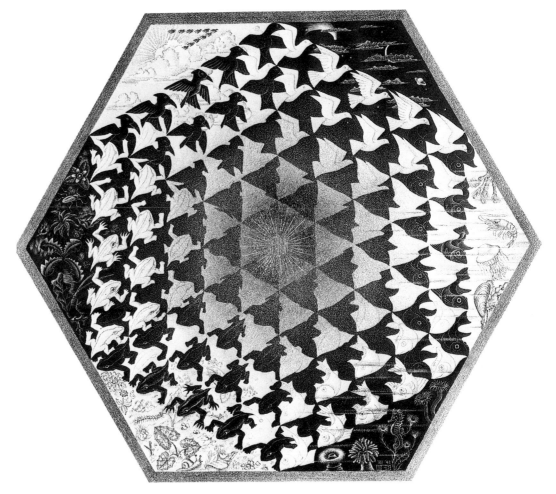

LEGENTES EXPELLIMUS CURAS

LABOR ET CONSTANTIA

EX LIBRIS ROODHUYZEN
DE VRIES–VAN DISHOECK

321 322
323

324 325
326

327
Reptiles. March 1943
Lithograph
334 × 385 (13^1/$_8$ × 15^1/$_8$")
Compare cat. nos. 310, 310A, 320 and 446

328
Ant. May 1943
Lithograph
182 × 249 (7^1/$_8$ × 9^3/$_4$")

329
Bookplate A. M. E. van Dishoeck. May 1943
Wood engraving
80 × 60 (3^1/$_8$ × 2^3/$_8$")

330
Blowball. July 1943
Wood engraving
178 × 180 (7 × 7^1/$_8$")

330A
Blowball. July 1943
Wood engraving, intaglio-printed
175 × 177 (6^7/$_8$ × 7")

331
Encounter. May 1944
Lithograph
342 × 464 (13^1/$_2$ × 18^1/$_4$")
Compare cat. nos. 370 and 384

332
Emblem for Restaurant Insulinde, The
Hague. April 1944
Woodcut in reddish brown
Diameter 120 (4³/₄")

333
Design for writing-paper for Chinese
script. June 1944
Woodcut in brown and ochre, printed
from two blocks
210 × 139 (8¹/₄ × 5¹/₂")

334
Balcony. July 1945
Lithograph
297 × 234 (11³/₄ × 9¹/₄")
Compare cat. no. 276

335
(Two) Doric Columns. August 1945
Wood engraving in black, brown and
blue-green, printed from three blocks
322 × 240 (12⁵/₈ × 9¹/₂")

336
Three Spheres I. September 1945
Wood engraving
279 × 169 (11 × 6⁵/₈″)

337
Diploma Tijdelijke Academie,
Eindhoven. December 1945
Woodcut, fourth state
342 × 240 (13¹/₂ × 9¹/₂″)

338
Magic Mirror. January 1946
Lithograph
280 × 445 (11 × 17¹/₂″)

339
Three Spheres II. April 1946
Lithograph
269 × 463 (10⁵/₈ × 18¹/₄″)
Compare cat. nos. 80, 267, 268 and 368

340
Dusk (Rome). May 1946
Mezzotint, second state
117 × 98 (4⁵/₈ × 3⁷/₈″)
Compare cat. no. 283

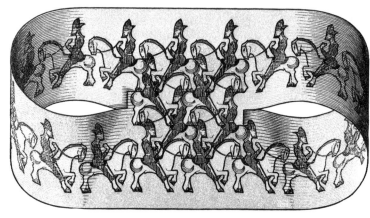

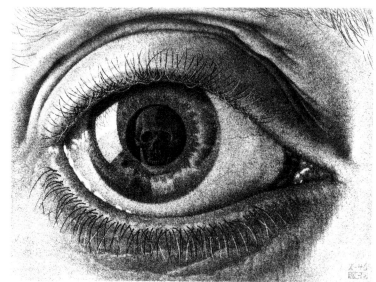

341
Bookplate J.C.de Bruyn van Melis- en
Mariekerke-Mackay. June 1946
Wood engraving
$80 \times 60 \, (3^1/_8 \times 2^3/_8'')$

342
Horseman. July 1946
Woodcut in red, black and grey,
printed from three blocks
$239 \times 449 \, (9^3/_8 \times 17^5/_8'')$
Compare cat. no. 418

343
Mummified Frog. August 1946
Mezzotint, third state
$135 \times 173 \, (5^3/_8 \times 6^3/_4'')$

344
Eye. October 1946
Mezzotint, seventh and final state
$141 \times 198 \, (5^1/_2 \times 7^3/_4'')$

345
New Year's greeting-card 1947,
Nederlandsche ExLibris-Kring, The
Hague. November 1946
Woodcut
$118 \times 101 \, (4^5/_8 \times 4'')$

346
Gallery. December 1946 (first
state)–April 1949 (further states)
Mezzotint, fourth state
$213 \times 159 \, (8^3/_8 \times 6^1/_4'')$
Compare cat. no. 348

347
Bookplate Albert Ernst Bosman.
[1946]
Wood engraving
$80 \times 60 \, (3^1/_8 \times 2^3/_8'')$

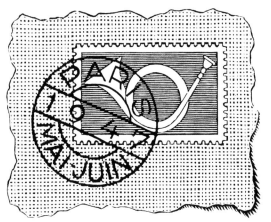

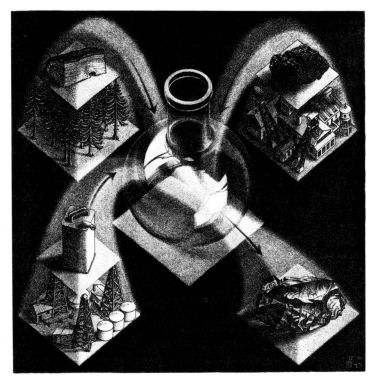

348
Other World. January 1947
Wood engraving and woodcut in black,
reddish brown and green, printed from
three blocks
318 × 261 (12¹/₂ × 10¹/₄″)
Compare cat. no. 346

349
XIIme Congrès Postal Universel:
vignette. April 1947
Woodcut
55 × 70 (2¹/₈ × 2³/₄″)

350
XIIme Congrès Postal Universel:
illustration. April 1947
Woodcut
156 × 181 (6¹/₈ × 7¹/₈″)

351
Synthesis. April 1947
Lithograph
310 × 310 (12¹/₄ × 12¹/₄″)

352
Up and Down. July 1947
Lithograph in brown
503 × 205 (19³/₄ × 8¹/₈″)

353
Crystal. December 1947
Mezzotint, second state
134 × 173 (5¹/₄ × 6³/₄″)

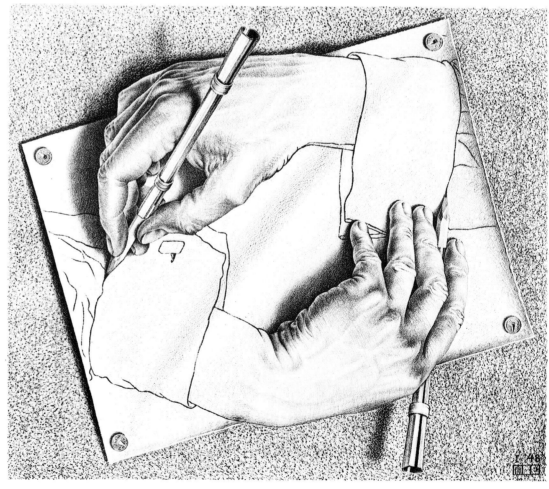

294

354
[Fish]. [1947]
Woodcut
$43 \times 55 \, (1^3/4 \times 2^1/8'')$
355
Drawing Hands. January 1948
Lithograph
$282 \times 332 \, (11^1/8 \times 13^1/8'')$
356
Drop (Dewdrop). February 1948
Mezzotint
$179 \times 245 \, (7 \times 9^5/8'')$

357
Sun and Moon. April 1948
Woodcut in blue, red, yellow and
black, printed from four blocks
$251 \times 270 \, (9^7/8 \times 10^5/8'')$
358
[Study for Stars]. August 1948
Woodcut
$370 \times 375 \, (14^5/8 \times 14^3/4'')$
Compare cat. no. 359
359
Stars. October 1948
Wood engraving
$320 \times 260 \, (12^5/8 \times 10^1/4'')$
Compare cat. no. 358

295

356   354   358
      355   357 359

360
New Year's greeting-card 1949, L. and
K. Asselbergs. November 1948
Woodcut
152 × 139 (6 × 5^1/$_2$″)
Compare cat. no. 446

361
[Plane-filling Motif with Birds]. April
1949
Wood engraving
54 × 68 (2^1/$_8$ × 2^5/$_8$″)

361A
[Regular Division of the Plane with
Birds]. [April 1949]
Wood engraving
115 × 208 (4^1/$_2$ × 8^1/$_8$″)

362
Sea-shells. July 1949
Mezzotint, first state
160 × 109 (6^1/$_4$ × 4^1/$_4$″)

363
Horses and Birds. September 1949
Wood engraving
87 × 72 (3^3/$_8$ × 2^7/$_8$″)
Compare cat. no. 446

364
Fish and Frogs. October 1949
Wood engraving
81 × 71 (3^1/$_4$ × 2^3/$_4$″)
Compare cat. no. 326

365
Double Planetoid (Double Planet).
December 1949
Wood engraving in green, dark blue,
black and white, printed from four
blocks, second state
Diameter 374 (14³/₄″)

366
Contrast (Order and Chaos). February
1950
Lithograph
280 × 280 (11 × 11″)

367
Rippled Surface. March 1950
Linoleum cut in black and grey-
brown, printed from two blocks
260 × 320 (10¹/₄ × 12⁵/₈″)

368
[Self-Portrait in Spherical Mirror].
April 1950
Woodcut
Diameter 82 (3¹/₄″)
Compare cat. nos. 80, 267, 268 and 339

299

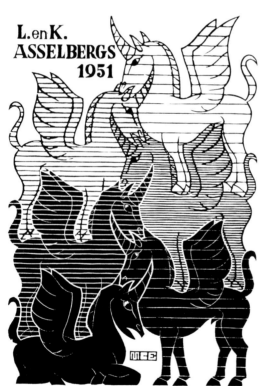

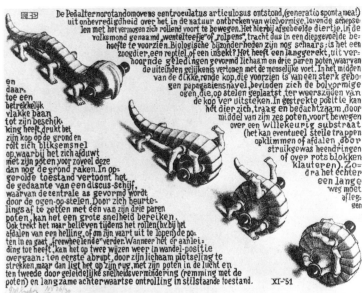

369
Butterflies. June 1950
Wood engraving
281 × 260 (11⅛ × 10¼″)

370
[Devils, vignette]. 1950
Wood engraving
97 × 59 (3⅞ × 2⅜″)
Compare cat. nos. 331 and 384

371
New Year's greeting-card 1951, L. and
K. Asselbergs. October 1950
Wood engraving
115 × 78 (4½ × 3⅛″)

372
Predestination (Topsy-Turvy World).
January 1951
Lithograph
294 × 422 (11⅝ × 16⅝″)
Compare cat. no. 416

373
Plane Filling I. March 1951
Mezzotint
146 × 192 (5¾ × 7¾″)

374
Curl-up. November 1951
Lithograph
170 × 232 (6¾ × 9⅛″)
Compare cat. no. 375

375
House of Stairs. November 1951
Lithograph
472 × 238 (18⅝ × 9⅜″)
Compare cat. no. 374

376
[Plane-filling Motif with Fish and Bird]. 1951
Linoleum cut
137 × 163 (5³/₈ × 6³/₈″)

377
Two Intersecting Planes. January 1952
Woodcut in green, brown and black, printed from three blocks
224 × 310 (8⁷/₈ × 12¹/₄″)

378
Puddle. February 1952
Woodcut in black, green and brown, printed from three blocks
240 × 319 (9¹/₂ × 12¹/₂″)
Compare cat. no. 230

379
Dragon. March 1952
Wood engraving
321 × 241 (12⁵/₈ × 9¹/₂″)

379A
Dragon. March 1952
Wood engraving; proof
217 × 212 (8¹/₂ × 8³/₈″)

380
Gravity. June 1952
Lithograph and watercolour
297 × 297 (11³/₄ × 11³/₄″)

381
[4 Graphic Artists, vignette]. (1952)
Woodcut
101 × 77 (4 × 3″)

382
[Earth, New Year's greeting-card
1953]. October 1952
Woodcut in blue-grey and brown,
printed from two blocks, with
letterpress in grey
155 × 135 (6¹/₈ × 5³/₈″)

383
[Air, New Year's greeting-card 1954].
October 1952
Woodcut in green and brown, printed
from two blocks, with letterpress in
grey
154 × 134 (6¹/₈ × 5³/₄″)

384
[Fire, New Year's greeting-card 1955].
October 1952
Woodcut in yellow and orange, printed
from two blocks, with letterpress in
grey
156 × 135 (6¹/₈ × 5³/₈″)
Compare cat. nos. 331 and 370

385
[Water, New Year's greeting-card
1956]. October 1952
Woodcut in green and blue, printed
from two blocks, with letterpress in
grey
155 × 135 (6¹/₈ × 5³/₈″)

386
Cubic Space Division (Cubic Space
Filling). December 1952
Lithograph
266 × 266 (10¹/₂ × 10¹/₂″)

387
Concentric Rinds (Concentric Space
Filling/Regular Sphere Division). May
1953
Wood engraving
241 × 241 (9¹/₂ × 9¹/₂″)

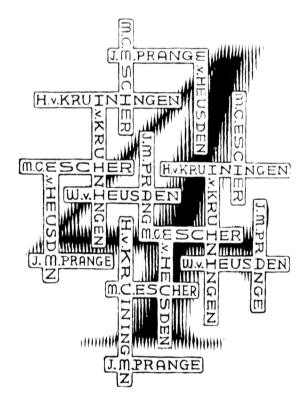

EUGÈNE & WILLY STRENS

FELICITAS 1956

FELICITAS 1955

EUGÈNE & WILLY STRENS

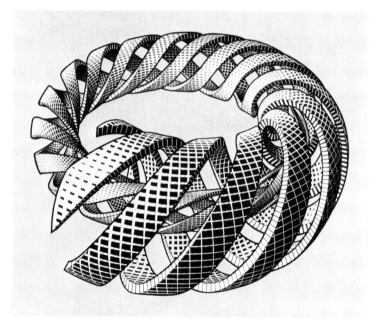

388
Relativity. July 1953
Woodcut
282 × 294 (11¹/₈ × 11⁵/₈″)
Compare cat. no. 389

389
Relativity. July 1953
Lithograph
277 × 292 (10⁷/₈ × 11¹/₂″)
Compare cat. no. 388

390
Spirals. December 1953
Wood engraving in black and grey,
printed from two blocks
270 × 333 (10⁵/₈ × 13¹/₈″)

391
[Trees and Animals]. [1953]
Wood engraving
44 × 99 (1³/₄ × 3⁷/₈″)

392
['E is een Ezel' [Donkey]]. 1953
Wood engraving
97 × 65 (3⁷/₈ × 2¹/₂″)

393
['M is een Muis' [Mouse]]. 1953
Woodcut
100 × 65 (3⁷/₈ × 2¹/₂″)

394
Bookplate A. R . A. Wertheim. March
1954
Woodcut
72 × 58 (2⁷/₈ × 2¹/₄″)

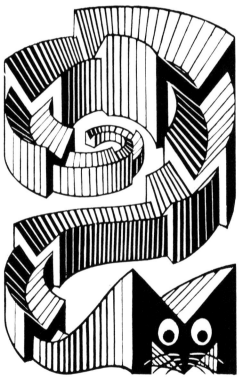

A.R.A.WERTHEIM

SEMPER IDEM

395
Tetrahedral Planetoid (Tetrahedral Planet). April 1954
Woodcut in green and black, printed from two blocks
430 × 430 (16⁷/₈ × 16⁷/₈″)

396
[Study for Rind]. May 1954
Wood engraving
305 × 210 (12 × 8¹/₄″)
Compare cat. nos. 401 and 409

397
Three Intersecting Planes. June 1954
Woodcut in green and black, printed from two blocks
324 × 375 (12³/₄ × 14³/₄″)

398
[Fish, vignette]. [August 1954]
Wood engraving
75 × 82 (3 × 3¹/₄″)
Compare cat. no. 417

399
Convex and Concave. March 1955
Lithograph
275 × 335 (10⁷/₈ × 13¹/₄″)

400
Liberation. April 1955
Lithograph
434 × 199 (17¹/₈ × 7⁷/₈″)

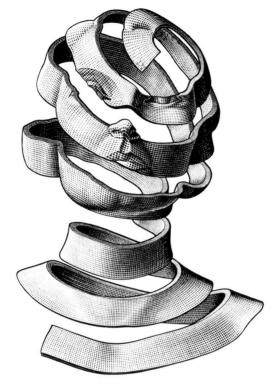

309

Vivo! Anima trepidans in me absumitur.

Ik ben mij zelf: een licht. Gij vindt
in mij uw eigen lot bepaald.
Blijf aldus niet voor 't wezen blind,
dat in mijn schijn U tegenstraalt.

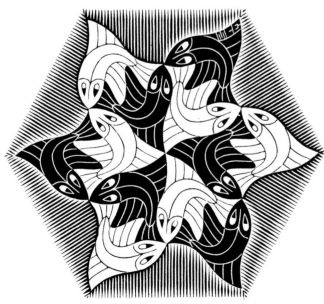

401
Rind. May 1955
Wood engraving and woodcut in black,
brown, blue-grey and grey, printed
from four blocks
345 × 235 (13⅝ × 9¼″)
Compare cat. nos. 396 and 409

402
Order and Chaos [II], (Compass Card).
August 1955
Lithograph
Diameter 272 (10¾″)

403
Depth. October 1955
Wood engraving and woodcut in
brown-red, grey-green and dark brown
printed from three blocks
320 × 230 (12⅝ × 9″)

404
Christmas card A K U. November 1955
Wood engraving
126 × 89 (5 × 3½″)

405
Three Worlds. December 1955
Lithograph
362 × 247 (14¼ × 9¾″)

406
[Fish, vignette]. [1955]
Woodcut
88 × 76 (3½ × 3″)

407
Candle Flame. January 1956
Woodcut
128 × 88 (5 × 3½″)
Compare cat. no. 172

408
Swans (White Swans, Black Swans).
February 1956
Wood engraving
199 × 319 (7⁷/₈ × 12¹/₂″)

409
Bond of Union. April 1956
Lithograph
253 × 339 (10 × 13³/₈″)
Compare cat. nos. 396 and 401

410
Print Gallery. May 1956
Lithograph
319 × 317 (12¹/₂ × 12¹/₂″)
Compare cat. no. 276

411
Division. July 1956
Woodcut, second state
Diameter 375 (14³/₄″)

412
New Year's greeting-card P T T.
September 1956
Wood engraving
136 × 152 (5³/₈ × 6″)
Compare cat. no. 446

413
Smaller and Smaller. October 1956
Wood engraving and woodcut in black
and brown, printed from four blocks
380 × 380 (15 × 15″)
Compare cat. no. 421

414
[Fish, vignette]. November 1956
Wood engraving
81 × 81 (3¹/₄ × 3¹/₄″)
Compare cat. no. 423

408 410   411 412

409   413 414

415
Cube with Ribbons. February 1957
Lithograph
$309 \times 305 \, (12^1/_8 \times 12'')$

416
[Regular Division of the Plane I]. June 1957
Woodcut in red
$240 \times 180 \, (9^1/_2 \times 7^1/_8'')$
Compare cat. no. 372

417
[Regular Division of the Plane II]. June 1957
Woodcut in red
$240 \times 180 \, (9^1/_2 \times 7^1/_8'')$
Compare cat. no. 398

418
[Regular Division of the Plane III].
June 1957
Woodcut in red
$240 \times 180 \, (9^1/_2 \times 7^1/_8'')$
Compare cat. no. 342

419
[Regular Division of the Plane IV].
June 1957
Woodcut in red
$240 \times 180 \, (9^1/_2 \times 7^1/_8'')$

420
[Regular Division of the Plane V]. June 1957
Woodcut in red
$240 \times 180 \, (9^1/_2 \times 7^1/_8'')$

421
[Regular Division of the Plane VI].
June 1957
Woodcut in red
$240 \times 180 \, (9^1/_2 \times 7^1/_8'')$
Compare cat. no. 413

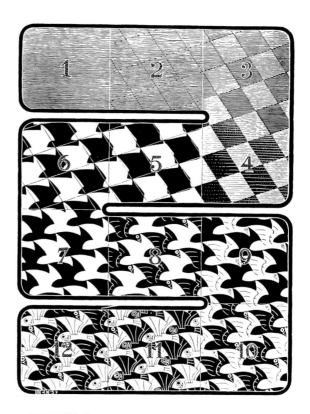

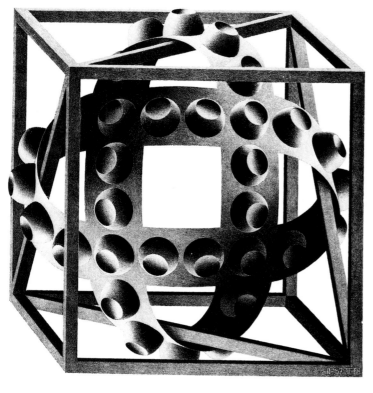

315

422
Plane Filling II. July 1957
Lithograph
315 × 370 (12³/₈ × 14⁵/₈″)

423
Whirlpools. November 1957
Wood engraving and woodcut, second
state, in red, grey and black, printed
from two blocks
438 × 235 (17¹/₄ × 9¹/₄″)
Compare cat. no. 414

424
Path of Life I. March 1958
Woodcut in red and black, printed
from two blocks
410 × 410 (16¹/₈ × 16¹/₈″)

425
Path of Life II. March 1958
Woodcut in grey-green and black,
printed from two blocks
370 × 370 (14⁵/₈ × 14⁵/₈″)

422   423   424
                              425

426
Belvedere. May 1958
Lithograph
462 × 295 (18¹/₄ × 11⁵/₈")
Compare cat. no. 430

427
Sphere Surface with Fish. July 1958
Woodcut in grey, gold and reddish
brown, printed from three blocks
340 × 340 (13³/₈ × 13³/₈")
Compare cat. no. 428

428
Sphere Spirals. October 1958
Woodcut in grey, black, yellow and
pink, printed from four blocks
Diameter 320 (12⁵/₈")
Compare cat. no. 427

429
Circle Limit I. November 1958
Woodcut
Diameter 418 (16¹/₂")

430
[Man with Cuboid]. [1958]
Wood engraving
64 × 64 (2¹/₂ × 2¹/₂")
Compare cat. no. 426

431
Flatworms. January 1959
Lithograph
338 × 412 (13¹/₄ × 16¹/₄")

432
Circle Limit II. March 1959
Woodcut in red and black, printed
from two blocks
Diameter 417 (16³/₈")

433
Fish and Scales. July 1959
Woodcut
378 × 378 (14⁷/₈ × 14⁷/₈")

434
Circle Limit III. December 1959
Woodcut, second state, in yellow,
green, blue, brown and black, printed
from five blocks
Diameter 415 (16³/₈")

435
Ascending and Descending. March
1960
Lithograph
355 × 285 (14 × 11¹/₄")

320

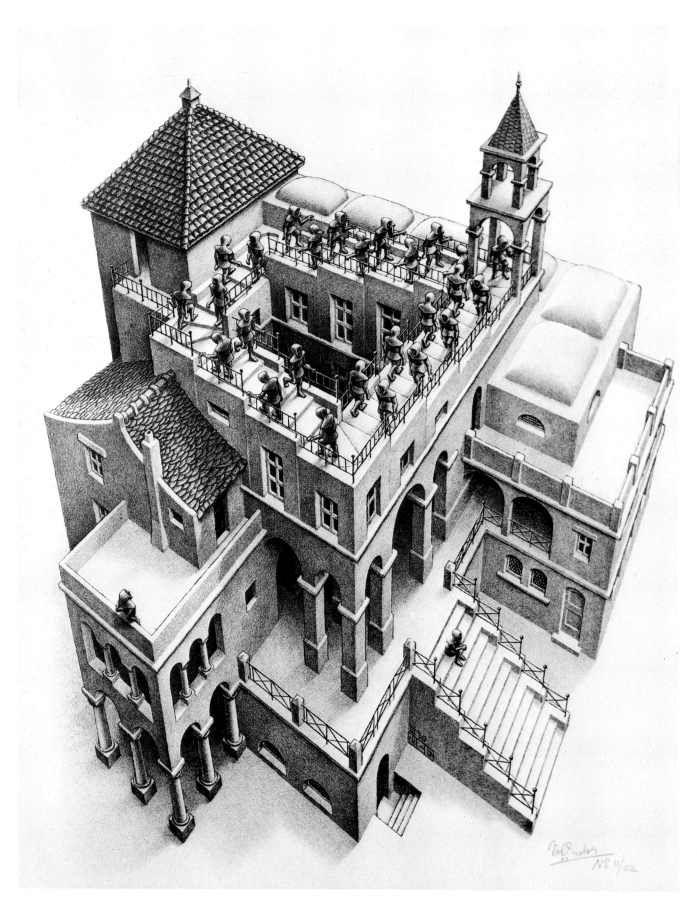

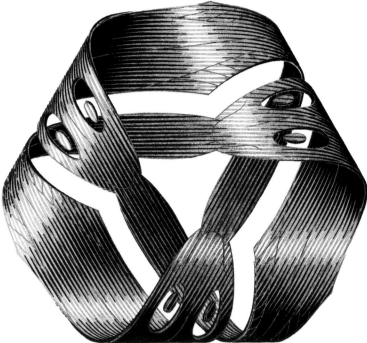

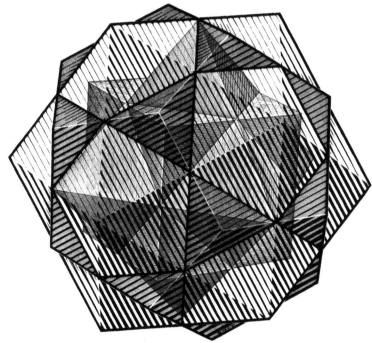

436
Circle Limit IV (Heaven and Hell). July
1960
Woodcut in black and ochre, printed
from two blocks
Diameter 416 (16³/₈″)

437
Möbius Strip I. March 1961
Wood engraving and woodcut in red,
green, gold and black, printed from
four blocks
238 × 259 (9³/₈ × 10¹/₄″)

438
Four Regular Solids. May 1961
Woodcut in black, yellow and red,
printed from three blocks
354 × 390 (13⁷/₈ × 15³/₈″)

322   Compare cat. no. 439

439
Waterfall. October 1961
Lithograph
380 × 300 (15 × 11³/₄″)
Compare cat. no. 438

436   437   439
438

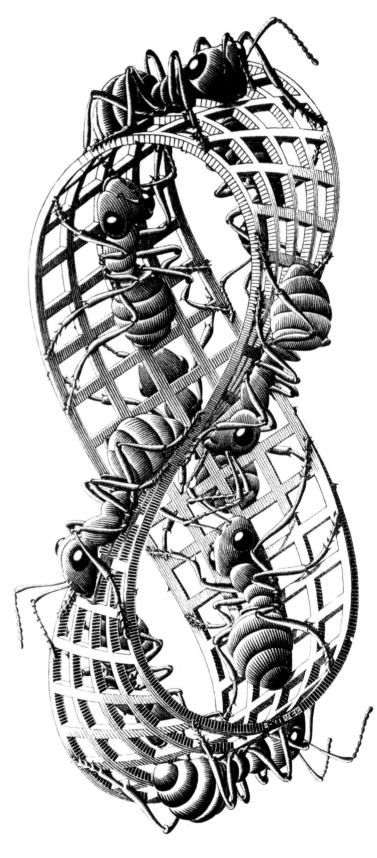

440
Larix [Apple]. 1961
Wood engraving
75 × 75 (3 × 3″)

441
Möbius Strip II (Red Ants). February
1963
Woodcut in red, black and grey-green,
printed from three blocks
453 × 205 (17⁷/₈ × 8¹/₈″)

442
Fish. 1963
Woodcut
109 × 109 (4¹/₄ × 4¹/₄″)

443
Square Limit. April 1964
Woodcut in red and grey-green,
printed from two blocks
340 × 340 (13³/₈ × 13³/₈″)

444
Knots. August 1965
Woodcut in black, green and brown,
printed from three blocks
430 × 320 (16⁷/₈ × 12⁵/₈″)

445
[Path of Life III]. November 1966
Woodcut in red and black, printed
from two blocks
366 × 371 (14³/₈ × 14⁵/₈″)

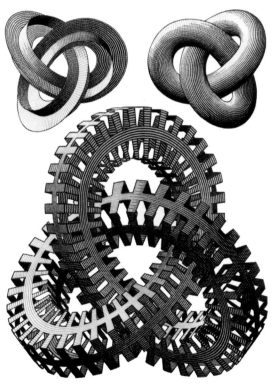

440 441   442 443
                  444 445

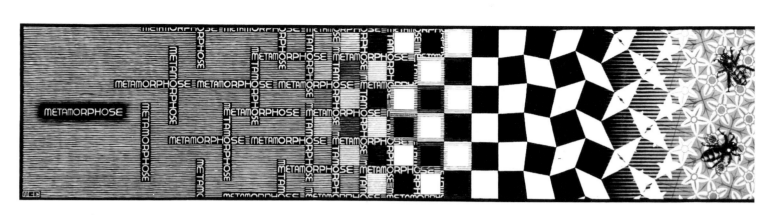

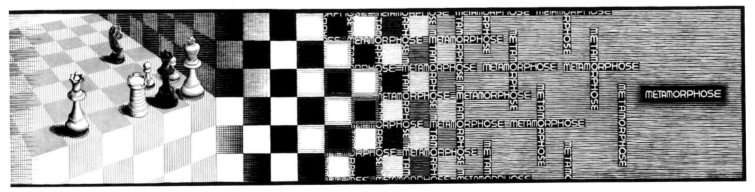

446
Metamorphosis III. 1967–68
Woodcut, second state, in black, green
and reddish brown, printed from
thirty-three blocks on six combined
sheets, mounted on canvas; partly
coloured by hand
192 × 6800 (7½ × 268″)
Compare cat. nos. 148, 298, 300, 310,
320, 327, 360, 363 and 412

447
[Study for part of Snakes]. [1969]
Woodcut
$117 \times 93 \, (4^5/_8 \times 3^5/_8'')$
448
Snakes. July 1969
Woodcut in orange, green and black,
printed from three blocks
$498 \times 447 \, (19^5/_8 \times 17^5/_8'')$

328

447
448

Notes on the Illustrations

See also page 177

1
Escher's Father
Added signature and date: bottom right
The print shown was cropped by Escher, left, right, top and bottom. There is also a copy measuring 226 × 164 mm (8⁷/₈ × 6¹/₂″) (Roosevelt Collection).

2
Bookplate Bastiaan Kist
Text in the print: BASTIAAN KIST
There are also copies in other colour combinations.

3
Chrysanthemum
There are also copies in brown.

5
Skull
Date based on the dated linoleum block
Signature in the print: top right

6
Railway Bridge
Date based on the diary of Escher's father
Signature in the print: bottom right
Added signature: bottom left

7
Mascot
Date based on the diary of Escher's father
Signature in the print: bottom right

8
Portrait of a Man
Added signature and date: bottom right

10
Hen with Egg
Date based on the dated linoleum block
Signature in the print: bottom left
There are also copies in more than one colour (from one block). The first state is without the egg. In the linoleum block a second (incomplete) signature has been cut, bottom right (□□E).

11
Still Life
Date based on the dated linoleum block
Signature in the print: bottom right
Added signature: bottom right
There are also copies in other colours than black. Copies dated '16 are also known.

12
Baby
Signature and date in the print: bottom right
There are also copies in other colours than black, and in more than one colour (from one block).

13
Young Thrush
Added signature and date: bottom right
Text in the print: JONGE LYSTER (Young thrush)
There are also copies in other colours than black.

14
Monogram MCE
Added signature and date: bottom right

15
Bookplate M.C. Escher
Date in the print: bottom
Added signature and date: bottom right
Text in the print: EX LIBRIS M.C. ESCHER 1917
There are also copies in other colours. Escher first cut the design legibly (that is, not in mirror image) in linoleum, then printed this linocut on another piece of linoleum, and from this made the definitive linocut.

16
Bookplate Heleen van Thienen
Date in the print: bottom centre
Text in the print: EX LIBRIS HELEEN VAN THIENEN 1917

17
Self-Portrait
Signature in the print: bottom right

Added signature and date: bottom right
There are also copies in light and dark brown. It is considered by some not to be a self-portrait but a portrait of Escher's eldest brother Eduard (Eddy) or of another brother (Nol or George).

18
Jug
Roosevelt Collection
Signature in the print: bottom right
Added signature: bottom right
Text in the print: JACOBA-KANNETJE (Jug)

19
The Rag Pickers
Date based on the diary of Escher's father
Added signature and date: bottom right
Text in the print: *The Rag Pickers*
There are also copies in other colour combinations. The print was made for a programme for a production of *The Rag Pickers* staged by interned British soldiers in aid of a children's home in Arnhem, on 12 January 1918.

20
Sunflowers
Date based on the diary of Escher's father
Added signature and date: bottom right

21
Fiet van Stolk
Signature in the print: bottom right
Date in the print: bottom
Added signature: bottom right
Text in the print: DOORN 8 AUGUSTUS 1918
In the first state the text is missing (the signature MCE is present). There are also copies in green.

22
Waves
Added signature and date: bottom right

There are also copies in other [col]our combinations and in a sin[gle] colour. It is possible that the sky above the waves was not coloured in, but printed from a separate block.

23
Two Bells
Added signature and date: bottom right
There are also copies in other colours and in two colours (printed from one block).

24
Self-Portrait
Added signature and date: bottom right
There are also copies in other colour combinations.

25
Bookplate T. de Ridder
Added signature and date: bottom right
Text in the print: TOOM DIT ROS T. DE RIDDER (Bridle this steed T. de Ridder)
There are also copies in greyish green.

26
Bookplate Tony de Ridder
Date based on cat. no. 25
Signature in the print: bottom right
Text in the print: TOOM DIT ROS TONY DE RIDDER (Bridle this steed Tony de Ridder)
There are copies with several prints on one sheet.

27
Bookplate R.I.H.
Roosevelt Collection
Date based on Escher's correspondence
Added signature: bottom right
Text in the print: R.I.H.

28
White Cat
Roosevelt Collection
Date based on the diary of Escher's father
Signature in the print: top left

329

Added signature and date: bottom
right

Other additions: no 2 (bottom left)

29

The Borger Oak, Oosterbeek

Added signature and date: bottom
right

There are also copies dated *1918*.

30

Portrait

Signature in the print: bottom right

Added signature and date: bottom
right

There are also copies in other colours
than black.

31

Portrait of a Bearded Man

Anonymous collection

Added signature and date: bottom
right

Reproduced from a photostat of
unknown provenance

32

Seated Man with a Cat

Signature in the print: top left

Date in the print: top right

Added signature: bottom left

33

Blocks of Basalt

Added signature and date: bottom
right

34

Tree

Signature and date in the print: bottom
left

There are also counterproofs of this
print.

35

Life Force

Signature in the print: bottom right

Text in the print: LEVENKRACHT (Life
force)

There are also dated copies and
counterproofs. In a number of prints
Escher blocked out the text with
black ink.

36

Self-Portrait

Added signature and date: bottom
right

37

Parrot

Date based on a preliminary study in a
sketchbook next to a dated drawing

Signature in the print: bottom left

38

White Cat

Date based on dated drawing

39

Skull

In a later state, shading and a signature

have been added in the square at
bottom left.

42

Sea-shell

Signature in the print: bottom right

This woodcut was possibly inspired by
Rembrandt's etching *The Shell* of
1650.

43

Sea-shell

Signature in the print: bottom left

44

Self-Portrait in a Chair

Added signature and date: bottom
right

46

Female Nude in a Landscape

There are also dated copies. One copy
is known dated *1921*. There are also
copies printed on textile.

47

Fairy-tale

Added signature and date: bottom
right

48

Wild West

Added signature and date: bottom
right

49

The Fall of Man

Signature and date in the print: bottom
right (in mirror image)

Added signature and date: bottom
right

50

Escher's Father with Magnifying Glass

Date based on the diary of Escher's
father

Signature in the print: top right

51

Portrait of a Man

Date based on dated drawing

There are also counterproofs of this
print.

52

Man Standing

Date based on dated drawing

Signature in the print: bottom centre
(upside-down)

There are also counterproofs of this
print.

54

Flower

Date based on the diary of Escher's
father

55

Seated Female Nude

There are no flowers in the first state.
There are also copies printed on
textile.

56

Seated Female Nude

Added signature: bottom left

57

Female Nude in a Chair

Signature in the print: bottom right

60

In Mesquita's Classroom

Signature in the print: bottom left

61

Sea-shells

Signature in the print: four times in the
centre (in the original print: top left)

The same block was printed four
times—twice recto, twice verso, on
transparent paper.

64

Poster

Added signature: at the bottom of the
picture, left of centre

Text in the print: HET AANGEZICHT
DES DOODS! ENORM!
SENSATIONEEL! YZIG! (The face of
death! Fantastic! Sensational!
Chilling!)

There exist proofs in various colours
and colour combinations.

66

Plane-filling Motif

Signature in the print: bottom centre

There exist proofs in black.

67

Paradise

Date based on Escher's
correspondence

Signature and date in the print: bottom
right

Added signature and date: bottom
right

This woodcut was possibly inspired by
a woodcut of 1918 by Gertraud
Brausewetter, Vienna.

68–83

The booklet *Flor de Pascua—Spreuken
14, vers 33* ('Flor de Pascua—
Proverbs 14, verse 33') by A. P. van
Stolk, with woodcuts by
M. C. Escher, was published in
November 1921 by Hollandia
Drukkerij, Baarn, in an edition of
222 copies. There are also sheets on
which 12 of the prints are printed
together (cat. nos. 69, 71, 73–82; 69
upside-down compared with the
print in the booklet).

81

'Never Think before You Act'

This woodcut was also printed (from
the original block) in an
introductory prospectus of 1921, in
which the opportunity was offered of
subscribing to *Flor de Pascua*.

83

Love

This woodcut was possibly inspired by
a woodcut by S. Jessurun de
Mesquita. The picture probably
shows Fiet van Stolk-Van der Does
de Willebois and her little son Jantje.

84

Blocks of Basalt

Added signature and date: bottom
right

85

Seated Female Nude

Added signature and date: bottom
right

86

Seated Female Nude

Roosevelt Collection

Date based on cat. no. 85

Added signature: bottom right

88

Hand with Fir Cone

Added signature: bottom left

There are also counterproofs of this
print.

89

St Francis

Date based on Escher's
correspondence

Signature in the print: top right

Added signature and date: bottom left

Other additions: *eigen druk* (own
printing), bottom right

90

Eight Heads

Added signature and date: bottom left

Other additions: *eigen druk* (own
printing), bottom right

90A

Eight Heads, basic block

Added signature: bottom centre

Added date: bottom left

91

Bookplate B. G. Escher

Beels Collection

Date based on the collector's notes

Text in the print: EX LIBRIS
B G ESCHER

There is also a version of 30 × 30 mm
($1\frac{1}{4} \times 1\frac{1}{4}''$) printed from a zinc
block.

92

Eagle

Date based on dated invitation

Escher made this woodcut for the
clubhouse De Arend (The Eagle) of
the Institute for the Mature Youth in
Rotterdam.

93

San Gimignano

Signature and date in the print: bottom
left

Added signature: bottom left
Other additions: *eigen druk* (own printing), bottom right

94

Siena

Date based on Escher's records

Signature in the print: bottom right

Added signature: bottom left

Text in the print: SIENA

The incorrect date 11–1920 has been blocked out with black ink. There are also copies printed on textile.

95

Serenade in Siena

Date based on Escher's correspondence

Signature in the print: bottom left

96

San Gimignano

Date based on the diary of Escher's father

Signature and date in the print: bottom left

Added signature: bottom left

Other additions: *eigen druk* (own printing), bottom right

97

Dolphins

Signature and date in the print: bottom left

Added signature: bottom left

Other additions: *eigen druk* (own printing), bottom right

98

Palm Tree

Signature in the print: bottom left

Date in the print: bottom right

99

Announcement card for exhibition

Date based on the date of the exhibition

Text in the print: CIRCOLO ARTISTICO SENESE AGOSTO 13–26 BIANCO E NERO MOSTRA D'ARTE PERSONALE DI M.C. ESCHER

100

Self-Portrait

Signature in the print: bottom right

Date in the print: bottom left

101

Portrait of Jetta

Signature and date in the print: top right

Added signature: bottom left

Other additions: *eigen druk* (own printing), bottom right

There is also a shortened version of this print of 286 mm (11 1/4″) high in which the hand with the flower is missing (cat. no. 101A). This was probably made by partially covering the paper.

102

Vitorchiano nel Cimino

Signature and date in the print: bottom right

Added signature: bottom left

Other additions: *eigen druk* (own printing), bottom right

103

St Vincent

Date based on Escher's records

Signature in the print: bottom left

Added signature: bottom left

Other additions: no 9 (top right)

This print was intended to be an illustration for the story of St Vincent and the miraculous raven from *Legenda Aurea*

104

The First Day of the Creation

Signature and date in the print: bottom left

Added signature: bottom left

Other additions: No 18 (bottom right)

Text in the print: GEN. I : I–5

105

The Second Day of the Creation

Signature and date in the print: top right

Added signature: bottom left

Text in the print: GEN. I : 6–8

In 1929 a special edition of three hundred copies was printed for the VAEVO (an association for the promotion of aesthetics in higher education).

106

The Third Day of the Creation

Signature and date in the print: bottom left

Added signature: bottom left

Other additions: *eigen druk* (own printing), bottom right

Text in the print: GEN. I : 9–13

107

The Fourth Day of the Creation

Signature and date in the print: top right

Added signature: bottom left

Text in the print: GEN. I : 14–19

108

The Fifth Day of the Creation

Signature and date in the print: bottom left

Added signature: bottom left

Text in the print: GEN. I : 20–23

109

The Sixth Day of the Creation

Signature and date in the print: bottom left

Added signature: bottom left

Other additions: *eigen druk* (own printing), bottom right

Text in the print: GEN. I : 24–31

110

Announcement card

Date based on the date of the exhibition

Text in the print: DU 2 AU 16 MAI DE 16 A 19 HEURES EXPOSITION M.C. ESCHER XYLOGRAPHE HOLLANDAIS BOIS GRAVES ESTAMPES DESSINS GRUPPO ROMANO INCISORI ARTISTI PALAZZETTO VENEZIA VIA DEGLI ASTALLI 3 ENTREE LIBRE

The exhibition was held in Rome, 2–16 May 1926. There are also copies in gold on dark-grey cardboard.

111

Tree

Date based on the date of the exhibition

Signature in the print: bottom left

Printed as a vignette on the invitation cards for the following exhibitions: of M.C. Escher in the Palazzetto Venezia in Rome, 2–16 May 1926; of Sophie van Stolk-Van der Does de Willebois, Maurits C. Escher, Gunth. Studemann and R. Stolk Soegina in the Amsterdamsche Ateliers voor Binnenhuiskunst, Amsterdam, 1 October–1 November 1927.

112

Birds

Date based on the date of the exhibition

Signature in the print: bottom left

Printed as a vignette in the catalogue for M.C. Escher's exhibition in the Palazzetto Venezia in Rome, 2–16 May 1926.

113

The Six Days of the Creation

Date based on the date of the exhibition

Signature in the print: centre right (in mirror image)

Text in the print: PRIMO GIORNO GEN. I: 1–5 CREAZIONE DELLA TERRA E DELLA LUCE. LO SPIRITO DI DIO SOPRA LE ACQUE SECONDO GIORNO GEN.I: 6–8 SEPARAZIONE DELLE ACQUE TERZO GIORNO GEN.I: 9–13 CREAZIONE DELLE PIANTE QUARTO GIORNO GEN.I: 14–19 CREAZIONE DEL SOLE E DELLA LUNA QUINTO GIORNO GEN I: 20–23 CREAZIONE DEGLI UCCELLI E DEI PESCI. SESTO GIORNO GEN. I: 24–31 CREAZIONE DEGLI ANIMALI E DELL'UOMO

In the text corrections have been made after printing (see picture): DEI was changed twice to DEGLI. This woodcut was printed on a folder containing a complete set of the six prints of the Creation that was for sale.

114

The Fall of Man

Signature and date in the print: bottom right

Added signature: bottom left

Other additions: *eigen druk* (own printing), bottom right

Text in the print: GEN. 3 : 6

115

Procession

Signature and date in the print: bottom left

Added signature: bottom left

Other additions: *eigen druk* (own printing), bottom right

116

Rome

Signature and date in the print: bottom right

Added signature: bottom left

Other additions: *eigen druk* (own printing), bottom right

There are also copies in gold and black.

117

Castle in the Air

Signature and date in the print: bottom right

Added signature: bottom left

Other additions: *eigen druk* (own printing), bottom right

118

Tower of Babel

Signature and date in the print: bottom left

Added signature: top left and bottom left

Other additions: *eigen druk* (own printing), bottom right

Text in the print: GEN. 11 : 7

119

Fara San Martino

Signature and date in the print: bottom right

Added signature: bottom left

120

Bonifacio

Signature and date in the print: bottom right

Added signature: bottom left

121
Citadel of Calvi
Signature and date in the print: top right
Added signature: bottom left
Other additions: *eigen druk* (own printing), bottom right
122
Birth announcement card of Arthur Escher
Text in the print: ROMA 8 DECEMBER 1928 VIA ALESSANDRO POERIO 94 ARTHUR EDUARD ESCHER
The 'stamped' text is possibly a linocut. There are also copies in other colour combinations.
123
Corte
Signature and date in the print: bottom left
Added signature: bottom left
124
La Cathédrale engloutie
Signature and date in the print: bottom right
Added signature: bottom left
Other additions: *eigen druk* (own printing), bottom right
This print was inspired by Debussy's Prelude *La Cathédrale engloutie*. The cathedral shown is probably Notre-Dame in Chartres, as 'adapted' by Escher.
125
Infant
Signature in the print: top right
Date in the print: top left
Added signature: bottom left
Other additions: *eigen druk* (own printing), bottom right
126
Goriano Sicoli
Signature and date in the print: bottom centre
Added signature: bottom left
Other additions: no 9/30 (bottom left)
127
Genazzano
Signature and date in the print: bottom left
Added signature: bottom left
Other additions: no 3/10 (bottom left)
128
Self-Portrait
Signature and date in the print: bottom left
Added signature: bottom left
Other additions: no 22/40 (bottom left)
129
Barbarano
Signature and date in the print: bottom left

Added signature: bottom left
Other additions: no 5/24 (bottom left)
130
Cerro al Volturno
Signature and date in the print: top right
Added signature: bottom left
Other additions: *eigen druk* (own printing), bottom right
131
Scanno
Signature and date in the print: bottom right
Added signature: bottom left
Other additions: no 5/45 (bottom left)
Text in the print: STAMPATO I. CRAIA. ROMA
132
Castrovalva
Signature and date in the print: top right
Added signature: bottom left
Other additions: no 39/50 (bottom left)
Text in the print: STAMPATO I. CRAIA. ROMA
133
Aragno
Signature in the print: bottom centre
Text in the print: ARAGNO MDCCCLXXX-MCMXXX
Escher was commissioned to make this lithograph, probably through the intervention of his printer I. Craia. The print was used for the anniversary menu of Il Caffè Aragno, which had been located in the Palazzo Marignoli in Rome since 20 September 1880.
134
The Bridge
Signature and date in the print: bottom left
Added signature: bottom left
Other additions: no 28/60 (bottom left)
Text in the print: STAMPATO I. CRAIA. ROMA
Escher called this print his first 'trifling work', a so-called Abruzzi composition.
135
Palizzi
Signature and date in the print: bottom right
Added signature: bottom left
136
Morano
Signature and date in the print: bottom right
Added signature: bottom left
137
Pentedattilo

Signature and date in the print: bottom right
Added signature: bottom left
Other additions: no 3/40 (bottom left)
138
Fiumara
Signature and date in the print: bottom left
Added signature: bottom left
Other additions: no 23/40 (bottom left)
139
Cattolica
Signature and date in the print: top right
Added signature: bottom left
Other additions: no 14/40 (bottom left)
140
Pentedattilo
Signature and date in the print: top right
Added signature: bottom left
141
Pentedattilo
Signature and date in the print: top left
Added signature: bottom left
142
Scilla
Signature and date in the print: bottom right
Added signature: bottom left
Other additions: no 5/40 (bottom left)
143
Tropea
Signature and date in the print: bottom left
Added signature: bottom left
Other additions: no 12/40 (bottom left)
144
Santa Severina
Signature and date in the print: bottom right
Added signature: bottom left
Other additions: no 10/40 (bottom left)
145
Rocca Imperiale
Signature and date in the print: bottom right
Added signature: bottom left
Other additions: no 13/40 (bottom left)
146
Rossano
Signature and date in the print: bottom right
147
Scilla
Signature and date in the print: top right
There are also copies in silver on black paper (147A).
148
Atrani

Signature and date in the print: top right
Added signature: bottom left
Other additions: no 10/30 (bottom left)
149
Invitation
Date based on the diary of Escher's father
Text in the print: KUNSTZAAL MARTINUS LIERNUR ZEESTRAAT 63 DEN HAAG TEL. 114581 TENTOONSTELLING VAN HOUTSNEDEN LITHO'S EN TEKENINGEN DOOR M. C. ESCHER GEOPEND VAN 1 TOT 31 OKTOBER 1931 OP WERKDAGEN VAN 10 TOT 6 UUR
According to his father's diary, Escher also made a poster for this exhibition of a linocut with the same picture and text.
150
Covered Alley
Signature and date in the print: top left
This print is also used on the cover of *De Graphicus M. C. Escher* by G. H. 's-Gravesande, *Halcyon* 3–4, The Hague, 1940
151
Atrani
Signature and date in the print: bottom right
Added signature: bottom left
Other additions: no 7/24 (bottom left)
152
Ravello
Signature and date in the print: bottom right
Added signature: bottom left
Other additions: no 14/23 (bottom left)
153
Coast of Amalfi
Signature and date in the print: bottom left
Added signature: bottom left
154
Cobwebs
Date based on the essay by G. H. 's-Gravesande mentioned below
Signature in the print: top right
After the first state, the two cobwebs centre right and top right have been added.
This print is an illustration for the poem 'Spinrag' (Cobwebs) by A. E. Drijfhout. The print and the poem were published in *De Graphicus M. C. Escher* by G. H. 's-Gravesande, *Halcyon* 3–4, The Hague, 1940.

155

Kite

Date based on Escher's records

Signature in the print: bottom right

Text in the print: *Ad summa nitens, nihil consequor. Stuwt mij een kracht omhoog, een kracht mij neerwaarts bindt: een doelloos ding voor 't oog, fier speelgoed van een kind.* (When a force pulls me up, a force holds me down: a useless thing to the eye, I am a child's proud toy.)

156

Flowers

Date based on Escher's records

Signature in the print: bottom left

Text in the print: *Gaudentes alienam mirantur tabem. U zij bewust hetgeen wij derven: ons vroeg versterven een oogenlust.* (Be aware of our privation: we die an early death to feast your eyes.)

This woodcut was also printed in *Elseviers geïllustreerd Maandschrift*, vol. 41, no. 10, October 1931, p. 224.

157

Sundial

Date based on Escher's records

Signature in the print: top right

Text in the print: PATET QUAELIBET ULTIMA LATET. EEN SCHADUW MEET HET SCHEIDEND UUR AAN MIJN ONWRIKBAARHEID VOORBIJ; ZOO WIJST HET WENTELEND GETIJ ZONDER RESPIJT UW EIGEN DUUR. (A shadow measures the parting hour as it passes by my unmoving presence: thus the changing tides ceaselessly point to your own transience.)

158

Squirrel

Date based on Escher's records

Signature in the print: top right

Text in the print: *Silva motum arcano continens silet. Het kraakt: er raakt iets los in 't bosch;—het rept,—dan staat het woud weer stil, in stilte.* (A crackling: something is moving in the wood; it stirs, and then the trees stand still again, in silence.)

159–86

The booklet *XXIV Emblemata dat zijn zinne-beelden*, with maxims in verse by A. E. Drijfhout and woodcuts by M. C. Escher, was published in 1932 by Van Dishoeck in Bussum, in an edition of three hundred copies. There are also separate prints of the second title page, the table of contents and the twenty-four emblem prints (cat. nos. 160–84).

159

Emblemata, first title page

Date based on the publication of the book

Signature in the print: bottom left

Text in the print: XXIV EMBLEMATA DAT ZIJN ZINNE-BEELDEN SPREUKVERZEN VAN A. E. DRIJFHOUT HOUTSNEDEN VAN M. C. ESCHER UITGEGEVEN IN HET JAAR MCMXXXII DOOR C. A. J. VAN DISHOECK N. V. TE BUSSUM

160

Emblemata, second title page

Date based on Escher's records and dated photographs

Signature in the print: centre left

Added signature: bottom left

Text in the print: XXIV EMBLEMATA DAT ZIJN ZINNE-BEELDEN SPREUKVERZEN VAN A. E. DRIJFHOUT HOUTSNEDEN VAN M. C. ESCHER

161

Emblemata, table of contents

Date based on Escher's records

Signature in the print: bottom right

Added signature: bottom left

Text in the print: XXIV EMBLEMATA BLOEMVAAS AANBEELD LUIT VLIEGER BOEI PALMBOOM WINDVAAN ZONNEWIJZER STOOMWALS VUURSLAG KAARSVLAM HANDWIJZER BIJENKORF KIKVORSCH EEKHOORN PADDESTOEL WEEGSCHAAL DOBBELSTEENEN VLINDER CACTUS WATERPUT SCHUILNEST GIETER HANGSLOT (Vase, anvil, lute, kite, buoy, palm tree, weather vane, sundial, steamroller, flint, candle flame, signpost, beehive, frog, squirrel, toadstool, balance, dice, butterfly, cactus, well, retreat, watering-can, padlock.)

162

Emblema I, Vase

Date based on Escher's records

Signature in the print: bottom right

Added signature: bottom left

Text in the print: GAUDENTES ALIENAM MIRANTUR TABEM. U ZIJ BEWUST HETGEEN WIJ DERVEN: ONS VROEG VERSTERVEN EEN OOGENLUST. (Be aware of our privation: we die an early death to feast your eyes.)

163

Emblema II, Anvil

Date based on Escher's records

Signature in the print: top left

Added signature: bottom left

Text in the print: FORTITUDO MALLEO CONTUNDENTI COMPAR. ZONDER MIJN WEDERSTAND, GESTAALDE LIJDZAAMHEID, MACHTELOOS WAAR UW HAND, VRUCHTELOOS UW BELEID. (Without my resistance and steeled patience, your hand would be powerless, your action fruitless.)

164

Emblema III, Lute

Date based on Escher's records

Signature in the print: top right

Text in the print: MINIME OPPRESSAE CONQUIESCUNT VOCES. GIJ HUNKERT NAAR WAT VREUGD EN NAAR VERSTOMD GEZANG? DE ACCOORDEN UWER JEUGD WEERKLINKEN EEUWEN LANG! (Do you pine for happiness and muted song? The chords of your youth will resound for centuries.)

165

Emblema IV, Kite

Date based on Escher's records

Signature in the print: top centre

Added signature: bottom left

Text in the print: AD SUMMA NITENS NIHIL CONSEQUOR. STUWT MIJ EEN KRACHT OMHOOG, EEN KRACHT MIJ NEERWAARTS BINDT: EEN DOELLOOS DING VOOR 'T OOG, FIER SPEELGOED VAN EEN KIND. (When a force pulls me up, a force holds me down: a useless thing to the eye, I am a child's proud toy.)

166

Emblema V, Buoy

Date based on Escher's records

Signature in the print: bottom right

Added signature: bottom left

Text in the print: NE MISERE IN VADA IMPACTUS PEREAS. VOLHARDEND, MACHTELOOS GETEISTERD DOOR DEN VLOED, WEERSTREEF IK, VRUCHTELOOS: —ZOO BLIJFT UW VAART BEHOED. (Persevering, helplessly harassed by the tide, I resist in vain: thus your voyage will be safe.)

167

Emblema VI, Palm Tree

Date based on Escher's records

Signature in the print: bottom left

Added signature: bottom left

Text in the print: PROCERA EX GRAMINE SURGENS MIRABILIS. *Van den grond vervreemde zonderlinge boom, sta ik rank en neem de wereld op in mijn droom.* (Curious tree, estranged from the ground, slender I stand, admitting the world to my dream.)

168

Emblema VII, Weather Vane

Date based on Escher's records

Signature in the print: bottom left

Added signature: bottom left

Text in the print: *Officium meum stabile agitari. Standvastig in mijn willoosheid wend ik mij, 't wenden nimmer moe. Gij smaalt mijn wispelturigheid? Dus is mijn taak, mijn trouw, zie toe!* (Steadfast in my lack of will, I turn, never tired of turning. You scoff at my fickleness? Such is my task, my faithfulness—just see!)

169

Emblema VIII, Sundial

Date based on Escher's records

Signature in the print: bottom left

Added signature: bottom left

Text in the print: PATET QUAELIBET ULTIMA LATET. EEN SCHADUW MEET HET SCHEIDEND UUR AAN MIJN ONWRIKBAARHEID VOORBIJ; ZOO WIJST HET WENTELEND GETIJ ZONDER RESPIJT UW EIGEN DUUR. (A shadow measures the parting hour as it passes by my unmoving presence: thus the changing tides ceaselessly point to your own transience.)

170

Emblema IX, Steamroller

Date based on Escher's records

Signature in the print: bottom left

Added signature: bottom left

Text in the print: *Vias pondere perseveranter exaequo. Wanstaltig en gezeuld, grommelend, afgebeuld, plet ik met norsch gedruisch mijn weg in 't gruis.* (Monstrous and dragging along, grumbling and worked to death, I roll my way through the grit with a gruff roaring.)

171

Emblema X, Flint

Date based on Escher's records

Signature in the print: top right

Added signature: bottom left

Text in the print: *Percute me, et eversione tenus, percute! Inwendig ben ik hard en koud, daar is in mij geen gloed noch vier, doch slaat mij 't lot, zoo menigvoud spatten de gensters ginds en hier.* (Inwardly I am hard and cold, there is no glow or fire in me, but if I am struck by fate, the sparks fly everywhere.)

172
Emblema XI, Candle Flame
Date based on Escher's records
Signature in the print: top right
Added signature: bottom left
Text in the print: *Vivo! Anima trepidans in me absumitur. Ik ben mij zelf: een licht.—Gij vindt in mij uw eigen lot bepaald. Blijf aldus niet voor 't wezen blind, dat in mijn schijn U tegenstraalt.* (I am myself: a light. In me you find your fate. So be not blind to the truth shining from my glow.)

173
Emblema XII, Signpost
Date based on Escher's records
Signature in the print: top right
Added signature: bottom left
Text in the print: *Omnes praeter unam praeclusae. Bedachtzaam,—achteloos,—neem vrij uw weg: U werd, welk pad ge straks verkoos, elk ander pad versperd.* (With thought or without care, choose your path freely: once you have chosen it, every other will be closed to you.)
There are also separate copies in which the last word is *ontzegd* ('denied') instead of *versperd*.

174
Emblema XIII, Beehive
Date based on Escher's records
Signature in the print: bottom left
Added signature: bottom left
Text in the print: IN ADVERSIS SEDULITAS INEPTA. BEDRIJVIGHEID GETROOST, ARBEIDZAAM, ONVERPOOSD, MITS HET GEWELD VAN 'T ZWERK NIET WOEDT OVER ONS WERK. (Industry comforts us, hard work with no respite, provided only that the elements do not rage while we are at work.)

175
Emblema XIV, Frog
Date based on Escher's records
Signature in the print: top left
Added signature: bottom left
Text in the print: SILENTIUM OMNI STREPITU MAIUS. DE KWAKERSCHAAR DOORRIJT DEN ZOMERNACHT OM 'T ZEERST; TOCH WELFT DE STILTE WIJD,

ROERLOOS,—EN OVERHEERSCHT. (The band of croakers pierces the summer night as best it can; yet silence envelops all, in stillness—and dominates.)

176
Emblema XV, Squirrel
Date based on Escher's records
Signature in the print: bottom right
Added signature: bottom left
Text in the print: *silva motum arcano continens silet. Het kraakt: er raakt iets los in 't bosch;—het rept,—dan staat het woud weer stil, in stilte.* (A crackling: something is moving in the wood; it stirs, and then the trees stand still again, in silence.)

177
Emblema XVI, Toadstool
Date based on Escher's records
Signature in the print: bottom left
Added signature: bottom left
Text in the print: *Dissolutionis ex humore speciose praefloresco. Wasdom van geheimenis, nabloei van de nacht, voos is mijn verrijzenis: een verwezen pracht.* (Secret growth, legacy of the night, spongily I rise, a serene beauty.)

178
Emblema XVII, Balance
Date based on Escher's records
Signature in the print: bottom right
Added signature: bottom left
Text in the print: ARBITRIUM PARI MOMENTO TEMPERANS. VERWILDERING ONTSTAAT, WAAR IK GEEN VREDE STICHT. HOE VOND DE WERELD BAAT, HIELD IK GEEN EVENWICHT! (Chaos is created where I do not make peace. How would the world profit if I did not keep its balance?)

179
Emblema XVIII, Dice
Date based on Escher's records
Signature in the print: bottom left
Added signature: bottom left
Text in the print: NEMINEM NISI STULTUM SUBMITTIMUS. ONS SCHONK MEN 'T VOOS GEZAG, DE WILLEKEUR VAN 'T LOT TE RICHTEN BIJ BEJAG, TE STIEREN TOT EEN SPOT. (We were assigned the dubious power of bending the arbitrariness of fate towards the pursuit of gain and making a mockery of it.)

180
Emblema XIX, Butterfly
Date based on Escher's records

Signature in the print: bottom left
Added signature: bottom left
Text in the print: *Signum immortalitatis fragile admodum. Zwenkend over de bloemen, bijster van een plicht, is mijn broosheid te roemen, die uw broosheid richt.* (Fluttering over the flowers without sense of duty, my fragility is to be praised, directing your fragility.)

181
Emblema XX, Cactus
Date based on Escher's records
Signature in the print: bottom right
Added signature: bottom left
Text in the print: EX MORSU TORMENTI CRETUS MORDENS. UIT DROEVEN DORREN GROND GEPIJNIGD EN VERSCHROEID, HOE KAN, WANNEER IK WOND, MIJN BITSHEID ZIJN VERFOEID? (Painfully scorched in the sad dry earth, how can I be detested for my spite when I inflict pain?)

182
Emblema XXI, Well
Date based on Escher's records
Signature in the print: bottom left
Added signature: bottom left
Text in the print: UBI AQUA NON PROFLUIT EXSATIO. WAAR BEEK EN BRON BEGEEFT, WAAR GANSCH GEEN LAAFNIS LEEFT, LESCH IK UIT DIEPTEN VERBORGEN: UW HEUL VOOR HEDEN EN MORGEN. (Where stream and source fail, where no refreshment exists, I quench your thirst from hidden depths: I am your sustenance today and tomorrow.)

183
Emblema XXII, Retreat
Date based on Escher's records
Signature in the print: bottom right
Added signature: bottom left
Text in the print: LATEBRA TUTA DEPRAVATIO ANIMI. EEN TOEVLUCHT OP ZIJN SCHOONST, ONTAARDING OP ZIJN BEST: EEN HALF KUNSTMATIG NEST, NAAR MENSCHENAARD EEN WOONST. (A refuge at its most beautiful, unearthly at its best; a semi-artificial nest, a human-like dwelling-place.)

184
Emblema XXIII, Watering-can
Date based on Escher's records
Signature in the print: bottom left
Added signature: bottom left
Text in the print: *Copiam non abunde redundans effundo. Een lafenis*

verstrekt met mate,—op haar tijd,—het leven kweekt, en rekt:—één regendrop verblijdt. (Refreshment furnished in moderation, in its due time, breeds life and extends it: a single drop of rain delights.)

185
Emblema XXIV, Padlock
Date based on Escher's records
Signature in the print: bottom centre
Added signature: bottom left
Text in the print: REPULSAE SUSPICIOSAE TORVA SUBOLES. VAN KWADE TROUW HET BEELD, VERSPERREND NAAR VERMOGEN; IN ONMIN EENS GETEELD, IN ACHTERDOCHT GETOGEN. (The image of bad faith, blocking the way as best it can; once born in enmity, bred in suspicion.)

186
Emblemata, colophon
Date based on the publication date of the book
Text in the print: VAN DIT BOEK, GEHEEL VAN DE OORSPRONKELIJKE HOUTBLOKKEN GEDRUKT DOOR G. J. VAN AMERONGEN & CO TE AMERSFOORT, OP SIMILI JAPON VAN VAN GELDER, IN EEN OPLAGE VAN 300 GENUMMERDE EXEMPLAREN, WERDEN DE EXEMPLAREN, GENUMMERD I–XXV, DOOR DEN HOUTSNIJDER GETEEKEND. N°32 (Of this book, printed from the original wood blocks by G. J. van Amerongen & Co at Amersfoort, on simili Japon of Van Gelder, in an edition of 300 numbered copies, the copies numbered I–XXV were signed by the artist. No. 32)
The number 32 has been stamped in.

187
Initial A
Vermeulen Collection
Date based on Escher's records
Signature in the print: top left
This woodcut was made for the book *De vreeselijke avonturen van Scholastica* (The Terrible Adventures of Scholastica), but was not printed in it. The initial A is for Aemilius, the priest in *Scholastica*.

188–205
The book *De vreeselijke avonturen van Scholastica* by Jan Walch, with woodcuts by M. C. Escher, was published in 1933 by C. A. J. van Dishoeck at Bussum. Of the edition

Spruyt at Enkhuizen; it was intended
to be wrapping-paper for the
Bijenkorf department store in
Amsterdam.

239
Fireworks
Signature and date in the print: bottom
right
Added signature: bottom left
Other additions: no 6/23 (bottom left)

240
Corte
Signature and date in the print: bottom
right
Added signature: bottom left

241
Calvi
Signature and date in the print: top left
Added signature: bottom left

242
Gulf of Porto
Signature and date in the print: top left
Added signature: bottom left
Other additions: no 11/24 (bottom left)

243
Old Olive Tree
Signature and date in the print: bottom
right
Added signature: bottom left

244
Tugboat
Signature and date in the print: bottom
right
Added signature: bottom left

245
Corsica, Calanche
Signature and date in the print: bottom
left
Added signature: bottom left
Other additions: no 1/26 (bottom left)

246
Calanche of Piana
Signature and date in the print: bottom
left, with incomplete date
Added signature: bottom left
Incorrect date 43' has been erased.
    There are also copies dated 2-'34 in
    which 43' has also been erased.

247
Nonza
Signature and date in the print: bottom
right
Added signature: bottom left
Other additions: no 21/30 (bottom left)

248
Still Life with Mirror
Signature and date in the print: bottom
left
Added signature: bottom left
Other additions: no 20/24 (bottom left)

249
Nocturnal Rome: Church Domes
Signature and date in the print: bottom
right
Added signature: bottom left

250
Nocturnal Rome: Colonnade of St
Peter's
Signature and date in the print: bottom
left
Added signature: bottom left

251
Nocturnal Rome: San Nicola
Signature and date in the print: bottom
left
Added signature: bottom left

252
Nocturnal Rome: Small Churches
Signature and date in the print: top left
Added signature: bottom left

253
Nocturnal Rome: Santa Francesca
Romana
Signature and date in the print: bottom
right
Added signature: bottom right

254
Nocturnal Rome: Santa Maria del
Popolo
Signature and date in the print: bottom
right
Added signature: bottom left

255
Nocturnal Rome: San Giorgio
Signature and date in the print: top
right
Added signature: bottom left

256
Nocturnal Rome: the 'Dioscuro'
Pollux
Signature and date in the print: top left
Added signature: bottom left

257
Nocturnal Rome: Trajan's Column
Signature and date in the print: bottom
right
Added signature: bottom left

258
Nocturnal Rome: Basilica of
Constantine
Signature and date in the print: top left
Added signature: bottom left

259
Nocturnal Rome: Castel Sant'Angelo
Signature and date in the print: top left
Added signature: bottom left

260
Nocturnal Rome: Colosseum
Signature and date in the print: bottom
left
Added signature: bottom left

261
St Bavo's, Ghent
Signature and date in the print: bottom
right
Added signature: bottom left
Other additions: no 16 (bottom right)
Escher sometimes incorrectly described
    this as St Nicholas' Church

262
Tournai Cathedral
Signature and date in the print: top
right
Added signature: bottom left
Other additions: *eigen druk* (own
printing), bottom right

263
Houses in Positano
Signature and date in the print: bottom
right
Added signature: bottom centre
Other additions: no 13/20 (bottom
centre)

264
Aeroplane above a Snowy Landscape
Text in the print: TIMOTHEUS
    WINTERNUMMER 1934–1935
Various proofs exist of this print in
    different colours and colour
    combinations, some without text;
    most of them are signed in the
    picture and dated *10-'34* (see 264A).

264A
Aeroplane above a Snowy Landscape
Signature and date in the print: top
right
Proof in grey and black, with a mistake
    in the lettering (*ü* instead of *u*)

265
Bookplate A. Rooseboom
Date based on Escher's records
Signature in the print: top left
Text in the print: A ROOSEBOOM
    EX LIBRIS

266
Coast of Amalfi
Signature and date in the print: bottom
left
Added signature: bottom left
Other additions: *eigen druk* (own
printing), bottom right

267
Still Life with Spherical Mirror
Signature and date in the print: bottom
right
Added signature: bottom left
Other additions: no 1/10 (bottom left)

268
Hand with Reflecting Sphere
Signature and date in the print: bottom
right
Added signature: bottom left

Other additions: no 5/30 (bottom left)
There are also copies in gold

269
St Peter's
Signature and date in the print: top left
Added signature: bottom left
Other additions: no 19 (bottom right)

270
Inside St Peter's
Signature and date in the print: bottom
left
Added signature: bottom left

271
Grasshopper
Signature and date in the print: bottom
right
Included as an original print in *De
Graphicus M. C. Escher* by G. H.
's-Gravesande, *Halcyon* 3–4, The
Hague, 1940

272
Dream
Signature and date in the print: bottom
left
Added signature: bottom left

273
Scarabs
Signature and date in the print: top
right
Added signature: bottom left
Other additions: *eigen druk* (own
printing), bottom right
Included as an original print in *De
Graphicus M. C. Escher* by G. H.
's-Gravesande, *Halcyon* 3–4, The
Hague, 1940

274
Portrait of G. A. Escher
Signature and date in the print: top
right
Added signature: bottom left
Other additions: *tegendruk*
(counterproof), bottom left
The print is signed, bottom right, by
    the subject of the portrait. There are
    also direct prints; that is, in mirror
    image.

275
Trademark
Date based on Escher's records
Added signature: bottom left
This print is designed as a trademark
    for the furnace construction factory
    of Anton Escher, M. C. Escher's
    cousin. Of this print, a zinc block of
    47 × 33 mm (1$^7/8$ × 1$^1/4$″) was made
    which was printed on the stationery
    of this factory. The illustration in
    this catalogue is from a signed proof
    of this block.

276
Senglea
Signature and date in the print: bottom right
Added signature: bottom left

277
Selinunte
Signature and date in the print: bottom left
Added signature: bottom left

278
'Hell'
Signature and date in the print: bottom right
Added signature: bottom left
Other additions: no 16/20 (bottom left)
Text in the print: EXCUD (between signature and date) H. BOSCH INVENTOR (bottom left)
The scene is a detail of the painting *The Garden of Delights* by Hieronymous Bosch. The female figure at top right can also be found in the lithograph *Belvedere* (cat. no. 426).

279
Snow
Signature and date in the print: bottom left
Added signature: bottom left
Other additions: no 1/10 (bottom left)

280
Prickly Flower
Signature and date in the print: bottom right
Alterations to the first and second states: the background has been elaborated; the plant at bottom left, the date and the signature have been added.

281
Libellula
Signature and date in the print: bottom right
Added signature: bottom left

282
Between St Peter's and the Sistine Chapel
Signature and date in the print: bottom right
Added signature: bottom left
Other additions: no 6/24 (bottom left)

283
S. S. Giovanni e Paolo
Signature in the print: top left
Added signature and date: bottom left
Other additions: *geschaafde litho eenig exemplaar* (scraped lithograph, only copy), bottom right
In 1946 Escher made a mezzotint of this picture (cat. no. 340).

284
Advertisement Chess Club Château-d'Oex
Date based on Escher's records
Text in the print: SEANCES TOUS LES LUNDIS DES 20 H. 30 CLUB D'ECHECS CHATEAU-D'OEX HOTEL DE LA GARE

285
House in the Lava
Signature and date in the print: bottom right
Added signature: bottom left
Other additions: no 17/20 (bottom left)

286
Freighter
Signature and date in the print: bottom left
Added signature: bottom left
Other additions: *eigen druk* (own printing), bottom right

287
Venice
Signature and date in the print: bottom left
Added signature: bottom left

288
Ancona
Signature and date in the print: bottom right

289
Catania
Signature and date in the print: bottom right

290
Marseilles
Signature and date in the print: bottom left
Added signature: bottom left

291
Poster
Date based on the date of the exhibition
Text in the print: EXPOSITION *Atelier de Riant-Chalet aux Bossons Peinture Art graphique J. Paschoud. M. C. Escher du 6 au 14 Janvier* ENTREE LIBRE *de 11 à 12¹/₂ et de 14 à 18 heures* CHATEAU-D'OEX

292
Invitation card
Date based on the date of the exhibition
Text in the print: *John Paschoud, peintre et M. C. Escher, graveur vous prient de leur faire l'honneur d'assister au vernissage de leur exposition le 5 Janvier dès 14 heures à l'Atelier de Riant-Chalet les Bossons, Château-d'Oex*

293
Announcement card
Date based on the date of the exhibition
Text in the print: PASCHOUD PEINTRE M. C. ESCHER GRAVEUR EXPOSITION DU 6 AU 14 JANVIER AUX BOSSONS À L'ATELIER DE RIANT-CHALET ENTREE LIBRE
The print shown (with the size given) was probably made from a zinc block that was considerably smaller than the original woodcut.

294
Leaning Tower, Pisa
Signature and date in the print: top right
Added signature: bottom left

295
Piano di Sant'Andrea, Genoa
Signature and date in the print: bottom right

296
Still Life and Street
Signature in the print: bottom right
Date in the print: bottom left
Added signature: bottom left
Other additions: *eigen druk* (own printing), bottom right

297
Porthole
Signature and date in the print: top right

298
Metamorphosis I
Signature and date in the print: bottom right
Added signature: bottom left
Other additions: *eigen druk* (own printing), bottom right

299
Het Bezwaarde Hart (The Troubled Heart)
Date based on Escher's records
Text in the print: HET BEZWAARDE HART GEDICHTEN J. G. ESCHER
Decorated title for J. G. Escher's *Het Bezwaarde Hart*, poems, C. A. J. van Dishoeck, Bussum, 1937

300
Development I
Signature and date in the print: bottom right
Added signature: bottom left
Other additions: *eigen druk* (own printing), bottom right

301
Study for cover of programme *St Matthew Passion*

Vermeulen Collection
Date based on cat. no. 302
Signature in the print: bottom centre
Text in the print:
DE NEDERLANDSCHE BACHVEREENIGING MATTHÄUS PASSION VAN JOHANN SEBASTIAN BACH 1685–1750 OP GOEDEN VRIJDAG IN DE GROOTE KERK TE NAARDEN

302
Programme *St Matthew Passion*
Date based on Escher's records
Signature in the print: bottom centre
Text in the print:
DE NEDERLANDSCHE BACHVEREENIGING MATTHÄUS PASSION VAN JOHANN SEBASTIAN BACH 1685–1750 OP GOEDEN VRIJDAG IN DE GROOTE KERK TE NAARDEN
This woodcut is printed (in purple from the original block) on the cover of a booklet containing the words of the *St Matthew Passion* by J. S. Bach.

303
Day and Night
Signature and date in the print: top right
Added signature: bottom left
Other additions: *eigen druk* (own printing), bottom right

304
Birth announcement card
Signature in the print: right below centre
Text in the print: JAN CHRISTOFFEL ESCHER UCCLE—BRUXELLES— AVENUE DE SATURNE 31 NÉ LE 6 MARS 1938
There are also copies in black, without text (but with the year 1938).

305
Cycle
Signature and date in the print: bottom right
Added signature: bottom left
Other additions: no 1/12 (bottom left)

306
Sky and Water I
Signature and date in the print: bottom centre
Added signature: bottom left
Other additions: *eigen druk* (own printing), bottom right

307
Birthday card for J. Greshoff
Date based on Escher's records
Signature in the print: top right
Text in the print:
1888–15 DEC.–1938

337

AAN JAN GRESHOFF VAN ZIJN
VRIENDEN

*Hier zijn mijn oude vrienden die het
leven*

*Versieren en er gloed en kleur aan
geven;*

Met wie ik lachen kan en debatteeren

*Zonder de kans dat ze mij ruw
bezeeren.*

*Laat mij die vrienden en de vreugde
om wie*

*Zijn hand legt onbaatzuchtig in mijn
hand.*

*Wie garandeert mij dat ik één twee
drie*

*Zulk goed gezelschap vind in 't andre
land?*

(To Jan Greshoff from his friends.
These are my old friends, who adorn
life and lend a glow and colour to it;
with whom I can laugh and debate
without the danger that they hurt me
harshly. Leave me these friends and
the joy of those who place their
hands in mine unselfishly. Who can
assure me that I shall find such good
company so quickly in the other
country?)

Escher was commissioned to make this
woodcut by friends of the poet Jan
Greshoff, on the occasion of the
latter's fiftieth birthday. The eight
lines of verse are from Greshoff's
poem 'Een bezoeker afgewezen' (A
Visitor Turned Away). The print
shows Greshoff's house in
Schaerbeek, near Brussels.

308
Sky and Water II
Signature and date in the print: bottom
centre
Added signature: bottom left
Other additions: *eigen druk* (own
printing), bottom right

309
Delft: Entrance to the Oude Kerk
Signature and date in the print: bottom
left
Added signature: bottom left

310
Development II
Date based on Escher's records
Added signature: bottom centre
Other additions: *eigen druk* (own
printing), bottom centre
There are also copies in other colour
combinations and on textile.

311
Delft: Grote Markt
Signature and date in the print: top left
Added signature: bottom left

Other additions: *eigen druk* (own
printing), bottom right

312
Delft: Nieuwe Kerk
Signature and date in the print: bottom
left
Added signature: bottom left

313
Delft: Voldersgracht
Signature and date in the print: bottom
right
Added signature: bottom left

314
Delft: Oostpoort
Signature and date in the print: top
right

315
Delft: (Interior) Nieuwe Kerk
Signature and date in the print: bottom
right
Added signature: bottom left

316
Delft: Town Hall
Signature and date in the print: top left

317
Delft: Voldersgracht
Signature and date in the print: bottom
right

318
Delft: (Seen from the Tower of the)
Oude Kerk
Signature and date in the print: bottom
left

319
Delft: Roofs
Signature and date in the print: bottom
left

320
Metamorphosis II
Signature in the print: bottom left
Date in the print: bottom right
Added signature: bottom left
Other additions: *eigen druk* (own
printing), bottom left
Text in the print: METAMORPHOSE
The first editions of this print were
printed in two colours (red and
black). The number of blocks is
based on a count made of the blocks
in 1980.

321
Bookplate Dr P. H. M. Travaglino
Date based on Escher's records
Signature in the print: bottom right
Added signature: bottom left
Text in the print: EX LIBRIS DR. P. H.
M. TRAVAGLINO
There are also copies dated *1939*.

322
Bookplate G. H. 's-Gravesande
Date based on Escher's records

Added signature: bottom left
Text in the print: EX LIBRIS G. H.
'S GRAVESANDE VAN DICHTEN
COMT MI CLEINE BATE. DIE LIEDE
RADEN MI DAT ICT LATE. (Writing
poetry profits me not. I am advised
to leave it alone.)
There are also copies dated *1942*.

323
Fish
Added signature and date: bottom left
Other additions: *eigen druk* (own
printing), bottom right

324
Plane-filling Motif with Reptiles
Date based on a dated study
Signature in the print: bottom right
The above-mentioned study is number
53 of Escher's own system for
regular divisions of the plane.

325
Bookplate D. H. Roodhuyzen de Vries
Date based on Escher's records
Signature in the print: top left
Added signature: bottom left
Text in the print: LEGENTES
EXPELLIMUS CURAS LABORE ET
CONSTANTIA EX LIBRIS
ROODHUYZEN DE VRIES-VAN
DISHOECK
There are also dated copies.

326
Verbum
Signature and date in the print: bottom
right
Added signature: bottom left
Other additions: no 3/40 (bottom left)
Text in the print: VERBUM

327
Reptiles
Signature and date in the print: bottom
left
Added signature: bottom left
Other additions: no 30/30 (bottom left)

328
Ant
Signature and date in the print: bottom
right
Added signature: bottom left
Other additions: no 8/20 (bottom left)

329
Bookplate A. M. E. van Dishoeck
Date based on Escher's records
Added signature: bottom left
Text in the print: A. M. E. VAN
DISHOECK EX LIBRIS
There are also dated copies.

330
Blowball
Date based on Escher's records
Signature in the print: bottom right

Added signature: bottom left
Other additions: *handdruk* (printed by
hand), bottom right

330A
Blowball
Signature and date in the print: bottom
right
An error in mirroring the year in the
date has been crossed out.

331
Encounter
Signature and date in the print: bottom
right
Added signature: bottom left
Other additions: no 13/30 (bottom left)
In April 1957 a special edition of two
hundred copies was printed for Arta,
The Hague/Zurich, to be sold to its
members; part of this edition was
sold through the sister organization
in the United States, IGAS.

332
Emblem for Restaurant Insulinde
Date based on Escher's records
Added signature: bottom centre
Other additions: *handdruk* (printed by
hand), bottom centre
Text in the print: CHINEESCH &
INDISCH RESTAURANT
'INSULINDE', plus a Chinese text
which can be translated as
'Indonesian Restaurant'.
Commissioned by Yates Wang of
Rijswijk, near The Hague. There are
also copies in red.

333
Design for writing-paper
Date based on Escher's records
Added signature: bottom left
Other additions: *handdruk* (printed by
hand), bottom right
Text in the print: *Gedicht door Yates
Wang 29 Mildemaand 4641 Anno
Imperatoris Flavi (21ste jaar van de
78ste Chinese tijdkring)*
NACHTEGAAL TEGEN GEWEMEL
VAN LENTEWOLKEN; PRIMULA'S
OP PAARLMOEREN
LANDSCHAPPEN. 21 MEI 1944
(Poem by Yates Wang 29 Mild-
month 4641 Anno Imperatoris Flavi
[21st year of the 78th Chinese
period]. Nightingale against
scudding spring clouds; primroses
on landscapes of mother-of-pearl.
21 May 1944)
Commissioned by Yates Wang of
Rijswijk, near The Hague. There are
also copies in other colour
combinations. There is a Chinese
text at the top and on both pillars,
and a Greek text in the iron railings.

334
Balcony
Signature and date in the print: top right
Added signature: bottom left
Other additions: *proefdruk* (proof), bottom left
There is also an (unfinished) wood-engraving block of this picture (see page 65).

335
Doric Columns
Signature and date in the print: top left
Added signature: bottom left
Other additions: *eigen druk* (own printing), bottom right
There are also copies printed only from the black block.

336
Three Spheres I
Signature in the print: bottom left
Date in the print: bottom right
Added signature: bottom left
Other additions: *eigen druk* (own printing), bottom right

337
Diploma Tijdelijke Academie, Eindhoven
Date based on Escher's records
Signature in the print: bottom left
Text in the print: TIJDELIJKE ACADEMIE EINDHOVEN 26 FEBR.–20 DEC. 1945 UITGEREIKT AAN

338
Magic Mirror
Signature and date in the print: top left
Added signature: bottom left
Other additions: no 2/36 (bottom left)

339
Three Spheres II
Signature and date in the print: bottom right
Added signature: bottom left
Other additions: no 39/40 (bottom left)

340
Dusk
Signature and date in the print: top right
Added signature: bottom left
Other additions: no 3 11 (bottom left); *eigen druk* (own printing), bottom right
The print shows SS. Giovanni e Paolo, Rome.

341
Bookplate J.C. de Bruyn
Date based on Escher's records
Signature in the print: bottom centre
Added signature: bottom left
Other additions: *handdruk* (printed by hand), bottom right

Text in the print: MANU FORTI J. C. DE BRUYN VAN MELIS- EN MARIEKERKE-MACKAY EX LIBRIS
There are also dated copies.

342
Horseman
Signature and date in the print: bottom right
Added signature: bottom left
Other additions: *eigen druk* (own printing), bottom right
There are also copies in other colour combinations and on textile. There also exist proofs of the individual blocks.

343
Mummified Frog
Signature and date in the print: top right
Added signature: bottom left
Other additions: no 24/24 (bottom left); *eigen druk* (own printing), bottom right
In the first state the signature and date are missing.

344
Eye
Signature and date in the print: bottom right
Added date: centre right

345
New Year's greeting-card 1947, Nederlandsche ExLibris-Kring
Date based on Escher's records
Signature in the print: bottom centre
Added signature: bottom left
Other additions: *handdruk* (printed by hand), bottom right
Text in the print: NEDERLANDSCHE EXLIBRIS-KRING 1 JAN. 1947 WIJ KOMEN ER UIT! (We shall come out!)

346
Gallery
Signature and date in the print: bottom right
Added signature: bottom left
Other additions: no 1 (bottom left); *eigen druk* (own printing), bottom right

347
Bookplate Albert Ernst Bosman
Date based on collector's notes
Signature in the print: bottom centre
Text in the print: ALBERT ERNST BOSMAN EX LIBRIS

348
Other World
Signature and date in the print: bottom left

Added signature: bottom left
Other additions: *eigen druk* (own printing), bottom right

349
XIIme Congrès Postal Universel
Date based on Escher's records
Added signature: bottom left
Other additions: *handdruk* (printed by hand), bottom right
Text in the print: PARIS 1947 MAI–JUIN
The booklet *XIIme Congrès Postal Universel* ('offert par la Délégation Néerlandaise') concerns an international post conference held in Paris in May–June 1947. Escher was commissioned to produce this booklet for the PTT (Post Office) in The Hague; he made two woodcuts for it. See A. G. C. Baert, 'Een onbekende zegel van Escher' (An Unknown Stamp by Escher) in *Nederlandsch Maandblad voor Philatelie*, vol. 45 (1968), no. 10, p. 574.

350
XIIme Congrès Postal Universel
Date based on Escher's records
Signature in the print: bottom right
Text in the print: DEUS MARE FECIT BATAVUS LITORA

351
Synthesis
Signature and date in the print: bottom right
Added signature: bottom left
Commissioned by NV Synthese, The Hague (manufacturers of synthetic plastics, a division of Sikkens Lakfabrieken, Sassenheim); copies were sent to business relations of this company. The print depicts the concept of 'synthesis'.

352
Up and Down
Signature and date in the print: bottom right
Added signature: bottom left
Other additions: no 13/36 (bottom left)
There exist proofs in black. In 1948 a special edition of four hundred copies was printed for the VAEVO.

353
Crystal
Signature and date in the print: top left
Added signature: bottom left
Other additions: no 18/25 (bottom left); *eigen druk* (own printing), bottom right

354
Fish

Date based on the date of the exhibition
This vignette was printed on the invitation card for the exhibition of Escher's work in the Scherft Art Gallery, The Hague, 29 November–19 December 1947.

355
Drawing Hands
Signature and date in the print: bottom right
Added signature: bottom left
Other additions: no 18/43 (bottom left)

356
Dewdrop
Signature and date in the print: bottom right
Added signature: bottom left
Other additions: no 5 (bottom left); *eigen druk* (own printing), bottom right

357
Sun and Moon
Signature and date in the print: bottom left
Added signature: bottom left
Other additions: *eigen druk* (own printing), bottom right
There exist proofs in the different colours and colour combinations.

358
Study for Stars
Signature in the print: top left
Date in the print: bottom right
Added signature: bottom left
Other additions: *eigen druk* (own printing), bottom right
There are also copies coloured by hand (watercolour).

359
Stars
Signature and date in the print: top right
Added signature: bottom left
Other additions: *eigen druk* (own printing), bottom right
There are also copies coloured by hand (watercolour). There is also a version in black, blue, yellow and pink, printed from four blocks. Of this version there exist proofs, printed from one or more blocks, in various colours or colour combinations.

360
New Year's greeting-card 1949
Date based on Escher's records
Signature in the print: bottom centre
Added signature: bottom left
Other additions: *handdruk* (printed by hand), bottom right

Text in the print: 1949—L. EN
K. ASSELBERGS
Commissioned by C.J. Asselbergs.

361
Plane-filling Motif with Birds
Added signature: bottom left
Added date: bottom right
Other additions: *handdruk* (printed by
hand), bottom right
This vignette was printed on the
invitation card for the exhibition of
Escher's work in the Van Lier Art
Gallery, Blaricum, 14 May–11 June
1949.

361A
Regular Division of the Plane with
Birds
Date based on cat. no. 361
Composed from six prints of the same
basic block (361).

362
Sea-shells
Signature and date in the print: top left
Added signature: bottom left
Other additions: no 2 (bottom left);
eigen druk (own printing), bottom
right
There exists a second state, which
Escher considered a failure.

363
Horses and Birds
Date based on Escher's records
Signature in the print: bottom left
Added signature: bottom left
Other additions: *handdruk* (printed by
hand), bottom right
This wood engraving was printed on
the invitation cards for the following
exhibitions of Escher's work:
Boymans Museum, Rotterdam,
15 October–15 November 1949;
Pictura, Dordrecht, 18 March–
8 April 1950; Leffelaar Art Gallery,
Haarlem, 26 September–17 October
1951.

364
Fish and Frogs
Date based on Escher's records
Signature in the print: centre left
This wood engraving was printed on
the invitation card for the exhibition
of Escher's work in the Goois
Museum, Hilversum, 12 June–
12 July 1954.

365
Double Planetoid
Signature and date in the print: left
above centre
Added signature: bottom centre
Other additions: *eigen druk* (own
printing), bottom centre

There exist proofs in other colour
combinations, and in black only.
One copy was mounted by Escher as
a rotating disc.

366
Contrast
Signature and date in the print: bottom
left
Added signature: bottom left
Other additions: no 36/43 (bottom left)
In june 1952 a special edition of four
hundred copies was printed for the
VAEVO.

367
Rippled Surface
Signature and date in the print: top left
Added signature: bottom left
Other additions: *eigen druk* (own
printing), bottom right
There are also copies in black and grey.

368
Self-Portrait in Spherical Mirror
Signature and date in the print: left
centre
This woodcut was printed on the
invitation cards for the following
exhibitions of Escher's works:
Moderne Boekhandel, Amsterdam,
15 April–6 May 1950; Leffelaar Art
Gallery, Haarlem, 26 September–
17 October 1951; Whyte Gallery,
Washington, D.C., 7 October—end
of November 1954.

369
Butterflies
Signature and date in the print: bottom
right
Added signature: bottom left
Other additions: *eigen druk* (own
printing), bottom right

370
Devils, vignette
Signature and date in the print: bottom
right
This wood engraving was printed on
the invitation card for the exhibition
of works by Escher and H. van
Kruiningen in Galerie Le Canard,
Amsterdam, 14 November–
14 December 1950, and (in green) on
the invitation card for the exhibition
of Escher's work in 't Oude
Wevershuys, Amersfoort,
3–29 October 1953.

371
New Year's greeting-card 1951
Date based on Escher's records
Signature in the print: bottom centre
Added signature: bottom left
Text in the print: L. *en* K. ASSELBERGS
1951
Commissioned by C.J. Asselbergs.

372
Predestination
Signature and date in the print: bottom
right
Added signature: bottom left
Other additions: *proefdruk* (proof),
bottom left

373
Plane Filling I
Signature in the print: bottom centre
Date in the print: top centre
Added signature: bottom left
Other additions: *proefdruk* (proof),
bottom left
There are also copies in blue.

374
Curl-up
Signature in the print: top left
Date in the print: bottom right
Added signature: bottom left
Other additions: *proefdruk* (proof),
bottom left
Translation of text in the print: The
Pedalternorotandomovens
centroculatus articulosus was
created (generatio spontanea!) out of
dissatisfaction with the fact that in
nature there are no wheel-shaped
creatures which are able to move by
rolling. The creature shown here,
popularly known as a 'curl-up', is an
attempt to fulfil this deeply felt need.
Its biological characteristics are still
uncertain: is it a mammal, a reptile
or an insect? It has an elongated
body consisting of horny articulated
plates and three pairs of legs, which
end in feet similar to the human foot.
In the middle of the fat, round head,
which has a sharply curved parrot
beak, there are two protruding eyes,
set on stalks and sticking out from
either side of the head. When it is
stretched out, the creature is able to
move over any substratum slowly
and thoughtfully, using its six legs (if
need be, it can climb up or go down
steep stairs, penetrate thick
undergrowth or clamber over rocks).
However, as soon as it has to travel
any distance along a relatively clear
path, it pushes down its head, curls
up as fast as lightning, pushing off
with its feet, if these are still touching
the ground. When it is rolled up it
has the appearance of a discus, of
which the central pivot is formed by
eyes on stalks. By pushing
successively with each of its three
pairs of legs, it can attain a high
speed. As it rolls along, it can pull in

its feet at will (for instance when
going down a slope or when
coasting) and thus freewheel. When
necessary, it is able to change back
to the walking position in two ways:
either, abruptly, by suddenly
stretching its body, but then it ends
up on its back with its feet in the air,
or by gradually reducing speed
(using its legs as a brake) and slowly
unrolling backwards when it has
come to a standstill.

375
House of Stairs
Signature and date in the print: bottom
left
Added signature: bottom left
Other additions: no 12/40 (bottom left)
Escher once joined together three
copies of this print to form a
continuous whole (see *The World of
M.C. Escher*, no. 173). There are
also smaller combinations made
from two copies.

377
Two Intersecting Planes
Signature and date in the print: bottom
centre
Added signature: bottom centre
Other additions: *eigen druk* (own
printing), bottom centre
There are also copies in yellow, brown
and black, and hand-coloured
proofs of the black block.

378
Puddle
Signature and date in the print: top left
Added signature: bottom left
Other additions: *eigen druk* (own
printing), bottom right
The reflected image comes from cat.
no. 230. There exist proofs in green
from one block and in green and
brown from two blocks.

379
Dragon
Signature and date in the print: bottom
left
Added signature: bottom left
Other additions: *eigen druk* (own
printing), bottom right
There exists a proof printed from a
block which Escher himself
considered a failure (379A).

380
Gravity
Signature and date in the print: left
above centre
Added signature: bottom right
Other additions: no 1/13 (bottom left)

381
4 Graphic Artists
Date based on the date of the exhibition
Text in the print: M. C. ESCHER
W. V. HEUSDEN   J. M. PRANGE
H. V. KRUININGEN
This woodcut was printed on the invitation cards for the exhibition '4 Grafici' in the Boymans Museum, Rotterdam, 27 September–2 November 1952, and in the Gemeentemuseum, Arnhem, 1 April–4 May 1953.

382
New Year's greeting-card 1953
Date based on Escher's records
Signature in the print: bottom left
Text in the print: EUGÈNE & WILLY
STRENS   FELICITAS 1953
The text on the back of the card shows that this is *Earth*, number 1 of the series *The Four Elements*.

383
New Year's greeting-card 1954
Date based on Escher's records
Signature in the print: bottom left
Text in the print: FELICITAS 1954
EUGÈNE & WILLY STRENS
The text on the back of the card shows that this is *Air*, number 2 of the series *The Four Elements*. There exist proofs without text.

384
New Year's greeting-card 1955
Date based on Escher's records
Signature in the print: bottom left
Text in the print: EUGÈNE & WILLY
STRENS   FELICITAS 1955
The text on the back of the card shows that this is *Fire*, number 3 of the series *The Four Elements*.

385
New Year's greeting-card 1956
Date based on Escher's records
Signature in the print: bottom left
Text in the print: FELICITAS 1956
EUGÈNE & WILLY STRENS
The text on the back of the card shows that this is *Water*, number 4 of the series *The Four Elements*.

386
Cubic Space Division
Signature and date in the print: bottom right
Added signature: bottom left
Other additions: no 10/20 (bottom left)

387
Concentric Rinds
Signature in the print: bottom right
Date in the print: bottom left

Added signature: bottom left
Other additions: *eigen druk* (own printing), bottom right
There are also copies coloured by hand (watercolour).

388
Relativity
Signature and date in the print: top left
There are also copies coloured by hand (coloured pencil).

389
Relativity
Signature and date in the print: top left
Added signature: bottom left
Other additions: no 1/20 (bottom left)

390
Spirals
Signature in the print: bottom right
Date in the print: bottom left
Added signature: bottom left
Other additions: *eigen druk* (own printing), bottom right

391
Trees and Animals
Date based on dated drawing
Signature in the print: bottom centre

392
Donkey
Date based on the publication date of the booklet
Signature in the print: bottom right
Printed from the original block in *Grafisch ABC*, 1953 premium for the donors of the Society for the Promotion of Graphic Art 'De Grafische', which published the booklet.

393
Mouse
Date based on the publication date of the booklet
Printed from the original block in *Grafisch ABC*.

394
Bookplate A. R. A. Wertheim
Roosevelt Collection
Date based on Escher's records
Added signature: bottom left
Text in the print: A.R.A. WERTHEIM
SEMPER IDEM

395
Tetrahedral Planetoid
Signature in the print: bottom right
Date in the print: bottom left
Added signature: bottom left
Other additions: *eigen druk* (own printing), bottom right

396
Study for Rind
Signature and date in the print: bottom centre
The print depicts Escher's wife, Jetta.

397
Three Intersecting Planes
Signature and date in the print: bottom centre
Added signature: bottom left
Other additions: *eigen druk* (own printing), bottom right
There are also copies in brown and black.

398
Fish, vignette
Date based on dated study and on the date of the exhibition
Signature in the print: top centre
Added signature: bottom right
The vignette was printed on the invitation card for the exhibition of Escher's work in the Stedelijk Museum, Amsterdam, 27 August–26 September 1954, on the occasion of the International Mathematical Conference, and on the catalogue of the exhibition of Escher's work at the Instituut voor Kunstgeschiedenis, Groningen, 7 May–15 June 1957. The above-mentioned study is number 99 of Escher's own system for regular divisions of the plane.

399
Convex and Concave
Signature and date in the print: top left
Added signature: bottom left
Other additions: no 20/56 (bottom left)

400
Liberation
Signature and date in the print: bottom right
Added signature: bottom left
Other additions: no 1/40 (bottom left)

401
Rind
Signature and date in the print: bottom centre
Added signature: bottom left
Other additions: *eigen druk* (own printing), bottom right
There exist proofs of the individual blocks. This print also exists in other colour combinations. It depicts Escher's wife, Jetta.

402
Order and Chaos
Date based on Escher's records
Signature and date in the print: bottom right
Commissioned by the Masonic Foundation 'Ritus en Tempelbouw', The Hague.

403
Depth

Signature and date in the print: bottom left
There are also copies in other colour combinations. There exist proofs printed from one block and from two blocks

404
Christmas card AKU
Vermeulen Collection
Date based on Escher's records
Signature in the print: bottom left
Commissioned by Algemene Kunstzijde Unie NV of Arnhem.

405
Three Worlds
Signature and date in the print: bottom left
Added signature: bottom left
Other additions: no 1/33 II (bottom left)
In May 1956 a special edition of seven hundred copies was printed for the VAEVO.

406
Fish, vignette
Date based on dated study
Signature in the print: top centre
The above-mentioned study is number 94 from Escher's own system for regular divisions of the plane.

407
Candle Flame
Collection C. J. van Vuure
Date based on Escher's records
Signature in the print: bottom right
Text in the print: *Vivo! Anima trepidans in me absumitur. Ik ben mij zelf: een licht. Gij vindt in mij uw eigen lot bepaald. Blijf aldus niet voor 't wezen blind, dat in mijn schijn U tegenstraalt.* (I am myself: a light. In me you find your fate. So be not blind to the truth shining from my glow.)
This woodcut was commissioned by C. J. van Vuure, of Hilversum; it was intended to be a vignette for the Collective Funeral Association 'Voorzorg'. It is a mirrored variant of an 'emblema' of 1931 (cat. no. 172).

408
Swans
Signature and date in the print: top right
Added signature: bottom left
Other additions: *eigen druk* (own printing), bottom right

409
Bond of Union
Signature and date in the print: bottom right

Added signature: bottom left
Other additions: no 25/52 II (bottom left)

410
Print Gallery
Signature and date in the print: centre
Added signature: centre
Other additions: no 15/43 (centre)

411
Division
Signature in the print: centre left
Date in the print: centre right
Added signature: bottom left
Other additions: *eigen druk* (own printing), bottom right

412
New Year's greeting-card PTT
Signature in the print: bottom right
Added date: bottom right
Commissioned by the PTT (Post Office), The Hague.

413
Smaller and Smaller
Signature in the print: left below centre
Date in the print: right below centre
Added signature: bottom left
Other additions: *eigen druk* (own printing), bottom right
There exist separate proofs of the centre and the edge of this print, in one and in two colours. There are also proofs in which the centre is printed in two colours and the edge only in black.

414
Fish, vignette
Date based on Escher's correspondence
This vignette was printed on the invitation cards for the following exhibitions: 4 Graphic Artists— Harry Disberg, M. C. Escher, H. van Kruiningen, Wout van Heusden, in the Stedelijk Museum, Amsterdam, 26 January–25 February 1957; *idem*, in the Printroom of the University of Leiden, 23 May–15 June 1957; Graphic Work by M. C. Escher, in the Singer Museum, Laren, 9 May—16 June 1958.

415
Cube with Ribbons
Signature and date in the print: bottom right
Added signature: bottom left
Other additions: no 20/30 (bottom left)

416–21
In 1957 the Foundation De Roos, in Utrecht, commissioned Escher to write and illustrate a book, entitled *Regelmatige vlakverdeling* (The

Regular Division of the Plane). It was published in 1958 in an edition of 175 numbered copies, and a few that were not numbered. This edition contained six separate prints in red of the woodcuts on pages 15, 19, 27, 31, 35 and 39 (which were also printed from the blocks). The text of this book is included in the present volume on pages 155–73.

416
Regular Division of the Plane I
Date based on Escher's records
Signature and date in the print: bottom left
Book 1958, page 15

417
Regular Division of the Plane II
Date based on Escher's records
Signature and date in the print: bottom left
Book 1958, page 19

418
Regular Division of the Plane III
Date based on Escher's records
Signature and date in the print: bottom left
Book 1958, page 27

419
Regular Division of the Plane IV
Date based on Escher's records
Signature and date in the print: bottom left
Book 1958, page 31

420
Regular Division of the Plane V
Date based on Escher's records
Signature and date in the print: bottom right
Book 1958, page 35

421
Regular Division of the Plane VI
Date based on Escher's records
Signature and date in the print: bottom left
Book 1958, page 39

422
Plane Filling II
Signature and date in the print: bottom left
Added signature: bottom left
Other additions: no 49/56 (bottom left)

423
Whirlpools
Signature in the print: bottom right
Date in the print: top left
Added signature: bottom left
Other additions: *eigen druk* (own printing), bottom right
In the first state, the signature is missing.

424
Path of Life I
Added signature: bottom left
Added date: bottom centre
Other additions: *eigen druk* (own printing), bottom right

425
Path of Life II
Added signature and date: bottom centre
Other additions: *eigen druk* (own printing), bottom centre

426
Belvedere
Signature and date in the print: bottom right
Added signature: bottom left
The woman at bottom right comes from cat. no. 278. The background comes from a 1929 scratch drawing (see *The World of M. C. Escher*, no. 35). In March 1965 Escher supplied sixty copies to the Ministry of Education, Arts and Sciences for use in schools in the Dutch West Indies.

427
Sphere Surface with Fish
Signature and date in the print: bottom centre
Added signature: bottom left
Other additions: *eigen druk* (own printing), bottom right
There is also a version in grey and black, printed from two blocks, without the background, so that it is circular; there exist proofs of this in different colour combinations, without signature or date. There exist separate proofs of the 'network of co-ordinates', including a 'three-dimensional' version in which the block is printed twice, once normally (in black) and once upside-down (in grey).

428
Sphere Spirals
Signature and date in the print: bottom right
Added signature: bottom left
Other additions: *eigen druk* (own printing), bottom right
There also exist proofs in other colour combinations. For the 'network of co-ordinates' the same block was used (printed twice) as for cat. no. 427.

429
Circle Limit I
Signature in the print: left below centre
Date in the print: right below centre
Added signature: bottom left

Other additions: *eigen druk* (own printing), bottom right

430
Man with Cuboid
Date based on cat. no. 426
Signature in the print: top right
This vignette was printed on the invitation card for the exhibition of Escher's work in the Institut Néerlandais in Paris, 12–28 March 1965.

431
Flatworms
Signature and date in the print: bottom left
Added signature: bottom left
Other additions: no 2/45 (bottom left)

432
Circle Limit II
Added signature and date: bottom left
Other additions: *eigen druk* (own printing), bottom right

433
Fish and Scales
Signature and date in the print: bottom right
Added signature: bottom left
Other additions: *eigen druk* (own printing), bottom right

434
Circle Limit III
Added signature and date: bottom left
Other additions: *eigen druk* (own printing), bottom right
There exists a large number of proofs of the first and second states, printed from one block and from two, four or five blocks, in which each block is printed once, twice or four times on the same sheet, in various colours.

435
Ascending and Descending
Signature and date in the print: bottom centre
Added signature: bottom right
Other additions: no 11/52 (bottom right)

436
Circle Limit IV
Signature and date in the print: bottom centre
Added signature: bottom left
Other additions: *eigen druk* (own printing), bottom right

437
Möbius Strip I
Signature and date in the print: centre right
Added signature: bottom left
Other additions: *eigen druk* (own printing), bottom right

Some copies have an extra gold edge along the bottom.

438
Four Regular Solids
Signature and date in the print: bottom centre
Added date: bottom left
Other additions: *proefdruk* (proof), bottom left
There are also copies in black, blue and red. There exist proofs printed from two blocks, in red and yellow.

439
Waterfall
Signature and date in the print: bottom right
Added signature: bottom left
Other additions: no 50/57 II (bottom left)
The 'plants' at bottom left come from a 1942 drawing (see *The World of M. C. Escher*, no. 256).

440
Larix
Roosevelt Collection
At the end of 1961 Escher sent this print to a number of friends as a Christmas card. In 1963 it was used for a Christmas card of the Henriëtte Roland Holst Foundation, Hilversum.

441
Möbius Strip II
Signature and date in the print: bottom centre
Added signature: bottom left
Other additions: *eigen druk* (own printing), bottom right
There exist proofs printed from the black block.

442
Fish
Date based on the publication date of the booklet
Signature in the print: bottom left
Printed from the original block in Pam G. Rueter's *De tekens van de dierenriem* (The Signs of the Zodiac), published in 1963 in an edition of five hundred copies; fifty numbered copies were intended for the donors of the Society for the Promotion of Graphic Art 'De Grafische', which published the booklet.

443
Square Limit
Signature and date in the print: left and right above centre and left and right below centre
Added signature: bottom left

Other additions: *eigen druk* (own printing), bottom right
There are also copies in red and blue.

444
Knots
Signature and date in the print: bottom left
Added signature: bottom left
Other additions: *eigen druk* (own printing), bottom right
There are copies with an incorrect year (*'56* instead of *'65*). There exist proofs printed from two blocks, in black and brown, and from one block, in brown and in green. There are separate prints, in black and in two colours, of each of the small knots (top left and top right).

445
Path of Life III
Signature and date in the print: bottom centre
Added signature: bottom left
Other additions: *eigen druk* (own printing), bottom right
Dated *66'* instead of *'66*. There exist proofs in black.

446
Metamorphosis III
Signature in the print: bottom left
Added signature: bottom left
Added date: bottom left *(XI '39–III '40 en VI '67–II '68)*
Other additions: *eigen druk* (own printing), bottom left
There are also copies of the first state, of the separate parts (sometimes signed), and proofs of the separate parts in various colour combinations. The number of blocks is based on a count made of the blocks in 1980.

447
Study for part of Snakes
Schwartz Collection
Date based on cat. no. 448
Signature in the print: bottom left
There are also hand-coloured copies.

448
Snakes
Signature and date in the print: bottom left, bottom right and top centre
Added signature: bottom centre
Other additions: *eigen druk* (own printing), centre.

Posthumous Prints

See also page 177
9
[Self-Portrait], May 1917
Linoleum cut
216 × 131 (8^1/$_2$ × 5^1/$_8$″)
Date based on dated linoleum block
Signature in the print: bottom right
There is an incomplete signature in mirror image at the bottom left of the print.

45
[Rabbits], August 1920
Woodcut
176 × 368 (6^7/$_8$ × 14^1/$_2$″)
Signature and date in the print: top right
Text in the print: TEXEL

87
[Wood near Menton], [1921]
Woodcut
283 × 353 (11^1/$_8$ × 13^7/$_8$″)
Date based on dated drawing

238
Design for wrapping-paper: Jelmoli [IV]
Woodcut
55 × 90 (2^1/$_8$ × 3^1/$_2$″)

310A
[Development II, first version], [1939]
Woodcut
480 × 480 (18^7/$_8$ × 18^7/$_8$″)
Date based on cat. no. 310
Black block for multicolour woodcut. Escher was obviously not satisfied with this version; he never printed the block.

Concordance

The heading *Cat* in the columns below designates the catalogue number in the present work. The heading *W* designates the corresponding number in *The World of M.C. Escher* (New York, 1972); the heading *G* that in *The Graphic Work of M.C. Escher* (New York, 1967).

Cat	W	G	Cat	W	G	Cat	W	G	Cat	W	G
69	3		226	54		326	116	17	390	191	42
74	2		228	55		327	120	28	395	194	58
80	4		230	56		328	121		397	195	36
82	5		231	57	5	331	127	30	399	198	56
89	9		239	58		334	130	70	400	199	15
90	7		245	59		335	131	71	401	200	45
90A	6		248	60		336	133	68	403	206	38
93	10		250	61		338	134	31	405	207	48
94	8		256	62		339	135	52	408	211	8
96	11		258	63		340	136		409	212	46
97	13		263	64		342	138	9	410	216	72
100	15		266	66		343	139		411	218	
101	16		267	65	50	344	140	54	413	219	18
102	17		268	67	51	346	141		415	221	55
103	18		270	69	6	348	142	63	422	222	35
105	19		271	70		352	146	64	423	224	21
108	20		272	76	7	353	147		424	225	
109	21		273	71		355	148	69	425	234	19
115	24		274	77	4	356	149	53	426	230	74
117	25		277	78		357	150	12	427	231	20
118	26	I	278	79		358	151		428	232	43
120	30		279	80		359	152	61	429	233	22
124	31		280	81		360	154		431	236	62
126	34		281	82		362	155		432	235	
127	36		285	90		365	156	57	433	242	26
128	37		286	91		366	157	59	434	239	24
130	38		289	94		367	160	47	435	243	75
132	39	2	296	97		369	161	27	436	247	23
134	40		297	95		372	165	33	437	248	41
136	43		298	99		373	166	34	438	249	
145	44		300	100	16	374	167	65	439	258	76
146	45		303	102	11	375	172	66	441	260	40
150	48		305	104	29	377	174	10	443	263	25
152	47		306	106	13	378	175	49	444	264	39
162	51		308	107	14	379	176	73	445	266	
164	52		310	108		380	178	60	446		32
194	46		311	109		382	182		448	270	
217	49		315	110		386	181	37			
218	50		320	111		387	185	44			
223	53	3	323	114		389	188	67			

List of Colour Plates

	Page
At the Mouth of the Ebro; watercolour	41
Mural mosaic in the Alhambra; drawing	41
Farmhouse, Ravello; drawing	42
View of Atrani; drawing	43
Corte, Corsica; drawing	44
Tiles in the Alhambra; drawing	53
One of Escher's first systematic studies for the division of the plane	54
Fish; woodcut on textile	63
Fish; woodcut in three colours (cat. no. 323)	64
Unfinished block for wood engraving *Balcony* (compare cat. no. 334)	65
Doric Columns; wood engraving in three colours (cat. no. 335)	66
Tapestry for the weavers Ed. de Cneudt in Baarn	75
Butterflies; coloured drawing (compare cat. no. 369)	76
Fond de Gaume, Les Eyzies; drawing	77
Ceiling decoration for the Philips company in Eindhoven	78
Whirlpools; woodcut in three colours (cat. no. 423)	95
Sphere Surface with Fish; woodcut in three colours (cat. no. 427)	96
Circle Limit III; woodcut in five colours (cat. no. 434)	97
Circle Limit IV; woodcut in two colours (cat. no. 436)	98
Tiled façade for the hall of a school in The Hague	115
Möbius Strip I; woodcut in four colours (cat. no. 437)	116
Four Regular Solids; woodcut in three colours (cat. no. 438)	117
Square Limit; woodcut in two colours (cat. no. 443)	118
Escher keeping his records	127
Knots; woodcut in three colours (cat. no. 444)	128
Two sections from the three-colour woodcut *Metamorphosis III* (cat. no. 446)	129
Snakes; woodcut in three colours (cat. no. 448)	130
Puddle; woodcut in three colours (cat. no. 378)	139
Detail of a textile print (kakemono)	140
A page from Escher's workbook showing his system for the regular division of the plane	149
Horsemen, study for the division of the plane no. 67; drawing	150
Horseman; woodcut in three colours (cat. no. 342)	150
The tin designed by Escher for the Verblifa company	151
Most of the three-colour woodcut *Senglea* (cat. no. 276) can be found in the lithograph *Print Gallery* (cat. no. 410)	152

Selected Bibliography

Writings by Escher

Grafiek en Tekeningen M.C.Escher.
Introduction by P.Terpstra. Zwolle,
1959
The Graphic Work of M.C.Escher.
London and New York, 1961.
Enlarged ed., New York, 1967
'Hoe ik er toe kwam, als graficus
ontwerpen voor wandversiering te
maken.' *De Delver*, vol. 14, no. 6
(1941), p. 81
'Introduction.' *Catalogus M.C.Escher.*
No. 118, Stedelijk Museum,
Amsterdam, 1954
*Mededelingenblad van de Nederlandse
Kring van Grafici en Tekenaars.* No.
3 (June 1950), pp. 5–7 and 19–20; no.
5 (December 1950), pp. 4–7
'Nederlandse grafici vertellen van hun
werk II.' *Phoenix*, vol. 2, no. 4
(1947), p. 90
'Oneindigheidsbenaderingen.' *De
Wereld van het Zwart en Wit.* Edited
by J.Hulsker. Amsterdam (1959), p.
41
Regelmatige Vlakverdeling. Utrecht,
1958 (limited ed., De Roos
Foundation)
'Samuel Jessurun de Mesquita.'
*Catalogus Tentoonstelling S.J.de
Mesquita en Mendes da Costa.*
Stedelijk Museum, Amsterdam,
1946
'Timbre-poste pour l'avion.' *Les
Timbres-poste des Pays-Bas de 1929
à 1939.* The Hague (1939), p. 59
*Wit-grijs-zwart. Mededelingen van 'De
Grafische'.* No. 13 (September 1951),
pp. 8–10; no. 20 (November 1953),
pp. 7–10; no. 24 (February 1956),
pp. 14–15 and 15–17
*The Writings and Lectures of Escher,
and His Collection of Clippings.* The
original texts, in addition to the
complete, authentic collection of all
2,100 drawings, held up to 1980 at
the Gemeentemuseum, The Hague
(4 vols.). Microfiche publication.
Zug, Switzerland, 1981

Books Illustrated by Escher

Drijfhout, E. E. *XXIV Emblemata dat
zijn zinne-beelden.* Bussum, 1932
Stolk, A.P.van. *Flor de Pascua.* Baarn,
1921
Walch, J. *De vreeselijke avonturen van
Scholastica.* Bussum, 1933

Books and Articles on Escher after 1950

Albright, T. 'Visuals—Escher.' *Rolling
Stone*, no. 52 (1970)
Chapelot, P. 'Une découverte: le
visionnaire Escher.' *Planète*, no. 8
(1963), p. 60
Ebbinge Wubben, J.C. 'M.C.Escher:
Noodlot.' *Openbaar Kunstbezit*, vol.
1, no. 6 (1957)
Ernst, Bruno. *De Toverspiegel van
M.C.Escher.* Amsterdam, 1976
'M.C.Escher lithographies.' *Caractère
Noël* (1963)
'Escher's Eerie Games.' *Horizon*, vol.
8, no. 4 (1966), p. 110
Flocon, Albert. 'A la frontière de l'art
graphique et des mathématiques:
Maurits Cornelis Escher.' *Jardin des
Arts*, no. 131 (1965), p. 9
'The Gamesman.' *Time*, vol. 65, no. 17
(1954), p. 68
Gardner, Martin. 'The Eerie
Mathematical Art of Maurits
C.Escher.' *Scientific American*, vol.
214, no. 4 (1966), p. 110
Gombrich, E.H. 'How to Read a
Painting.' *The Saturday Evening
Post*, vol. 234, no. 30 (1961), p. 20
Hofmeijer, D.H. 'The Wondrous
World of M.C.Escher.' *Circuit*, no.
26 (1969)
Hofstadter, R. *Gödel, Escher, Bach: An
Eternal Golden Braid.* New York,
1979
Locher, J.L. *Catalogus Overzichtsten-
toonstelling M.C.Escher* (with
contributions by C.H.A.Broos,
G.W.Locher, M.C.Escher,
H.S.M.Coxeter, Bruno Ernst),
Gemeentemuseum, The Hague, 1968

Locher, J. L., C. H. A. Broos,
M. C. Escher, G. W. Locher,
H. S. M. Coxeter. *The World of
M.C.Escher.* New York, 1972
Loveland, R.J. *Graphic Imagery of
M.C.Escher.* Master's thesis.
University of Wyoming, 1967
Maas, J. 'The Stately Mansions of the
Imagination.' *Horizon*, vol. 5, no. 7
(1963), p. 10
Nemerov, H. 'The Miraculous
Transformations of Maurits
Cornelis Escher.' *Artist's Proof*, vol.
3, no. 2 (1963–64), p. 32
Platt, C. 'Expressing the Abstract.'
New Worlds, vol. 51, no. 173 (1967),
p. 44
'Prying Dutchman.' *Time*, vol. 57, no.
14 (1951), p. 50
Severin, M.F. 'The Dimensional
Experiments of M. C. Escher.' *The
Studio*, vol. 141, no. 695 (1951), p. 50
Sheldon-Williams, P.M.T. 'Graphic
Work of M.C.Escher.' *Apollo*, vol.
76, no. 82 (1962)
'Speaking of Pictures.' *Life*, vol. 5, no.
18 (1961), p. 18
'Tricks Played on Hand and Eye.' *The
UNESCO Courier*, vol. 19, no. 5
(1964), p. 14
Wennberg, G. 'Tillvaron som synvilla.'
Ord och Bild, no. 1 (1962), p. 52
Wilkie, Kenneth. 'The Weird World of
Escher.' *Holland Herald*, vol. 9
(1974)

Index of Works Illustrated

Index of Names